Cloud Computing: Security and Management

Cloud Computing: Security and Management

Edited by **Conor Suarez**

New York

Published by Willford Press,
118-35 Queens Blvd., Suite 400,
Forest Hills, NY 11375, USA
www.willfordpress.com

Cloud Computing: Security and Management
Edited by Conor Suarez

International Standard Book Number: 978-1-68285-140-1 (Hardback)

Contents

Preface — VII

Chapter 1 — **A quantitative analysis of current security concerns and solutions for cloud computing** — 1
Nelson Gonzalez, Charles Miers, Fernando Redígolo, Marcos Simplício, Tereza Carvalho, Mats Näslund and Makan Pourzandi

Chapter 2 — **Trust mechanisms for cloud computing** — 19
Jingwei Huang and David M Nicol

Chapter 3 — **A survey on securing the virtual cloud** — 33
Robert Denz and Stephen Taylor

Chapter 4 — **Increasing virtual machine security in cloud environments** — 42
Roland Schwarzkopf, Matthias Schmidt, Christian Strack, Simon Martin and Bernd Freisleben

Chapter 5 — **A design space for dynamic service level agreements in OpenStack** — 54
Craig A Lee and Alan F Sill

Chapter 6 — **Improving the performance of Hadoop Hive by sharing scan and computation tasks** — 67
Tansel Dokeroglu, Serkan Ozal, Murat Ali Bayir, Muhammet Serkan Cinar and Ahmet Cosar

Chapter 7 — **Architecture-based integrated management of diverse cloud resources** — 78
Xing Chen, Ying Zhang, Gang Huang, Xianghan Zheng, Wenzhong Guo and Chunming Rong

Chapter 8 — **Towards full network virtualization in horizontal IaaS federation: security issues** — 93
Anant V Nimkar and Soumya K Ghosh

Chapter 9 — **Fine-grained preemption analysis for latency investigation across virtual machines** — 106
Mohamad Gebai, Francis Giraldeau and Michel R Dagenais

Chapter 10 — **A framework for cloud-based context-aware information services for citizens in smart cities** — 121
Zaheer Khan, Saad Liaquat Kiani and Kamran Soomro

A quantitative analysis of current security concerns and solutions for cloud computing

Nelson Gonzalez[1*], Charles Miers[1,4], Fernando Redígolo[1], Marcos Simplício[1], Tereza Carvalho[1], Mats Näslund[2] and Makan Pourzandi[3]

Abstract

The development of cloud computing services is speeding up the rate in which the organizations outsource their computational services or sell their idle computational resources. Even though migrating to the cloud remains a tempting trend from a financial perspective, there are several other aspects that must be taken into account by companies before they decide to do so. One of the most important aspect refers to security: while some cloud computing security issues are inherited from the solutions adopted to create such services, many new security questions that are particular to these solutions also arise, including those related to how the services are organized and which kind of service/data can be placed in the cloud. Aiming to give a better understanding of this complex scenario, in this article we identify and classify the main security concerns and solutions in cloud computing, and propose a taxonomy of security in cloud computing, giving an overview of the current status of security in this emerging technology.

Introduction

Security is considered a key requirement for cloud computing consolidation as a robust and feasible multi-purpose solution [1]. This viewpoint is shared by many distinct groups, including academia researchers [2,3], business decision makers [4] and government organizations [5,6]. The many similarities in these perspectives indicate a grave concern on crucial security and legal obstacles for cloud computing, including service availability, data confidentiality, provider lock-in and reputation fate sharing [7]. These concerns have their origin not only on existing problems, directly inherited from the adopted technologies, but are also related to new issues derived from the composition of essential cloud computing features like scalability, resource sharing and virtualization (e.g., data leakage and hypervisor vulnerabilities) [8]. The distinction between these classes is more easily identifiable by analyzing the definition of the essential cloud computing characteristics proposed by the NIST (National Institute of Standards and Technology) in [9], which also introduces the SPI model for services (SaaS, PaaS, and IaaS) and deployment (private, public, community, and hybrid).

Due to the ever growing interest in cloud computing, there is an explicit and constant effort to evaluate the current trends in security for such technology, considering both problems already identified and possible solutions [10]. An authoritative reference in the area is the risk assessment developed by ENISA (European Network and Information Security Agency) [5]. Not only does it list risks and vulnerabilities, but it also offers a survey of related works and research recommendations. A similarly work is the security guidance provided by the Cloud Security Alliance (CSA) [6], which defines security domains congregating specific functional aspects, from governance and compliance to virtualization and identity management. Both documents present a plethora of security concerns, best practices and recommendations regarding all types of services in NIST's SPI model, as well as possible problems related to cloud computing, encompassing from data privacy to infrastructural configuration. Albeit valuable, these studies do not focus on quantifying their observations, something important for developing a comprehensive understanding of the challenges still undermining the potential of cloud computing.

*Correspondence: nmimura@larc.usp.br
[1] Escola Politécnica at the University of São Paulo (EPUSP), São Paulo, Brazil
Full list of author information is available at the end of the article

The main goal of this article is to identify, classify, organize and quantify the main security concerns and solutions associated to cloud computing, helping in the task of pinpointing the concerns that remain unanswered. Aiming to organize this information into a useful tool for comparing, relating and classifying already identified concerns and solutions as well as future ones, we also present a taxonomy proposal for cloud computing security. We focus on issues that are specific to cloud computing, without losing sight of important issues that also exist in other distributed systems. This article extends our previous work presented in [11], providing an enhanced review of the cloud computing security taxonomy previously presented, as well as a deeper analysis of the related work by discussing the main security frameworks currently available; in addition, we discuss further the security aspects related to virtualization in cloud computing, a fundamental yet still underserved field of research.

Cloud computing security

Key references such as CSA's security guidance [6] and top threats analysis [12], ENISA's security assessment [5] and the cloud computing definitions from NIST [9] highlight different security issues related to cloud computing that require further studies for being appropriately handled and, consequently, for enhancing technology acceptance and adoption. Emphasis is given to the distinction between services in the form of software (SaaS), platform (PaaS) and infrastructure (IaaS), which are commonly used as the fundamental basis for cloud service classification. However, no other methods are standardized or even employed to organize cloud computing security aspects apart from cloud deployment models, service types or traditional security models.

Aiming to concentrate and organize information related to cloud security and to facilitate future studies, in this section we identify the main problems in the area and group them into a model composed of seven categories, based on the aforementioned references . Namely, the categories are: network security, interfaces, data security, virtualization, governance, compliance and legal issues. Each category includes several potential security problems, resulting in a classification with subdivisions that highlights the main issues identified in the base references:

1. Network security: Problems associated with network communications and configurations regarding cloud computing infrastructures. The ideal network security solution is to have cloud services as an extension of customers' existing internal networks [13], adopting the same protection measures and security precautions that are locally implemented

and allowing them to extend local strategies to any remote resource or process [14].

   (a) Transfer security: Distributed architectures, massive resource sharing and virtual machine (VM) instances synchronization imply more data in transit in the cloud, thus requiring VPN mechanisms for protecting the system against sniffing, spoofing, man-in-the-middle and side-channel attacks.
   (b) Firewalling: Firewalls protect the provider's internal cloud infrastructure against insiders and outsiders [15]. They also enable VM isolation, fine-grained filtering for addresses and ports, prevention of Denial-of-Service (DoS) and detection of external security assessment procedures. Efforts for developing consistent firewall and similar security measures specific for cloud environments [16,17] reveal the urge for adapting existing solutions for this new computing paradigm.
   (c) Security configuration: Configuration of protocols, systems and technologies to provide the required levels of security and privacy without compromising performance or efficiency [18].

2. Interfaces: Concentrates all issues related to user, administrative and programming interfaces for using and controlling clouds.

   (a) API: Programming interfaces (essential to IaaS and PaaS) for accessing virtualized resources and systems must be protected in order to prevent malicious use [19-23].
   (b) Administrative interface: Enables remote control of resources in an IaaS (VM management), development for PaaS (coding, deploying, testing) and application tools for SaaS (user access control, configurations).
   (c) User interface: End-user interface for exploring provided resources and tools (the service itself), implying the need of adopting measures for securing the environment [24-27].
   (d) Authentication: Mechanisms required to enable access to the cloud [28]. Most services rely on regular accounts [20,29,30] consequently being susceptible to a plethora of attacks [31-35] whose consequences are boosted by multi-tenancy and resource sharing.

3. Data security: Protection of data in terms of confidentiality, availability and integrity (which can

be applied not only to cloud environments, but any solution requiring basic security levels) [36].

(a) Cryptography: Most employed practice to secure sensitive data [37], thoroughly required by industry, state and federal regulations [38].

(b) Redundancy: Essential to avoid data loss. Most business models rely on information technology for its core functionalities and processes [39,40] and, thus, mission-critical data integrity and availability must be ensured.

(c) Disposal: Elementary data disposal techniques are insufficient and commonly referred as deletion [41].In the cloud, the complete destruction of data, including log references and hidden backup registries, is an important requirement [42].

4. Virtualization: Isolation between VMs, hypervisor vulnerabilities and other problems associated to the use of virtualization technologies [43].

(a) Isolation: Although logically isolated, all VMs share the same hardware and consequently the same resources, allowing malicious entities to exploit data leaks and cross-VM attacks [44]. The concept of isolation can also be applied to more fine-grained assets, such as computational resources, storage and memory.

(b) Hypervisor vulnerabilities: The hypervisor is the main software component of virtualization. Even though there are known security vulnerabilities for hypervisors, solutions are still scarce and often proprietary, demanding further studies to harden these security aspects.

(c) Data leakage: Exploit hypervisor vulnerabilities and lack of isolation controls in order to leak data from virtualized infrastructures, obtaining sensitive customer data and affecting confidentiality and integrity.

(d) VM identification: Lack of controls for identifying virtual machines that are being used for executing a specific process or for storing files.

(e) Cross-VM attacks: Includes attempts to estimate provider traffic rates in order to steal cryptographic keys and increase chances of VM placement attacks. One example consists in overlapping memory and storage regions initially dedicated to a single virtual

machine, which also enables other isolation-related attacks.

5. Governance: Issues related to (losing) administrative and security controls in cloud computing solutions [45,46].

(a) Data control: Moving data to the cloud means losing control over redundancy, location, file systems and other relevant configurations.

(b) Security control: Loss of governance over security mechanisms and policies, as terms of use prohibit customer-side vulnerability assessment and penetration tests while insufficient Service Level Agreements (SLA) lead to security gaps.

(c) Lock-in: User potential dependency on a particular service provider due to lack of well-established standards (protocols and data formats), consequently becoming particularly vulnerable to migrations and service termination.

6. Compliance: Includes requirements related to service availability and audit capabilities [47,48].

(a) Service Level Agreements (SLA): Mechanisms to ensure the required service availability and the basic security procedures to be adopted [49].

(b) Loss of service: Service outages are not exclusive to cloud environments but are more serious in this context due to the interconnections between services (e.g., a SaaS using virtualized infrastructures provided by an IaaS), as shown in many examples [50-52]. This leads to the need of strong disaster recovery policies and provider recommendations to implement customer-side redundancy if applicable.

(c) Audit: Allows security and availability assessments to be performed by customers, providers and third-party participants. Transparent and efficient methodologies are necessary for continuously analyzing service conditions [53] and are usually required by contracts or legal regulations. There are solutions being developed to address this problem by offering a transparent API for automated auditing and other useful functionalities [54].

(d) Service conformity: Related to how contractual obligations and overall service requirements are respected and offered based on the SLAs predefined and basic service and customer needs.

7. Legal issues: Aspects related to judicial requirements and law, such as multiple data locations and privilege management.

    (a) Data location: Customer data held in multiple jurisdictions depending on geographic location [55] are affected, directly or indirectly, by subpoena law-enforcement measures.

    (b) E-discovery: As a result of a law-enforcement measures, hardware might be confiscated for investigations related to a particular customer, affecting all customers whose data were stored in the same hardware [56-58]. Data disclosure is critical in this case.

    (c) Provider privilege: Malicious activities of provider insiders are potential threats to confidentiality, availability and integrity of customers' data and processes' information [59,60].

    (d) legislation: Juridical concerns related to new concepts introduced by cloud computing [61].

Cloud computing security taxonomy

The analysis of security concerns in the context of cloud computing solutions shows that each issue brings different impacts on distinct assets. Aiming to create a security model both for studying security aspects in this context and for supporting decision making, in this section we consider the risks and vulnerabilities previously presented and arrange them in hierarchical categories, thus creating a cloud security taxonomy. The main structure of the proposed taxonomy, along with its first classification levels, are depicted in Figure 1.

The three first groups correspond to fundamental (and often related) security principles [7] (Chapters 3-8).

The *architecture* dimension is subdivided into network security, interfaces and virtualization issues, comprising both user and administrative interfaces to access the cloud. It also comprises security during transferences of data and virtual machines, as well as other virtualization related issues, such as isolation and cross-VM attacks. This organization is depicted in Figure 2. The architecture group allows a clearer division of responsibilities between providers and customers, and also an analysis of their security roles depending on the type of service offered (Software, Platform or Infrastructure). This suggests that the security mechanisms used must be clearly stated before the service is contracted, defining which role is responsible for providing firewalling capabilities, access control features and technology-specific requirements (such as those related to virtualization).

The *compliance* dimension introduces responsibilities toward services and providers. The former includes SLA concerns, loss of service based on outages and chain failures, and auditing capabilities as well as transparency and security assessments. The latter refers to loss of control over data and security policies and configurations, and also lock-in issues resulting from lack of standards, migrations and service terminations. The complete scenario is presented in Figure 3.

The *privacy* dimension includes data security itself (from sensitive data, regulations and data loss to disposal and redundancy) and legal issues (related to multiple jurisdictions derived from different locations where data and services are hosted). The expansion of this group is represented in Figure 4. We note that the concerns in this dimension cover the complete information lifecycle (i.e., *generation, use, transfer, transformation, storage, archiving,* and *destruction*) inside the provider perimeter and in its immediate boundaries (or interfaces) to the users.

A common point between all groups is the intrinsic connection to data and service lifecycles. Both privacy and compliance must be ensured through all states of data, including application information or customer assets, while security in this case is more oriented towards how the underlying elements (e.g., infrastructural hardware and software) are protected.

Current status of cloud security

A clear perspective of the main security problems regarding cloud computing and on how they can be organized

Figure 1 Cloud computing security taxonomy. Top level overview of the security taxonomy proposed, highlighting the three main categories: security related to privacy, architecture and compliance.

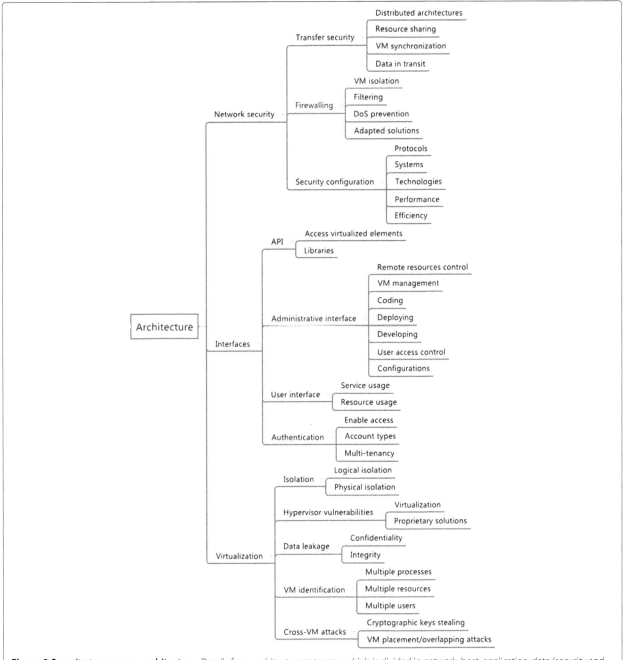

Figure 2 Security taxonomy - architecture. Details from architecture category, which is divided in network, host, application, data (security and storage), security management, and identity and access controls – all these elements are directly connected to the infrastructure and architecture adopted to implement or use a cloud solution.

to ease decision making is the primary step for having a comprehensive overview of the current status of cloud security. In this section, we analyze industry and academia viewpoints focusing on strategic study areas that need to be further developed. This study is based on more than two hundred different references including white papers, technical reports, scientific papers and other relevant publications. They were analyzed in terms of security problems and solutions by evaluating the number of citations for each case. We used a quantitative approach to identify the amount of references related to each category of concerns or solutions. Our goal is not to determine if the presented solutions completely solve an identified concern, since most of the referenced authors agree that this is an involved task. Nonetheless, we identify the number of references dealing with each concern, providing

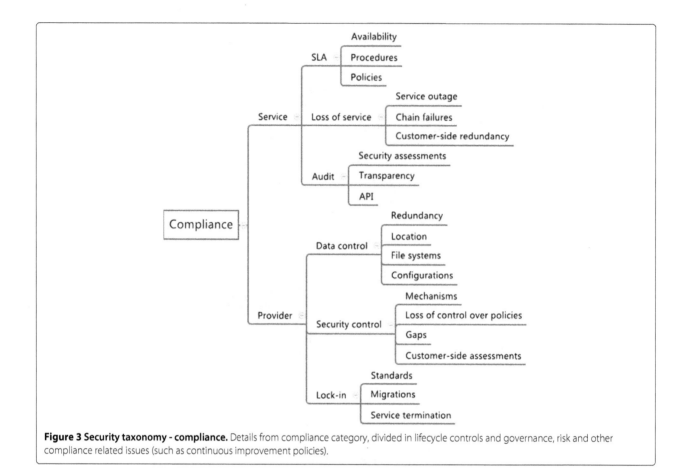

Figure 3 Security taxonomy - compliance. Details from compliance category, divided in lifecycle controls and governance, risk and other compliance related issues (such as continuous improvement policies).

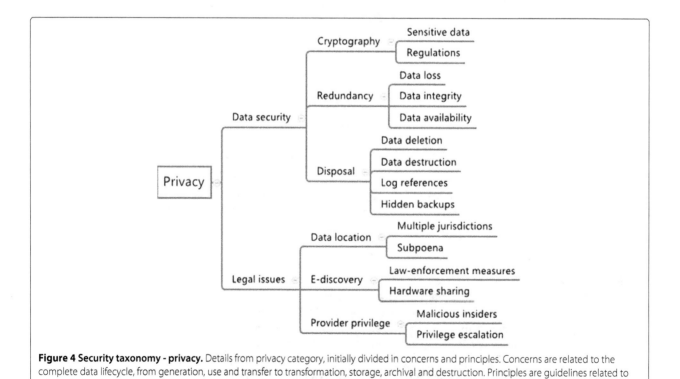

Figure 4 Security taxonomy - privacy. Details from privacy category, initially divided in concerns and principles. Concerns are related to the complete data lifecycle, from generation, use and transfer to transformation, storage, archival and destruction. Principles are guidelines related to privacy in the cloud.

some useful insight on which are the concerns that have received more attention from the research community and which have not been so extensively analyzed. Some observations about the analysis method:

1. The references consulted came from different research segments, including academia, organizations, and companies. Due to the article's length limitations, we did not include all the consulted references in the References section. In the following we present some of the main sources of consultation:

    (a) Academia: conference papers and journals published by IEEE, ACM, Springer, Webscience, and Scipress.
    (b) Organizations: reports, white papers, and interviews from SANS Institute, CSA, NIST, ENISA, Gartner Group, KVM.org, OpenGrid, OpenStack, and OpenNebula.
    (c) Companies: white papers, manuals, interviews, and web content from ERICSSON, IBM, XEROX, Cisco, VMWare, XEN, CITRIX, EMC, Microsoft, and Salesforce.

2. Each reference was analyzed aiming to identify all the mentioned concerns covered and solutions provided.

Therefore, one reference can produce more than one entry on each specified category.

3. Some security perspectives were not covered in this paper, as each security/concern category can be sub-divided in finer-grained aspects such as: authentication, integrity, network communications, etc.

We present the security concerns and solutions using pie charts in order to show the representativeness of each category/group in the total amount of references identified. The comparison between areas is presented using radar graphs to identify how many solutions address each concern category/group.

Security concerns

The results obtained for the number of citations on security issues is shown in Figure 5. The three major problems identified in these references are legal issues, compliance and loss of control over data. These legal- and governance-related concerns are followed by the first technical issue, isolation, with 7% of citations. The least cited problems are related to security configuration concerns, loss of service (albeit this is also related to compliance, which is a major problem), firewalling and interfaces.

Grouping the concerns using the categories presented in section "Cloud computing security" leads to the

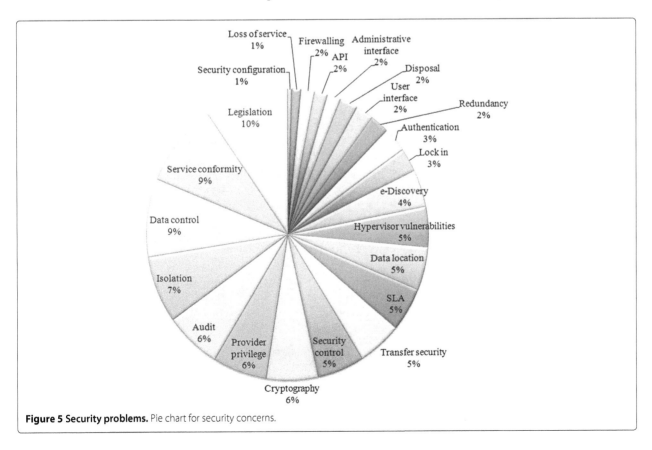

Figure 5 Security problems. Pie chart for security concerns.

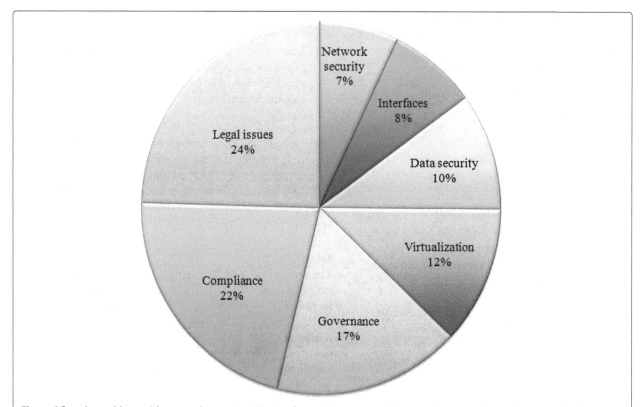

Figure 6 Security problems with grouped categories. Pie chart for security concerns with grouped categories (seven altogether: legal issues, compliance, governance, virtualization, data security, interfaces and network security).

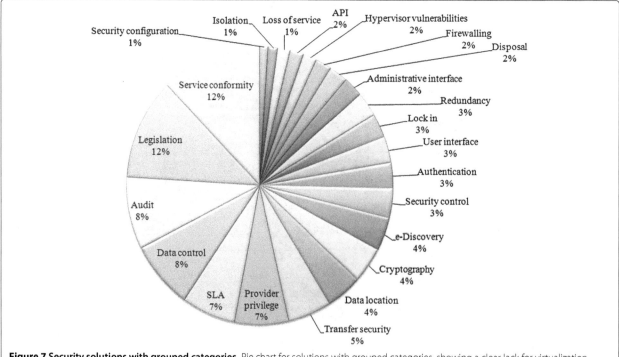

Figure 7 Security solutions with grouped categories. Pie chart for solutions with grouped categories, showing a clear lack for virtualization security mechanisms in comparison to its importance in terms of concerns citations.

construction of Figure 6. This figure shows that legal and governance issues represent a clear majority with 73% of concern citations, showing a deep consideration of legal issues such as data location and e-discovery, or governance ones like loss of control over security and data. The technical issue more intensively evaluated (12%) is virtualization, followed by data security, interfaces and network security.

Virtualization is one of the main novelties employed by cloud computing in terms of technologies employed, considering virtual infrastructures, scalability and resource sharing, and its related problems represent the first major technical concern.

Security solutions

When analyzing citations for solutions, we used the same approach described in the beginning of this section. The results are presented in Figure 7, which shows the percentage of solutions in each category defined in section "Cloud computing security", and also in Figure 8, which highlights the contribution of each individual sub-category.

When we compare Figures 6 and 7, it is easy to observe that the number of citations covering security problems related to legal issues, compliance and governance is high (respectively 24%, 22%, and 17%); however, the same also happens when we consider the number of references proposing solutions for those issues (which represent respectively 29%, 27%, and 14% of the total number of citations). In other words, these concerns are higly relevant but a large number solutions are already available for tackling them.

The situation is completely different when we analyze technical aspects such as virtualization, isolation and data leakage. Indeed, virtualization amounts for 12% of problem references and only 3% for solutions. Isolation is a perfect example of such discrepancy as the number of citations for such problems represents 7% in Figure 5, while solutions correspond to only 1% of the graph from Figure 8. We note that, for this specific issue, special care has been taken when assessing the most popular virtual machine solution providers (e.g., XEN, VMWARE, and KVM) aiming to verify their concerns and available solutions. A conclusion that can be drawn from this situation is that such concerns are also significant but yet little is available in terms of solutions. This indicates the need of evaluating potential areas still to be developed in order to provide better security conditions when migrating data and processes in the cloud.

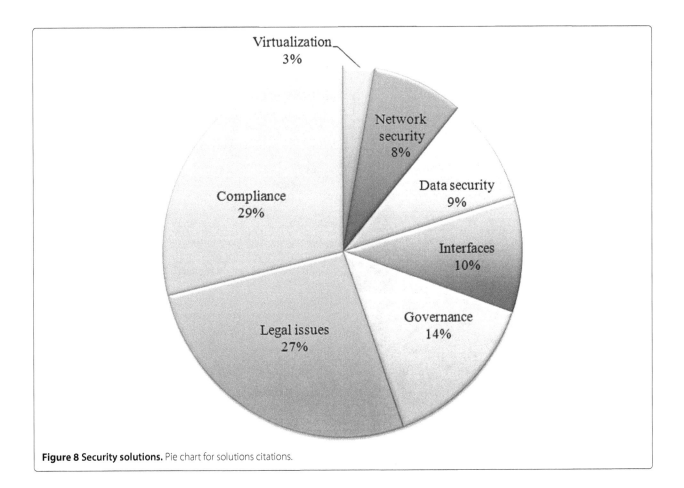

Figure 8 Security solutions. Pie chart for solutions citations.

Comparison

The differences between problem and solution citations presented in the previous sections can be observed in Figure 9.

Axis values correspond to the number of citations found among the references studied. Blue areas represent concern citations and lighter red indicates solutions, while darker red shows where those areas overlap. In other words, light red areas are problems with more citations for solutions than problems – they might be meaningful problems, but there are many solutions already addressing them – while blue areas represent potential subjects that have received little attention so far, indicating the need for further studies.

Figure 9 clearly shows the lack of development regarding data control mechanisms, hypervisor vulnerabilities assessment and isolation solutions for virtualized environments. On the other hand, areas such as legal concerns, SLAs, compliance and audit policies have a quite satisfactory coverage. The results for grouped categories (presented in section 4) are depicted in Figure 10.

Figure 10 shows that virtualization problems represent an area that requires studies for addressing issues such as isolation, data leakage and cross-VM attacks; on the other hand, areas such as compliance and network security encompass concerns for which there are already a considerable number of solutions or that are not considered highly relevant.

Finally, Considering virtualization as key element for future studies, Figure 11 presents a comparison focusing on five virtualization-related problems: isolation (of computational resources, such as memory and storage

capabilities), hypervisor vulnerabilities, data leakage, cross-VM attacks and VM identification. The contrast related to isolation and cross-VM attacks is more evident than for the other issues. However, the number of solution citations for all issues is notably low if compared to any other security concern, reaffirming the need for further researches in those areas.

Related work

An abundant number of related works and publications exist in the literature, emphasizing the importance and demand of security solutions for cloud computing. However, we did not identify any full taxonomy that addresses directly the security aspects related to cloud computing. We only identified some simplified models that were developed to cover specific security aspects such as authentication. We were able to recognize two main types of works: (1) security frameworks, which aim to aggregate information about security and also to offer sets of best practices and guidelines when using cloud solutions, and (2) publications that identify future trends and propose solutions or areas of interest for research. Each category and corresponding references are further analyzed in the following subsections.

Security frameworks

Security frameworks concentrate information on security and privacy aiming to provide a compilation of risks, vulnerabilities and best practices to avoid or mitigate them. There are several entities that are constantly publishing material related to cloud computing security, including ENISA, CSA, NIST, CPNI (Centre for the Protection of

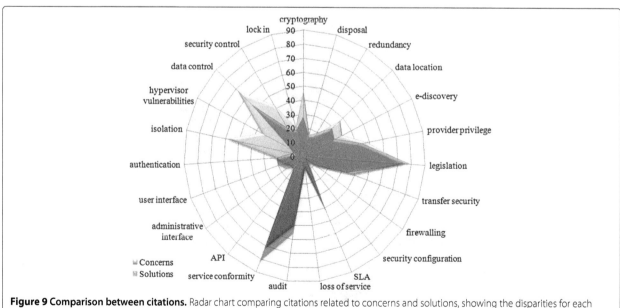

Figure 9 Comparison between citations. Radar chart comparing citations related to concerns and solutions, showing the disparities for each security category adopted.

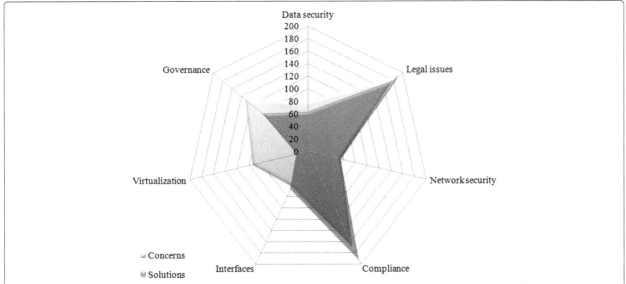

Figure 10 Comparison between citations with grouped categories. Radar chart grouping the categories, showing the difference between citations about concerns and solutions regarding each category.

National Infrastructure from UK government) and ISACA (the Information Systems Audit and Control Association). In this paper we focus on the first three entities, which by themselves provide a quite comprehensive overview of issues and solutions and, thus, allowing a broad understanding of the current status of cloud security.

ENISA

ENISA is an agency responsible for achieving high and effective level of network and information security within the European Union [62]. In the context of cloud computing, they published an extensive study covering benefits

and risks related to its use [5]. In this study, the security risks are divided in four categories:

- Policy and organizational: issues related to governance, compliance and reputation;
- Technical: issues derived from technologies used to implement cloud services and infrastructures, such as isolation, data leakage and interception, denial of service attacks, encryption and disposal;
- Legal: risks regarding jurisdictions, subpoena and e-discovery;

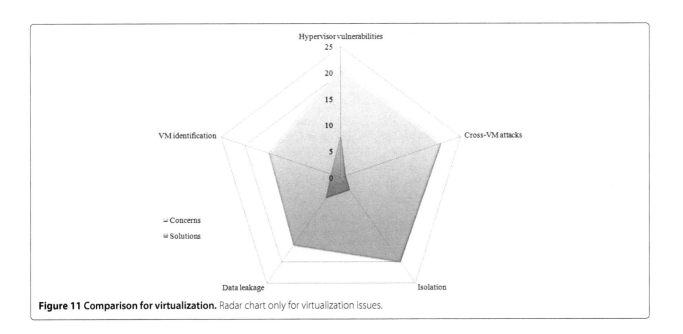

Figure 11 Comparison for virtualization. Radar chart only for virtualization issues.

- Not cloud specific: other risks that are not unique to cloud environments, such as network management, privilege escalation and logging;

As a top recommendation for security in cloud computing, ENISA suggests that providers must ensure some security practices to customers and also a clear contract to avoid legal problems. Key points to be developed include breach reporting, better logging mechanisms and engineering of large scale computer systems, which encompass the isolation of virtual machines, resources and information. Their analysis is based not only on what is currently observed, but also on what can be improved through the adoption of existing best practices or by means of solutions that are already used in non-cloud environments. This article aims at taking one step further by transforming these observations into numbers – a quantitative approach.

CSA

CSA is an organization led by a coalition of industry practitioners, corporations, associations and other stakeholders [63], such as Dell, HP and eBay. One of its main goals is to promote the adoption of best practices for providing security within cloud computing environments.

Three CSA documents are analyzed in this paper – the security guidance [6], the top threats in cloud computing [12] and the Trusted Cloud Initiative (TCI) architecture [64] – as they comprise most of the concepts and guidelines researched and published by CSA.

The latest CSA security guidance (version 3.0 [65]) denotes multi-tenancy as the essential cloud characteristic while virtualization can be avoided when implementing cloud infrastructures – multi-tenancy only implies the use of shared resources by multiple consumers, possibly from different organizations or with different objectives. They discuss that, even if virtualization-related issues can be circumvented, segmentation and isolated policies for addressing proper management and privacy are still required. The document also establishes thirteen security domains:

1. Governance and risk management: ability to measure the risk introduced by adopting cloud computing solutions, such as legal issues, protection of sensitive data and their relation to international boundaries;
2. Legal issues: disclosure laws, shared infrastructures and interference between different users;
3. Compliance and audit: the relationship between cloud computing and internal security policies;
4. Information management and data security: identification and control of stored data, loss of physical control of data and related policies to minimize risks and possible damages;

5. Portability and interoperability: ability to change providers, services or bringing back data to local premises without major impacts;
6. Traditional security, business continuity and disaster recovery: the influence of cloud solutions on traditional processes applied for addressing security needs;
7. Data center operations: analyzing architecture and operations from data centers and identifying essential characteristics for ensuring stability;
8. Incident response, notification and remediation: policies for handling incidents;
9. Application security: aims to identify the possible security issues raised from migrating a specific solution to the cloud and which platform (among SPI model) is more adequate;
10. Encryption and key management: how higher scalability via infrastructure sharing affects encryption and other mechanisms used for protecting resources and data;
11. Identity and access management: enabling authentication for cloud solutions while maintaining security levels and availability for customers and organizations;
12. Virtualization: risks related to multi-tenancy, isolation, virtual machine co-residence and hypervisor vulnerabilities, all introduced by virtualization technologies;
13. Security as a service: third party security mechanisms, delegating security responsibilities to a trusted third party provider;

CSA also published a document focusing on identifying top threats, aiming to aid risk management strategies when cloud solutions are adopted [12]. As a complete list of threats and pertinent issues is countless, the document targets those that are specific or intensified by fundamental characteristics of the cloud, such as shared infrastructures and greater flexibility. As a result, seven threats were selected:

1. Abuse and nefarious used of cloud computing: while providing flexible and powerful resources and tools, IaaS and PaaS solutions also unveil critical exploitation possibilities built on anonymity. This leads to abuse and misuse of the provided infrastructure for conducting distributed denial of service attacks, hosting malicious data, controlling botnets or sending spam;
2. Insecure application programming interfaces: cloud services provide APIs for management, storage, virtual machine allocation and other service-specific operations. The interfaces provided must implement security methods to identify, authenticate and protect

against accidental or malicious use, which can introduce additional complexities to the system such as the need for third-party authorities and services;

3. Malicious insiders: although not specific to cloud computing, its effects are amplified by the concentration and interaction of services and management domains;

4. Shared technology vulnerabilities: scalability provided by cloud solutions are based on hardware and software components which are not originally designed to provide isolation. Even though hypervisors offer an extra granularity layer, they still exhibit flaws which are exploited for privilege escalation;

5. Data loss and leakage: insufficient controls concerning user access and data security (including privacy and integrity), as well as disposal and even legal issues;

6. Account, service and traffic hijacking: phishing and related frauds are not a novelty to computing security. However, not only an attacker is able to manipulate data and transactions, but also to use stolen credentials to perform other attacks that compromise customer and provider reputation.

7. Unknown risk profile: delegation of control over data and infrastructure allows companies to better concentrate on their core business, possibly maximizing profit and efficiency. On the other hand, the consequent loss of governance leads to obscurity [66]: information about other customers sharing the same infrastructure or regarding patching and updating policies is limited. This situation creates uncertainty concerning the exact risk levels that are inherent to the cloud solution;

It is interesting to notice the choice for cloud-specific issues as it allows the identification of central points for further development. Moreover, this compilation of threats is closely related to CSA security guidance, composing a solid framework for security and risk analysis assessments while providing recommendations and best practices to achieve acceptable security levels.

Another approach adopted by CSA for organizing information related to cloud security and governance is the TCI Reference Architecture Model [64]. This document focuses on defining guidelines for enabling trust in the cloud while establishing open standards and capabilities for all cloud-based operations. The architecture defines different organization levels by combining frameworks like the SPI model, ISO 27002, COBIT, PCI, SOX and architectures such as SABSA, TOGAF, ITIL and Jericho. A wide range of aspects are then covered: SABSA defines business operation support services, such as compliance, data governance, operational risk management,

human resources security, security monitoring services, legal services and internal investigations; TOGAF defines the types of services covered (presentation, application, information and infrastructure; ITIL is used for information technology operation and support, from IT operation to service delivery, support and management of incidents, changes and resources; finally, Jericho covers security and risk management, including information security management, authorization, threat and vulnerability management, policies and standards. The result is a tri-dimensional relationship between cloud delivery, trust and operation that aims to be easily consumed and applied in a security-oriented design.

NIST

NIST has recently published a taxonomy for security in cloud computing [67] that is comparable to the taxonomy introduced in section "Cloud computing security taxonomy". This taxonomy's first level encompass typical roles in the cloud environment: cloud service provider, responsible for making the service itself available; cloud service consumer, who uses the service and maintains a business relationship with the provider; cloud carrier, which provides communication interfaces between providers and consumers; cloud broker, that manages use, performance and delivery of services and intermediates negotiations between providers and consumers; and cloud auditor, which performs assessment of services, operations and security. Each role is associated to their respective activities and decomposed on their components and subcomponents. The clearest difference from our taxonomy is the hierarchy adopted, as our proposal primarily focuses on security principles in its higher level perspective, while the cloud roles are explored in deeper levels. The concepts presented here extend NIST's initial definition for cloud computing [9], incorporating a division of roles and responsibilities that can be directly applied to security assessments. On the other hand, NIST's taxonomy incorporates concepts such as deployment models, service types and activities related to cloud management (portability, interoperability, provisioning), most of them largely employed in publications related to cloud computing – including this one.

Frameworks summary

Tables 1 and 2 summarize the information about each framework.

Books, papers and other publications

Rimal, Choi and Lumb [3] present a cloud taxonomy created from the perspective of the academia, developers and researchers, instead of the usual point of view related to vendors. Whilst they do provide definitions and concepts such as cloud architecture (based on SPI model),

Table 1 Summary of CSA security frameworks

Framework	Objectives	Structure and comments
CSA Guidance	• Recommendations for reducing risks • No restrictions regarding specific solutions or service types • Guidelines not necessarily applicable for all deployment models • Provide initial structure to divide efforts for researches	• One architectural domain • Governance domains: risk management, legal concerns, compliance, auditing, information management, interoperability and portability • Operational domains: traditional and business security, disaster recovery, data center operations, encryption, application security, identification, authorization, virtualization, security outsourcing • Emphasis on the fact that cloud is not bound to virtualization technologies, though cloud services heavily depend on virtualized infrastructures to provide flexibility and scalability

CSA Top Threats	• Provide context for risk management decisions and strategies
	• Focus on issues which are unique or highly influenced by cloud computing characteristics
		• Seven main threats:
		  – Abuse and malicious use of cloud resources
		  – Insecure APIs
		  – Malicious insiders
		  – Shared technology vulnerabilities
		  – Data loss and leakage
		  – Hijacking of accounts, services and traffic
		  – Unknown risk profile (security obscurity)
		• Summarizes information on top threats and provide examples, remediation guidelines, impact caused and which service types (based on SPI model) are affected

CSA Architecture	• Enable trust in the cloud based on well-known standards and certifications allied to security frameworks and other open references • Use widely adopted frameworks in order to achieve standardization of policies and best practices based on already accepted security principles	• Four sets of frameworks (security, NIST SPI, IT audit and legislative) and four architectural domains (SABSA business architecture, ITIL for services management, Jericho for security and TOGAF for IT reference) • Tridimensional structure based on premises of cloud delivery, trust and operations • Concentrates a plethora of concepts and information related to services operation and security

Table summarizing information related to CSA security frameworks (guidance, top threats and TCI architecture).

virtualization management, service types, fault tolerance policies and security, no further studies are developed focusing on cloud specific security aspects. This characteristic is also observed in other cloud taxonomies [68-70] whose efforts converge to the definition of service models and types rather than to more technical aspects such as security, privacy or compliance concerns – which are the focus of this paper.

In [7], Mather, Kumaraswamy and Latif discuss the current status of cloud security and what is predicted for the future. The result is a compilation of security-related subjects to be developed in topics like infrastructure, data security and storage, identity and access management, security management, privacy, audit and compliance. They also explore the unquestionable urge for more transparency regarding which party (customer or cloud provider) provides each security capability, as well as the need for standardization and for the creation of legal agreements reflecting operational SLAs. Other issues discussed are the inadequate encryption and key management capabilities currently offered, as well as the need for multi-entity key management.

Many publications also state the need for better security mechanisms for cloud environments. Doelitzscher et al. [71] emphasize security as a major research area in cloud computing. They also highlight the lack of flexibility of classic intrusion detection mechanisms to handle virtualized environments, suggesting the use of special security audit tools associated to business flow modeling through security SLAs. In addition, they identify abuse of cloud resources, lack of security monitoring in cloud infrastructure and defective isolation of shared resources as focal points to be managed. Their analysis of top security concerns is also based on publications from CSA, ENISA and others, but after a quick evaluation of issues their focus switch to their security auditing solution, without offering a deeper quantitative compilation of security risks and areas of concern.

Table 2 Summary of ENISA and NIST security frameworks

Framework	Objectives	Structure and comments
ENISA Report		
	• Study on benefits and risks when adopting cloud solutions for business operations • Provide information for security assessments and decision making	• Three main categories of cloud specific risks (policy and organizational, technical, legal) plus one extra category for not specific ones • Offers basic guidelines and best practices for avoiding or mitigating their effects • Presents recommendations for further studies related to trust building (certifications, metrics and transparency), large scale data protection (privacy, integrity, incident handling and regulations) and technical aspects (isolation, portability and resilience) • Highlights the duality of scalability (fast, flexible and accessible resources versus concentrations of data attracting attackers and also providing infrastructure for aiding their operations) • Extensive study on risks considering their impact and probability
NIST Taxonomy		

	• Define what cloud services should provide rather than how to design and implement solutions
	• Ease the understanding of cloud internal operations and mechanisms
		• Taxonomy levels:
		  – First level: cloud roles (service provider, consumer, cloud broker, cloud carrier and cloud auditor)
		  – Second level: activities performed by each role (cloud management, service deployment, cloud access and service consumption)
		  – Third and following levels: elements which compose each activity (deployment models, service types and auditing elements)
		• Based on publication SP 500-292, highlighting the importance of security, privacy and levels of confidence and trust to increase technology acceptance
		• Concentrates many useful concepts, such as models for deploying or classifying services

Table summarizing information on ENISA and NIST security frameworks.

Associations such as the Enterprise Strategy Group [72] emphasize the need for hypervisor security, shrinking hypervisor footprints, defining the security perimeter virtualization, and linking security and VM provisioning for better resource management. Aiming to address these requirements, they suggest the use of increased automation for security controls, VM identity management (built on top of Public Key Infrastructure and Open Virtualization Format) and data encryption (tightly connected to state-of-art key management practices). Wallom *et al.* [73] emphasize the need of guaranteeing virtual machines' trustworthiness (regarding origin and identity) to perform security-critical computations and to handle sensitive data, therefore presenting a solution which integrates Trusted Computing technologies and available cloud infrastructures. Dabrowski and Mills [74] used simulation to demonstrate virtual machine leakage and resource exhaustion scenarios leading to degraded performance and crashes; they also propose the addition of orphan controls to enable the virtualized cloud environment to offer higher availability levels while keeping overhead costs under control. Ristenpart *et al.* [44] also explore virtual machine exploitation focusing on information leakage, specially sensitive data at rest or in transit.

Finally, Chadwick and Casenove [75] describe a security API for federated access to cloud resources and authority delegation while setting fine-grained controls and guaranteeing the required levels of assurance inside cloud environments. These publications highlight the need of security improvements related to virtual machines and virtualization techniques, concern that this paper demonstrates to be valid and urgent.

Discussion

Considering the points raised in the previous section, a straightforward conclusion is that cloud security includes old and well-known issues – such as network and other infrastructural vulnerabilities, user access, authentication and privacy – and also novel concerns derived from new technologies adopted to offer the adequate resources (mainly virtualized ones), services and auxiliary tools. These problems are summarized by isolation and hypervisor vulnerabilities (the main technical concerns according to the studies and graphics presented), data location and e-discovery (legal aspects), and loss of governance over data, security and even decision making (in which the cloud must be strategically and financially considered as a decisive factor).

Another point observed is that, even though adopting a cloud service or provider may be easy, migrating to another is not [76]. After moving local data and processes to the cloud, the lack of standards for protocols and formats directly affects attempts to migrate to a different provider even if this is motivated by legitimate reasons such as non-fulfillment of SLAs, outages or provider bankruptcy [77]. Consequently, the first choice must be carefully made, as SLAs are not perfect and services outages happen at the same pace that resource sharing, multi-tenancy and scalability are not fail proof. After a decision is made, future migrations between services can be extremely onerous in terms of time and costs; most likely, this task will require an extensive work for bringing all data and resources to a local infrastructure before redeploying them into the cloud.

Finally, the analysis of current trends for cloud computing reveals that there is a considerable number of well-studied security concerns, for which plenty solutions and best practices have been developed, such as those related to legal and administrative concerns. On the other hand, many issues still require further research effort, especially those related to secure virtualization.

Considerations and future work

Security is a crucial aspect for providing a reliable environment and then enable the use of applications in the cloud and for moving data and business processes to virtualized infrastructures. Many of the security issues identified are observed in other computing environments: authentication, network security and legal requirements, for example, are not a novelty. However, the impact of such issues is intensified in cloud computing due to characteristics such as multi-tenancy and resource sharing, since actions from a single customer can affect all other users that inevitably share the same resources and interfaces. On the other hand, efficient and secure virtualization represents a new challenge in such a context with high distribution of complex services and web-based applications, thus requiring more sophisticated approaches. At the same time, our quantitative analysis indicates that virtualization remains an underserved area regarding the number of solutions provided to identified concerns.

It is strategic to develop new mechanisms that provide the required security level by isolating virtual machines and the associated resources while following best practices in terms of legal regulations and compliance to SLAs. Among other requirements, such solutions should employ virtual machine identification, provide an adequate separation of dedicated resources combined with a constant observation of shared ones, and examine any attempt of exploiting cross-VM and data leakage.

A secure cloud computing environment depends on several security solutions working harmoniously together. However, in our studies we did not identify any security solutions provider owning the facilities necessary to get high levels of security conformity for clouds. Thus, cloud providers need to orchestrate / harmonize security solutions from different places in order to achieve the desired security level.

In order to verify these conclusions in practice, we deployed testbeds using OpenNebula (based on KVM and XEN) and analyzed its security aspects; we also analyzed virtualized servers based on VMWARE using our testbed networks. This investigation lead to a wide research of PaaS solutions, and allowed us to verify that most of them use virtual machines based on virtualization technologies such as VMWARE, XEN, and KVM, which often lack security aspects We also learned that Amazon changed the XEN source code in order to include security features, but unfortunately the modified code is not publicly available and there appears to be no article detailing the changes introduced. Given these limitations, a deeper study on current security solutions to manage cloud computing virtual machines inside the cloud providers should be a focus of future work in the area. We are also working on a testbed based on OpenStack for researches related to identity and credentials management in the cloud environment. This work should address basic needs for better security mechanisms in virtualized and distributed architectures, guiding other future researches in the security area.

Competing interests
The authors declare that they have no competing interests.

Author's contributions
NG carried out the security research, including the prospecting for information and references, categorization, results analysis, taxonomy creation and analysis of related work. CM participated in the drafting of the manuscript as well as in the analysis of references, creation of the taxonomy and revisions of the text. MS, FR, MN and MP participated in the critical and technical revisions of the paper including the final one, also helping with the details for preparing the paper to be published. TC coordinated the project related to the paper and also gave the final approval of the version to be published. All authors read and approved the final manuscript.

Acknowledgements
This work was supported by the Innovation Center, Ericsson Telecomunicações S.A., Brazil.

Author details
[1] Escola Politécnica at the University of São Paulo (EPUSP), São Paulo, Brazil. [2] Ericsson Research, Stockholm, Sweden. [3] Ericsson Research, Ville Mont-Royal, Canada. [4] State University of Santa Catarina, Joinville, Brazil.

References

1. IDC (2009) Cloud Computing 2010 – An IDC Update. slideshare.net/JorFigOr/cloud-computing-2010-an-idc-update
2. Armbrust M, Fox A, Griffith R, Joseph AD, Katz RH, Konwinski A, Lee G, Patterson DA, Rabkin A, Stoica I, Zaharia M (2009) Above the Clouds:

A Berkeley View of Cloud Computing. Technical Report UCB/EECS-2009-28, University of California at Berkeley, eecs.berkeley.edu/Pubs/TechRpts/2009/EECS-2009-28.html

3. Rimal BP, Choi E, Lumb I (2009) A Taxonomy and, Survey of Cloud Computing Systems. In: Fifth International Joint Conference on INC, IMS and IDC, NCM '09, CPS. pp 44–51

4. Shankland S (2009) HP's Hurd dings cloud computing, IBM. CNET News

5. Catteddu D, Hogben G (2009) Benefits, risks and recommendations for information security. Tech. rep., European Network and Information Security Agency, enisa.europa.eu/act/rm/files/deliverables/cloud-computing-risk-assessment

6. CSA (2009) Security Guidance for Critical Areas of Focus in Cloud Computing. Tech. rep., Cloud Security Alliance

7. Mather T, Kumaraswamy S (2009) Cloud Security and privacy: An Enterprise Perspective on Risks and Compliance. 1st edition. O'Reilly Media

8. Chen Y, Paxson V, Katz RH (2010) What's New About Cloud Computing Security? Technical Report UCB/EECS-2010-5, University of California at Berkeley, eecs.berkeley.edu/Pubs/TechRpts/2010/EECS-2010-5.html

9. Mell P, Grance T (2009) The NIST Definition of Cloud Computing. Technical Report 15, National Institute of Standards and Technology, www.nist.gov/itl/cloud/upload/cloud-def-v15.pdf

10. Ibrahim AS, Hamlyn-Harris J, Grundy J (2010) Emerging Security Challenges of Cloud Virtual Infrastructure. In: Proceedings of APSEC 2010 Cloud Workshop, APSEC '10

11. Gonzalez N, Miers C, Redígolo F, Carvalho T, Simplício M, Naslund M, Pourzandi M (2011) A quantitative analysis of current security concerns and solutions for cloud computing. In: Proceedings of 3rd IEEE CloudCom. Athens/Greece: IEEE Computer Society

12. Hubbard D, Jr LJH, Sutton M (2010) Top Threats to Cloud Computing. Tech. rep., Cloud Security Alliance. cloudsecurityalliance.org/research/projects/top-threats-to-cloud-computing/

13. Tompkins D (2009) Security for Cloud-based Enterprise Applications. http://blog.dt.org/index.php/2009/02/security-for-cloud-based-enterprise-applications/

14. Jensen M, Schwenk J, Gruschka N, Iacono LL (2009) On Technical Security Issues in Cloud Computing. In: IEEE Internation Conference on Cloud Computing. pp 109–116

15. TrendMicro (2010) Cloud Computing Security - Making Virtual Machines Cloud-Ready. Trend Micro White Paper

16. Genovese S (2009) Akamai Introduces Cloud-Based Firewall. http://cloudcomputing.sys-con.com/node/1219023

17. Hulme GV (2011) CloudPassage aims to ease cloud server security management. http://www.csoonline.com/article/658121/cloudpassage-aims-to-ease-cloud-server-security-management

18. Oleshchuk VA, Køien GM (2011) Security and Privacy in the Cloud - A Long-Term View. In: 2nd International Conference on Wireless Communications, Vehicular Technology, Information Theory and Aerospace and Electronic Systems Technology (Wireless VITAE), WIRELESS VITAE '11. pp 1–5, http://dx.doi.org/10.1109/WIRELESSVITAE.2011.5940876

19. Google (2011) Google App Engine. code.google.com/appengine/

20. Google (2011) Google Query Language (GQL). code.google.com/intl/en/appengine/docs/python/overview.html

21. StackOverflow (2011) Does using non-SQL databases obviate the need for guarding against SQL injection? stackoverflow.com/questions/1823536/does-using-non-sql-databases-obvia te-the-need-for-guarding-against-sql-injection

22. Rose J (2011) Cloudy with a chance of zero day. www.owasp.org/images/1/12/Cloudy_with_a_chance_of_0_day_Jon_Rose-Tom_Leavey.pdf

23. Balkan A (2011) Why Google App Engine is broken and what Google must do to fix it. aralbalkan.com/1504

24. Salesforce (2011) Salesforce Security Statement. salesforce.com/company/privacy/security.jsp

25. Espiner T (2007) Salesforce tight-lipped after phishing attack. zdnet.co.uk/news/security-threats/2007/11/07/salesforce-tight-lipped-a fter-phishing-attack-39290616/

26. Yee A (2007) Implications of Salesforce Phishing Incident. ebizq.net/blogs/security_insider/2007/11/-implications_of_salesforc e_phi.php

27. Salesforce (2011) Security Implementation Guide. login.salesforce.com/help/doc/en/salesforce_security_impl_guide.pdf

28. Li H, Dai Y, Tian L, Yang H (2009) Identity-Based Authentication for Cloud Computing. In: Proceedings of the 1st International Conference on Cloud Computing, CloudCom '09

29. Amazon (2011) Elastic Compute Cloud (EC2). aws.amazon.com/ec2/

30. Kaufman C, Venkatapathy R (2010) Windows Azure Security Overview. go.microsoft.com/?linkid=9740388, [August]

31. McMillan R (2010) Google Attack Part of Widespread Spying Effort. PCWorld

32. Mills E (2010) Behind the China attacks on Google. CNET News

33. Arrington M (2010) Google Defends Against Large Scale Chinese Cyber Attack: May Cease Chinese Operations. TechCrunch

34. Bosch J (2009) Google Accounts Attacked by Phishing Scam. BrickHouse Security Blog

35. Telegraph T (2009) Facebook Users Targeted By Phishing Attack. The Telegraph

36. Pearson S (2009) Taking account of privacy when designing cloud computing services. In: Proceedings of the 2009 ICSE Workshop on Software Engineering Challenges of Cloud Computing, CLOUD '09

37. Musthaler L (2009) Cost-effective data encryption in the cloud. Network World

38. Yan L, Rong C, Zhao G (2009) Strengthen Cloud Computing Security with Federal Identity Management Using Hierarchical Identity-Based Cryptography. In: Proceedings of the 1st International Conference on Cloud Computing, CloudCom '09

39. Tech C (2010) Examining Redundancy in the Data Center Powered by the Cloud and Disaster Recovery. Consonus Tech

40. Lyle M (2011) Redundancy in Data Storage. Define the Cloud

41. Dorion P (2010) Data destruction services: When data deletion is not enough. SearchDataBackup.com

42. Mogull R (2009) Cloud Data Security: Archive and Delete (Rough Cut). securosis.com/blog/cloud-data-security-archive-and-delete-rough-cut/

43. Messmer E (2011) Gartner: New security demands arising for virtualization, cloud computing. http://www.networkworld.com/news/2011/062311-security-summit.html

44. Ristenpart T, Tromer E, Shacham H, Savage S (2009) Hey, you, get off of my cloud: exploring information leakage in third-party compute clouds. In: Proceedings of the 16th ACM conference on Computer and communications security, CCS '09. New York, NY, USA, ACM, pp 199–212, doi.acm.org/10.1145/1653662.1653687

45. Chow R, Golle P, Jakobsson M, Shi E, Staddon J, Masuoka R, Molina J (2009) Controlling data in the cloud: outsourcing computation without outsourcing control. In: Proceedings of the 2009 ACM workshop on, Cloud computing security, CCSW '09. New York, NY, USA, ACM, pp 85–90, http://doi.acm.org/10.1145/1655008.1655020

46. Sadeghi AR, Schneider T, Winandy M (2010) Token-Based Cloud Computing - Secure Outsourcing of Data and Arbitrary Computations with Lower Latency. In: Proceedings of the 3rd international conference on Trust and trustworthy computing, TRUST '10

47. Brandic I, Dustdar S, Anstett T, Schumm D, Leymann F (2010) Compliant Cloud Computing (C3): Architecture and Language Support for User-driven Compliance Management in Clouds. In: 2010 IEEE 3rd International Conference on Cloud Computing. pp 244–251, http://dx.doi.org/10.1109/CLOUD.2010.42

48. Brodkin J (2008) Gartner: Seven cloud computing security risks. http://www.infoworld.com/d/security-central/gartner-seven-cloud-computing-security-risks-853

49. Kandukuri BR, Paturi R, Rakshit A (2009) Cloud Security Issues. In: Proceedings of the 2009 IEEE International Conference on Services Computing, SCC '09

50. Winterford B (2011) Amazon EC2 suffers huge outage. http://www.crn.com.au/News/255586,amazon-ec2-suffers-huge-outage.aspx

51. Clarke G (2011) Microsoft BPOS cloud outage burns Exchange converts. http://www.theregister.co.uk/2011/05/13/

52. Shankland S (2011) Amazon cloud outage derails Reddit, Quora

53. Young E (2009) Cloud Computing - The role of internal audit

54. CloudAudit (2011) A6 - The automated audit, assertion, assessment and assurance API. http://cloudaudit.org/

55. Anand N (2010) The legal issues around cloud computing. http://www.labnol.org/internet/cloud-computing-legal-issues/14120/

56. Hunter S (2011) Ascending to the cloud creates negligible e-discovery risk. http://ediscovery.quarles.com/2011/07/articles/information-technology/ascending-to-the-cloud-creates-negligible-ediscovery-risk/

57. Sharon D, Nelson JWS (2011) Virtualization and Cloud Computing: benefits and e-discovery implications. http://www.slaw.ca/2011/07/19/virtualization-and-cloud-computing-benefits-and-e-discovery-implications/

58. Bentley L (2009) E-discovery in the cloud presents promise and problems. http://www.itbusinessedge.com/cm/community/features/interviews/blog/e-discovery-in-the-cloud-presents-promise-and-problems/?cs=31698

59. Zierick J (2011) The special case of privileged users in the sloud. http://blog.beyondtrust.com/bid/63894/The-Special-Case-of-Privileged-Users-in-the-Cloud

60. Dinoor S (2010) Got Privilege? Ten Steps to Securing a Cloud-Based Enterprise. http://cloudcomputing.sys-con.com/node/1571649

61. Pavolotsky J (2010) Top five legal issues for the cloud. http://www.forbes.com/2010/04/12/cloud-computing-enterprise-technology-cio-network-legal.html

62. ENISA (2011) About ENISA. http://www.enisa.europa.eu/about-enisa

63. CSA (2011) About. https://cloudsecurityalliance.org/about/

64. CSA (2011) CSA TCI Reference Architecture. https://cloudsecurityalliance.org/wp-content/uploads/2011/11/TCI-Reference-Architecture-1.1.pdf

65. CSA (2011) Security Guidance for Critical Areas of Focus in Cloud Computing V3.0. Tech. rep., Cloud Security Alliance. [Http://www.cloudsecurityalliance.org/guidance/csaguide.v3.0.pdf]

66. Ramireddy S, Chakraborthy R, Raghu TS, Rao HR (2010) Privacy and Security Practices in the Arena of Cloud Computing - A Research in Progress. In: AMCIS 2010 Proceedings, AMCIS '10. http://aisel.aisnet.org/amcis2010/574

67. NIST (2011) NIST Cloud Computing Reference Architecture: SP 500-292. http://collaborate.nist.gov/twiki-cloud-computing/pub/CloudComputing/ReferenceArchitectureTaxonomy/NIST_SP_500-292_-_090611.pdf

68. Youseff L, Butrico M, Silva DD (2008) Toward a Unified Ontology of Cloud Computing. In: Grid Computing Environments Workshop, 2008. GCE '08. pp 10, 1, http://dx.doi.org/10.1109/GCE.2008.4738443

69. Johnston S (2008) Sam Johnston: taxonomy: the 6 layer cloud computing stack. http://samj.net/2008/09/taxonomy-6-layer-cloud-computing-stack.html]

70. Linthicum D (2009) Defining the cloud computing framework. http://cloudcomputing.sys-con.com/node/811519

71. Doelitzscher F, Reich C, Knahl M, Clarke N (2011) An autonomous agent based incident detection system for cloud environments. In: Third IEEE International Conference on Cloud Computing Technology and Science, CloudCom 2011, CPS. pp 197–204, http://dx.doi.org/10.1109/CloudCom.2011.35

72. Oltsik J (2010) Information security, virtualization, and the journey to the cloud. Tech. rep., Cloud Security Alliance

73. Wallom D, Turilli M, Taylor G, Hargreaves N, Martin A, Raun A, McMoran A (2011) myTrustedCloud: Trusted Cloud Infrastructure for Security-critical Computation and Data Managment. In: Third IEEE International Conference on Cloud Computing Technology and Science, CloudCom 2011, CPS. pp 247–254

74. Dabrowski C, Mills K (2011) VM Leakage and Orphan Control in Open-Source Clouds. In: Third IEEE International Conference on Cloud Computing Technology and Science, CloudCom 2011, CPS. pp 554–559

75. Chadwick DW, Casenove M (2011) Security APIs for My Private Cloud. In: Third IEEE International Conference on Cloud Computing Technology and Science, CloudCom 2011, CPS. pp 792–798

76. Claybrook B (2011) How providers affect cloud application migration. http://searchcloudcomputing.techtarget.com/tutorial/How-providers-affect-cloud-application-migration

77. CSA (2011) Interoperability and portability

2

Trust mechanisms for cloud computing

Jingwei Huang* and David M Nicol

Abstract

Trust is a critical factor in cloud computing; in present practice it depends largely on perception of reputation, and self assessment by providers of cloud services. We begin this paper with a survey of existing mechanisms for establishing trust, and comment on their limitations. We then address those limitations by proposing more rigorous mechanisms based on evidence, attribute certification, and validation, and conclude by suggesting a framework for integrating various trust mechanisms together to reveal chains of trust in the cloud.

Keywords: Trust, Cloud computing, Trust mechanisms, Reputation, QoS, SLA, Transparency-based trust, Formal accreditation, Cloud audit, Policy-based trust, Evidence-based trust, Attribute certification

Introduction

Cloud computing has become a prominent paradigm of computing and IT service delivery. However, for any potential user of cloud services, they will ask "can I trust this cloud service?" Furthermore, what exactly does "trust" mean in the context of cloud computing? What is the basis of that trust? If the attributes of a cloud service (or a service provider) are used as evidence for trust judgment on the service (or provider respectively), on what basis should users believe the attributes claimed by cloud providers? Who are authorities to monitor, measure, assess, or validate cloud attributes? The answers to those questions are essential for wide adoption of cloud computing and for cloud computing to evolve into a trustworthy computing paradigm. As addressed in [1], "the growing importance of cloud computing makes it increasingly imperative that we grapple with the meaning of trust in the cloud and how the customer, provider, and society in general establish that trust."

The issues and challenges of trust in cloud computing have been widely discussed from different perspectives [2-10]. A number of models and tools have been proposed [11-13]. Each contributes a partial view of cloud trust, but lacking still is a complete picture illustrating how cloud entities work together to form a "societal" system, with a solid grounding in trust, serving to facilitate trusted paths to trusted cloud services. The NIST Cloud Computing Reference Architecture [14] identified cloud

brokers and cloud auditors as entities who conduct assessment of cloud services; however, there are few studies on trust relation analysis and the chains of trust from cloud users to cloud services (or providers) through those intermediary cloud entities. In this paper, we investigate trust mechanisms for the cloud, present our vision of the "societal systems mechanisms" of trust and a framework for analyzing trust relations in the cloud, and suggest trust mechanisms which combine attribute certification, evidence-based trust and policy-based trust.

Because of the criticality of many computing services and tasks, some cloud clients cannot make decisions about employing a cloud service based solely on informal trust mechanisms (e.g. web-based reputation scores); these decisions need to be based on formal trust mechanisms, which are more certain, more accountable, and more dependable. Here, the word "formal" is meant to carry the sense of "official" assessment in a society. In our suggested cloud trust mechanisms, the attributes of a cloud service (or its provider) are used as evidence for the user's trust judgment on the service (or provider), and the belief in those attributes is based on "formal" certification and chains of trust for validation.

In this paper, we focus somewhat informally on the conceptual basis for analysis of trust in the cloud; we do not at this time address mathematical modeling, which would involve many more precise details, formal languages, and specific use cases. With respect to terminology, an "entity" is an autonomous agent; a "cloud entity" refers to an entity in the cloud, such as a cloud provider, a cloud user, a cloud broker, and a cloud auditor; "semantics of trust" refers to

*Correspondence: jingwei@iti.illinois.edu
Information Trust Institute, University of Illinois at Urbana-Champaign 1308 West Main Street, Urbana, Illinois 61801, USA

precisely defined meaning of trust, including the relations among the components of trust.

This paper is organized as the following sections: (1) we define the *semantics of trust*; (2) we review the *state-of-the-art trust mechanisms* for cloud computing; (3) we discuss *policy-based trust judgment*, which is a real formal trust mechanism used in Public Key Infrastructure (PKI) practice. By policy-based trust, a cloud service or service provider can be trusted if it conforms to a trusted policy; (4) we present a general structure of *evidence-based trust*, by which particular attributes of a cloud service or attributes of a service provider are used as evidence for trust judgment; (5) we discuss *attribute assessment and attribute certification*, by which some attributes of a cloud service (or service provider) are formally certified, and the belief in those attributes is based on formal certification and chains of trust for validation; (6) we present an integrated view of the trust mechanisms for cloud computing, and analyze the trust chains connecting cloud entities; (7) finally, we give a summary and identify further research.

Semantics of trust

The term "trust" is often loosely used in the literature on cloud trust, frequently as a general term for "security" and "privacy", such as [4]. What exactly does "trust" mean?

Trust is a complex social phenomenon. Based on the concepts of trust developed in social sciences [15,16], we use the following definition [17]:

Trust is a mental state comprising: (1) **expectancy** *- the trustor expects a specific behavior from the trustee (such as providing valid information or effectively performing cooperative actions); (2)* **belief** *- the trustor believes that the expected behavior occurs, based on the evidence of the trustee's competence, integrity, and goodwill; (3)* **willingness to take risk** *- the trustor is willing to take risk for that belief.*

It is important to understand that the expected behavior of trustee is beyond the trustor's control; the trustor's belief in that expected behavior of trustee is based on the trustee's capability, goodwill (including intension or motivation), and integrity. The integrity of the trustee gives the trustor confidence about the predictability of the trustee's behavior.

We identify two types of trust, based on the trustor's expectancy: *trust in performance* is trust about what the trustee performs, whereas *trust in belief* is trust about what the trustee believes. The trustee's performance could be the truth of what the trustee says or the successfulness of what the trustee does. For simplicity, we represent both as a statement, denoted as a Boolean-type term, x, called a reified proposition [18]. For the first case, x is what the trustee says; for the second, x represents a successful

performance, which is regarded as a statement that the trustee made, describing his or her performance. A *trust in performance* relationship, $trust\_p(d,e,x,k)$, represents that trustor d trusts trustee e regarding e's performance x in context k. This relationship means that if x is made by e in context k, then d believes x in that context. In first-order logic (FOL),

$$trust\_p(d,e,x,k) \equiv madeBy(x,e,k) \supset believe(d,k\dot\supset x)$$
(1)

where $\dot\supset$ is an operator used for reified propositions to mimic the logical operator for implication, $\supset$. A *trust in belief* relationship, $trust\_b(d,e,x,k)$, represents that trustor d trusts trustee e regarding e's belief (x) in context k. This trust relationship means that if e believes x in context k, then d also believes x in that context:

$$trust\_b(d,e,x,k) \equiv believe(e,k\dot\supset x) \supset believe(d,k\dot\supset x).$$
(2)

Trust in belief is transitive; *trust in performance* is not; however, *trust in performance* can propagate through *trust in belief*. A more detailed account can be found in [17,19].

From the definition above, the trustor's mental state of belief in his expectancy on the trustee is dependent on the evidence about the trustee's competency, integrity, and goodwill. This leads to logical structures of reasoning from belief in evidence to belief in expectancy. We will discuss this later in § 'Evidence-based trust'.

The semantics of trust in the context of cloud computing has the same semantic structure as stated above; what still needed are the specific expectancy and the specific characteristics of cloud entities's competency, integrity, and goodwill in the context of cloud computing. We will discuss further in § 'Evidence-based trust'.

State-of-the-art trust mechanisms in clouds

In this section, we discuss existing trust mechanisms in the cloud. From the discussion, we will see that each of the mechanisms addresses one aspect of trust but not others.

Reputation based trust

Trust and reputation are related, but different. Basically, trust is between two entities; but the reputation of an entity is the aggregated opinion of a community towards that entity. Usually, an entity that has high reputation is trusted by many entities in that community; an entity, who needs to make trust judgment on an trustee, may use the reputation to calculate or estimate the trust level of that trustee.

Reputation systems are widely used in e-commerce and P2P networks. The reputation of cloud services or cloud service providers will undoubtably impact cloud users' choice of cloud services; consequently, cloud providers try to build and maintain higher reputation. Naturally, reputation-based trust enters into the vision of making trust judgment in cloud computing [11,13,20].

Reputation is typically represented by a comprehensive score reflecting the overall opinion, or a small number of scores on several major aspects of performance. It is unrealistic to ask a large number of cloud users to rate a cloud service or service provider against a large set of complex and fine-grained criteria. The reputation of a cloud service provider reflects the overall view of a community towards that provider, therefore it is more useful for the cloud users (mostly individual users) in choosing a cloud service from many options without particular requirements. Reputation may be helpful when initially choosing a service, but is inadequate afterwards. In particular, as a user gains experience with the service, the trust placed on that service meeting performance or reliability requirements will evolve based on that experience.

SLA verification based trust

"Trust, but verify" is a good advice for dealing with the relationships between cloud users and cloud service providers. After establishing the initial trust and employing a cloud service, the cloud user needs to verify and reevaluate the trust. A service level agreement (SLA) is a legal contract between a cloud user and a cloud service provider. Therefore, quality of service (QoS) monitoring and SLA verification is an important basis of trust management for cloud computing. A number of models that derive trust from SLA verification have been proposed [12,13].

A major issue is that SLA focuses on the "visible" elements of cloud service performance, and does not address "invisible" elements such as security and privacy. Another issue is that many cloud users lack the capability to do fine grained QoS monitoring and SLA verification on their own; a professional third party is needed to provide these services. In a private cloud, there may be a cloud broker or a trust authority (e.g. RSA's CTA, to be discussed later in § 'Cloud transparency mechanisms'), whom is trusted in the trust domain of the private cloud; so the trusted broker or trust authority can provide the users in the private cloud the services of QoS monitoring and SLA verification. In a hybrid cloud or interclouds, a user within a private cloud might still rely on the private cloud trust authority to conduct QoS monitoring and SLA verification; however, in a public cloud, individual users and some small organizations without technical capability may use a commercial professional cloud entity as trust broker. We discuss this in § 'Trust as a service'.

Cloud transparency mechanisms

Transparency and accountability are a recognized basis for gaining trust on cloud providers. To increase transparency of the cloud, the Cloud Security Alliance (CSA) launched the "Security, Trust & Assurance Registry (STAR)" program [21], a free publicly accessible registry which allows cloud service providers to publish self-assessment of their security controls, in either a "Consensus Assessments Initiative Questionnaire (CAIQ)" or a "Cloud Controls Matrix (CCM)", which embody CSA published best practices. CAIQ contains over 140 questions which cloud users or auditors may ask; CCM is a framework describing how a cloud provider aligns with the CSA security guide [22]. Examples of cloud providers' self-assessments can be found at the CSA STAR website [23]. STAR is a useful source for users seeking cloud services. However, the information offered is a cloud provider's *self*-assessment; cloud users may want assessments performed by some independent third-party professional organizations.

Different from STAR, CSC.com proposed [24] and CSA adopted the CloudTrust Protocol (CTP) [25], a request-response mechanism for a cloud user to obtain specific information about the "elements of transparency" applied to a specific cloud service provider; the elements of transparency cover aspects of configuration, vulnerability, audit log, service management, service statistics, and so forth. "The primary purpose of the CTP and the elements of transparency is to generate evidence-based confidence that everything that is claimed to be happening in the cloud is indeed happening as described, ..., and nothing else" [26]. CTP provides an interesting channel between cloud users and cloud service providers, allowing users internal observations of cloud service operations. However, like STAR, an essential weakness of CTP is that its information is provided by cloud service provider itself. Dishonest cloud service providers can filter out or change the data. From the point of view of a trust judgement, it raises questions of the data's reliability.

Trust as a service

We have already noted the need for employing third-party professionals for QoS monitoring and SLA verification. Independent assessment has utility in other aspects of cloud computing, as well.

RSA announced the *Cloud Trust Authority* (CTA) [27] as a cloud service, called Trust as a Service (TaaS) to provide a single point for configuring and managing security of cloud services from multiple providers. The initial release of the CTA includes: *identity service*, enabling single sign-on among multiple cloud providers, and *compliance profiling service*, enabling a user to view the security profiles of multiple cloud providers against a common benchmark. The CTA is a tool specialized on cloud trust management, and is developed from RSA's philosophy of "trust = visibility + control" [28]. As a cloud-based tool, the CTA could largely simplify cloud users' trust management. However, a cloud user must still make trust judgment about the cloud service assertions streamed in the CTA, because those assertions were made by cloud service providers themselves. Most importantly, a cloud user needs to judge the trustworthiness of the CTA in role as an intermediary.

The essential issue of any TaaS mechanism is about what is the basis of the trust relation between cloud users and those commercial trust brokers. We will discuss the answers later in subsections 'Trust judgement on a cloud broker' and 'Trust judgment on a cloud service provider'.

Formal accreditation, audit, and standards

Because self-assessment exercises may be compromised by dishonesty, some argue that formal accreditation from a trusted independent authority is necessary for a healthy cloud market; some others argue that formal accreditation "would stifle industry innovation" [2].

External audits, attestations, or certifications for more general purpose (not specific to clouds) have been used in practice. Examples include: the ISO/IEC 27000 series, which are international information security management standards [29]; "Statement on Standards for Attestation Engagements No. 16" (SSAE 16) [30], which is an attestation standard for service organizations, put forth by the Auditing Standards Board (ASB) of the American Institute of Certified Public Accountants (AICPA). SSAE 16 is replacing the older standard "Statement on Auditing Standards No. 70" (SAS 70); "The International Standard on Assurance Engagements 3402" (ISAE 3402) [31], which is a globally recognized standard for assurance reporting on service organizations.

Specific to cloud computing, in addition to CTP and STAR (for self-assessment), CSA also launched the CloudAudit initiative, which provides a common interface and namespace for cloud providers to produce audit assertions, and allows cloud users to automate use of that data in their own audit processes. CloudAudit could facilitate automated cloud audit, conducted by cloud providers (for self-audit), cloud users (for cloud user-audit), and cloud auditors (for formal audit). CloudAudit, CCM, CAIQ, and CTP form the CSA Governance, Risk Management and Compliance (GRC) stack.

To ensure trustworthiness, the International Grid Trust Federation (IGTF) issued GFD-I.169 as guidelines for auditing the cloud/grid assurance bodies – the certification authorities (CAs) issuing X.509 certificates [32].

A formal process for assessment of cloud services and their providers by independent third parties, acceptable to both cloud users and providers, does not yet exist. Formal accreditation specific to independent third-party cloud assessors also does not exist.

Further discussion

A reputation-based trust mechanism reflects the overall view of a community towards a cloud service provider. It can help with cloud service selection; but is insufficient for other important purposes.

After establishing an initial trust on a cloud service, a cloud user needs to verify and re-evaluate that trust. QoS monitoring and SLA verification based trust mechanism can help to manage the existing cloud trust relations. The QoS/SLA mechanism can manage "visible" elements of the black box of a cloud service, such as performance; but it cannot help to manage the "invisible" elements inside a cloud service, such as privacy protection.

Cloud transparency mechanisms provide channels for cloud users to "observe" how cloud service providers operate. The mechanisms help to establish trust by making the cloud services more "visible". The essential issue of the transparency mechanisms is that the information is provided by cloud service providers themselves; thus we need to identify the basis for cloud users to trust them.

The TaaS mechanism provides cloud users a solution where the sophisticated tasks of cloud trust management can be delegated to third-party professionals. However similarly the basis for cloud users to trust them needs to be estabulished.

One possible solution to the problems posed in the above mechanisms is formal accreditation and audit. The mechanisms of formal accreditation and audit in the cloud do not exist yet and are still in discussion.

In the rest of this paper, we continue to explore the cloud trust mechanisms by borrowing policy-based trust mechanism from PKI, combined with evidence-based trust and attribute certification and validation.

Policy-based trust

We earlier identified the need for "formal" trust mechanisms in cloud computing. In a related sphere, PKI is a widely used mature technology that employs "formal" trust mechanisms to support digital signature, key certification and validation, as well as attribute certification and validation. Can we apply trust ideas used in PKI to establish "formal" trust mechanisms to the cloud?

To simplify the discussion, consider the example illustrated in Figure 1. Alice has a digital document supposedly signed by Bob using his private key K_b'. To validate, she needs Bob's public key K_b. Assume that Alice trusts only her trust anchor certification authority CA_1, and she knows only K_1, her trust anchor's public key. In order for her to verify the signature on the document as being Bob's, she needs to discover a certification path (a chain of certificates) from CA_1 to CA_3 who has issued Bob's public key certificate. As shown in the figure, Alice uses CA_1's public key K_1 to validate CA_2's public key K_2; because Alice trusts CA_1 on public key certification, and CA_2's public

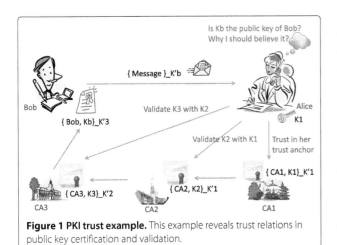

Figure 1 PKI trust example. This example reveals trust relations in public key certification and validation.

key is certified by CA_1, Alice can believe that CA_2's public key is K_2; then Alice uses K_2 to validate CA_3' public key K_3; and finally uses K_3 to validate Bob's public key K_b. The main issue is *why Alice should believe K_3 is CA_3's public key and K_b is Bob's public key?*

Essentially, to infer belief in a statement "Bob's key is K_b", Alice needs to trust CA_3, the creator of that assertion, with respect to the truth of the statement; however, this raises questions that ask about the foundation of that trust, and how the trust is inferred or calculated. Some research suggests that the trust comes from recommendations along the chain of certificates by those certificate issuers [33]; but the practice of digital certification and validation in real PKI systems suggests that *the trust comes from compliance with certain certificate policies.*

As specified in IETF RFC 5280 [34], in addition to the basic statement that binds a public key with a subject, a public key certificate also contains a certificate policy (CP) extension. For a public key certificate issued to a CA, the certificate means that the issuing CA who conforms to the specified CP asserts that the subject CA has the certified public key, and the subject CA also adheres to the specified CP. As a result, to infer Alice's belief in CA_3's key and Bob's key, she must trust that CP in the sense that any CA conforming to that CP will generate valid public key certificates. There are more complex and interesting issues in PKI trust [35], but for the purpose of this paper, we will not go further.

In summary, as PKI is currently practiced, trust in a certification authority (CA) with respect to issuing and maintaining valid public key certificates is based on the CA's conformance with certain certificate policies. Certificate policies play a central role in PKI trust. We call this trust mechanism as *policy-based trust.*

Evidence-based trust
We now discuss using attributes as evidence to make trust decision.

From the definition of trust given in § 'Semantics of Trust', a trustor's belief in the expected behaviour of trustee is based on the evidence about the trustee's attributes of competency, goodwill, and integrity, with respect to that expectation. Formally, we could express a general form of evidence-based trust as follows:

$$believe(u, attr_1(s, v_1)) \land ... \land believe(u, attr_n(s, v_n))$$
$$\rightarrow trust\_ * (u, s, x, c) \qquad (3)$$

which states that if an individual u believes a subject s has attribute $attr_1$ with value v_1, ..., attribute $attr_n$ with value v_n, then u trusts (either *trust in belief* or *trust in performance*) s with respect to x, the performance of s or information created or believed by s, in a specific context c.

An entity's belief in an attribute assessment is dependent on whether the entity trusts the entity who makes that attribute assessment. Formally, based on the definition of trust-in-performance, formula (1) in § 'Semantics of Trust', we could have

$$trust\_p(u, a, attr(s, v), c) \land madeBy(attr(s, v), a, c)$$
$$\land inContext(c) \rightarrow believe(u, attr(s, v)), \qquad (4)$$

which states that if an individual u trusts an attribute authority a to make assertions about a subject s has attribute $attr$ with value v in a specific context c, a specific assertion $attr(s, v)$ is made by a in context c, and the context c is the case, then u believes that assertion. In the formula, $attr(s, v)$ is a reified proposition represented as a term. Since not only the attributes of a cloud service may be assessed and certified, but also the attributes of a cloud entity may be assessed and certified, in the above formula, we may use $attr(e, v)$ to state that cloud entity e has attribute $attr$ with value e. In this way, a logic formula similar to (4) can describe the relation from trust in a cloud auditor to the belief in the certified attribute of a cloud entity such as a service provider.

To use attributes as evidence in trust judgment, we organize the relevant attributes in a two-dimension space: (1) one dimension goes along the domain of the trustor's expectation on the trustee, in the context of cloud computing, including aspects of performance, security, and privacy; (2) another dimension goes along the source of trust, that is, what makes the trustor trust the trustee, including the trustee's competency (capability), integrity (consistency in performance and principles), and goodwill (motivation or intension).

Figure 2 illustrates a spectrum of attributes in cloud computing. Most commonly considered ones fall in the category of competency; attributes that reflect integrity and goodwill are frequently neglected, and should be included in trust judgment. To neglect these is to implicity assume that trust does not depend on them, or if it

Domain-specific expectation	Sources of trust		
	Competency	Good will / intention	Integrity / consistency
Performance	Availability; Reliability; ...	\<Constant efforts to improve performance>	\<Consistency shown by historic data>
Security	Security cert; Security breach rate; ...	\<Constant efforts to improve security>	\<Consistency shown by historic data>
Privacy	Privacy regulation compliance; Privacy violation rate; ...	\<Constant efforts to improve privacy>	\<Consistency shown by historic data>

Figure 2 Attributes for evidence-based trust. The attributes used for evidence-based trust judgment can be organized in two dimensions: (1) sources of trust, including competency, goodwill, and integrity; (2) domain-specific expectation.

does, that dependence is satisfied. Characterization and quantification of integrity and goodwill is an interesting research challenge. A trustee's historical behavior might reflect integrity; goodwill might be quantified as performance improvements are measured, and cloud users' feedback.

Different cloud users may have different trust policies, involving different trust attributes. A common trust *framework* supports evidence-based trust judgment for different users and different policies. The connection between evidence-based trust and policy-based trust is that the belief that an entity conforms to a trusted policy implies the belief that the entity has a set of attributes associated with that policy.

Attribute assessment and certification

When the attributes of a cloud service (or cloud entity) are used as evidence to make trust judgment on the service (or entity), the sources of attribute assessment must be trustworthy, and those attributes need to be distributed in a trustworthy way. In the following, we first discuss the source of attribute assertions and then we discuss attribute certification as a formal approach to deliver cloud attributes.

Sources of cloud attribute assessment

Assessment of attributes may come from several sources: the cloud user, other peer users, the service provider, cloud auditor/accreditator, and cloud broker. We discuss each of them in turn.

Cloud user observation

If a cloud user has already interacted with a cloud service or a cloud service provider, then the experience will be the user's direct basis for cloud attribute assessment. Experience is a fundamental factor of trust, and this kind of trust, called "interpersonal trust", has long been studied in both social sciences and computing science.

The advantage of using direct interaction experience is that the data used are first-hand and may be most relevant; the disadvantage is that the data accumulated are limited with respect to the sample size and the range of the usage of the cloud service. A specific user's experience is just one piece of the information revealing the trustworthiness of a cloud service.

Opinions of other peer users

When a cloud user has only limited direct experience with a cloud service (or none at all), other peer users' opinions could be an important source of cloud attribute assessment. The major issues are: can those peer reviewers be trusted with respect to their opinions on the cloud service? and how can those different opinions be aggregated?

There are at least two basic approaches to solving the problem: social network based and reputation based.

Social network based approach A cloud user takes one or more trusted friends' opinions, and combines them with that user's personal trust in each of those friends. That user may not have a direct trust relation with a "popular" reviewer, but the user may derive an indirect trust relation with that reviewer through a trust network [17,36], which is a specific form of social networks, comprising of only trust relations. The social network based approach is an analogue of how a person initially trusts an entity, unknown before in the real world. Models in this category are heuristic. Typically, one asks only a small number of trusted friends for their opinions. When a large number of peer users' opinions are involved, the approach becomes reputation based.

Reputation based approach A typical methodology is to aggregate a large number of peer user's ratings, often seen in e-commerce product/service ratings. The advantage is that the data used for assessment may cover many more situations and have a wider time-window of observations; this approach can have a much wider view on the cloud service (or its provider) than a single user does. On the other hand, some weaknesses exist: a large number of raters are required for meaningful and objective ratings; the raters and users should have a common understanding of the attribute semantics and the corresponding measurement; this approach is suitable for the purpose of overall rating, or is limited to rating a small number of attributes; the trustworthiness of individual voter are rarely taken into account; usually, as in e-commerce, the reputation of product/service is calculated by an organization in a centralized manner, so the organization may manipulate the calculation, and the calculating service may become a single point of attack.

Statements from cloud service provider

Some cloud service attributes may be specified, promised, or revealed by its provider. In "service specification" and advertisements, a service provider will specify the featured attributes of a cloud service; the attributes of the service stated in a SLA are the promises of that service provider to that user. Through the CloudTrust Protocol (CTP) [26], cloud users can request and get a response from the provider about "the elements of transparency", the information concerning the compliance, security, privacy, integrity, and operational security history.

However, information about the attributes of a service given by the service provider are usually not directly believed by the first-time users. Sometimes a user may believe a service provider's statements or promises, based on the brand name or reputation of that service provider, or based on the user's past experience of interaction. In any case, the stated attributes are an important part of the watch-list in cloud service monitoring, and they are used to verify whether the service provider behaves as trusted. The conclusion of the verification will be used by the users to build or revise their trust in that service provider.

In general, the statements or promises about the attributes of a cloud service given by a cloud service provider itself need to be verified before used for decision making, and cloud attribute assertions from third party independent professional organizations are expected, which we discuss in the following subsections 'Assessment of cloud auditor/accreditor' and 'Observation of cloud brokers'.

Assessment of cloud auditor/accreditor

NIST identifies a cloud auditor as "a party that can conduct independent assessment of cloud services, information system operations, performance, and security of a cloud implementation. A cloud auditor can evaluate the services provided by a cloud provider in terms of security controls, privacy impact, performance, etc." [14]. Obviously, cloud audit is an important channel of cloud attribute assessment. A limitation of cloud auditing is that the trust assessment reflects only the state at the time of the audit. Trust changes dynamically, as a function of dynamic monitoring of behavior.

A cloud auditor's assessment is usually regarded as a reliable information source for trust judgment. To some cloud users, a cloud auditor as a third-party professional organization may be a satisfactory trust root. However, to some others, the trustworthiness of a cloud auditor also needs to be evaluated by looking into the auditor's attributes and/or policies. Since cloud audit is an important mechanism to ensure trustworthiness of clouds,

each cloud auditor should be periodically audited and/or accredited by a professional association such as Auditing Standards Board of AICPA.

In formal accreditation, an entity who provides a professional service is assessed against official standards, and is issued with certification of its competency, authority, or credibility. The certification is provided by an accreditor, who is a third party independent authorized accreditation organization, and who is also accredited by a national standard body or professional association. If formal accreditation is applied to clouds, the cloud attribute assessment from a formal accreditation will be another important information source for cloud trust judgment.

Accreditation is somewhat similar to audit. In both cases an entity is assessed by an independent third party; however, there are subtle differences. First, they may have different focusing aspects of assessment. Accreditation focuses on the qualification of the accredited entity with respect to conducting a specific type of professional services; audit focuses on assessing the performance of the audited entity with respect to the common requirements of a society and/or the professional standards of a professional community. Secondly, audit typically takes place annually or once per half year; accreditation takes place in a longer period (e.g. every 5 years).

In summary, in context of cloud computing, the assessments by audit and accreditation are objective and "formal", but they are not real-time information as from real-time monitoring.

Observation of cloud brokers

Cloud brokers play an important role. By the NIST definition [14], a cloud broker is "an entity that manages the use, performance, and delivery of cloud services, and negotiates relationships between Cloud Providers and Cloud Consumers." A cloud broker may provide services in three categories [14]: (1) service intermediation: for a given cloud service, to provide value-added additional services such as performance monitoring and security management; (2) service aggregation: to provide an integrated service by aggregating several cloud services from different providers; (3) service arbitrage: to select proper cloud services in an integrated service, based on the quantified evaluation of the alternative cloud services. The observation of a cloud broker can be an important source of cloud attribute assessment.

The advantages of broker observation include: real-time cloud service performance monitoring; feedback from many peer users; an ability to monitor and evaluate a collection of the same category of cloud services from different providers. A cloud broker potentially has a relatively complete picture of a cloud service.

However, again the question arises whether a cloud broker can be trusted with respect to assessing cloud attributes. This depends on the relationship between broker and providers, and between broker and users. A tight business relation with some cloud providers may make the brokers' opinion be not as objective as the one made in formal audit or accreditation.

From the perspective of cloud market mechanism we imagine that if a cloud broker represents a cloud provider, then the cloud broker may provide information which favors that cloud provider; however, if a broker is independent, and its business depends on the trust relations with users, the broker is more motivated to find and provide information being truly helpful for cloud users. This situation may occur when a cloud broker serves as a gateway for a large number of cloud users in the cloud market. Consistent with the above view, we further imagine that if a cloud broker is highly trusted by some cloud users (especially, end cloud users), the broker may become those cloud users' trust anchor, taking care of trust management for those cloud users.

In order to ensure that a cloud broker behaves as a trustworthy cloud entity, cloud users will expect to learn how a cloud broker works, whether the broker is neutral, what policies the broker follows, and whether the broker has certain attributes that can be used as evidence to judge its trustworthiness. Therefore, essentially a cloud broker is also expected to be formally audited and/or accredited either.

Attribute certification
In addition to X.509 identity (public key) certification, there also exists X.509 *attribute certification* [37]. Public key certification is used in authentication; attribute certification is used for both authentication and authorization. An attribute certificate (AC) is a statement digitally signed by the AC issuer to certify that the AC holder has a set of specified attributes. The certified attributes can be access identity, authentication information (e.g. username/password pairs), group membership, role, and security clearance [37]. An AC mainly contains the following fields: unique AC identifier, AC holder, AC issuer, attribute-value pairs, valid period, the Id of the algorithm used to verify the signature of the AC, and extensions, which mainly include AC targeting – a list of specified servers or services where the AC can be used, and CRL (Certificate Revocation List) distribution points.

The current IETF X.509 AC standard [37] might be considered for use in cloud attribute certification, but it has several limitations.

First, the standard does not include important attributes needed in the cloud context. Extensions are possible to deal with this, but still no standards regarding service performance, security, and privacy. Second, with respect to attribute certification, the real authority behind attribute assertion is the entity who really knows the certified

entity. For example, with respect to the role or membership of an entity in a specific organization, that organization is naturally the authority to state that attribute. From this point of view, we should discern the difference between "*attribute assertion authority*" (AAA) and *attribute certification authority* (ACA, i.e. AC issuer). We use AA (Attribute Authority) to refer to an entity who is both AAA and ACA. In the context of clouds, who plays the role of AA? From our earlier discussion, it is obvious that the most reliable sources for attribute assertion/assessment are independent third-party professional organizations such as cloud auditors and accreditors, and even cloud brokers.

Finally, current IETF X.509 AC standard [37] adopts a simple trust structure where "one authority issues all of the ACs for a particular set of attributes". In cloud applications (except for small scale private clouds) an AC issuer may be frequently outside the trust boundary of an AC user. Therefore, mechanisms for cross-domain attribute certification and validation are necessary for both hybrid cloud and public cloud.

An integrated view
Earlier, we envisioned that the attributes of a cloud service (or cloud entity) can be used as evidence for a cloud user to make trust judgment on the service (or entity); we discussed the sources of cloud attribute assessment and *attribute certification*; we also revealed that PKI in practice uses policy-based trust mechanism, which might be used in cloud computing either. In this section, we put together all those mechanisms, including: reputation based, SLA verification based, transparency based, formal accreditation and audit, as well as the suggested policy-based, evidence-based, and cloud attribute certification, to construct an overall framework for analyzing and modeling trust chains among cloud entities.

Figures 3, 4, 5 and 6 illustrate the dependence between the trust placed in various cloud entities and the sources of evidence for trust judgment. In these figures, the left part illustrates trust placed on different types of cloud entities; the right part illustrates trust mechanisms to be used, which are also the sources of evidence to support trust judgment; the arrows represent dependence relations between them; the dependence relations together form the chains of trust in the cloud. The six mechanisms shown in those pictures are an abstraction of typical mechanisms; a real system support trust judgment in practice may involve several mechanisms. For example, a cloud reputation system may calculate reputation scores, and also provide assessed attributes from brokers and users' reviews. The three mechanisms in the lower-right part with dotted border-lines are suggested ones and do not exist yet. Most mechanisms may support trust judgment on different types of cloud entities, but note that for

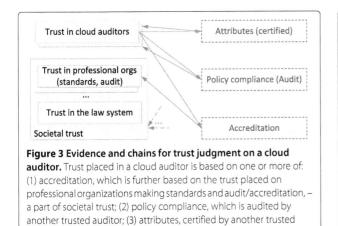

Figure 3 Evidence and chains for trust judgment on a cloud auditor. Trust placed in a cloud auditor is based on one or more of: (1) accreditation, which is further based on the trust placed on professional organizations making standards and audit/accreditation, – a part of societal trust; (2) policy compliance, which is audited by another trusted auditor; (3) attributes, certified by another trusted auditor.

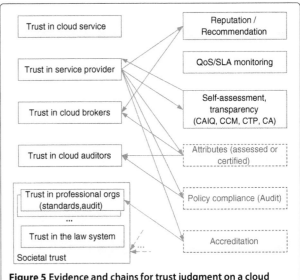

Figure 5 Evidence and chains for trust judgment on a cloud service provider. Similar to the structure of trust judgment on cloud broker showed in Figure 4.

a same mechanism, the contents to be examined for a specific type of cloud entity could be different from the ones for another types of entities. For example, when applied to a cloud service provider, "policy compliance audit", refers to evaluation of a cloud service provider's conformance to its cloud service policy; however, when applied to a cloud auditor, it refers to the evaluation of a cloud auditor conformance to a cloud audit policy.

Now we discuss each trust judgment task in turn.

Societal trust

Societal trust is foundational in all trust models that include individuals and organizations; cloud computing is no exception. Each individual in a society has to place

trust in some basic parts of the society. Examples include: trust in the law system and government to maintain social order; trust in some professional services; trust in professional organizations with respect to creating and maintaining specific professional services standards. In the cloud context, examples of professional organizations might include AICPA, NIST (National Institute of Standards and Technology), IGTF (International Grid

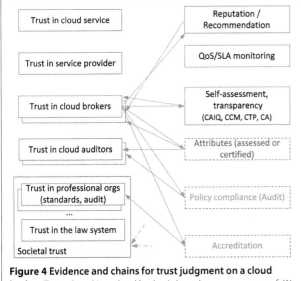

Figure 4 Evidence and chains for trust judgment on a cloud broker. Trust placed in a cloud broker is based on one or more of: (1) accreditation; (2) policy compliance; (3) certified attributes; (4) self-assessment and information revealing, which is based on the trust placed in this broker with respect to telling truth; (5) reputation calculated or recommendation made by another trusted broker.

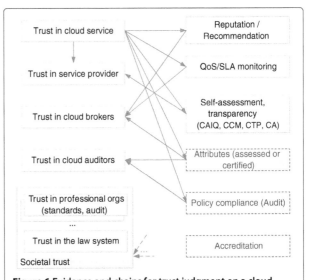

Figure 6 Evidence and chains for trust judgment on a cloud service. Trust placed in a cloud service is based on one or more of: (1) cloud service provider, whom is trusted; (2) policy compliance; (3) certified attributes; (4) QoS monitoring and SLA verification, which are conducted by a trusted party such as a trusted broker; (5) reputation calculated or recommendation made by a trusted broker.

Trust Federation), and CSA (Cloud Security Alliance). We specifically assume that societal trust leads cloud users to put their trust in the accreditation of cloud entities including auditors, brokers, and service providers, with respect to the qualification of a cloud entity on corresponding professional services.

While we recognize societal trust as a root of cloud trust, a deeper treatment of societal trust is beyond the scope of our overview of trust in clouds.

Trust judgment on a cloud auditor

A cloud auditor is a professional independent assessor of cloud entities. An auditor conforms to professional policies and/or standards in his operations. Cloud auditors should be also externally audited periodically by audit professional organizations, to ensure they comply with established policies and standards.

One cloud user might place a cloud auditor in his trusted societal root, i.e., simply assume the auditor is trustworthy; another user may choose instead to make a trust judgment on a cloud auditor as they do on other cloud entities. By the semantics of trust given in § 'Semantics of Trust', for "trust in a cloud auditor", the **expectancy** of a cloud user on a cloud auditor is the objective and professional assessment on a cloud entity with respect to its cloud services against a specific set of standards; the belief in that expectancy is based on some **evidence** with respect to the auditor's competency, goodwill, and integrity. For this judgment, there may be several sources of information as shown in Figure 3, and they are discussed as follows:

- **Accreditation:** A cloud user may check whether a specific cloud auditor is formally accredited by an professional audit organization and/or a cloud computing professional organization. Belief in accreditation is further dependent on whether the cloud user trusts the formal accreditor – an audit professional organization such as ASB of AICPA.
- **Policy compliance audit:** A cloud auditor should conform to professional policies and/or standards in its audit operations, such as SAS 70, SSAE 16, and ISAE 3402; the auditor should assess a cloud entity against widely accepted policies; the quality of the audit operations of an auditor is also assessed through audit, conducted by a different auditor appointed by an professional audit organization. A cloud user may use the audit results as evidence for trust judgment. The cloud user's belief in the audit result is further dependent on the user's trust in the auditor conducting the audit.
- **Certified attributes:** In addition to accreditation and policy compliance, a cloud user may want to check the auditor's other attributes, such as the

history of the auditor, experiences of those previously audited by that auditor, the history of the audit applied to the auditor. Some attributes may be contained in audit documents; some others may be certified (or assessed, verified, and digitally signed) by a peer auditor. The cloud user's belief in the certified attributes is dependent on the user's trust in the issuer of the certified attributes.

Trust judgment on a cloud broker

As discussed in § 'Observation of cloud broker', a cloud broker provides various intermediate services. Any cloud entity offering intermediated services may be regarded as a broker. Examples may include: "market" for cloud services such as SpotCloud [38], and TaaS such as CTA [27]. Note that an online reputation and ranking system for cloud services can also be regarded as a cloud broking service.

For the concept of "trust in a cloud broker", the **expectancy** of a cloud user on a cloud broker includes trustworthy value-added services such as bridging and aggregating services, security and identity management services, objective and precise evaluation of cloud services and their providers. To make evidence-based trust judgments, as illustrated by Figure 4, the evidence may include:

- **Accreditation:** Similar to cloud auditors, a cloud broker should be qualified for providing cloud broking services, through formally accreditation by a cloud computing professional organization.
- **Policy compliance audit:** A cloud broker should conform to certain policies and/or standards widely adopted or accepted by the cloud in the broker's operations; the quality of its operations should be audited by a cloud auditor. A cloud user may use the audit result as evidence for trust judgment. The cloud user's belief in the audit result is further dependent on the user's trust in the auditor conducting the audit.
- **Attributes (assessed or certified):** The attributes of a cloud broker on competency, goodwill, and integrity are important evidence for cloud users' trust judgment. In addition to the attributes assessed with respect to policy compliance, other attributes regarding performance, security, and privacy as discussed in § 'Evidence-based trust' may be also audited by a cloud auditor, or assessed and digitally signed by other cloud brokers, or reviewed and digitally signed by some cloud users. The cloud user's belief in the certified/assessed attributes is dependent on the user's trust in the issuer of the certified/assessed attributes.
- **Self-assessment and information revealing:** Cloud brokers as a special type of intermediated cloud

service providers should also adopt the CSA cloud transparency mechanisms to exercise self-assessment such as CAIQ and CCM, and information revealing as does in CTP (discussed in § 'Cloud transparency mechanisms'). The cloud user's belief in the information revealed by the broker is dependent on the user's trust in that broker with respect to telling the truth, which may be verified in a formal audit.

- **Reputation/recommendation:** Reputation and recommendation can be very helpful to new cloud users and/or the users who are planning to recompose their cloud services. The cloud user's belief in the reputation scores and recommendation is dependent on the user's trust in the source of the information, typically, a cloud broker.

Trust judgment on a cloud service provider

The trust **expectancy** of a user with respect to a provider is that the provider offers trustworthy cloud services. The evidence for trust judgment on a cloud service provider may include the following sources, as shown in Figure 5:

- **Accreditation**
- **Policy compliance audit**
- **Attributes (assessed or certified)**
- **Self-assessment and information revealing**
- **Reputation/recommendation**

All of the above mechanisms are similar to the ones applied to cloud brokers, save that the trustee is a cloud service provider rather than a cloud broker.

Trust judgment on a cloud service

We view a cloud service as an autonomous agent; and that "a cloud user trusts a cloud service" means that the user has the **expectancy** that the cloud service is trustworthy, which means that the cloud service has a set of attributes including reliability, availability, confidentiality, integrity, safety, and privacy; the user believes the expectancy to be true based on some **evidence**, from diverse sources, shown in Figure 6:

- **Trust based on the service provider:** by *trust in performance*, a user trusts a cloud service with respect to performance, security, and privacy, based on the identity of the provider. If the user trusts that the provider gives trustworthy cloud services, then the cloud service is trusted.

- **Policy compliance audit:** A cloud user may examine specific policies and/or standards applied to the service, and investigate the results of formal audits of the provider.

- **Attributes (assessed or certified):** A cloud user may examine the attributes of a cloud service regarding performance, security, and privacy, which may be audited by a cloud auditor, or assessed and digitally signed by cloud brokers, or reviewed and digitally signed by some cloud users. The belief in those attributes is dependent on the trust in the corresponding attribute assessor.

- **Self-assessment and information revealing:** A cloud user may study information about the service which is revealed by the service provider through cloud transparency mechanisms. The user's belief in the information is dependent on the user's trust in the cloud service provider with respect to telling the truth.

- **QoS monitoring and SLA verification:** QoS monitoring and SLA verification (a shorter term "QoS/SLA monitoring" is used in Figure 6) is an important source to verify trust and to adjust trust. If the monitoring is conducted by a cloud broker, then the belief in the results of monitoring is dependent on the trust in that broker with respect to objective and professional monitoring.

- **Reputation/recommendation:** a cloud user may trust a cloud service, based on a trusted cloud broker's recommendation. Similar to PKI trust, recommendation may be handled in two ways: one regards the "recommendation" as the broker's trust in that recommended service, and then derives indirect trust on that service through using *trust in belief* relation with the broker; another is (as in PKI practice) that the broker only certifies that that cloud service has certain attributes or conforms to certain policies, and cloud users to make their own decision whether to trust that service.

Further discussion

As seen above, the trust placed on a cloud entity may be dependent on several sources of evidence; however, it is unnecessary to use all of them; a cloud user may use one or more sources of evidence for trust judgment, dependent on the user's trust policy. For example, to decide whether to trust a cloud service provider, a cloud user may simply just check whether the provider passed the formal audit of a widely accepted cloud service policy, conducted by a trusted auditor.

In the discussion above, the trust mechanisms of reputation/recommendation, QoS monitoring and SLA verification, self-assessment and information revealing are already in development; formal accreditation is in discussion, but it does not exist yet; trust mechanisms of attribute assessment/certification, which is used for evidence-based trust judgment, and policy compliance

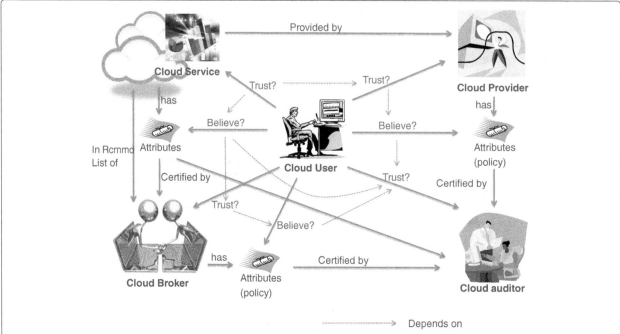

Figure 7 Chains of trust relations in clouds. This figure provides an integrated picture to illustrate the chains of trust relations from a cloud user to a cloud service and related cloud entities, where accreditation is omitted for simplicity.

audit, which is used for policy-based trust judgment, are what we suggest, and do not exist in the cloud yet; however policy-based trust has been successfully (more or less) used in PKI practice, and the practice is a proof of feasibility.

The mechanism of using attribute assessment/certification and evidence-based trust judgment could be complex, due to a possibly large set of attributes to consider and a possibly long chains of trust relations. Nevertheless, the policy-based trust judgment can be actually regarded as a simplified version of the attribute/evidence-based mechanism, in the sense that a widely accepted policy captures a set of key attributes.

In the above figures, the trust relations with various cloud entities, shown in the left part of the figures, are dependent on various sources of evidence, shown in the right part of figures; and the derivation of a source of evidence is dependent on some trust relations either. All those dependence relations form the chains of trust. Figure 7 illustrates some chains of trust focusing on policy-based and attribute/evidence-based mechanisms.

Summary and further research

Trust is a critical aspect of cloud computing. We examined and categorized existing research and practice of trust mechanisms for cloud computing in five categories—reputation based, SLA verification based, transparency mechanisms (self-assessment and information revealing),

trust as a service, and formal accreditation, audit, and standards. Most current work on trust in the cloud focus narrowly on certain aspects of trust; our thesis is that this is insufficient. Trust is a complex social phenomenon, and a systemic view of trust mechanism analysis is necessary. In this paper we take a broad view of trust mechanism analysis in cloud computing and develop a somewhat informal and abstract framework as a route map for analyzing trust in the clouds. In particular, we suggest: (1) a policy-based approach of trust judgment, by which the trust placed on a cloud service or a cloud entity is derived from a "formal" audit proving that the cloud entity conforms to some trusted policies; (2) a "formal" attribute-based approach of trust judgment, by which particular attributes of a cloud service or attributes of a service provider are used as *evidence* for trust judgment, and the belief in those attributes is based on formal certification and chains of trust for validation. To support this mechanism, we propose a general structure of evidence-based trust judgment, which provides a basis to infer the trust in a cloud entity from the belief in the attributes that entity has, and in which, based on the semantics of trust, we define the attributes to be examined are in a space of two-dimensions – domain of expectancy and source of trust including competency, integrity, and goodwill.

Future research will focus on mathematically formal frameworks for reasoning about trust, including modeling, languages, and algorithms for computing trust.

Abbreviations

AA: Attribute Authority; AC: Attribute Certificate; AICPA: American Institute of Certified Public Accountants; ASB: Auditing Standards Board; CA: Certification Authority; CAIQ: Consensus Assessment Initiative Questionnaire; CCM: Cloud Control Matrix; CP: Certificate Policy; CSA: Cloud Security Alliance; CTA: Cloud Trust Authority; CTP: CloudTrust Protocol; GRC: Governance, Risk Management and Compliance; IETF: Internet Engineering Task Force; IGTF: International Grid Trust Federation; ISAE 3402: The International Standard on Assurance Engagements 3402; NIST: National Institute of Standards and Technology; PKI: Public Key Infrastructure; QoS: Quality of Service; SLA: Service Level Agreement; SSAE 16: Statement on Standards for Attestation Engagements No. 16; STAR: Security, Trust & Assurance Registry; TaaS: Trust as a Service.

Competing interests

The authors declare that they have no competing interests.

Authors' contributions

JH carried out the study of trust in clouds and drafted the manuscript; DMN helped develop the concepts, reviewed, and revised the manuscript. Both authors read and approved the final manuscript.

Authors' information

Jingwei Huang is a research scientist in Information Trust Institute, University of Illinois at Urbana-Champaign. He received his PhD from University of Toronto in 2008, and is a member of ACM and IEEE. His research mainly focuses on (1) formal theories of trust, including the formal semantics of trust, measurement of trust, calculus of trust, trust evolution, and trust mechanisms; (2) applications of formal trust models in distributed computing and open networks, such as trust in cloud computing; (3) information assurance, including security policies for cross-domain information sharing, and formal models combining role-based access control, mandatory access control, and attribute-based access control.
David M. Nicol is the Franklin W. Woeltge Professor of Electrical and Computer Engineering at the University of Illinois at Urbana-Champaign, and Director of the Information Trust Institute. Previously he held faculty positions at the College of William and Mary and at Dartmouth College. His research interests include high-performance computing, simulation modeling and analysis, and security. He was elected Fellow of the IEEE and Fellow of the ACM for his contributions in those areas. He is co-author of the widely used textbook Discrete-Event Systems Simulation and was the inaugural awardee of the ACM Special Interest Group on Simulation's Distinguished Contributions Award, for his contributions in research, teaching, and service in the field of simulation.

Acknowledgements

This material is based upon research sponsored by the U.S. Air Force Research Laboratory (AFRL) and the U.S. Air Force Office of Scientific Research (AFSOR), under agreement number FA8750-11-2-0084. The U.S. Government is authorized to reproduce and distribute reprints for Governmental purposes notwithstanding any copyright notation thereon. We would like to thank Professor Roy Campbell, Professor Ravishankar K. Iyer, Scott Pickard, and many others in ACC-UCoE (Assured Cloud Computing University Center of Excellence, a joint effort of AFSOR, AFRL, and UIUC) for their valuable discussion.

References

1. Michael B (2009) In clouds shall we trust? IEEE Security and Privacy 7(5): 3–3. http://dx.doi.org/10.1109/MSP.2009.124
2. Everett C (2009) Cloud computing: A question of trust. Computer Fraud Security 2009(6): 5–7. http://dx.doi.org/10.1016/S1361-3723(09)70071-5
3. Garrison G, Kim S, Wakefield RL (2012) Success factors for deploying cloud computing. Commun ACM 55(9): 62–68. http://doi.acm.org/10.1145/2330667.2330685
4. Ghosh A, Arce I (2010) Guest editors' introduction: In cloud computing we trust - but should we? Secur Privacy, IEEE 8(6): 14–16. doi:10.1109/MSP.2010.177
5. Habib S, Hauke S, Ries S, Muhlhauser M (2012) Trust as a facilitator in cloud computing: a survey. J Cloud Comput Adv Syst Appl 1(1): 19.

doi:10.1186/2192-113X-1-19, http://www.journalofcloudcomputing.com/content/1/1/19
6. Khan K, Malluhi Q (2010) Establishing trust in cloud computing. IT Prof 12(5): 20–27. doi:10.1109/MITP.2010.128
7. Michael B, Dinolt G (2010) Establishing trust in cloud computing. IANewsletter 13(2): 4–8. http://iac.dtic.mil/iatac/download/Vol13_No2.pdf
8. Park J, Spetka E, Rasheed H, Ratazzi P, Han K (2012) Near-real-time cloud auditing for rapid response. In: In: 26th International conference on advanced information networking and applications workshops (WAINA), pp 1252–1257. IEEE Computer Society, Washington, DC, USA. doi:10.1109/WAINA.2012.78
9. Pearson S (2011) Toward accountability in the cloud. Internet Comput IEEE 15(4): 64–69. doi:10.1109/MIC.2011.98
10. Takabi H, Joshi J, Ahn G (2010) Security and privacy challenges in cloud computing environments. Secur Privacy IEEE 8(6): 24–31. doi:10.1109/MSP.2010.186
11. Abawajy J (2011) Establishing trust in hybrid cloud computing environments. In: Proceedings of the 2011 IEEE 10th International Conference on Trust, Security and Privacy in Computing and Communications,. IEEE Computer Society, Washington, DC, USA. TRUSTCOM '11, pp 118–125. doi:10.1109/TrustCom.2011.18. http://dx.doi.org/10.1109/TrustCom.2011.18
12. Haq IU, Alnemr R, Paschke A, Schikuta E, Boley H, Meinel C (2010) Distributed trust management for validating sla choreographies. In: Wieder P, Yahyapour R, Ziegler W (eds). Grids and service-oriented architectures for service level agreements. Springer, US. pp 45–55. http://dx.doi.org/10.1007/978-1-4419-7320-7_5
13. Pawar P, Rajarajan M, Nair S, Zisman A (2012) Trust model for optimized cloud services(Dimitrakos T, Moona R, Patel D, McKnight D, eds.). Springer, Berlin Heidelberg. pp 97–112. http://dx.doi.org/10.1007/978-3-642-29852-3_7
14. NIST (2011) NIST cloud computing standards roadmap, NIST CCSRWG-092. first edition. NIST, Gaithersburg, MD,USA. http://www.nist.gov/itl/cloud/upload/NIST_SP-500-291_Jul5A.pdf
15. Blomqvist K (1997) The many faces of trust. Scand J Manage 13(3): 271–286
16. Mayer R, Davis J, Schoorman F (1995) An integrative model of organizational trust: Past, present, and future. Acad Manage Rev 20(3): 709–734
17. Huang J, Nicol D (2010) A formal-semantics-based calculus of trust. Internet Comput IEEE 14(5): 38–46. doi:10.1109/MIC.2010.83
18. Shaoham Y (1987) Temporal logics in ai: Semantical and ontological considerations. Artif Intell 33: 89–104
19. Huang J, Fox MS (2006) An ontology of trust: formal semantics and transitivity. In: Proceedings of the ICEC'06, 259–270. ACM, New York, NY, USA. doi:10.1145/1151454.1151499
20. Hwang K, Kulkareni S, Hu Y (2009) Cloud security with virtualized defense and reputation-based trust mangement. In: Dependable, Autonomic and Secure Computing, 2009. DASC '09. IEEE Computer Society, Washington, DC, USA. Eighth IEEE International Conference on, pp 717–722. doi:10.1109/DASC.2009.149
21. CSA (2011) STAR (security , trust and assurance registry) program. Cloud Security Alliance. https://cloudsecurityalliance.org/star/. Accessed on 16 Oct. 2012
22. CSA (2011) Security guidance for critical areas of focus in cloud computing v3.0. Cloud Security Alliance. www.cloudsecurityalliance.org/guidance/csaguide.v3.0.pdf
23. CSA (2011) CSA: Security, trust and assurance registry. Cloud Security Alliance. https://cloudsecurityalliance.org/research/initiatives/star-registry/, Accessed on 16 Oct. 2012
24. Knode R (2009) Digital trust in the cloud. CSC.COM. http://assets1.csc.com/au/downloads/0610_20_Digital_trust_in_the_cloud.pdf
25. CSC (2011) Cloudtrust protocol (CTP). Cloud Security Alliance. https://cloudsecurityalliance.org/research/ctp/. Accessed on 16 Oct. 2012
26. Knode R, Egan D (2010) Digital trust in the cloud – A precis for the CloudTrust protocol (V2.0). CSC. https://cloudsecurityalliance.org/wp-content/uploads/2011/05/cloudtrustprotocolprecis_073010.pdf
27. RSA (2011) RSA establishes cloud trust authority to accelerate cloud adoption. RSA. http://www.rsa.com/press_release.aspx?id=11320

28. EMC (2011) Proof, not promises: Creating the trusted cloud. EMC. http://www.emc.com/collateral/emc-perspective/11319-tvision-wp-0211-ep.pdf

29. ISO (2005) ISO/IEC 27001:2005 information technology – security techniques – information security management systems – requirements. ISO. http://www.iso.org/iso/catalogue_detail?csnumber=42103. Accessed on 16 Oct. 2012

30. AICPA (2010) SSAE 16. AICPA. http://www.aicpa.org/Research/Standards/AuditAttest/Pages/SSAE.aspx. Accessed on 16 Oct. 2012

31. IAASB (2009) ISAE 3402. International Auditing and Assurance Standards Board. http://www.ifac.org/sites/default/files/downloads/b014-2010-iaasb-handbook-isae-3402.pdf. Accessed on 16 Oct. 2012

32. IGTF (2010) Guidelines for auditing grid cas version 1.0. IGTF. http://www.ogf.org/documents/GFD.169.pdf

33. Maurer UM (1996) Modelling a public-key infrastructure. In: In: ESORICS '96: Proceedings of the 4th European symposium on research in computer security. Springer-Verlag, London, pp 325–350

34. Cooper D, Santesson S, Farrell S, Boeyen S, Housley R, Polk W (2008) Internet x.509 public key infrastructure certificate and certificate revocation list (CRL) profile. IETF. http://www.ietf.org/rfc/rfc5280.txt

35. Huang J, Nicol D (2009) Implicit trust, certificate policies and formal semantics of PKI. Information Trust Institute, University of Illinois at Urbana-Champaign

36. Ziegler CN, Lausen G (2005) Propagation models for trust and distrust in social networks. Inf Syst Front 7(4–5): 337–358. http://dx.doi.org/10.1007/s10796-005-4807-3

37. Farrell S, Housley R, Turner S (2010) An internet attribute certificate profile for authorization. IETF. http://www.ietf.org/rfc/rfc5755.txt

38. Enomaly Inc. (2010) SportCloud: Global market for cloud capacity. Enomaly Inc. http://spotcloud.com. Accessed on 18 Jan. 2013

3

A survey on securing the virtual cloud

Robert Denz[*] and Stephen Taylor

Abstract

The paper presents a survey and analysis of the current security measures implemented in cloud computing and the hypervisors that support it. The viability of an efficient virtualization layer has led to an explosive growth in the cloud computing industry, exemplified by Amazon's Elastic Cloud, Apple's iCloud, and Google's Cloud Platform. However, the growth of any sector in computing often leads to increased security risks. This paper explores these risks and the evolution of mitigation techniques in open source cloud computing. Unlike uniprocessor security, the use of a large number of nearly identical processors acts as a *vulnerability amplifier*: a single vulnerability being replicated thousands of times throughout the computing infrastructure. Currently, the community is employing a diverse set of techniques in response to the perceived risk. These include *malware prevention and detection*, *secure virtual machine managers*, and *cloud resilience*. Unfortunately, this approach results in a disjoint response based more on detection of known threats rather than mitigation of new or *zero-day* threats, which are often left undetected. An alternative way forward is to address this issue by leveraging the strengths from each technique in combination with a focus on *increasing attacker workload*. This approach would make malicious operation time consuming and deny persistence on mission time-scales. It could be accomplished by incorporating migration, non-determinism, and resilience into the fabric of virtualization.

Keywords: Vulnerability amplifier; Malware prevention and detection; Secure virtual machine managers; Cloud resilience; Zero-day; Increasing attacker workload; Virtual machine; View comparison-based malware detection

Introduction

Virtualization of servers in the cloud operates by adding a new layer to the software stack known as the hypervisor [1] or Virtual Machine Monitor (VMM) [2]. The hypervisor encapsulates the hardware, allowing it to be used by multiple operating system instances concurrently. This flexibility, coupled with the cost and performance advantages of sharing the underlying hardware, has revolutionized the computing industry: large numbers (i.e. hundreds of thousands) of generic hardware platforms, using multi-core blade technology, are now coupled through high-performance networking to produce a generic computing surface. Any subset of this collection can be combined to operate in tandem for a particular application using a multitude of operating systems.

Conceptually, the hypervisor presents a *virtual machine* abstraction that restricts malicious code, executing within one instance of an operating system, from affecting a different instance. Unfortunately, hypervisors have introduced their own new security challenges: Adversaries now actively attempt to detect the presence of an operating hypervisor in order to tailor attacks accordingly [3]. A wide range of hypervisor detection techniques have already appeared against popular systems such as VMWare, VirtualPC, Bochs, Hydra, Xen, and QEMU [4]. Often, these techniques operate by exploiting timing differences between virtualized and non-virtualized operations [5]. Alternatively, they detect unusual memory locations associated with key operating system data structures [6]. For example, the Red Pill technique works by using the SIDT X-86 instruction to determine the location in memory of the interrupt descriptor table; a machine running above a hypervisor will return a location much higher in memory than one that is not [7]. Following hypervisor detection, the adversary then attacks either the operating system, the virtual switch (vSwitch) sharing network connectivity between virtual machines, or the hypervisor itself [8].

The presence of a hypervisor has no impact on the vulnerabilities associated with the operating system. As a result, any exploit that leverages a known vulnerability will still operate successfully [9]. Although, a remote exploit gives the adversary control of a single virtual machine, by

* Correspondence: Robert.M.Denz.TH@Dartmouth.edu
Thayer School of Engineering at Dartmouth College, Hanover, NH, America

using the exploit in a virus the entire cloud could be compromised. It is this *vulnerability amplification* that poses the most significant threat to the future of cloud computing.

Direct attacks against a vSwitch may undermine the operation of multiple virtual machines on a single host by denying connectivity to all of them simultaneously. The vSwitch provides the same functionality as a physical switch and in consequence exhibits the same vulnerabilities, enabling the same exploits [10]. For example, Address Resolution Protocol (ARP) spoofing, involves the interception of valid network packets by sending fake ARP packets to a switch [11].

Hypervisor attacks involve the direct exploitation of vulnerabilities in the hypervisor. All virtual machines executing on a hypervisor have distinct data structures, separated in hardware. This separation forms a semantic gap [12] that prevents virtual machines from having visibility or impact upon each other's data structures [13]. Direct Kernel Structure Manipulation (DKSM) bridges the semantic gap by patching virtual machine data structures and redirecting hypervisor accesses to shadow copies. This allows the virtual machine to present false information to the hypervisor regarding the virtual machine state, allowing implants, such as rootkits [14], to persist without detection.

Virtualization provides inherent redundancy and appears to provide robust, large-scale, cost-effective availability of shared resources [15]. However, this perception is tempered by the known risk of vulnerability amplification and the paucity of knowledge regarding zero-day exploitation in clouds: history has shown that lack of detection does not imply lack of infection. Current mitigation techniques reviewed by this paper have already evolved based on *malware detection and prevention, secure virtual machine managers,* and *cloud resilience.* These three categories and their roles in preventing an attacker from gaining access to the cloud is illustrated in Figure 1. Omitted from Figure 1 are cloud services that provide authentication such as lightweight active directory protocol servers and trusted computing techniques as they are outside the scope of this survey. Initially, the attacker has to overcome or bypass the intrusion detection and prevention systems typically employed at the cloud boundary. They are then faced with a secure hypervisor usually installed on a single host; whose purpose is to restrict access to kernel and hypervisor data structures. Finally, cloud resilience is used by a host to restore a single compromised or failed virtual machine to a known good state. Although not currently prevalent throughout the industry, hypervisors offer the opportunity to restrict the attacker's access to the base of the software stack. Since typically the number of vulnerabilities is directly related to the number of source

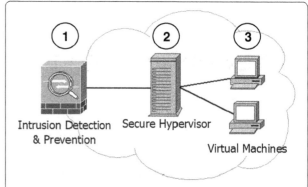

Figure 1 The three cloud security techniques reviewed by this paper: intrusion detection & prevention, secure hypervisors, and virtual machines.

lines of code [16], this would allow tight control of the hardware and allow operating system designers to build successive layers on a secure base of trust. The small size of the hypervisor also opens the door to formal reasoning concerning its security properties [17]. Unfortunately, these ideas have yet to be cohesively integrated and their impact upon security quantified. In the sections that follow we explore the building blocks that are available for improving cloud security and assess them on the basis of their *performance impact,* ability to *reduce the attack surface, detect known and zero-day threats, resolve detected threats,* and *increase attacker workload* by denying either surveillance or persistence.

Threat model

The security implementation analyzed in this survey address the threat model for intrusions employing remote control outlined in Figure 2. It may involve several steps including surveillance to determine if a vulnerability exists [18], use of an appropriate exploit or other access method [18], privilege escalation [19], removing exploit artifacts, and hiding behavior [14]. Surveillance may involve obtaining a copy of the binary code and using reverse engineering [20,21] or fuzzing [22] to facilitate a broad range of attack vectors including return oriented programming [23]. The implant then persists for a time sufficient enough to carry out some malicious effect, obtain useful information, or propagate intrusion to other systems.

Unlike the time to execute an exploit, the time spent in surveillance and persistence may range from minutes to months or even years depending upon the intended effect. Moreover, the presence of an intrusion may never be detected by network defenses but instead may be recognized indirectly due to either a deviation from expected behavior, or may be derived from intelligence sources.

Nevertheless, each cloud security technique represents an integral building block in the multilayered defense of

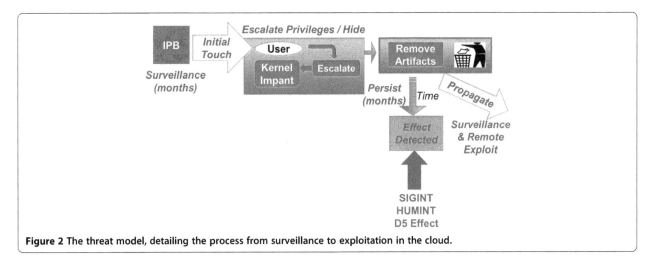

Figure 2 The threat model, detailing the process from surveillance to exploitation in the cloud.

the cloud. Malware detection and prevention systems are the initial line of defense in preventing an attacker from gaining a foothold on a cloud. The secure hypervisors present a hardened code base that restricts access to hardware to all, but the most privileged operations. Lastly, cloud resilient solutions are present to protect against the unknown exploits, which may allow an attacker to operate on a cloud indefinitely.

Malware detection and prevention

Malware detection was one of the first techniques implemented after the introduction of hypervisors. To achieve this, researchers paired the proven technology of Intrusion Detection Systems (IDS) with the ability to hide in a virtual machine. In this scenario, the IDS still performs the same function of identifying patterns of malicious behavior on a system that may be compromised [24]; for example a proof of concept based on the Snort IDS successfully prevented a Distributed Denial of Service (DDoS) attack [25]. This implementation installed a virtual machine that ran Snort on top of the VMware hypervisor to monitor network traffic to all guest virtual machines attached to a virtual switch. Once running, the IDS dealt with DDoS attacks in two steps: Initially, attacking computers were blocked by Snort; subsequently, the virtual server automatically moved the application under attack to a new location in the cloud. This demonstrated that an IDS can function inside the cloud; however, the implementation was just as vulnerable to zero-day attacks as non-virtualized IDS's [26]: attacks were missed due to IDS configuration and the failure of signatures to detect new attacks.

The Hybrid Virtual IDS is a solution that leverages the strengths of the cloud and improves upon the previous Snort implementation [27]. The approach combines resilience of a virtual IDS and the versatility offered by a host based IDS. This is possible through the use of integrity checking [28] and system call trace analysis

[29]. Integrity checking is a static detection process in which a changed file is compared to a gold standard to determine if the change is malicious. System call trace analysis dynamically flags anomalous system call behavior as potentially dangerous. These two approaches are implemented inside of a virtual machine to provide an isolated environment. A custom hypervisor is then used to ensure the isolation between all virtual machines. To provide functionality to the IDS, the hypervisor has hooks that allow the inspection of other guest virtual machines running on the hypervisor. This allows the hybrid virtual IDS to remain isolated from other running virtual machines, while still allowing it to access data from the virtual machines it is monitoring. This technique performed well in testing conducted by the authors of the Hybrid Virtual IDS, but returned unexpected performance results: as the IDS decreases the length of time between inspecting of the monitored virtual machine, the workload processing time did not increase linearly as to be expected and instead became erratic. The cause of this erratic performance is open to additional research.

With the introduction of a hypervisor and a virtualized IDS, it was only a matter of time before firewalls were moved into the cloud. One of these virtual firewall implementations is VMwall [30], which runs in the privileged virtual machine that controls the Xen hypervisor and uses virtual machine introspection [31]. This is the process of inspecting the data structures of a separate virtual machine. To enable this functionality, the Xen hypervisor has added hooks that capture all network connections created by a process. The data pertaining to these connections is then passed to VMwall for analysis. The connection is either allowed or blocked by using a whitelist (a list of approved processes and connection types). To deter false data during introspection, kernel integrity checking [32] is used to verify the state of kernel data structures in the guest virtual machines. This is necessary, as the primary method of inspecting traffic is through these data structures; malicious modification may compromise the monitoring of traffic. However, VMwall may be vulnerable to hijacking of a whitelisted process or an already established connection. The only method of detection against the compromise of an approved process is through the checksumming of the in-memory image of that process. This is performed by ensuring that the hash of a process has not changed from that of one contained in the whitelist. Due to the performance impact of hash analysis, this method is generally not implemented. Hijacking an established connection can be partially prevented through time outs associated with kernel rules contained in the whitelist. To fully prevent this type of compromise, deep packet inspection could be used, but is not currently employed by VMwall. Importantly, the employed introspection techniques cause a minimal performance impact: the additional overhead is 7% for file transfers from hypervisor to guest and 1% for file transfers from a guest to the hypervisor. Added overhead for Transmission Control Protocol (TCP) and User Data Protocol (UDP) connections are negligible; increases are measured in microseconds.

An alternative approach to detection techniques, like VMwall and hybrid IDS, are prevention methods. One security appliance that performs prevention is Malaware, which is designed to prevent malware that tailors attacks upon detection of a hypervisor [33]. To deter this initial identification of a virtual environment, a signature based method is used. In this instance, a signature is an instruction that should not be executed by an unprivileged process. As an example, when a process such as Red Pill attempts to run the SIDT instruction, it will be flagged as malicious. However, as the authors of Malaware have stated, a signature based approach is only effective against known types of malware. To combat zero-day threats, two behavior based approaches that utilize dynamic analysis are proposed [34]. This could be accomplished by first learning the current process and its page table base address. With this, it is possible to check if the current instruction register belongs to the process' code pages. If this mapping does not exist, Malaware could flag the process as malicious. The second dynamic analysis method suggested is taint tracking. Changes to the system, otherwise known as taint, are created, when a process modifies any code or memory location. Accordingly, when taint is created in monitored locations, the offending process is immediately flagged as malicious. An added benefit of taint tracking is it defeats malicious code that has been transformed to look harmless, also known as code obfuscation [35]. Once loaded into a monitored region, the obfuscated code is immediately marked as tainted and the associated process is flagged as malicious. Unfortunately, only the signature based piece of the detection has been implemented and

no data relating to added overhead has been collected. However, the initial detection results were promising with a malware detection rate of 76%. Lastly, it is important to note that techniques that alter known memory states, such as address space layout randomization (ASLR) may increase the difficulty of this type of taint tracking [36].

Another prevention method, guest view casting [37], moves malware prevention from the guest virtual machine to the hypervisor. This approach reconstructs the data structures of the guest for analysis at the hypervisor level. This is achieved by translating guest virtual memory addresses to physical memory addresses, then reading the raw data from the guest's virtual hard drive. The reassembled state in the hypervisor can then be compared to the guest's state using viewing tools such as Windows Task Manager and memory dump to display all processes in memory. The presence of discrepancies between the two states may indicate the existence of malware in the guest. The authors have labeled this method of searching for discrepancies between states as *view comparison-based malware detection*. An outgrowth of this method is to use anti-virus software to scan the guest's state from inside of the hypervisor. The use of anti-virus outside of the guest shows that it identifies malware more effectively than anti-virus running inside a virtual machine. Additionally, performance of anti-virus is improved outside of the virtual machine. The primary drawback to this approach is the assumption that the hypervisor has not been compromised. The authors agree that malicious code that targets the hypervisor [38] can compromise their approach.

Although detection and prevention are important, the last two decades have demonstrated that it is unlikely that malware can be eliminated completely [39]. Security researchers in an attempt to understand these attacks have to rely on system logs that lack integrity [40] and are often incomplete [41]. The ReVirt IDS [42], which runs on UMLinux [43]; was created in an attempt to improve upon these inadequacies. This is accomplished by creating logs for all of the relevant system level information needed to replay what transpired at an instruction by instruction level for a specific virtual machine. This allows administrators to determine all the relevant information pertaining to an attack. The overhead of performing these functions is 13-58% for kernel tasks and up to 8% for logging tasks.

Secure virtual machine managers
Hypervisors have afforded researchers with new security capabilities. However, the hypervisor itself has come under attack as a way of gaining control of a system [44]. This has led to the introduction of Secure Hypervisors that reduce the attack surface and increase reliability by reducing the number of lines of code [16]. sHype [45],

designed by IBM, increases security by taking the idea of control flow enforcement first seen in SELinux [46] and applying those controls on information flows between virtual machines through a mandatory access control model. Using intricate security policies; unfortunately, these make it difficult to guarantee security and can be over 50,000 lines of code [47]. To remove this level of complexity, sHype affords the same control flow protections, but at the hypervisor level and without the need of a policy administrator. These information flows are maintained through the use of a reference monitor that decides what connections to accept and deny between virtual machines. The sHype approach creates a flexible architecture, which allows it to support many different security modules [48]. This is accomplished in around 11,000 lines of code; SELinux alone is over 85,000 lines of code.

The performance impact of sHype enforcement policies is less than 1% [45]. However, sHype's primary shortfall is that it does not completely protect against unauthorized transfer of information between two virtual machines that are not allowed to share information. Figure 3 illustrates the problem: nodes A, B, and C represent three different virtual machines and all are connected to a reference monitor. Virtual machines A and B are not allowed to share information, but both are allowed to share information with virtual machine C. A covert channel is created, when virtual machine C acts as an intermediary and passes information between A and B. In this case the reference monitor would not intervene, as it only sees information being transferred from A to C and from C to B. Fortunately, the addition of a Chinese wall (communication rules) can be added to sHype to protect against this covert channel [49]. In this case, the rule would only allow two of the three virtual machines to run at any one time. However, this method has the drawback of causing a decrease in performance of up to 9.1% [50].

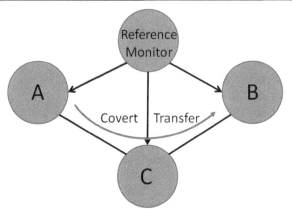

Figure 3 An example of a covert channel, where node A transfers information to node B, through the intermediary node C.

This performance impact can be mitigated by performing Chinese wall policy checks at virtual machine creation and then caching these decisions. Since, policy changes are infrequent, this configuration reduces the performance impact to less than 1% [51].

A different direction from control flow enforcement is used in the noHype hypervisor [52]. This minimalist approach removes as much as possible from the hypervisor; unfortunately, no published numbers for lines of code are available. However, the first prototype was based on a stripped down version of Xen 4.0; implying that it falls somewhere less than 1.6 million lines of code [53]. The code count was reduced by shrinking the size of the hypervisor by following four rules. First, noHype pre-allocates processor cores and memory to virtual machines. This allows the virtual machine to control its own hardware, which improves performance. Second, each virtual machine is assigned its own I/O device. Being in the cloud, it is assumed that these virtual machines only need network interface cards (NIC). The issue here is that servers have a limited number of NICs. Thankfully, newer NICs take advantage of Single-Root I/O Virtualization [54], which allows them to present themselves as multiple NICs. Thus, each virtual machine on a server is able to receive its own NIC, even if there are more virtual machines than NICs. Third, noHype provides the user with a predefined guest virtual machine in order to control the discovery of hardware. This also prevents a user from uploading a malicious guest virtual machine, which could attack the hypervisor. Lastly, noHype avoids indirection that occurs through the creation of virtual cores and memory, since cores and memory are assigned directly to each virtual machine. These four principles were tested against a standard Xen 4.0 install and startup time was reduced by 1% in the noHype implementation. However, noHype loses the ability to perform any introspection of the guest virtual machines as the hypervisor is limited in functionality. Thus, a virtual machine in the noHype cloud could become infected without noHype being aware of the infection.

Another popular feature of the cloud is live migration of virtual machines [55]. This can be seamlessly accomplished with little downtime thanks to virtualization. However, migrations lose the states maintained by stateful firewalls [56] and IDS' [57]. These states can be maintained using a network security enabled hypervisor (NSE-H) designed on top of the Xen hypervisor [58]. This builds on the concepts used in secure hypervisors, but adds support for secure file transfers. The performance impact of this method is measured in downtime, which is the time a virtual machine is not available during transfer. The cost of securing these migrations is up to a 15% increase in downtime versus downtime of non-secure transfers [58]. This downtime occurs for two reasons when maintaining the security context of the virtual machines being migrated. The first is the additional time needed to securely copy a virtual machine's memory space from one host to another. The second is the NSE-H security additions, as they are using additional resources on the system.

Cloud resilience

An often over-looked aspect of cloud computing is *Resilience*, defined as the ability for a system to recover and continue to provide services when a loss of hardware or software occurs [59]. One such system, Cloud Resilience for Windows (CReW) [60], expands the idea of resilience to the security domain through the use of strong security in guest virtual machines [61], and introspection [62]. Implementation is on top of the 270,000 plus lines of code that comprise the kernel-based virtual machine hypervisor [63]. This has enabled CReW to effectively prevent attacks from some rootkits and repair any damage they may have caused, but at a cost to performance as the number of virtual machines increases or security level is raised. At a strict level with three virtual machines, CReW adds ~48% increase in time needed for CPU tasks and ~279% increase in time required for I/O related tasks. For the paranoid setting, CReW adds ~116% increase in time for CPU related tasks and adds ~347% increase in time for I/O related tasks [60].

A technique that builds upon the ideas presented in CReW and supports other operating systems is that of *hypervisor-based efficient proactive recovery* [64]. This approach makes the assumption that no matter what defense is implemented on the cloud, a machine will eventually be maliciously compromised or taken offline. Thus, after particular failure conditions are met, the guest virtual machine is refreshed from a gold standard. A prototype of these concepts was developed using a modified Xen hypervisor [65]. Testing has shown there is a balance between throughput and availability. Thus, a user of this method can choose between lower throughput and higher availability or higher throughput and lower availability when faults occur.

The Bear operating system is a minimalist implementation that builds resiliency on top of a secure hypervisor [66]. A key design choice is the strong enforcement of separating core functionality into four layers, which is typical of modern micro kernels, like the MINIX operating system [67]. Importantly, the attack surface is reduced with a shared code base (>50%) of 10,903 lines of code shared between the Bear Hypervisor and Kernel. The size is attributable to a small custom hypervisor and small custom kernel. Resiliency is derived from non-deterministically refreshing the virtual machines on the

hypervisor to a gold standard after a period of time. This refresh is done by starting a second virtual machine from the known valid state and then transferring functionality to it, all while simultaneously tearing down the first virtual machine. By using this method, control is seamlessly transferred between virtual machines and without an impact to performance. Also, any known or zero-day malware present on the torn down virtual machine will not be present on the newly started virtual machine.

Comparative analysis

Table 1 presents a summary comparison, of the approaches based on reduction of the attack surface, prevention of zero-day threats, and overhead. The "Reduces Attack Surface" category shows that all of the technologies other than sHype and Bear rely on a large code base. This poses a concern, as demonstrated by the authors of "Reliability Issues in Open Source Software", who have shown that errors occur at a rate of .09 defects per thousand lines of open source code. This problem is worse for closed source systems, with .57 defects per thousand lines of code. Although the numbers will vary with code base naturally, this result that indicates Xen will have 144 defects, KVM 25, UMLinux 162, sHype and Bear each present a single defect. An interesting comparison was provided between open source software and closed source software. Due to the partial unintended release of 300,000 lines of VMware kernel code; the code could contain up to 171 defects, which is more defects then a full install of UMLinux. Obviously, sHype and Bear systems are a bare minimum install and have less functionality when compared to the other hypervisors. This has led to the sHype architecture being ported to the Xen hypervisor by the authors of *"Building a MAC-Based Security Architecture for the Xen Open-Source Hypervisor"*, which has the net effect of increasing functionality and potential number of defects. The key takeaway is that a small code size and open source distribution are desirable to prove a system to be reliable and secure. However, closed source systems, which are outside of the purview of this article, do exist and provide similar security features. Two such commercial hypervisors not reviewed are Citrix XenClient and HyTrust.

After evaluating each system on its abilities to perform "Malware Detection" and "Prevents Zero-Days"; there were two clear outliers. Malware detection and prevention methods primarily protect against known threats, because of their use of whitelists and signatures. However, ReVirt is the outlier in this category, as it provides capabilities to remove zero-days; unlike its counterparts, it has no ability to detect malware. Secure hypervisors restrict access to the hypervisor but generally provide no malware detection abilities or zero-day prevention. Lastly, resilient systems

Table 1 Comparison summary of surveyed systems

Cloud security implementation	Reduces attack surface (lines of code)	Malware detection	Mitigates zero-day threats	Added overhead (%)
Malaware	> 725 K	Yes	No	No data
Guest view casting	> 1,600 K	Yes	No	Reduced up to 70%
Virtual snort	> 300 K	Yes	No	No data
Hybrid IDS	> 300 K	Yes	No	~4-36%
VMwall	~ 1,600 K	Yes	No	1-7%
ReVirt	~ 1,800 K	No	Yes	8-58%
NSE-H	> 1,600 K	No	No	15%
Shype	~ 11 k	No	No	< 1%
Shype with Chinese wall in critical path	> 1,600 K	No	No	9.1%
Shype with Chinese wall outside critical path	> 1,600 k	No	No	< 1%
NoHype	< 1,600 K	No	No	Reduced up to 1%
CReW	> 270 K	Yes	Yes	~48-347%
Hypervisor-based proactive recovery	~ 1,600 K	Yes	Yes	~8-12.7%
Bear	~ 11 k	Not applicable	Yes	< 1%

such as CReW and hypervisor based proactive recovery have shown promising results in both categories. The model of whitelists and signatures is replaced with restoration upon detection of anomalous system behavior. Thus, both known malware and zero-days are removed from the system when it is restored to a valid state. Resilient systems do not prevent the initial compromise from known threats, unlike malware prevention and detection systems. The outlier in this group is Bear, which makes no attempt to check for anomalous behavior. Instead, it assumes the system will eventually be compromised and therefore refreshes the system non-deterministically. This has the same end result of removing any known or zero-day attacks that may be present, but also invalidates surveillance and prevents persistence. Nevertheless, the effectiveness of resilient systems warrants further research.

The final category of "Added Overhead" is important, as no technique should overly impact system performance. Both secure hypervisors and malware prevention and detection schemes can minimally impact and in some cases improve performance. The larger resilient prototypes such as CReW and hypervisor proactive recovery have not yet reached this level of performance. Bear however, has had a negligible impact on performance when refreshing virtual machines. Research into future resilient system implementations should aim to maintain the performance levels set by intrusion detection and prevention systems, secure hypervisors, and the Bear operating system. This can be achieved by leveraging the proven practices of either adding functionality to the hypervisor as seen in Guest View Casting or reducing the hypervisor foot print as accomplished by NoHype and Bear. Once this performance requirement is met, further

capabilities can be added to resilient systems, which allow for the creation of a new cloud security architecture.

Related fields of work

One field of study that has not been included in this survey is the idea of trust [68] in regards to the unauthorized access of data. One approach to handle trust in data security is that of security labels in the cloud [69]. The goal of this approach is to isolate customer virtual machines from each other to prevent data leakage across virtual machines. This work is an enhancement of a trusted hypervisor that extends trust to network storage [70]. In regards to privacy, customers are concerned that their personal information will be leaked to those who should not have access to it. A current solution to this problem is the use of encryption with access control [71]. Using public key cryptography in the cloud, the user can be sure that their data is safe and only they have access to it.

Conclusion

All of the techniques reviewed in this paper have produced gains in making cloud computing more secure. Most of the solutions strive to race to the bottom of the software stack to combat known risks, rather than unknown zero-day risks. Moreover, it is currently left up to the cloud provider to pick from a grab bag of techniques to secure their infrastructure. This has led to a diverse set of approaches in cloud security, each with its own goals. The most successful approaches could be combined to build new cloud infrastructure. A starting point would be to begin with the idea of resilience as discussed in this paper. Non-determinism could then be added through process specific virtual machines. Multiple copies of these machines could refresh some processes in a non-deterministic manner. Lastly, secure migrations of processes and whole virtual machines can be added. Combining all these techniques could provide a cloud computing environment that drastically increases attacker workload.

Notice

The U.S. Government is authorized to reproduce and distribute reprints for Governmental purposes notwithstanding any copyright notation thereon. The views and conclusions contained herein are those of the authors and should not be interpreted as necessarily representing the official policies or endorsements, either expressed or implied, of the Defense Advanced Research Projects Agency (DARPA) or the U.S. Government.

Competing interests
The authors of this paper have no competing interests.

Authors' contributions
RD carried out the survey of the available literature and drafted the manuscript. Both authors read and approve the final manuscript.

Acknowledgements
This material is based on research sponsored by the Defense Advanced Research Projects Agency (DARPA) under agreement number: FA8750-11-2-0257.

References
1. Barham P, Dragovic B, Fraser K, Hand S, Harris T, Ho A, Neugebauer R, Pratt I, Warfield A (2003) "Xen and the Art of Virtualization. In: Proceedings of the nineteenth ACM symposium on Operating systems principles, pp 164–177
2. Goldberg RP (1974) A survey of virtual machine research. In: Proceedings of Computer, 7th edn., pp 34–45
3. Paleari R, Martignoni L, Roglia GF, Bruschi D (2009) A fistful of red-pills: how to automatically generate procedures to detect CPU emulators. In: Proceedings of the 3rd USENIX conference on Offensive technologies
4. Ferrie P (2006) "Attacks on Virtual Machine Emulators". Symantec Advanced Threat Research
5. Fitzgibbon N, Wood M, Conficker C (2009) A Technical Analysis. SophosLabs, Sophos Inc
6. Quist D, Smith V (2006) "Detecting the Presence of Virtual Machines Using the Local Data Table". http://www.offensivecomputing.net/files/active/0/vm.pdf
7. Rutkowska J (2006) "Red Pill"., http://www.hackerzvoice.net/ouah/Red_%20Pill.html
8. Ibrahim AS, Hamlyn-Harris J, Grundy J (2010) "Emerging Security Challenges of Cloud Virtual Infrastructure". In: Proceedings of APSEC Cloud Workshop
9. Corregedor M, Von Solms S (2011) "Implementing Rootkits to Address Operating System Vulnerabilities". Proceeding of Information Security South Africa, pp 1–8
10. Cabuk S, Dalton CI, Edwards A, Fischer A (2008) "A Comparative Study on Secure Network Virtualization". Technical Report HPL-2008-57, HP Laboratories
11. De Vivo M, De Vivo GO, Isern G (1998) "Internet Security Attacks at the Basic Levels". 32nd edn. ACM SIGOPS Operating Systems Review, pp 4–15
12. Chen PM, Noble BD (2001) "When virtual is better than real". Proceedings of the Eighth Workshop on Hot Topics in Operating Systems, pp 133–138
13. Bahram S, Jiang X, Zi W, Grace M, Li J, Srinivasan D, Rhee J, Xu D (2010) "DKSM: subverting virtual machine introspection for fun and profit". 29th IEEE International Symposium on Reliable Distributed Systems, pp 82–91
14. Hoglund G, Butler J (2005) Rootkits: subverting the windows Kernel. Addison-Wesley Professional, USA
15. Neal L (2009) Is Cloud Computing Really Ready for Prime Time? 42nd edn, of Computer 42:15–20
16. Pandey RK, Tiwari V (2011) "Reliability issues in open source software". In: Proceedings of the International Journal of Computer Applications, 34th edn., p 1
17. Klein G, Elphinstone K, Heiser G, Andronick J, Cock D, Derrin P, Elkaduwe D, Engelhardt K, Kolanski R, Norrish M, Sewell T, Tuch H, Winwood S (2009) "seL4: formal verication of an OS Kernel". In: Proceedings of 22nd ACM Symposium on Operating Systems Principles
18. Kennedy D, O'Gorman J, Kearns D, Aharoni M (2011) Metasploit: the penetration testers guide. No Starch Press
19. Davi L, Dmitrienko A, Sadeghi AR, Winandy M (2011) Privilage escalation attacks on android. Information Security, Springer
20. Eagle C (2011) The IDA Pro Book. No Starch Press, San francisco, USA
21. Eilam E (2005) Reversing. Wiley, New York, USA
22. Forresterm JE, Miller BP (2000) "An Empirical Study of the Robustness of Windows NT Applications Using Random Testing". 4th USENIX Windows Systems Symposium, Seattle, Appears (in German translation) as "Empirische Studie zur Stabilität von NT-Anwendungen", iX, September 2000
23. Checkoway S, Halderman JA, Feldman AJ, Felten EW, Kantor B, Shacham H (2009) "Can DREs provide long-lasting security? The case of return-oriented programming and the AVC advantage". In: Proceedings of the USENIX/AC-CURATE/IAVoSS Electronic Voting Technology Workshop, August 2009
24. Denning D (1987) "An intrusion-detection model". Proc IEEE Trans Softw Eng SE-13(2):222–232
25. Bakshi A, Yogesh B (2010) "Securing cloud from DDOS Attacks using Intrusion Detection System in Virtual Machine". Second International Conference on Communication Software and Networks, pp 26–264
26. Lippmann R, Haines JW, Fried DJ, Korba J, Das K (2000) "The 1999 DARPA Off-Line Intrusion Detection Evaluation". In: Proceedings The International Journal of Computer and Telecommunications Networking - Special issue on recent advances in intrusion detection systems, vol 4, 34th edn., pp 579–595
27. Garfinkel T, Rosenblum M (2003) "A Virtual Machine Introspection Based Architecture for Intrusion Detection". In: Proceedings of Network and Distributed Systems Security Symposium
28. Kim GH, Spafford EH (1994) "The design and implementation of tripwire: a file system integrity checker". In: Proceedings of the 2nd ACM Conference on Computer and communications security., pp 18–29
29. Hofmeyr SA, Forrest S, Somayaji A (1998) Intrusion detection using sequences of system calls. J Comput Secur 6:151–180
30. Srivastava A, Giffin J (2008) "Tamper-Resistant, Application-Aware Blocking of Malicious Network Connections". In: Proceedings of the 11th international symposium on Recent Advances in Intrusion Detection., pp 39–58
31. Pfoh J, Schneider C, Eckert C (2009) "A Formal Model for Virtual Machine Introspection". In: Proceedings of the 1st ACM workshop on Virtual machine security., pp 1–10
32. Loscocco PA, Wilson PW, Pendergrass JA, McDonell CD (2007) "Linux Kernel Integrity Measurement Using Contextual Inspection". In: Proceedings of the ACM workshop on Scalable trusted computing., pp 21–29
33. Zhu D, Chin E (2007) "Detection of vm-aware malware"
34. Egele M, Kruegel C, Kirda E, Yin H, Song D (2007) "Dynamic Spyware Analysis". In: Proceedings USENIX Annual Technical Conference on Proceedings of the USENIX Annual Technical Conference, 18th edn
35. You I, Yim K (2010) "Malware obfuscation techniques: a brief survey". In: Proceedings of International Conference on Broadband, Wireless Computing, Communication and Application
36. Livshits B (2012) "Dynamic taint tracking in managed runtimes". Microsoft Research Technical Report, MSR-TR-2012-114
37. Jiang X, Wang X, Xu D (2007) "Stealthy Malware Detection Through VMM-Based "Out-of-the-Box" Semantic View Reconstruction". In: Proceedings of the 14th ACM conference on Computer and communications security., pp 128–138
38. Klein T (2003) "Scooby Doo-VMware Fingerprint Suite", http://www.trapkit.de/research/vmm/scoopydoo/index.html
39. Giffin J (2010) "The Next Malware Battleground Recovery after Unknown Infection". In: Proceedings of IEEE Journal on Security and Privacy, pp 74–76
40. CERT Coordination Center (2001) "CERT/CC security improvement modules: analyze all available information to characterize an intrusion"
41. Dittrich D (2000) "Report on the Linux Honeypot Compromise", http://project.honeynet.org/challenge/results/dittrich/evidence.txt
42. Dunlap GW, King ST, Cinar S, Basrai MA, Chen PM (2002) "ReVirt: enabling intrusion analysis through virtual-machine logging and replay".

In: Proceedings of the 5th symposium on Operating systems design and implementation., pp 211–224

43. Buchacker K, Buchacker K, Sieh V, Sieh V, Alexander F, Universität Erlangen-nürnberg (2001) "Framework for testing the fault-tolerance of systems including OS and network aspects". In: Proceedings IEEE High-Assurance System Engineering Symposium

44. Rutkowska J, Tereshkin A (2008) "Bluepilling the Xen Hypervisor". Black Hat, USA

45. Sailer R, Valdez E, Jaeger T, Perez R, Van Doorn L, Griffin JL, Berger S, Sailer R, Valdez E, Jaeger T, Perez R, Doorn L, Linwood J, Berger GS (2005) "sHype: Secure Hypervisor Approach to Trusted Virtualized Systems". IBM Research Report RC23511

46. Loscocco P, Smalley S (2001) "Integrating Flexible Support for Security Policies into the Linux Operating System". In: Proceedings of the FREENIX Track: 2001 USENIX Annual Technical Conference., pp 29–42

47. Jaeger T, Sailer R, Zhang X (2003) "Analyzing integrity protection in the SELinux example policy". In: Proceedings of the 12th conference on USENIX Security Symposium, 12th edn., p 59, 74

48. Vogl S (2010) "Secure hypervisors". In: Proceedings of 12th International Conference on Enterprise Information System

49. Cheng G, Jin H, Zou D, Ohoussou AK, Zhao F (2008) "A Prioritized Chinese Wall Model for Managing the Covert Information Flows in Virtual Machine Systems". In: Proceedings of The 9th International Conference for Young Computer Scientists., pp 1481–1487

50. Wang G, LI M, Weng C (2010) "Chinese Wall Isolation Mechanism and Its Implementation on VMM". In: Proceedings of Systems and Virtualization Management: standards and the cloud, 71st edn., pp 13–18

51. Sailer R, Jaeger T, Valdez E, Cáceres R, Perez R, Berger S, Griffin JL, Van Doorn L (2005) "Building a MAC-Based Security Architecture for the Xen Open-Source Hypervisor". In: Proceedings of Computer Security Applications Conference, 21st Annual

52. Szefer J, Keller E, Lee RB, Rexford J (2011) "Eliminating the Hypervisor Attack Surface for a More Secure Cloud". In: Proceedings of the 18th ACM conference on Computer and communications security., pp 401–412

53. Murray D, Milos G, Hand S (2008) "Improving Xen Security through Disaggregation". In: Proceedings of the Proceedings of the fourth ACM SIGPLAN/SIGOPS international conference on Virtual execution environments., pp 151–160

54. Dong Y, Yu Z, Rose G (2008) "SR-IOV networking in Xen: architecture, design and implementation". In: Proceedings of the First conference on I/O virtualization

55. Clark C, Fraser K, Hand S, Hansen JG, July E, Limpach C, Pratt I, Warfield A (2005) "Live Migration of Virtual Machines". In: Proceedings of the 2nd conference on Symposium on Networked Systems Design & Implementation, 2nd edn., pp 273–286

56. Gouda MG, Liu AX (2005) "A Model of Stateful Firewalls and its Properties". In: Proceedings of the IEEE International Conference on Dependable Systems and Networks

57. Kruegel C, Valeur F, Vigna G, Kemmerer R (2002) "Stateful Intrusion Detection for High-Speed Networks". In: Proceedings of the 2002 IEEE Symposium on Security and Privacy

58. Xianqin C, Han W, Sumei W, Xiang L (2009) "Seamless Virtual Machine Live Migration on Network Security Enhanced Hypervisor". In: Proceedings of Broadband Network & Multimedia Technology., pp 847–853

59. Laprie J, T LAAS-CNRS (2005) "Resilience for the scalability of dependability". In: Proceedings of ISNCA., pp 5–6

60. Lombardi F, Di Pietro R, Soriente C (2010) "CReW: cloud resilience forwindows guests through monitored virtualization". In: Proceedings of the 29th IEEE Symposium on Reliable Distributed Systems., pp 338–342

61. Lombardi F, Di Pietro R (2009) "Kvmsec: a security extension for linux kernel virtual machines". In: Proceedings of the ACM symposium on Applied Computing., pp 2029–2034

62. Lombardi F, Di Pietro R (2011) "Secure virtualization for cloud computing". In: Proceedings of the Journal of Network and Computer Applications., pp 1113–1122

63. Russel R (2007) "lguest: implementing the little Linux hypervisor". In: Proceedings of the Linux Symposium, 2nd edn., pp 173–178

64. Reiser HP, Kapitza R (2007) "Hypervisor-Based Efficient Proactive Recovery". In: Proceedings of the 26th IEEE International Symposium on Reliable Distributed Systems., pp 83–92

65. Reiser HP, Kapitza R (2007) "VM-FIT: supporting intrusion tolerance with virtualisation technology". In: Proceedings of the 1st Workshop on Recent Advances on Intrusion-Tolerant Systems., pp 18–22

66. Taylor S, Henson M, Kanter M, Kuhn S, McGill K, Nichols C (2011) "Bear–a resilient operating system for scalable multi-processors". Submitted for publication in IEEE Security and Privacy, Nov/Dec 2011

67. Tanenbaum A, Woodhull A (2006) "Operating systems: design and implementation. Prentice Hall, Upper Saddle River, USA

68. Lehtinen R, Russell D, Gangemi GT Sr (2006) "Computer security basics", 2nd edn. O'Reilly Media, Sebastopol, USA

69. Berger S, Cáceres R, Goldman K, Pendarakis D, Perez R, Rao JR, Rom E, Sailer R, Schildhauer W, Srinivasan D, Tal S, Valdez E (2009) "Security for the cloud infrastructure: trusted virtual data center implementation". In: Proceedings of the IBM Journal of Research and Development, 53rd edn., pp 560–571

70. Berger S, Cáceres R, Pendarakis D, Sailer R, Valdez E (2008) "TVDc: managing security in the trusted virtual datacenter". In: Proceedings of ACM SIGOPS Operating Systems Review, 42nd edn., pp 40–47

71. Yu S, Wang C, Ren K, Lou W (2010) "Achieving Secure, Scalable, and Fine-grained Data Access Control in Cloud Computing". In: Proceedings of the 29th conference on Information communications., pp 534–542

4

Increasing virtual machine security in cloud environments

Roland Schwarzkopf[*], Matthias Schmidt, Christian Strack, Simon Martin and Bernd Freisleben

Abstract

A common approach in Infrastructure-as-a-Service Clouds or virtualized Grid computing is to provide virtual machines to customers to execute their software on remote resources. Giving full superuser permissions to customers eases the installation and use of user software, but it may lead to security issues. The providers usually delegate the task of keeping virtual machines up to date to the customers, while the customers expect the providers to perform this task. Consequently, a large number of virtual machines (either running or dormant) are not patched against the latest software vulnerabilities. The approach presented in this article deals with these problems by helping users as well as providers to keep virtual machines up to date. Prior to the update step, it is crucial to know which software is actually outdated or affected by remote security vulnerabilities. While these tasks seem to be straightforward, developing a solution that handles multiple software repositories from different vendors and identifies the correct packages is a challenging task. The Update Checker presented in this article identifies outdated software packages in virtual machines, regardless if the virtual machine is running or dormant on disk. The proposed Online Penetration Suite performs pre-rollout scans of virtual machines for security vulnerabilities using established techniques and prevents execution of flawed virtual machines. The article presents the design, the implementation and an experimental evaluation of the two components.

Introduction

Infrastructure-as-a-Service (IaaS) Clouds [1] and virtualized Grid computing are based on the idea that users build individual virtual machines as execution environments for their tasks, allowing them to provide the required software stack without having to deal with Cloud or (multiple) Grid site administrators [2].

While the use of virtual machines is beneficial for service and infrastructure providers (users and providers in the Cloud nomenclature), by lowering the costs for the former and improving utilization and management capabilities for the latter, there are also some drawbacks. Since virtual machines are cheap and easy to create, users tend to create distinct virtual machines for different tasks. Users can branch new virtual machines based on old ones, snapshot machines or even rollback machines to a previous state. While these features provide great flexibility for users, they pose an enormous security risk for providers. A machine rollback, for example, could reveal

an already fixed security vulnerability [3]. What makes the task of keeping the software stack up-to-date even more time-consuming is the the increasing number of virtual machines, a phenomenon called virtual machine sprawl [4].

More problems arise because some of the virtual machines are likely to be dormant (not running) at some point in time. These virtual machines cannot be easily kept up-to-date, because typically this would require the virtual machines to be started, updated and shut down again, which is not only time-consuming, but may also be a tedious process. Different solutions [4-6] have been developed to solve the maintenance problem of (dormant) virtual machines. While these solutions can be used to update dormant machines, they suffer from a potential compatibility problem. They "forcibly" install updates, either by changing an underlying layer [5] or by replacing files [4,6], and there is no guarantee that the updates can be safely applied and that they are compatible to the software stack and the configuration of all affected virtual machines.

Moreover, all of these solutions lack the ability to properly identify which applications are truly outdated. Since

*Correspondence: rschwarzkopf@mathematik.uni-marburg.de
Department of Mathematics and Computer Science, University of Marburg, Hans-Meerwein-Str. 3, D-35032 Marburg, Germany

this information is a prerequisite for the actual update process, it is a crucial step in the process of keeping (dormant) virtual machines in a Cloud or a virtualized Grid computing environment up-to-date. While such a check is easy to perform for running virtual machines, because of the commonly used package management systems on Linux platforms and automatic update facilities on Windows platforms, it is again a problem with dormant virtual machines. Even if virtual machines are kept up to date, the installed software might still contain design flaws or software vulnerabilities not fixed with the latest update. Thus, only checking for updates alone is not sufficient. Furthermore, machines used in a public IaaS environment are subject to external attacks, i.e., they might be a selected or random target chosen by scripts. Therefore, it is indispensable to continuously analyze the used virtual machines and take proactive countermeasures such as patching the revealed flaws.

In this article a combined approach that checks for software updates and scans virtual machines for known security vulnerabilities is presented. The first component called *Update Checker* is proposed to check a potentially huge number of Linux-based virtual machines for the necessity of updates. Since the Update Checker copies the information about installed packages to a central database, the check can be executed on the central instance without booting the virtual machine beforehand and shutting it down afterwards, which is the most time-consuming part of checking for updates of a virtual machine. Thus, the check is independent of the status of the virtual machine (running or dormant). Both apt/dpkg and yum/rpm are supported and therefore all major Linux distributions. The solution allows easy checking of all registered virtual machines, returning either the number of available updates or details about each of the available updates. The second component called *Online Penetration Suite* (OPS) is proposed to perform periodic or pre-rollout online-scanning of virtual machines. While periodic scans can be done in idle times, pre-rollout scans are executed before machines go live, delaying the start of a machine but using the latest version of the scanners for up-to-date results. Virtual machines are scanned for software vulnerabilities, using a combination of well-known security products.

Furthermore, the proposed solutions can inform the owners about relevant findings via e-mail. Using an API, other management tools can utilize the results. To leverage existing software, our proposal is based on the Xen Grid Engine (XGE) [2] and the Image Creation Station (ICS) [7] introduced in previous publications. The XGE is a software tool to create either virtualized Grid environments on-demand or to act as a Cloud IaaS middleware. The ICS offers an easy way for users to create, maintain and use virtual machines in the previously mentioned

environments. An exemplary integration into the ICS, marking virtual machines that contain obsolete packages in virtual machine lists and providing details about available updates in detail views, and the XGE, preventing virtual machines containing obsolete packages from being started, is provided. The OPS scan process is triggered either by the ICS as a periodic maintenance operation or, if the additional overhead is acceptable, by the XGE as a pre-rollout check that might prevent a virtual machine from being started. As an alternative to preventing virtual machines from being started, those virtual machines can be started as usual and the owner is informed that his/her running machine is potentially unsafe. This can help administrators by giving them an overview of their dormant virtual machines, but also users without experience in the area of system maintenance (e.g. scientists that build custom virtual machines to execute their jobs), by making them aware of the problem.

The article is organized as follows. The next section presents the proposed design. Then, its implementation is discussed, followed by the presentation of experimental results. Afterwards, related work is discussed. The final section concludes the article and outlines areas for future research.

Design
The following sections present the design of the proposed approach. The first section outlines the Update Checker, a solution for checking for updates in virtual machines. The second section describes the Online Penetration Suite, an approach for online-scanning virtual machines for known software vulnerabilities.

Update checker
Since the primary goal of the Update Checker is detecting obsolete software in (dormant) virtual machines, the term virtual machine is used throughout this article. Nevertheless, the solution is applicable to physical machines as well.

The concept of the Update Checker is to build a central database that contains all the information required for the task of checking for updates. This includes the list of installed packages, including the exact version of the installed package as well as the list of repositories that are used for each virtual machine. This information has to be imported into the central database when the virtual machine is first registered, and updated after each change of the virtual machine, i.e., after the installation of new software or the update of already installed software.

Since the Update Checker is not targeted at a single Linux distribution (compared to, e.g., Landscape for Ubuntu [8]), at least the two prevalent software management solutions are supported: apt/dpkg, used for example in Debian and Ubuntu, as well as yum/rpm, used for example in Red Hat and Fedora as well as SuSE. Both solutions use a specific package database format as well as a specific repository format. While apt/dpkg uses the same plaintext file format both as package database and as repository database, yum/rpm uses a Berkeley database as package database and an XML file as repository database. Nevertheless, this has no influence on the structure of the database used to store the required information, since both systems have the concept of distinct package names and a consistent versioning scheme in common.

The design of the solution is shown in Figure 1. There are specific importers for the package databases and for the repository databases of the different software management solutions. This makes the Update Checker easily adaptable to other software management solutions. Information about the installed packages of a virtual machine is stored in the Package DB. Metadata about the VM, i.e., the time stamp of the import, the repositories used, etc., is stored in the Metadata DB. Information about the available packages on the different repositories is stored in the Repository Cache. When invoked, the Update Checker takes the information from these databases and

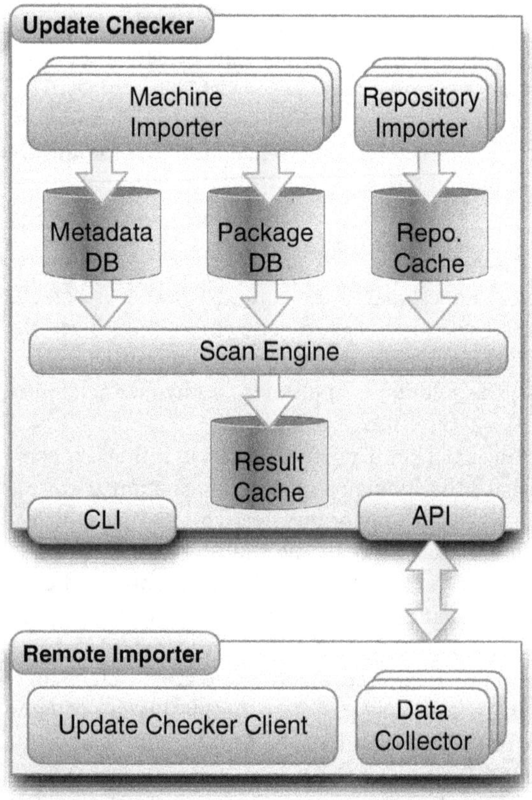

Figure 1 Update Checker architecture. The architecture of the Update Checker.

the Repository Cache and matches installed and available packages to detect obsolete software and stores the results in the Result Cache.

When a query for the state of one or more virtual machines is issued, the Update Checker first checks to see if the result of that query is already available in the Result Cache and returns the cached result if it is not obsolete. Cached results are considered obsolete after a configurable amount of time, depending on factors such as the frequency of updates or the need for security. Otherwise, it checks if the package lists of all repositories assigned to the virtual machine are available in the Repository Cache and not obsolete, i.e., the configured validity period has not yet expired. If this is not the case, the package lists are downloaded from the software vendor's repository, parsed and stored in the Repository Cache for future use. When using the Repository Cache instead of the real repositories, there is the chance that the Update Checker fails to identify an outdated package. Nevertheless, the Repository Cache is very useful for checking many virtual machines and by using a small validity period, the risk can be minimized. Finally, the actual check of the virtual machine is started, comparing the version of each installed package with the version available at the repository. Information about outdated packages is then stored in the Result Cache, so that subsequent queries regarding the same virtual machine can be answered faster.

To help the user to judge whether the identified outdated software poses a risk to the virtual machine, the Update Checker infers information about the priority of an update. Unfortunately, there is no common way to do this for multiple distributions. As a first approach, the source repository of the updated packages is evaluated, since distributions like Debian or Ubuntu use special repositories for security updates. The source of an update can therefore be used as a hint of its significance.

The Update Checker allows to query for the number of available updates for a single or multiple virtual machines as well as for details about the outdated packages and available updates for a single virtual machine. The former query allows a good estimation of the state of the virtual machine, where zero means the virtual machine is up to date, while a number greater than zero means that there are updates available. If significance information is available, individual numbers for each level of significance as well as the sum of the numbers are returned. This can either be used in situations where an overview over a number of virtual machines is required, e.g. , a list of virtual machines in a management tool like the ICS, or as a status check for a specific virtual machine, e.g., before it is started by the XGE.

Since the availability of updates itself allows no judgment about the threat resulting from the outdated packages, even when significance information is available, the latter query allows a detailed examination of the status of a virtual machine, by giving a list of outdated packages. This allows the user of the virtual machine to do a threat analysis based on the outdated packages and decide whether immediate action is required or not. The described functionality is used as an example of the integration of the Update Checker with other components. The complete solution is shown in Figure 2.

Two different interfaces are provided by the Update Checker: a command line interface (CLI) and an API for use by other software. The former can be used, when an administrator manually wants to execute an update check or register a virtual machine. The latter is provided for other tools like the ICS or XGE, allowing them to easily access the status information. This interface is provided using the language-independent protocol XML-RPC [9], to be available to tools written in any language.

The Update Checker can also be configured to run the checks at regular intervals, e.g., daily or weekly. This speeds up queries by other tools, because the information is already available. Users can be informed about obsolete software in their virtual machines via email. Additionally, administrators can also be informed about all virtual machines using obsolete software, to get an overview of the security of all virtual machines running on their infrastructure.

To ease the registration of virtual machines, the remote importer is provided (see Figure 1). It uses software management solution specific Data Collectors to gather the information required for the Update Checker, sends it to the machine the Update Checker is running on and triggers the registration process.

It might seem cumbersome to manually re-register virtual machines after every change, but with the remote importer it is merely a single command. Furthermore, it

can be easily automated when software for management and maintenance of virtual machines is used.

Online penetration suite

This section presents the Online Penetration Suite (OPS) to scan an arbitrary number of virtual machines for security vulnerabilities utilizing multiple security scanners. The OPS combines and interprets the different results and generates a machine-readable and a human-readable report. Furthermore, the OPS is able to manage (start, stop, migrate, etc.) virtual machines if necessary. This allows automatic testing of virtual machines in a virtualized infrastructure to detect known security vulnerabilities. Once the vulnerabilities are known, the administrators and users can fix them to protect their systems with respect to unwanted attacks.

Architecture

The OPS is divided into two parts: the *logic* part, containing the flow control and the report generator, and the *backend* part, operating the registered vulnerability scanners and the virtual machines. The architecture of the OPS is shown in Figure 3, containing two adapters for OpenVAS [10] and Nessus [11].

The *OPS Logic* module controls the processes of the OPS. It configures the security scanners, boots the virtual machines to test (if required) and starts the actual scans. Since the vulnerability scanners are basically third-party products with individual characteristics and modes of operation, they are abstracted by *Adapters* that hide the differences and provide an unified interface to start and monitor the vulnerability scanners. They allow the OPS not only to start the actual scans, but also to watch the scanners during the execution to detect any failures and react accordingly.

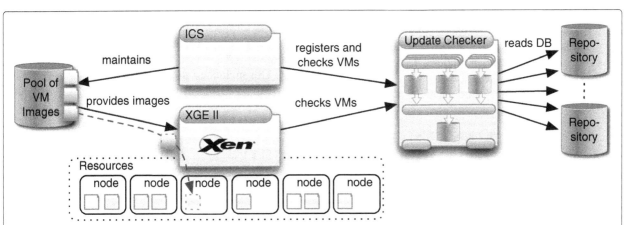

Figure 2 Usage scenario. The architecture of a complete system for virtualized Grid computing, consisting of the ICS, the XGE and the Update Checker. The figure shows the XGE deploying and starting a virtual machine, after the Update Checker has attested the virtual machine as being up-to-date.

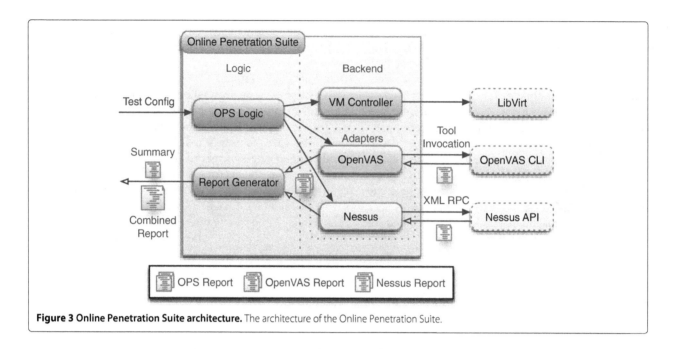

Figure 3 Online Penetration Suite architecture. The architecture of the Online Penetration Suite.

For a scan, the OPS needs two input parameters: the names of the target virtual machines and the name(s) of one or more vulnerability scanners. If no scanners are provided, the OPS chooses all scanners by default. A name uniquely identifies a virtual machine and allows the OPS to obtain further information like the IP and MAC address, path to the disk image(s), etc.

The *Report Generator* module collects the reports from the different scanners and generates the final result: a summary, containing the number of detected vulnerabilities categorized by a risk factor, and a combined report, containing the results from the security scanners in a unified format. To enable the Report Generator to analyze and understand the reports, the adapters have to convert the reports from the native format of the scanner to the unified OPS format.

The *backend* part of OPS consists of adapters to the required tools and libraries. It provides a module to control virtual machines using the libvirt [12] library as well as the vulnerability scanner adapters. Currently, the OPS supports two different scanners: OpenVAS [10] and Nessus [11], both well-known and established security-products.

Running vulnerability scans

OpenVAS is built as a client-server-architecture. The server is divided into three parts: administrator, manager and scanner. All clients communicate with either the manager or the administrator that both call the scanner. The OPS uses omp, a tool from the OpenVAS command line client for interaction. In order to guarantee a seamless scan, some of the countless options of OpenVAS are

preset by the OpenVAS adapter module using a configuration file. This prevents the user from choosing wrong options that could possibly lead to false results. Nevertheless, by modifying the adapter configuration file it is possible for an administrator to enable/disable tests or set/unset options.

Nessus, being the ancestor of OpenVAS, is also built as a client-server-architecture. To control it, an XML-RPC interface is used. Nessus needs a number of parameters to start the scan process: the IP address of the server, authentication data and a scan configuration. Similar to the OpenVAS adapter, the Nessus adapter module presets a number of options to guarantee a seamless scan process.

Structure of the reports

The combined report generated by the *Report Generator* is hierarchically divided into several parts. It starts with a summary of all reports and contains the results of each scanner structured by each tested virtual machine. Finally, the machine-specific report contains the vulnerabilities of this host. This includes a detailed description of the vulnerability, the severity level and if applicable, port number and transport protocol. The following paragraph shows an excerpt of a report:

```
<vulnerability>
<title>Microsoft Outlook SMB
Attachment
Remote Code Execution Vulnerability
(978212)</title>
<port>general/tcp</port>
<risk_factor>HIGH</risk_factor>
<description>
```

```
Overview: This host has critical
security
update missing according to Microsoft
Bulletin MS10-045.
[...]
CVE : CVE-2010-0266
BID : 41446
</description>
</vulnerability>
```

Implementation
In this section, the implementation of the Update Checker and the OPS is outlined.

Update checker
This section describes important parts of the implementation of the Update Checker, working from the top to the bottom of Figure 1. First, the machine and repository importers and their sources of information are described using the Debian Package Manager (dpkg) and the Advanced Packaging Tool (apt) of Debian and its derivates as an example. Afterwards, the internal databases and caches, the Scan Engine and the different interfaces are described. This section is concluded with details about the remote importer and the integration with other components. Further implementation details can be found in a previously published paper [13] of the authors. The implementation of the Update Checker has been done using the Ruby programming language.

Machine importer
A machine importer is responsible for importing the list of installed packages and enabled repositories of a machine into the Package DB and Metadata DB, respectively. This information is collected from the package database, that keeps track of installed packages, versions, files belonging to each package, etc., and from the configuration files of the software management solution.

The package database of dpkg is stored in /var/lib/dpkg and consists of several text files, of which the file status is of particular interest, because it contains the metadata for each package that has ever been installed on the system. For each package it contains about a dozen key-value-pairs, of which three are required to extract the information: Package, which contains the package name, Status, which contains the state of the package (installed or not installed), and Version, which contains the exact version of the package. The following snippet shows the parsed parts of a dpkg package management database entry:

```
Package: openssh-server
Status: install ok installed
Version: 1:5.1p1-5
```

The repositories used by apt are stored in /etc/apt/sources.list. This file contains multiple definitions, one per line, in the following format:

```
deb ROOT ARCHIVE COMPONENT
(COMPONENT...)
```

The meaning of these fields is explained in the next section. They are required to build the URL for the actual repository that is required to load the list of available packages.

Repository importers
A repository importer is responsible for importing the list of available packages in a repository into the Repository Cache. This information is gathered from the repository database of the software management solution. The repository database of an apt repository can be found using the following URL that is built using information from the fields in the config file.

```
ROOT/dists/ARCHIVE/COMPONENT/ ⤸
    binary-ARCHITECTURE/Packages.TYPE
```

The ROOT field contains the root URL of the repository or mirror. The next two fields partition the repository: Debian and Ubuntu use ARCHIVE to divide the repository by the release (e.g. *stable* or *testing*) and COMPONENT to divide by license type and level of support (e.g. *main, contrib* or *non-free*). The last two fields specify the system architecture and the compression format of the repository database.

The repository database uses the same format as the package database of dpkg. Thus, parsing can be done using the same technique.

Internal databases and caches
The Package DB is used to store a name-version-pair for each installed package on every machine. Its counterpart is the Repository Cache that stores a name-version-pair for each available package on every repository. Initially, it was planned to store this information in a database. Unfortunately, importing a virtual machine or updating the list of available packages of a repository was very slow using this technique. As a faster alternative, a hash encoded in JSON [14] was chosen, written to an individual file per virtual machine or repository, respectively. This was faster by a factor of more than 23 when measured for the import of two Debian repositories (2.16 sec using the hash versus 50.02 sec using the database). The equivalent to the database snippets shown above in the internal format is the following:

```
...,"openssh-server":"1:5.1p1-5",...
```

Information about outdated packages is stored in the Result Cache. It stores name-old version-new version-priority-quadruplets in a JSON encoded list, written to an individual file per virtual machine.

The Metadata DB stores a list of all registered virtual machines and repositories as well as the mapping between them. Furthermore, it stores the names of all files that build the Package DB, Repository Cache and Result Cache, together with an expiration date for each file of the two caches.

Scan engine

In this component, the actual identification of outdated packages takes place. Whenever a query for available updates of a virtual machine is submitted and there is no current result in the result cache, the Update Checker first determines the required repositories using the Metadata DB. If the repository cache does not contain current versions of the required repositories, a repository importer is used to update the cache. Afterwards, the list of installed packages is retrieved from the Package DB and the version of each package is compared with the version of that package stored in the repository cache. Outdated packages are stored in the result cache with installed and available version, so that subsequent queries can be handled faster. Finally, the number of outdated packages or the list of outdated packages is returned to the issuer of the query.

One particular problem discovered during the implementation of the Update Checker is the format of the version numbers used by the different package management systems or distributions, respectively. While most of the distributions use versions composed of the fields epoch, version and release, there are subtle differences between the distributions, e.g., separators, format of the release field, etc. Even the versionomy gem, a Ruby library especially designed for version comparisons, failed to correctly compare Debian version numbers.

One possibility is the use of the dpgk binary which provides an option to compare versions. This is very slow, since each comparison requires forking a new process. A Ruby library named dpkg-ruby implements version comparison using a native library. An old version of this library contains a Ruby-only version of the version comparison. Although slower, this solution is preferred to be independent of native libraries. By using an additional string comparison beforehand, performance losses can be cut down. Except for some minor tweaks, this version comparison library worked with all version numbers that were encountered in Debian and Fedora.

A daemon is used to provide some automation. All virtual machines can be checked for updates automatically at regular intervals. As described above, this frequently updates the cached repository databases and caches the results for all virtual machines. Queries using the API or the command line interface can then be served from the cache, requiring almost no time (only a file has to be read). The daemon also allows to notify users by email about outdated packages in their virtual machines. Additionally, the daemon can be configured to send emails about the status of all virtual machines to administrators.

Online penetration suite

The Online Penetration Suite is implemented in the Java programming language. Virtual machines are controlled using the Java binding of the libvirt library, the Nessus scanner is invoked using the Apache XML-RPC library and the reports of the vulnerability scanners are processed and converted using the Java API for XML Processing (JAXP).

Depending on the test configuration specified via the command line, the OPS frontend selects the required vulnerability scanners, starts their server components (if required), boots the virtual machines to scan (if they are not running already) and finally initiates and monitors the actual scan processes. All of these operations are hidden behind an interface that is implemented by the adapters, making the OPS easily extensible with new scanners. Since the report generation process is based entirely on reports in the unified OPS format, no vulnerability scanner dependent code is required for this step in the frontend.

The adapters use different techniques to control and monitor the actual vulnerability scanners. OpenVAS provides a command line interface, so its adapter needs to create a test configuration in the form of an XML file and pass it as an argument to the omp binary. Monitoring of OpenVAS requires analyzing the output of its client. For Nessus, the provided XMLRPC API is used. It contains methods to start and monitor the actual scan process. Both adapters contain code to convert the proprietary report formats into the unified OPS format.

Experimental results

The following section presents an evaluation of the presented components.

Update checker

Measurements have been conducted to evaluate the Update Checker on an Intel Xeon E5220 machine with 1 GB memory. The first measurement is a local measurement testing all components of the Update Checker, i.e., machine import, repository import and update checking. Three Debian and three Fedora virtual machines have been used in this test, with varying numbers of installed packages and enabled repositories. Each test has been executed 20 times and average values have been calculated. The results are shown in Table 1.

In the first part of this evaluation, the different machine importers were tested. All required files were copied to the

Table 1 Update Checker component benchmark

Distribution	Installed packages	Machine import	Repository import	Update import
Debian	563	0.04 secs	2.39 secs	0.44 secs
Debian	867	0.06 secs	2.80 secs	0.44 secs
Debian	1493	0.07 secs	2.68 secs	0.78 secs
Fedora	591	0.03 secs	13.59 secs	0.38 secs
Fedora	1063	0.04 secs	14.84 secs	1.00 secs
Fedora	2159	0.05 secs	15.38 secs	2.10 secs

Benchmark of all individual components of the Update Checker.

machine the test was executed on prior to the evaluation, thus no network communication is involved. Furthermore, before the measurement `rpm -qa` was executed on the source machine to generate a list of installed packages including their version. This is required to work around incompatibilities (i.e., the rpm binary on Debian squeeze could not read the rpm database of a Fedora 15 installation).

The growing import times can be explained with the growing number of installed packages that must be parsed.

The second part of the test measured the time required to download and parse all repository databases for the virtual machines (each machine had between 2 and 4 repositories configured) without using the repository cache. The times measured are thus artificial and are only of little relevance for actual usage, but allow evaluating the repository import and update checking. While the times for the Debian machines are quite stable, the increase of the time for Fedora is caused by the number of repositories used (2, 3 and 4, respectively). The very bad performance of the Fedora repository import is caused by the use of XML in the repository database.

The last part of the test evaluates the algorithm that actually checks for updates. Again, the increase in the times is caused by the growing number of packages. The reason for the worse results for Fedora are probably the longer and more complex version numbers used in Fedora, making the comparison harder and more time-consuming.

The measured values are promising. Checking for updates is a very fast process with the Update Checker. Because of the individual files used for the Package DB and Repository Cache, we do not expect performance degradation when the number of virtual machines increases. The relatively long time required for importing yum repositories is compensated by the repository cache, that results in every repository being downloaded and parsed only once during the configurable validity period of the cache.

To evaluate the influence of the repository cache, another measurement has been conducted that represents a more realistic scenario: checking all imported virtual machines for updates. The six machines from the last measurement were checked at once, taking advantage of the repository cache. The experiment was repeated 20 times and the average times are shown in Figure 4. The results indicate that the repository cache is very effective in cutting down the time required to check multiple virtual machines for updates.

To evaluate the scalability (and applicability for physical machines) of the Update Checker, 115 physical nodes from our compute cluster were imported. All machines were checked at once using the repository cache. The experiment was repeated 20 times and the time required to check all virtual machines was calculated. The results shown in Figure 5 provide evidence for the scalability of the Update Checker. The average check time was 34.53 seconds for all 115 machines, that is 0.30 seconds per machine.

Another measurement was conducted to evaluate the import time of the virtual machines, when the remote importer is used. This involves gathering all required files, executing `rpm -qa` in the case of rpm based distributions, sending everything to the Update Checker and starting the import process. For each virtual machine, 10 imports were executed. The results are shown in Figure 6.

As expected, the amount of time the import process requires grows with the number of packages in the database. Generally, the import process is faster for apt/dpgk based virtual machines than for yum/rpm based virtual machines. The source of this problem seems to be the use of the rpm binary to extract the information from the database.

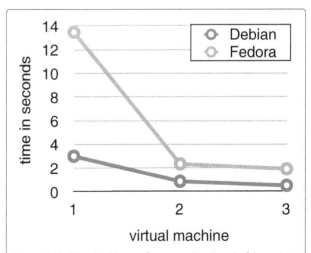

Figure 4 Update checking performance. Benchmark of the update checking process for multiple virtual machines using the repository cache.

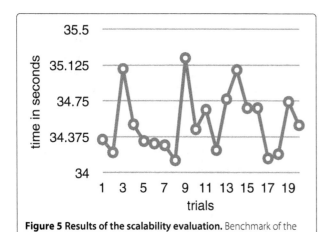

Figure 5 Results of the scalability evaluation. Benchmark of the update checking process for 115 machines using the repository cache.

Online penetration suite

The following section presents measurements related to the OPS. All tested systems are Xen domainU virtual machines running Debian Squeeze and located on Pentium IV systems with 1 GB memory. The OPS node is an Intel Xeon E5220 machine and 1 GB memory. All systems are interconnected with switched fast Ethernet.

The first experiment measures the total runtime of the OPS depending on the number of virtual machines. Figure 7 shows the results. The OPS used both vulnerability scanners in parallel while the number of target virtual machines was increased with every run. To get a robust mean, 100 trials were performed. Testing one virtual machine took 684 seconds on average, testing two machines took 859 seconds, testing three machines

1056 seconds, and it took 1279 seconds to test all four machines. Obviously, the measurement reveals that the runtime increases linearly with the number of tested systems. Furthermore, it reveals that it is more efficient to test multiple targets in parallel instead of scanning one after another.

In order to test the efficiency of the OPS, multiple tests against virtual machines running different versions of the Debian operating systems were conducted. The unpatched release version of Debian *Etch* (released April 2007), *Lenny* (released February 2009), *Squeeze* (released February 2011) and *Wheezy* (current unstable version) were used. The results of the tests are shown in Table 2.

The OPS successfully revealed a number of security vulnerabilities in all tested versions, including two high-risk flaws in each version. Debian *Etch* is the oldest release and contains the lowest number of vulnerabilities because it contains less features (in terms of installed services) than all other versions. Other flaws are related to the installed kernel version. The flaws appeared with newer kernel versions and thus, only in newer Debian versions.

Related work

The Cloud computing risk report written by ENISA [15] mentions the failure of customer hardening procedures as one of the research problems needed to be solved. Customers failing to secure the computing environment may pose a vulnerability to the Cloud infrastructure.

Automation of system administration, including system administration and updating systems is one of the relevant research topics mentioned in the Expert Group Report [16] created by the European Commission.

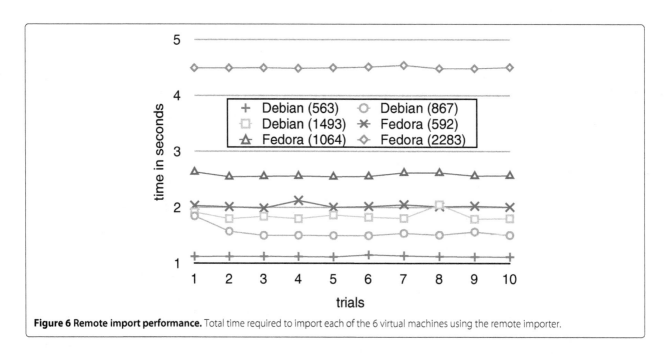

Figure 6 Remote import performance. Total time required to import each of the 6 virtual machines using the remote importer.

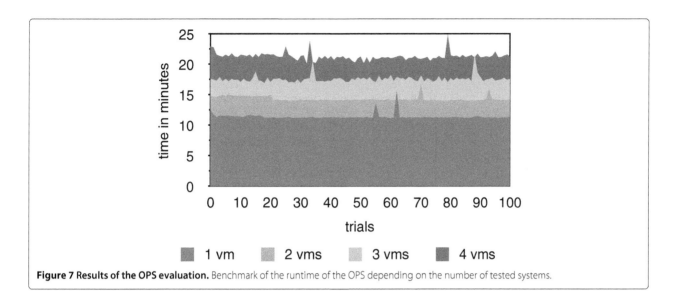

Figure 7 Results of the OPS evaluation. Benchmark of the runtime of the OPS depending on the number of tested systems.

An image management system, called Mirage, is presented by Wei et al. [6]. Mirage addresses security concerns of a virtual machine image publisher, customer and administrator. To reduce the publisher's risk, an access control framework regulates the sharing of virtual machines images. Image filters remove unwanted information (e.g., logs, sensitive information, etc) from images prior to publishing. The authors also present a mechanism to update dormant images and apply security updates. While Mirage offers a complete solution for virtual disk image maintenance, it lacks the features presented in this article. Mirage cannot show whether the packages in a system are outdated and work with multiple package management systems.

Based on Mirage, Reimer et al. [4] present the Mirage image format (MIF), a new storage format for virtual machine disk images. MIF solves the problem of *virtual machine image sprawl*, i.e., the complexity of maintaining disk image content that changes continuously due to cloning or snapshotting. MIF stores the disk image content in a central repository and supports searching, installing and updating applications in all images. By using a special storage device, disk images share common blocks

and thus take up only a fraction of the actual disk space. Using MIF it is also possible to update packages on a system although the update procedure is quite complex. At first, it is quite unclear how the system determines whether there is a need for an update. Furthermore, the system needs a modified version of dpkg, thus, it is not usable with off-the-shelf installations or other package management solutions. The authors state that "the optimized Dpkg does not support some of Dpkg's features".

A system for unscheduled system updates, called Auto-Pod, was presented by Potter et al. [17]. AutoPod is based on system call interposition and the chroot utility and is able to create file system namespaces, called pods. Every process in a pod can be offline-migrated to another physical machine by using a checkpoint mechanism. Unfortunately, AutoPod is bound to Debian Linux and cannot be used with other package managers. Furthermore, it also updates a system automatically, which could lead to problems in case of an incomplete update. In contrast to the presented solution, AutoPod is based on chroot, which is known for having several major security flaws in the past.

Sapuntzakis et al. [18] developed a utility, called the Collective, which assigns virtual appliances to hardware dynamically and automatically. By keeping software up to date, their approach prevents security break-ins due to fixed vulnerabilities. While their approach allow updating whole virtual machine appliances, it does not allow the update of certain packages within the appliance. Furthermore, it is not possible to determine whether certain packages are outdated.

Layered virtual machines [5] can be used to solve the maintenance problem of dormant virtual machines. These machines are split up in different layers, such as a common base layer, containing a base system with some commonly required libraries and tools, an user layer containing

Table 2 OPS results for Debian

Distribution	Risk level *none*	Risk level *Low*	Risk level *medium*	Risk level *high*
Debian Etch	14	2	0	2
Debian Lenny	43	2	3	2
Debian Squeeze	44	2	3	2
Debian Wheezy	43	2	3	2

Number of security vulnerabilities the OPS detected in different versions of Debian Linux.

specific applications required by the user and potentially other layers. Besides benefits when it comes to storage and transfer of those virtual machines, considering shared layers that need to be stored and transferred only once and reused by many virtual machines, this architecture also helps with the problem of keeping machines up-to-date. Because a base layer is shared by many virtual machines, updating the base layer will affect all virtual machines built on top. Although not the complete software stack is affected by those updates, some of the most important parts of the system (e.g., the SSH libraries, which were affected by a serious bug in the Debian implementation back in 2008 [19]) can be fixed this way.

Canonical, the company behind Ubuntu Linux, offers a commercial product called Landscape [8]. Landscape can be used to manage Ubuntu (virtual) machines, including package management and monitoring. While Landscape is able to detect and update outdated applications within virtual machines, it can only handle the Debian package format and is not able to update dormant machines. However, Landscape can update outdated machines once they are live the next time.

SAVEly, a tool to check Amazon Machine Images (AMIs) for vulnerabilities was presented by Bleikertz et al. [20]. The authors construct an attack graph based on the security polices used in EC2. These policies are used to group machines while restricting the communication between them. Based on the graph, the authors use the OpenVAS scanner to check the AMI for remote vulnerabilities. Their approach is tightly coupled to Amazon's EC2 and cannot be used with other IaaS implementations or in virtualized Grid environments.

Yoon and Sim [21] present an automated network vulnerability assessment framework. It uses a combination of a scan manager, message relay server and scanners to check the hosts in a network for vulnerabilities. Their approach uses similar techniques as the ones presented, but it lacks the ability to work in a Cloud computing environment. It is neither able to control virtual machines, nor to instrument an IaaS solution like the XGE.

Conclusions

In this article, a new approach to increase the security of virtual machines in either virtualized Grid or Cloud computing environments has been presented. It is based on two components: a first component called Update Checker to identify outdated packages can check either running or dormant virtual machine images efficiently. It supports the two major Linux software management solutions, namely apt/dpkg and yum/rpm, and thus all major Linux distributions currently used in Grid or Cloud environments. Due to its flexible design, plugins for other software management solutions can be easily added. The use of multiple caches speeds up the check process, resulting

in a time less than a second for a complete check of an average virtual machine. A second component called Online Penetration Suite scans virtual machines for software vulnerabilities using established security techniques. It can identify flaws in software components listening on the network. Both components are integrated into two already existing solutions (XGE and ICS) that leverage their capabilities to deny running too outdated machines or provide the user with the ability to update his or her machines.

There are several areas for future work. For example, the current implementation of the Update Checker only supports software installed using the package management systems of current Linux distributions. Nevertheless, there are cases where software is installed in other ways, either by compiling it manually or by installing software from binary packages that are not available in repositories. The idea of a generic framework with software specific plugins that can determine the installed version seems to be promising. Problems to solve are binaries without a version parameter and even more locating the software that was installed without using the package management system. Furthermore, the current approach to infer the significance of updates is a very basic approach. Comparing the list of outdated packages to the security advisories of the distribution, if available, seems to be promising. This would require distribution specific parsers for the advisories, since there is no unified advisory format, and manual configuration of the advisory sources for each distribution. The OPS currently controls two vulnerability scanners. In the future, it would be desirable to support a larger number of scanners.

Competing interests
The authors declare that they have no competing interests.

Authors' contributions
All authors contributed equally. All authors read and approved the final manuscript.

Acknowledgements
This work is partly supported by the German Ministry of Education and Research (BMBF) (D-Grid Initiative and HPC-Call) and the Hessian Ministry of Science and Art (HMWK).

References
1. Armbrust M, Fox A, Griffith R, Joseph A (2009) Above the Clouds: A Berkeley View of Cloud Computing, Technical Report UCBEECS200928 53(UCB/EECS-2009-28). EECS Department University of California Berkeley
2. Smith M, Schmidt M, Fallenbeck N, Dörnemann T, Schridde C, Freisleben B (2009) Secure On-demand Grid Computing. J Future Generation Comput Syst 25(3): 315–325
3. Garfinkel T, Rosenblum M (2005) When Virtual is Harder than Real: Security Challenges in Virtual Machine Based Computing. In 10th Workshop on Hot Topics in Operating Systems 121–126

4.   Reimer D, Thomas A, Ammons G, Mummert T, Alpern B, Bala V (2008) Opening Black, Boxes: Using Semantic Information to Combat Virtual Machine Image Sprawl. In Proceedings of the Fourth ACM SIGPLAN/SIGOPS International Conference on Virtual Execution Environments 111–120. Seattle: ACM

5.   Schwarzkopf R, Schmidt M, Fallenbeck N, Freisleben B (2009) Multi-Layered Virtual Machines for Security Updates in Grid Environments. In Proceedings of 35th Euromicro Conference on Internet Technologies, Quality of Service and Applications (ITQSA) 563–570. Patras: IEEE Press

6.   Wei J, Zhang X, Ammons G, Bala V, Ning P (2009) Managing Security of Virtual Machine Images in a Cloud Environment. In Proceedings of the 2009 ACM Workshop on, Cloud Computing Security, CCSW '09 91–96. New York: ACM

7.   Fallenbeck N, Schmidt M, Schwarzkopf R, Freisleben B (2010) Inter-Site Virtual Machine Image Transfer in Grids and Clouds. In Proceedings of the 2nd International ICST Conference on Cloud Computing (CloudComp 2010) 1–19. Barcelona: Springer, LNICST

8.   Canonical Inc (2011) Ubuntu Advantage Landscape. http://www.canonical.com/enterprise-services/ubuntu-advantage/landscape

9.   Winer D (2003) XML-RPC Specification. http://www.xml-rpc.com/spec

10. OpenVAS Developers (2012) The Open Vulnerability Assessment System (OpenVAS). http://www.openvas.org/

11. Tenable Network Security (2012) Nessus Security Scanner. http://www.nessus.org/products/nessus

12. Libvirt Developers (2012) Libvirt - The Virtualization API. http://libvirt.org/

13. Schwarzkopf R, Schmidt M, Strack C, Freisleben B (2011) Checking Running and Dormant Virtual Machines for the Necessity of Security Updates in Cloud Environments. In Proceedings of the 3rd IEEE International Conference on Cloud Computing Technology and Science (CloudCom) 239–246. Athens: IEEE Press

14. Crockford D (2006) The application/json Media Type for JavaScript Object Notation (JSON). http://www.ietf.org/rfc/rfc4627

15. ENISA European Network and Information Security Agency (2009) Cloud Computing Risk Assessment. http://www.enisa.europa.eu/act/rm/files/deliverables/cloud-computing-risk-assessment

16. Lillard TV, Garrison CP, Schiller CA, Steele J (2010) The Future of Cloud Computing. In Digital Forensics for Network, Internet, and Cloud Computing 319–339. Boston: Syngress

17. Potter S, Nieh J (2005) AutoPod: Unscheduled System Updates with Zero Data Loss. In Autonomic Computing, International Conference on 367–368

18. Sapuntzakis C, Brumley D, Chandra R, Zeldovich N, Chow J, Lam MS, Rosenblum M (2003) Virtual Appliances for Deploying and Maintaining Software. In Proceedings of the 17th USENIX Conference on System Administration 181–194. Berkeley: USENIX Association

19. Debian Security Advisory 1576-1 OpenSSH (2008) Predictable Random Number Generator. http://www.debian.org/security/2008/dsa-1576

20. Bleikertz S, Schunter M, Probst CW, Pendarakis D, Eriksson K (2010) Security Audits of Multi-tier Virtual Infrastructures in Public Infrastructure Clouds. In Proceedings of the 2010 ACM Workshop on Cloud Computing Security, CCSW '10 93–102. Chicago

21. Yoon J, Sim W (2007) Implementation of the, Automated Network Vulnerability Assessment Framework. In Proceedings of the 4th International Conference on Innovations in Information Technology 153–157. Dubai: IEEE

5

A design space for dynamic service level agreements in OpenStack

Craig A Lee[1]* and Alan F Sill[2]

Abstract

This paper does a systematic review of the possible design space for cloud-hosted applications that may have changing resource requirements that need to be supported through dynamic service level agreements (SLAs). The fundamental SLA functions are reviewed: Admission Control, Monitoring, SLA Evaluation, and SLA Enforcement – a classic autonomic control cycle. This is followed by an investigation into possible application requirements and SLA enforcement mechanisms. We then identify five basic Load Types that a dynamic SLA system must manage: Best Effort, Throttled, Load Migration, Preemption and Spare Capacity. The key to meeting application SLA requirements under changing surge conditions is to also manage the spare surge capacity. The use of this surge capacity could be managed by one of several identified load migration policies. A more detailed SLA architecture is presented that discusses specific SLA components. This is done in the context of the OpenStack since it is open source with a known architecture. Based on this SLA architecture, a research and development plan is presented wherein fundamental issues are identified that need to be resolved through research and experimentation. Based on successful outcomes, further developments are considered in the plan to produce a complete, end-to-end dynamic SLA capability. Executing on this plan will take significant resources and organization. The NSF Center for Cloud and Autonomic Computing is one possible avenue for pursuing these efforts. Given the growing importance of cloud performance management in the wider marketplace, the cloud community would be well-served to coordinate cloud SLA development across organizations such as the IEEE, Open Grid Forum, and the TeleManagement Forum.

Keywords: Service level agreements; Autonomic computing; Live migration; OpenStack

Introduction

Service level agreements (SLAs) are used to define the necessary Quality of Service (QoS) for an application or user in an IT system. SLAs originally were defined as a contractual document between IT resource providers and consumers that involved cost analysis and pricing, along with financial incentives or penalties. For performance-critical applications, though, such contractual SLAs are not sufficient. Performance-critical applications require SLAs whereby the computing infrastructure monitors, detects, and responds to changes in demand to ensure that application-level processing requirements are met. Furthermore, changes in demand may be caused not just by new applications being instantiated, but also by changes in demand by the running applications themselves. Some

applications may have unpredictable changes in their processing demands and associated service levels. Even if changes in demand are somewhat predictable, it would still be desirable for the cloud service provider to be able to accommodate such changes without having to renegotiate a new SLA.

Hence, *dynamic* SLAs are required. This will be particularly necessary in computing cloud that are, by nature, multi-tenant environments where many applications may have changing service level requirements. What we want to avoid is forcing users to over-specify their service level requirements in order to satisfy future changes in their demand. If users were allowed to do so, then applications would simply acquire excess resource capacity and then let it sit idle the vast majority of the time. This would effectively *fragment* the cloud capacity and reduce the overall utilization.

By providing dynamic SLAs, we are attempting to satisfy competing goals: (a) ensure that every running application

*Correspondence: lee@aero.org
[1] Computer Systems Research Department, The Aerospace Corporation, P.O. Box 92957, El Segundo, CA 90009, USA
Full list of author information is available at the end of the article

component meets its deadlines, while (b) enabling the cloud scheduler to maximize resource utilization, thereby "doing more with less". By maximizing resource utilization, and understanding the possible aggregate surge requirements, it should be possible to do better overall capacity planning. That is to say, it should be possible to better determine the minimum amount of excessive surge capacity that needs to be available at any time. Doing so should help minimize the necessary overall cloud size, and reduce all associated costs, e.g., footprint, power, HVAC, staffing, etc.

Much work in cloud SLAs involves enforcing non-functional properties, such as compute node locality (zones), long-term storage preservation, and storage redundancy. For this white paper, however, we will focus just on performance metrics. Addressing non-functional properties will be addressed at a later time.

As noted already, the SLA mechanisms presented and discussed here will not be contractual in nature. That is to say, they will not involve two human organizations entering into an agreement for specific service levels between a provider and a consumer that carry penalties and rewards. We will also be considering performance management from both the consumer's and provider's perspective. We will not be considering one-sided goals, such as optimizing revenue. While many optimization problems, such as optimizing revenue [1], can be NP-hard requiring heuristic solutions, they do not address the performance requirements of individual user applications.

Hence, we will be developing technical, *machine-enforceable* SLA mechanisms, that a cloud provider can offer as a service, and a consumer can choose to use or not. These machine-enforceable mechanisms for dynamic SLAs will provide a probabilistic guarantee for performance. *The goal is to provide the user with a reasonable expectation that performance requirements will be met, through mechanisms that are reasonable for the provider to implement and support for multiple applications.*

In this paper, we begin by reviewing the fundamental functions necessary for SLAs and their enforcement. We then survey and investigate the possible design choices and implementation options. We conclude with a draft research and development for SLAs in OpenStack. While this particular R&D plan targets OpenStack as the test vehicle for planned work, any research results should be widely applicable to other cloud software stacks.

Fundamental SLA functions

Dynamic SLAs are actually an instance of an *autonomic control cycle: monitoring, analysis, planning, execution* – whereby systems can monitor themselves and maintain a target behavior [2]. In the context of dynamic SLAs, however, we will use the following four major functions:

- **Admission Control.** When a user wishes to instantiate a new application, the user must specify the required performance parameters for each of the application components to be instantiated. The cloud provider must then make a determination whether if sufficient capacity is available to adequately service the new application once started. An application component may consist of multiple servers that communicate in a specific topology. Hence, the cloud provider must determine if there are adequate cycles, memory space, disk space, and disk bandwidth for each application server, along with adequate network bandwidth among them. If there is, then the application can be started.

- **Monitoring – Metrics Collection.** While applications are running, the cloud infrastructure and the applications must be monitored. Monitoring must be as unobtrusive as possible, but must also capture essential data to determine if performance goals are being met. One or more monitoring systems could be used to collect data from different levels of the entire computing infrastructure. In a cloud environment, this could include monitoring the physical servers, hypervisors, the guest OSs, and the virtual applications themselves. While different monitoring systems could be used, all collected information must be collated and made available for the next functions.

- **SLA Evaluation.** Once an SLA has been established, the application has been started, and various performance metrics are being collected, there must be an agent that compares the SLA targets with the observed metrics, and determines when an application's performance has gone, or is going, "out of spec". For contractual SLAs, this could be termed an *SLA violation*, but for dynamic SLAs, this more accurately denotes that simply a threshold has been crossed requiring a response. A key issue for this agent is how to map the SLA metrics to the observable metrics. SLA metrics may be expressed in units that are meaningful at the application level and a *semantic gap* may exist between the metrics that are actually being collected.

- **SLA Enforcement – Violation Response.** An important issue for SLA Enforcement is whether an application's resource demands are expected to be static throughout its execution, or whether they can vary in a predictable or unpredictable manner. If an application's demands are expected to be relatively constant, then *static throttling* methods can be used. However, if an application's demands can vary, perhaps unpredictably, then it's behavior must be monitored to determine if it has gone "out of spec". For a performance-critical application, the primary goal of a machine-enforceable, dynamic SLA is to pro-actively bring the application back into compliance. This requires some type of "control knobs" on the infrastructure or on the application itself.

SLA design options and approaches

Within each one of these fundamental SLA functions, there are further technical design issues that must be addressed. For each there are usually several implementation options with different challenges and trade-offs. We now put these fundamental functions into a general SLA architecture, as illustrated in Figure 1, and discuss them in more depth.

Admission control

Admission Control must maintain a *total cloud capacity document*, from which the currently available capacity can be derived or maintained. A total cloud capacity document must capture the capacity of all resources within a cloud data center, in addition to their network topology. Hence, in the most general case, all servers must be identified, along with their clock speeds, amounts of memory, local disk, and total network bandwidth. These resources must be placed in a network topology that includes routers and switches that have their own performance capabilities. Such network topologies are typically represented as a graph.

Likewise when a user submits an application for admission, the user must submit a service level request that captures the desired performance requirements that could be in a similar graph structure. Clearly for many applications, these resource graph structures may be simple, such as an individual server, or have a well-known, stereotypical structure. An example of this might be simply streaming a

movie to a viewer. Some applications, however, may have detailed, highly structured, and even hierarchical SLA requests.

When the Admission Control agent receives a service request, it must consult the available capacity document and determine if the service request can be supported by the available capacity. When expressing network capacity and requirements as graph structures, this entails a *graph embedding* or *graph matching* problem. This is a well-known problem encountered in many other areas of computer science and IT. Timberwolf [3], for example, is a successful tool for doing die layout for integrated circuits consisting of millions of transistors and the wire runs that must connect them. Metis [4] is graph partitioning tool that might be applicable in this application domain. Also, a Network Calculus [5] could be used to provide a theoretical framework from which to model resource allocations and service guarantees. In computer networks, the concept of *service curves* are used that determines the relationship between arriving and departing network flows.

Admission control could, however, be greatly simplified by avoiding explicit graph presentations. The network switches connecting servers in a data center are often arranged in a hierarchy to achieve scalable bandwidth. That is to say, the switches are arranged in a *fat tree* where more bandwidth is available higher up in the tree, thereby avoiding *tree saturation* for network flows closer to the root, or backbone, switches. Under such conditions, the topology of the switch fabric becomes less important. Hence, we could ensure that the switch fabric does not become saturated simply by managing the aggregate BW demand in to and out of each of the servers. In this case, Admission Control only requires that each application

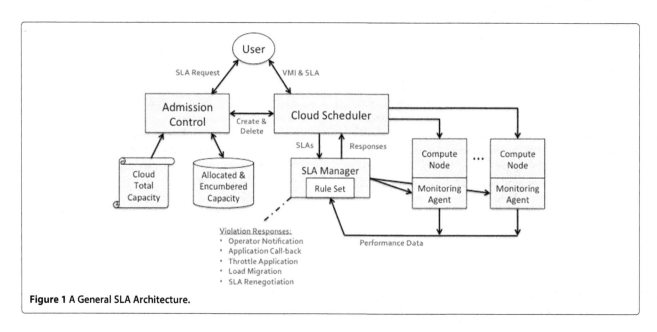

Figure 1 A General SLA Architecture.

process is allocated where there are sufficient cycles and network bandwidth at the network interfaces.

While this addresses the issue of network bandwidth, an application may also have network latency constraints between pairs of servers. In this case, then Admission Control must ensure that the servers are allocated "close" to one another by some metric, e.g., the number of network hops. While using a graph structure to represent sets of latency requirements is most general, latency requirements could be addressed by evaluating such a distance metric for simple pair-wise allocations.

In terms of existing standards, WS-Agreement [6] could be used to represent SLA service terms. WS-Agreement defines a domain-agnostic protocol whereby agreements can be established. This means that WS-Agreement can be used with different *term languages* as needed by the application domain. Hence, the challenge here is to define a term language that could capture the necessary application component performance characteristics, be they graph structures or simpler sums. WS-Agreement provides a formal definition for SLA representations and defines a single round of *offer-accept* message exchange. The provider offers an initial *template* of possible service terms. A service consumer replies with a completed template. The provider must then accept or reject the offer. There are a growing number of implementations for WS-Agreement, along with some valuable lessons learned [7].

Building on this, WS-Agreement Negotiation [8] defines a protocol for multiple rounds of negotiation, whereby a tree of offers and counter-offers is built. The tree root is the initial offer. Tree branches represent different sequences of offers and counter-offers, where service terms are adjusted in an effort to find mutually satisfactory terms.

It is actually very important that tools like WS-Agreement are domain-agnostic, since application domains can have widely different terms that are relevant to possible SLAs. Nae et al. [9], for example, present an interesting collection of SLA terminology and parameters for Massively Multiplayer Online Games that are of interest to providers and users. Given that many other domains will have similar but different sets of parameters, we can conclude that a flexible, pluggable architecture for SLA monitoring and reporting of performance metrics is highly preferable. While it might be possible to define a very basic SLA nomenclature, taxonomy and terminology, some degree of extension and customization will have to be allowed.

An outstanding issue here that we do not directly address in this paper is how to map high-level system requirements into lower-level metrics that can be measured and managed. Work has been done in this area, however. As part of the SLA@SOI project [10], the

EVEREST Reasoning Engine translates SLA Abstract Syntax Objects into events in an Event Calculus [11]. This Event Calculus specifies patterns of events that should, or should not, occur within a specified period of time. The Detecting SLA Violation infrastructure (DeSVi) also enables mappings between SLA parameters and resource metrics by utilizing mapping rules with domain specific languages [12]. Similarly, the Quality Assurance for Distributed Services project (Qu4DS) manages the translation of SLA parameters by profiling the service provider [13]. Further work in managing the translation of application-oriented SLA requirements needs to be addressed as future work. For near-term experimental purposes, such translations can be managed by hand, since we will be focusing on the effectiveness of the SLA enforcement mechanisms themselves.

Another key challenge here is how to represent and manage the notion of *encumbered surge capacity* for dynamic SLAs. Many applications and application domains can be managed by static SLAs. A prime example here is simply streaming a video to a consumer. The consumer wants to watch the video with smooth performance, i.e., no pauses or drop-outs. The resource allocation necessary to accomplish this is known and constant. In multi-tenant clouds, however, with complex applications that will have varying computational needs, the challenge is how to dynamically meet these requirements within the context of an existing agreement, without having to resort to a heavy weight renegotiation and reinstantiation process. In a very real sense, a dynamic SLA is a quintessential use of the on-demand resources and flexibility offered by cloud computing.

This notion of encumbered surge capacity is also key for overall capacity management. Many dedicated systems are currently sized based on their expected *worst case* behavior rather than their *average case* behavior. This means there is dedicated excess capacity only to be used during worst case surge processing requirements. Having this dedicated excess capacity drives the overall system size, and total cost of ownership and operation, e.g., footprint, power, staffing, etc. One of the value propositions for cloud computing is the available of on-demand resources. That is to say, a cloud should be able to offer a joint pool of spare capacity to all tenant applications. Hence, a smaller pool of excess capacity should be needed, rather than having dedicated excess capacity for each application.

An alternative to maintaining surge capacity, however, is simply to allow resource *overbooking* [14]. An application's usage patterns for CPU, memory use, storage, and networking can be profiled and factored into the model for overbooking to achieve optimal packing of applications into a given set of virtualized resources. That is to say, the expected usage patterns can be used as an aid for the opportunistic packing of different types of applications (or differently-behaving instances of the same application) onto resources in order to achieve balanced overall utilization of the resources over all types of utilization within the application portfolio. As a simple example, I/O intensive applications might be booked with cpu-intensive ones that do not require a lot of I/O, to achieve an optimal overbooking. As reported in [14], though, a combination of modeling, monitoring, and prediction techniques must be used to avoid exceeding the total infrastructure capacity. In any case, application scheduling schemes should be sufficiently flexible to recognize performance degradation in a given metric that may come from overuse reported in another metric, and the SLA control scheme must be sufficiently powerful to allow for dynamic control over application types that can be mixed for optimal overall usage.

Once the cloud manager has determined that there is sufficient capacity to host the new application component – by whatever means used – the user can actually submit the component VMs, along with the SLA document, to the Cloud Scheduler. At this point, the Cloud Scheduler informs Admission Control that the components are actually being instantiated. This "inks the deal". The SLA is not in force until this point. The Scheduler starts the VMs on one or more Compute Nodes, and informs the SLA Manager of the new processes and the load that is expected. The SLA Manager may inform one or more Monitoring Agents on each Compute Node of metrics that need to be collected.

Monitoring

The actual monitoring could be done by a number of different existing tool sets. These include Ceilometer [15], Ganglia [16], Nagios [17], and Zenoss [18], to name a few. We will not review the details of these tools here. Rather, we identify key design alternatives that can determine the effectiveness and responsiveness of any SLA enforcement mechanism.

These design alternatives involve *what*, *where*, and *when* to monitor. The Monitoring Agents could monitor at different levels in the system stack on each Compute Node:

- *Host OS/Hypervisor.* Here the Monitoring Agent could capture all traditional operating system metrics at the hardware level, e.g., percentage CPU time per VM, memory usage, disk I/O, network I/O, etc.
- *Guest OS.* Monitoring here enables the Agent to collect operating system information specific to one VM.
- *Application Level.* As opposed to the previous two levels, this requires that the application be modified to provide a monitoring interface whereby application-level performance metrics can be obtained.

After this data is initially captured, it can be used at different times. All of the monitored data is archived in a database that can be queried by the SLA Manager. The Manager can periodically apply a rule set from the SLA information, provided by the Cloud Scheduler when VMs were instantiated, to determine if an SLA is being violated, or requires any corrective action. Given the amount of data in the database, the SLA Manager could also do *long-term trending analyses* that could not be identified from single metrics or events. However, rather than waiting for information to be deposited in the database, the SLA Manager could also set *stream triggers* as close to the meters themselves in the Monitoring Agents. These stream triggers are lightweight, state-less (or very low state) triggers that are easy to evaluate. Hence, they could provide the SLA Manager with an earlier notification of a potential problem.

These monitoring options, however, are all *reactive* – they only react to SLA violations after the fact. It is possible to do more *pro-active* SLA enforcement by monitoring further up in an application's processing chain. By doing so, the conditions that cause an SLA violation might be detectable before the violation actually occurs.

Consider that an application consists of an Input Buffer that partitions work units over a number of servers, as illustrated in Figure 2. After processing, these work units are collected by a Collector that monitors the how long it took each work unit to get processed after entering the Input Buffer. If work units are exceeding the application's latency requirement, additional servers could be spun-up to process more work units and reduce overall latency. This is reactive downstream monitoring since the SLA Manager can only decide to add more servers after latencies have exceeded some threshold. However, if the depth of the Input Buffer were monitored, then more pro-active SLA enforcement could be done, where more servers could be added when the buffer depth exceeds a threshold, but before the work unit latency actually starts to exceed application requirements.

Figure 2 also illustrates the fact that a large cloud data center may require and be composed of multiple SLA Managers to address issues of scalability. SLA Managers could be distributed across the cloud infrastructure, and also the applications themselves. These managers could communicate, or gossip, in a peer-to-peer fashion, be organized into hierarchies, or into other useful structures. This notion of distributed SLA managers implies that there must also be distributed SLA models by which overall system behavior, and individual application behavior, can be managed. The development and evaluation of such distributed SLA models is an outstanding goal.

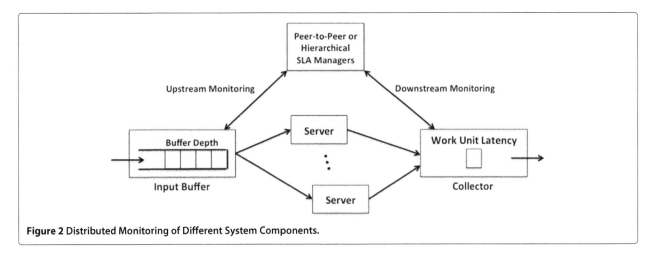

Figure 2 Distributed Monitoring of Different System Components.

SLA evaluation

Deciding when a server has crossed a load threshold is not a simple numerical comparison. A server's load at any one instant in time may fluctuate about a fixed threshold value. Basing decisions on each fluctuation could cause load migrations and VM instantiations that involve more overhead than the benefits realized. To prevent such behavior, more robust statistical methods are typically employed. Such methods include *Median Absolute Deviation, Interquartile Range,* and *Iterative Local Regression.*

In addition to dampening out some of the "high frequency" noise in system measurements, some amount of *hysteresis* should be built into SLA evaluations. This will prevent the SLA Manager from trashing between different enforcement mechanisms, such as load migration and load consolidation, in a cascading chain reaction.

We also note that if the surge probability of each application component is known, then the *joint probability* of any process on the server going into SLA violation could be determined. This joint probability could possibly be used to determine the best amount of spare capacity to maintain on a server, in order to minimize overall application impact due to load migration.

Developing such predictive models of system behavior is a common application of *machine learning* techniques. While machine learning has been a central topic in Artificial Intelligence for decades, the use of *reinforcement learning* in autonomic applications has been getting renewed attention [19]. A reinforcement learning system is essentially exposed to a sequence of *state-action pairs* to converge on a model of system behavior and optimal management policies. While reinforcement learning can be used "in the absence of explicit system models, with little or no domain-specific initial knowledge", *model-based* reinforcement learning can shorten the training process, but can also be constrained by the defined model. Thus, reinforcement learning is commonly recognized as having the following issues:

- The number of observed state-action pairs needed to converge on optimal policies may be huge,
- When in an initial training period, the results might be very poor, which can be very problematic for use on an operational system,
- Some number of *exploration* actions need to be taken that may produce sub-optimal results in the short-term, but enable better results in the long-term, and
- Real-world applications must not exhibit *incomplete observability* – that is to say, the RL system must be able to monitor all system metrics that are relevant to understanding and controlling the target system's behavior.

To address some of these concerns, hybrid reinforcement algorithms have been developed to shorten the training process and improve the overall quality of system management [20]. Reinforcement learning has also been recently applied to cloud computing [21]. In this work, a reinforcement learning algorithm was used to configure sets of VMs for their (1) number of virtual cpus, (2) number scheduler credits, and (3) the available memory capacity to optimize the response time and throughput when servicing a canonical, three-tiered web application. Efforts are also being made to commercialize this technology. Numenta's *Grok* architecture, for example, uses a bio-inspired *cortical* learning algorithm implemented using a modified Hadoop engine that is hosted on Amazon EC2 [22]. This provides *automated streaming analytics* that can be used for system behavior prediction and anomaly detection.

While such approaches to managine cloud-based SLAs are intriguing, much work needs to be done to establish how well this would work in practical applications. Such predictive modeling could be coupled with monitoring system behavior from widely different parts of the cloud and its applications. Learning algorithms

could also be used to do on-the-fly load classification and comparison to established system models.
The SLA mechanisms should also be able to deal
with inaccurate or untruthful estimations of application requirements being provided by users [23]. Ultimately, the ability to serve both behavior prediction and
anomaly detection is an advantage that should also be
investigated.

SLA enforcement

Once it has been determined that an SLA in not in spec,
what can the system do to bring it back into spec? We
discuss some options here.

- **Notification or Call-back.** This is the simplest
  option. The SLA Manager simply notifies an operator
  who manually changes application parameters to
  reduce resource demand. While this is not a
  machine-enforceable mechanism, it will nonetheless
  be a practical alternative in many situations.
- **Throttling.** Throttling mechanisms exist in modern
  operating systems that can limit the amount of
  resources a process can consume. Under throttling,
  applications have no dynamic options and an SLA
  violation is not possible. This is suitable for
  applications that have very stable service level
  requirements, or where being throttled will not
  adversely affect application goals. (An example is
  processing a work load "over night" where there is
  significant lee-way in how long the processing
  actually takes.)
- **Load Migration.** If a server becomes overloaded by
  any metric, e.g., cpu load, memory usage, disk IO or
  network IO, this can be remedied by migrating some
  of the load to other servers with more available
  capacity. This can be done by either *process migration*
  or *live VM migration*. Clearly the overhead of either
  migration technique would limit how quickly service
  levels could be effectively re-established. Process
  migration may take less time since a smaller memory
  volume may have to be transferred, but migrating
  entire VMs allows sets of processes to be transferred.
  While migration can be done without interaction
  with the running application, the application is
  "down" during the migration. Hence, migration itself
  may precipitate, or contribute to, an SLA violation.
  Some clouds currently support *live VM migration*.
- **Acquiring Additional Resources On-Demand.**
  Rather than moving load, the offending application
  could be notified (through a call-back) that it needs
  to acquire more resources on demand. This requires
  that the application know how to incorporate more
  servers into its processing chain, i.e., how to partition
  its workload across more servers. That is to say, the

application developer must design the application to
be able to incorporate additional servers.
- **SLA Renegotiation.** As a final option, SLA
  renegotiation could be done. This is obviously a
  heavy-weight option of last choice since it could
  potentially entail restarting parts of the application
  on newly acquired resources.

While these are all options for managing SLAs, in this
paper we are focusing on those mechanisms whereby
dynamic SLAs can be managed. Users must have confidence that if they don't over-specify their average SLA
requirements, the infrastructure will be able to gracefully
respond to changes in requirements. This fundamental
requirement affects how SLA must be defined, evaluated, and enforced. SLAs must be defined in a *term language* whereby the relevant terms and parameters can be
expressed. These terms and parameters must be evaluated
with regards to the available enforcement mechanisms.

For the SLA mechanisms that have been identified, we
now can define the following *Server Load Types* that can
be used by the Cloud Scheduler and SLA Manager to
enforce SLAs (as illustrated in Figure 3):

Type I Service Loads are simply *Best Effort*, i.e., application VMs that are allocated using existing methods with
no SLAs. As a practical matter, not all user applications
may need or want an SLA, and the cloud provider may
not want to require that all tenants must specify an SLA.
These processes may change their processing, memory,
disk and network demand whenever they want. All tenant processes on a particular server, however, but will be
constrained by the physical capabilities of that server. If
a server becomes resource-bound in any way (compute,
memory, disk, or network), then all processes on that
server will simply slow down, depending on their profile
of resource demands.

Type II Server Loads are strictly throttled. As noted
before, this is appropriate for those application processes
that have known and stable resource requirements. By
knowing those requirements, the cloud scheduler can co-
locate such processes and maximize server utilization.
Since each process is throttled, each is guaranteed a minimum level of service.

Type III Server Loads depend on live migration to remedy an SLA violation. By identifying those processes that
can be migrated, the cloud scheduler can better manage
server utilization. When a server exceeds a load threshold (by some metric), either a process or entire VM can be
migrated to another server that has sufficient capacity to
reduce the load on the local server. However, some processes or VMs may tolerate migration better than others.

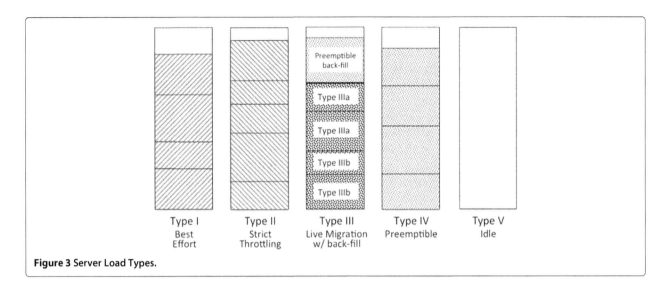

Figure 3 Server Load Types.

Since migration may take a non-trivial amount of time, migration itself may contribute to, or even cause, an SLA violation.

Hence, we can partition Type III Server Loads into **Type IIIa** and **Type IIIb Server Loads** that can, and can not, tolerate migration, respectively. For Type IIIb Server Loads that are less tolerant of live migration, a cloud scheduler could *delay* or *reduce* the number of necessary migrations by maintaining some amount of spare capacity on servers with migratable loads. The amount of this spare capacity could be managed to perhaps hit the "sweet spot" in the trade-off between wasting capacity and avoiding (or delaying) migration. Consider the policy whereby the cloud scheduler ensures there is enough spare capacity on a server such that any one application process can surge without triggering a migration. This can be expressed as:

$$\sum_{i=0}^{k-1} NormLoad_i + max_{0 \leq i \leq k-1}(SurgeLoad_i) \leq MaxLoad$$

By ensuring that enough capacity is available for the maximum surge requirements of any process on that server, then any one process can surge without triggering migration. If multiple processes surge, then migration would be triggered at some time. (For this reason, it is important when application processes may surge for correlated reasons.) Of course, enough spare capacity could be maintained to enable $j < k$ processes to surge simultaneously, but this raises the amount of excess capacity that is maintained and its associated costs.

To limit the amount of excess capacity that is wasted, less than $max(SurgeLoad_i)$ spare capacity could be maintained. In this case, migration may not be avoidable for any one process, but at least migration would be delayed, depending on how long or how bad a surge is. The number of migrations over time might also be reduced.

For Type III SLAs (both a and b), it must be decided which process to migrate and to which target server. Such decisions must be codified as *migration policy*. Different migration policies can be defined that attempt to optimize different system or application metrics, sometimes defined as an *objective function*. For commercial operators that are concerned about power consumption and server utilization, this can be a monetized objective function based on the cost of power and the cost of SLA violations. This has been called the *Dynamic VM Consolidation* problem [24].

For performance-sensitive applications, however, migration policies could be based on a variety of different metrics to choose which process or VM to migrate:

- Fastest Migration Time (least time needed)
- Application Value (priority)
- Application Availability
- Maximum Load Reduction
- Load Reduction to Just Below Maximum
- Highest Correlation with Causing Excessive Load

Also, managing applications with non-stationary workloads with dynamic SLAs represents a fundamental autonomic control challenge. Given these applications' dynamic behavior, simple threshold comparisons will clearly be inappropriate. Methods will be needed for building *hysteresis* into the decision mechanisms. This has been investigated using *multi-size sliding window algorithms* whereby the *mean intermigration time* can be maximized [25].

It is clear that effectively using load migration for Type IIIa and IIIb SLAs will require extensive experimentation and experience. Which processes are appropriate for Type

IIIa and IIIb SLAs, which migration policies work the best, and how to manage their parameters, such as local surge capacity, are all open questions.

Rather than simply wasting the spare capacity to delay or reduce the number of live migrations, however, a similar technique to that used in [26] could be used to *back-fill* the spare capacity with *preemptible* processes or VMs. These are called **Type IV Server Loads**. Type IV Server Loads can be preempted without warning, and possibly restarted somewhere else at a later time, without significantly affecting the user's overall requirements. Thus, when a Type IIIb load goes into a surge, Type IV loads resident on the same physical server can be terminated, on-demand, to delay or reduce any necessary migrations.

Finally, **Type V Server Loads** simply represent spare capacity that is available on-demand, for both live migrations and for new VM instantiations. The amount of this spare capacity depends on the aggregate surge requirements of all applications.

Overall, the goal is to ensure that all application processes can meet their processing requirements, while minimizing the resources that must be maintained. This means strictly managing the excess capacity that must be maintained for surge requirements. It also means managing the spare capacity that is fragmented across all servers that are not fully loaded, and the total spare capacity available within the cloud as a whole. Theoretically, server load could be managed completely dynamically by live migration and on-demand instantiation, but stating Service Levels gives the cloud scheduler valuable information concerning the expected demands. Ideally this should enable the cloud scheduler to minimize the number of live migrations and instantiations that are necessary.

An SLA research and development plan

Having reviewed the fundamental SLA functions, and identified the available SLA enforcement mechanisms for OpenStack, along with the resulting Load Types, we now put all of this together into an architecture and a development plan.

An SLA architecture for OpenStack

Figure 4 presents an integrated SLA architecture for OpenStack. The User begins by sending an SLA request to the Nova-AC (Admission Control) service, using the standard WS-Agreement format. When Nova-AC is booted, it is initialized with the Total Capacity Document for this cloud. This document specifies the cloud's current total capacity, e.g., number and type of servers, amount of storage, network bandwidth, etc. The exact format of this document needs to be defined, but presumably it could follow the *SLA template* that the Nova-AC provides to potential users as part of the WS-Agreement process.

Based on the incoming SLA request, Nova-AC consults its database of allocated and available capacity. According to the discussion in Section 'Admission control', an admission control decision could be made simply by identifying a host where there is sufficient cycles and network bandwidth available, according to the requested Load Type (without having to maintain more complicated, graphical representations). If multiple rounds of negotiation are required, the WS-Agreement Negotiation [8] standard defines how this can be done.

Once the User essentially has an "SLA offer", the Virtual Machine Image and the SLA are submitted through the Nova-API to the Nova-Scheduler. Like all OpenStack services, the Nova-API is designed using a configurable

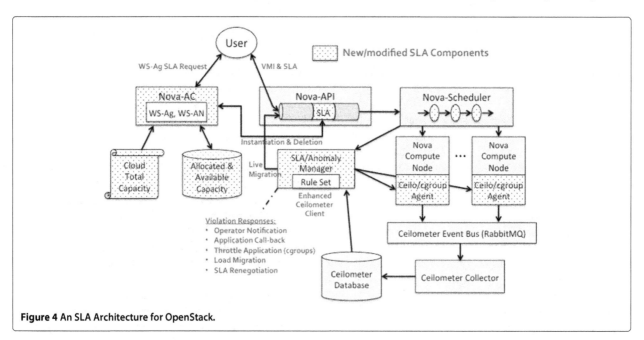

Figure 4 An SLA Architecture for OpenStack.

command pipeline. When booted, the command pipeline can be configured with different pipeline stages to include or omit different functionalities. To support SLAs, a new SLA pipeline stage will be included. When any operation involving an SLA is encountered, Nova-API will inform Nova-AC of the change in resources being allocated or released. It will likewise inform the SLA Manager of the same changes.

When VMs are actually being allocated, the Nova-Scheduler uses a *Filter and Weight* approach, as illustrated in Figure 5. To choose the host on which to allocate a VM, Nova-Scheduler first applies a set of filters to identify which hosts are possible candidates. A set of weighting functions are then applied to rank the candidates and identify the best one. This design allows OpenStack to support many different scheduling paradigms, depending on the filters and weighting functions available. Open-Stack currently support several basic scheduling algorithms, e.g., random placement, random placement within an availability zone, and placement on the least loaded host. To support SLAs, additional SLA Filtering and Weighting functions will need to be written that makes the correct selections based on the SLA Load Type and capacity requested.

Once instantiated on a host compute node, a monitoring agent will have to be used to acquire the necessary performance information. Ceilometer is the OpenStack monitoring service under development. This uses the same RabbitMQ [27] instance used by Nova to collect all performance information and deposit it in a database. Other monitoring tools, besides Ceilometer, could be used. Zenoss, for instance, is much more mature than Ceilometer and offers many *ZenPacks* that can be installed to monitor many different parts of a system software stack, e.g., Apache Tomcat servers, PostgresSQL databases, and Java SNMP, just to name a few examples. Nonetheless, for

initial development and evaluation purpose, Ceilometer could be used completely adequate.

Based on the Load Type requested, the SLA Manager will look for specific performance metrics from different host servers. For Type II throttled work loads, a mechanism, such as *cgroups* [28] in Linux, could be used. Linux cgroups allow hierarchical *control groups* to be defined. Each control group is associated with a limit on the amount of resources that can be consumed on that server, e.g., the percentage of cpu time, memory, disk IO, and network IO. These limits are actually enforced by tools such as Linux *CPUsets* [29]. User processes are assigned to different control groups based on the limit of resources they are allowed to consume. The operating system then enforces those limits when scheduling a process to run. To use this mechanism, the SLA Manager will have to manage the available cgroups on a specific servers, and which VM processes are assigned to them.

For Type IIIa and IIIb work loads, the SLA Manager will need to employ live migration to enforce policy. Live VM migration can generally be done transparently to the running applications. However, the time required for a live migration depends on the amount of memory currently in use by a VM, *Mem*, the number of open file descriptors (i.e., open files and network connections), *nOpenConn*, and the available network bandwidth, *BW*, between the current host and the migration target host.

$$T_{migration} = O(nOpenConn + (Mem/BW))$$

Further refinements to this relationship can be made. The performance costs of live migration can also depend on the internal details of the cloud implementation, such as the type of hypervisor used, as well as the storage and memory architectures [30]. A truly flexible SLA control

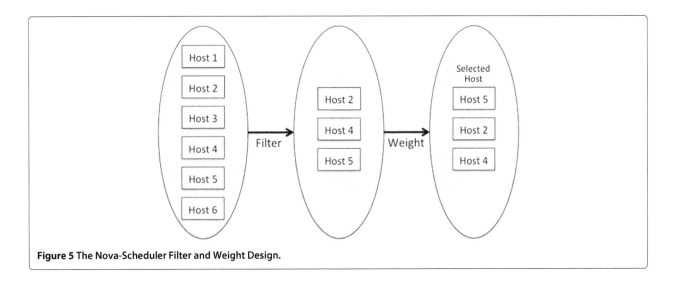

Figure 5 The Nova-Scheduler Filter and Weight Design.

architecture will allow for selection of the application parameters for which the cost model should be tuned.

Even if live migration is otherwise transparent to the application, this time delay may precipitate, or contribute to, an SLA violation. This underscores the importance of accurately evaluating $T_{migration}$ that applications may encounter, and how it may affect their SLAs. It may also be the case that CPU-intensive applications may be easier to migrate than ones that are highly inter-connected. Hence, a key goal will be to develop an accurate and predictive model of live migration that takes in all of these possible factors, and can be used to support different migration policies.

Finally we note that using the SLA architecture described here to effectively manage cloud resources will require a certain *population* of Load Types. That is to say, processes and VMs of each Load Type must be represented in some number and distribution whereby a cloud scheduler can effectively use them to manage the overall cloud utilization, while ensuring that individual application performance requirements are being met. This will be especially true for Load Types III and IV where back-fill scheduling is used to improve utilization. Experimentally determining workable Load Type populations will only be possible once there is a significant SLA architecture in place.

A research and development plan

With these design options and goals in mind, we now present a draft development and test plan. Clearly this SLA system will depend on Linux cgroups and live migration in OpenStack. cgroups are an established capability, so that is considered to be low risk. Live migration in OpenStack, however, is still maturing.

Live migration has been demonstrated in the OpenStack Folsom release, using KVM with libvert on ubuntu 10.09 or 12.04. Live migration using Xen has also been reported. The initial use for live migration in OpenStack, however, is not load balancing or SLA enforcement. Rather it will be used for *VM evacuation*. This is for basic server maintenance purposes, where all running VMs can be moved off of a server to allow software upgrades, hardware replacement, or other routine maintenance functions to be done. Server evacuation is currently intended to be manually managed by cloud administrators.

Given that the basic live migration capability has been demonstrated in OpenStack (since Folsom) for manual maintenance purposes, it should be possible to add the SLA "intelligence" whereby live migration can be used for performance management. Hence, we defined the sequence of tasks for the Research and Development Plan given below. This plan starts by building and evaluating just the core SLA enforcement mechanisms (Tasks 1

and 2). We must first show that these mechanisms are effective in providing reasonable guarantees of application performance. Once that is established, we can then consider building the rest of the supporting SLA management tools, i.e., Tasks 3, 4, 5 and 6. Proposing specific schedule milestones and budget are outside the scope of this paper.

A Research and Development Plan
1. Build Core Enforcement Infrastructure

- Install Ceilometer on existing OpenStack cloud
- Build a basic SLA Manager by enhancing the Ceilometer client

  - Periodically queries database for specific metrics
  - Applies rule sets to detect specific performance conditions on a per application basis

- Demonstrate process throttling with cgroups
- Demonstrate processes and VMs live migration

2. Demonstrate SLA Manager Capabilities

- Build/construct synthetic/manufactured work loads

  - Provide work loads programmed to go through variable changes in demand
  - Build work load scenarios relevant to various application domains

- Develop and evaluate migration policies

  - Assess migration parameters: spare capacity, migration time, load reduction/correlation, etc.
  - Evaluate how well live migration can be managed (inter-migration time)
  - Develop accurate, predictive model(s) of migration overhead
  - Compare process migration vs. VM migration

- Evaluate overhead, responsiveness, and stability

  - How much overhead does monitoring incur to produce useful information
  - Evaluate how quickly can the system respond to and maintain SLA targets
  - Evaluate responsiveness vs. stability trade-off

3. Develop Nova-AC Service

- Develop common WS-Agreement term language

- Develop Total Cloud Capacity Document
- Develop Allocated Capacity Document
- Investigate semantic mapping from application-level requirements to infrastructure-level metrics

4. **Develop Nova-API Pipeline Stage**

- Establish interaction with Nova-AC and SLA Manager when instantiating application VMs

    – Enable accurate tracking of allocated and available capacity
    – Enable live migration managed by SLA Manager

5. **Develop Nova-Scheduler SLA Functions**

- Develop the filtering and weighting functions to identify the best host for relevant Load Types

6. **Demonstrate End-to-End Integrations**

- Develop or acquire non-trivial "operational-like" work loads
- Manage SLAs for multiple apps simultaneously
- Demonstrate that individual application requirements can be met while managing overall cloud requirements, e.g., utilization
- Evaluate minimal population of Load Types (number and distribution) to effectively manage overall cloud resources

7. **Develop and Evaluate Learning Algorithms**

- Identify all relevant system metrics necessary understand and control system behavior
- Evaluate the trade-off between the length of training period versus eventual effectiveness
- Develop and evaluate methods for enabling exploration actions that do not adversely affect operational systems

8. **Develop and Evaluate Distributed SLA Managers**

- Evaluate P2P and hierarchical organizations
- Develop and evalaute distributed SLA models, ultimately including learning algorithms
- Evaluate overhead, responsiveness, stability of distributed SLA methods

Summary and recommendations

This paper has reviewed the basic requirements for providing dynamic service-level agreements, and developed a draft plan for implementing and evaluating such dynamic SLAs in OpenStack. This SLA architecture does require that applications understand what their own resource requirements are. For some existing applications, this information may be difficult to acquire. When an application is deployed on dedicated hardware, there may have been no provision for determining the actual requirements of each application component. As long as an application component never became an egregious bottleneck, everything was fine.

The proposed SLA architecture could, in fact, be used to determine a application's actual requirements. Without specifying or enforcing SLAs in a separate test environment, the monitoring infrastructure could simply catalog the application's behavior over time and various "operational" conditions. Once known, the application could be moved to an SLA-controlled infrastructure with appropriate SLAs in force. In any case, any further work should leverage other relevant projects in the overall cloud marketplace. The NSF Center for Cloud and Autonomic Computing has a number of projects concerning cloud SLAs [31].

The European Union has reported the results of a number of research projects, ranging from business-level SLAs to scientific SLAs [32]. These include the OPTIMIS [33], CONTRAIL [34], and SLA@SOI [10] projects. Given the wide interest in SLAs and the recognition that SLAs will be critical for a wide segment of the cloud marketplace, the TeleManagement Forum (TMF) has started an SLA working group [35] to develop industry best practices and standards, using the OGF WS-Agreement and WS-Agreement Negotiation as a starting point [36]. With these developments, the OpenStack community might eventually incorporate support for some form of dynamic SLAs.

Acknowledgments
The authors gratefully acknowledge the many useful comments from the organizers and participants of the *3rd International Workshop on Intelligent Techniques and Architectures for Autonomic Clouds (ITAAC 2013)* that improved the scope and completeness of this paper.

Competing interests
The authors declared that they have no competing interests.

Authors' contributions
CL produced an earlier version of this paper that laid out the fundamental capabilities necessary for dynamic service level agreements, identified possible control mechanisms based on the load types, and cast this as potential augmentations to the OpenStack service architecture. AS greatly improved this earlier version by clarifying and emphazing key concepts, identifying highly relevant citations, and fleshing out the research and development plan, as relevant to the new NSF Center for Cloud and Autonomic Computing at Texas Tech University. The authors read and approved the final manuscript.

Author details
[1]Computer Systems Research Department, The Aerospace Corporation, P.O. Box 92957, El Segundo, CA 90009, USA. [2]High Performance Computing Center, Texas Tech University, Lubbock, TX 79409, USA.

References

1. Casalicchio E, Menascé DA, Aldhalaan A (2013) Autonomic resource provisioning in cloud systems with availability goals. In: Proceedings of the 2013 ACM cloud and autonomic computing conference. CAC '13. ACM, New York. pp 1:1–1:10
2. Kephart JO, Chess DM (2003) The vision of autonomic computing. IEEE Comput 36(1):41–52
3. Sechen C, Sangiovanni-Vincentelli A (1985) The Timberwolf placement and routing package. IEEE J Solid-State Circuits 20(2):510–522
4. Karypis G METIS: Serial Graph Partitioning and Fill-Reducing Matrix Ordering. http://glaros.dtc.umn.edu/gkhome/metis/metis/overview
5. Jiang Y, Liu Y (2009) Stochastic network calculus. Springer, London, 2008. doi:10.1007/978-1-84800-127-5, ISBN 978- 1-84800-126-8
6. Waeldrich O, Battré D, Brazier F, Clark K, Oey M, Papaspyrou A, Wieder P, Ziegler W (2011) Web services agreement negotiation, Version 1.0. OGF GFD-R-P.193. http://www.ogf.org/documents/GFD.193.pdf
7. Battre D, Hovestadt M, Wäldrich O (2010) Lessons learned from implementing WS-agreement. In: Wieder P etal. (ed). Grids and service-oriented architectures for service level agreements. Springer
8. Andrieux A, Czajkowski K, Dan A Keahey K, Ludwig H, Nakata T, Pruyne J, Rofrano J, Tuecke S, Xu M (2011) Web services agreement specification (WS-Agreement). OGF GFD-R.192. http://www.ogf.org/documents/GFD.192.pdf
9. Nae V, Prodan R, Iosup A (2013) Autonomic operation of massively multiplayer online games in clouds. In: Proceedings of the 2013 ACM Cloud and Autonomic Computing conference. CAC '13. ACM, New York. pp 10:1–10:10
10. The SLA@SOI Project. http://www.sla-at-soi.eu
11. Mahbub K, Spanoudakis G, Tsigkritis T (2011) Translation of SLAs into monitoring specifications. In: Wieder P, Butler JM, Theilmann W, Yahyapour R (eds). Service level agreements for cloud computing. Springer
12. Emeakaroha VC, Netto MAS, Calheiros RN, Brandic I, Buyya R, De Rose CAF (2011) Towards autonomic detection of SLA violations in cloud infrastructures. Future Generat Comput Syst 28(7):1017–1029. doi:10.1016/j.future.2011.08.018
13. Freitas AL, Parlavantzas N, Pazat J-L (2012) An integrated approach for specifying and enforcing slas for cloud services. In: 5th IEEE intl. conf. on cloud computing. IEEE
14. Tomás L, Tordsson J (2013) Improving cloud infrastructure utilization through overbooking. In: Proceedings of the 2013 ACM Cloud and Autonomic Computing conference. CAC '13. ACM, New York. pp 5:1–5:10
15. The OpenStack Foundation. Welcome to the Ceilometer Developer Documentation! http://docs.openstack.org/developer/ceilometer/
16. The Ganglia Monitoring System. http://ganglia.sourceforge.net
17. Nagios Enterprises. Nagios. http://www.nagios.org
18. Zenoss Inc. Zenoss. http://www.zenoss.com
19. G Tesauro (2007) Reinforcement learning in autonomic computing: a manifesto and case studies. IEEE Internet Comput 11(1):22–30
20. Z Wang, X Qiu, T Wang (2012) A hybrid reinforcement learning algorithm for policy-based autonomic management. In: 9th International Conference on Service Systems and Service Management (ICSSSM). IEEE
21. C-Z Xu, J Rao, X Bu (2012) URL: A unified reinforcement learning approach for autonomic cloud management. J Parallel Distrib Comput 72(2):95–105
22. Ahmad S (2012) Automated machine learning for autonomic computing. In: 9th ACM International Conference on Autonomic Computing (ICAC). New York
23. Mashayekhy L, Nejad MM, Grosu D (2013) A truthful approximation mechanism for autonomic virtual machine provisioning and allocation in clouds. In: Proceedings of the 2013 ACM Cloud and Autonomic Computing conference. CAC '13. ACM, New York. pp 9:1–9:10
24. Beloglazov A, Buyya R (2012) Optimal online deterministic algorithms and adaptice heuristics for energy and performance efficient dynamic consolidation of virtual machines in cloud data centers. Concurrency Comput Pract Ex 24:1397–1420
25. Belograz A, Buyya R (2013) Managing overloaded hosts for dynamic consolidation of virtual machines in cloud data centers under quality of service constraints. IEEE Trans Parallel Distr Syst 24(7):1366–1379
26. Marshall P, Keahey K, Freeman T (2011) Improving utilization of infrastructure clouds. In: CCGRID '11 Proceedings of the 2011 11th IEEE/ACM international symposium on cluster, cloud and grid computing. pp 205–214
27. GoPivotal, Inc. RabbitMQ. http://www.rabbitmq.com
28. Menage P, Jackson P, Lameter C (2006) CGroups. http://www.kernel.org/doc/Documentation/cgroups/cgroups.txt
29. Derr S, Jackson P, Lameter C, Menage P, Seto H (2006) CPUSets. http://www.kernel.org/doc/Documentation/cgroups/cpusets.txt
30. Hu W, Hicks A, Zhang L, Dow EM, Soni V, Jiang H, Bull R, Matthews JN (2013) A quantitative study of virtual machine live migration. In: Proceedings of the 2013 ACM Cloud and Autonomic Computing conference. CAC '13. ACM, New York. pp 11:1–11:10
31. The NSF Center for Cloud and Autonomic Computing. http://www.nsfcac.org
32. Kyriazis D (ed) (2013) Cloud computing service level agreements: exploitation of research results. http://ec.europa.eu/digital-agenda/en/news/cloud-computing-service-level-agreements-exploitation-research-results
33. The OPTIMUS Project. http://www.optimis-project.eu
34. The CONTRAIL Project. http://www.contrail-project.eu
35. The TeleManagement Forum. SLA Management. http://www.tmforum.org/SLAManagement/1690/home
36. (2013) The TeleManagement Forum. Enabling End-to-End Cloud SLA Management, TR 178, Version 0.7. http://www.tmforum.org/TechnicalReports/TR178EnablingEndtoEnd/50148/article.html

6

Improving the performance of Hadoop Hive by sharing scan and computation tasks

Tansel Dokeroglu[1*], Serkan Ozal[1], Murat Ali Bayir[2], Muhammet Serkan Cinar[3] and Ahmet Cosar[1]

Abstract

MapReduce is a popular programming model for executing time-consuming analytical queries as a batch of tasks on large scale data clusters. In environments where multiple queries with similar selection predicates, common tables, and join tasks arrive simultaneously, many opportunities can arise for sharing scan and/or join computation tasks. Executing common tasks only once can remarkably reduce the total execution time of a batch of queries. In this study, we propose a Multiple Query Optimization framework, SharedHive, to improve the overall performance of Hadoop Hive, an open source SQL-based data warehouse using MapReduce. SharedHive transforms a set of correlated HiveQL queries into a new set of *insert queries* that will produce all of the required outputs within a shorter execution time. It is experimentally shown that SharedHive achieves significant reductions in total execution times of TPC-H queries.

Keywords: Hadoop; Hive; Data warehouse; Multiple-query optimization

Introduction

Hadoop is a popular open source software framework that allows the distributed processing of large scale data sets [1]. It employs the MapReduce paradigm to divide the computation tasks into parts that can be distributed to a commodity cluster and therefore, provides horizontal scalability [2-9]. The MapReduce functions of Hadoop uses (*key,value*) pairs as data format. The input is retrieved in chunks from Hadoop Distributed File System (HDFS) and assigned to one of the *mappers* that will process data in parallel and produce the (k_1,v_1) pairs for the reduce step. Then, (k_1,v_1) pair goes through *shuffle* phase that assigns the same k_1 pairs to the same reducer. The reducers gather the pairs with the same k_1 values into groups and perform aggregation operations (see Figure 1). HDFS is the underlying file system of Hadoop. Due to its simplicity, scalability, fault-tolerance and efficiency Hadoop has gained significant support from both industry and academia; however, there are some limitations in terms of its interfaces and performance [10]. Querying the data with Hadoop as in a traditional RDBMS infrastructure is one of the most common problems that Hadoop users face. This affects a majority of users

who are not familiar with the internal details of MapReduce jobs to extract information from their data warehouses.

Hadoop Hive is an open source SQL-based distributed warehouse system which is proposed to solve the problems mentioned above by providing an SQL-like abstraction on top of Hadoop framework. Hive is an SQL-to-MapReduce translator with an SQL dialect, HiveQL, for querying data stored in a cluster [11-13]. When users want to benefit from both MapReduce and SQL, mapping SQL statements to MapReduce tasks can become a very difficult job [14]. Hive does this work by translating queries to MapReduce jobs, thereby exploiting the scalability of Hadoop while presenting a familiar SQL abstraction [15]. These attributes of Hive make it a suitable tool for data warehouse applications where large scale data is analyzed, fast response times are not required, and there is no need to update data frequently [4].

Since most data warehouse applications are implemented using SQL-based RDBMSs, Hive lowers the barrier to moving these applications to Hadoop, thus, people who already know SQL can easily use Hive. Similarly, Hive makes it easier for developers to port SQL-based applications to Hadoop. Since Hive is based on a

*Correspondence: tansel@ceng.metu.edu.tr
[1] Middle East Technical University Computer Engineering Department, Cankaya, Ankara, Turkey
Full list of author information is available at the end of the article

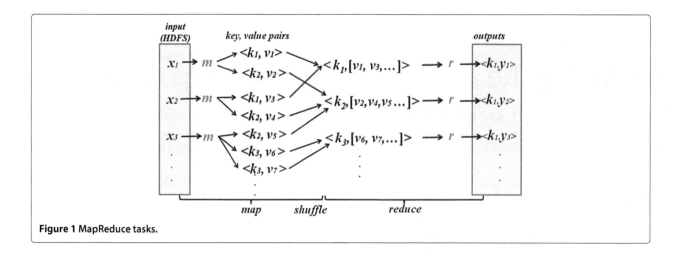

Figure 1 MapReduce tasks.

query-at-a-time model and processes each query independently, issuing multiple queries in close time interval decreases performance of Hive due to its execution model. From this perspective, it is important to note that there has been no study, to date, that incorporates the Multiple-query optimization (MQO) technique for Hive to reduce the total execution time of a batch of queries [16-18].

Studies concerning MQO for traditional warehouses have shown that it is an efficient technique that dramatically increases the performance of time-consuming decision support queries [2,19-21]. In order to improve the performance of Hadoop Hive in massively issued query environments, we propose SharedHive, which processes HiveQL queries as a batch and improves the total execution time by merging correlated queries before passing them to the Hive query optimizer [6,15,22]. By analyzing the common tasks of correlated HiveQL queries we merge them to a new set of *insert queries* with an optimization algorithm and execute as a batch. The developed model is introduced as a novel component for Hadoop Hive architecture.

In Related work Section, brief information is presented concerning the related work on MQO, SQL-to-MapReduce translators that are similar to Hive, and recent query optimization studies on MapReduce framework. SharedHive system architecture Section explains the traditional architecture of Hive and introduces our novel MQO component. The next Section (Sharing scan and computation tasks of HiveQL queries) explains the process of generating a set of merged *insert queries* from correlated queries. Experimental setup and results Section discusses the experiments conducted to evaluate the SharedHive framework for HiveQL queries that have different correlation levels. The Section before the conclusion presents the comparison of SharedHive with the other MapReduce-based MQO methods. Our

concluding remarks are given in Conclusions and future work Section.

Related work

The MQO problem was introduced in the 1980s and finding an optimal global query plan using MQO was shown to be an NP-Hard problem [16,23]. Since then, a considerable amount of work has been undertaken on RDBMSs and data analysis applications [24-26]. Mehta and DeWitt considered CPU utilization, memory usage, and I/O load variables in a study during planning multiple queries to determine the degree of intra-operator parallelism in parallel databases to minimize the total execution time of declustered join methods [27]. A proxy-based infrastructure for handling data intensive applications has been proposed by Beynon [28]; however, this infrastructure was not as scalable as a collection of distributed cache servers available at multiple back-ends. A data integration system that reduces the communication costs by a multiple query reconstruction algorithm is proposed by [29]. IGNITE [30] and QPipe [31] are important studies that use the micro machine concept for query operators to reduce the total execution time of a set of queries. A novel MQO framework is proposed for the existing SPARQL query engines [32]. A cascade-style optimizer for Scope, Microsoft's system for massive data analysis, is designed in [33]. CoScan [34,35] shows how sharing scan operations can benefit multiple MapReduce queries.

In recent years, a significant amount of research and commercial activity has focused on integrating MapReduce and structured database technologies [36]. Mainly there are two approaches, either adding MapReduce features to a parallel database or adding database technologies to MapReduce. The second approach is more attractive because no widely available open source parallel database system exists, whereas MapReduce is available as an open source project. Furthermore, MapReduce is accompanied by a plethora of free tools as well as having cluster availability and support. Hive [11], Pig [37], Scope [20], and HadoopDB [10,38] are projects that provide SQL abstractions on top of MapReduce platform to familiarize the programmers with complex queries. SQL/MapReduce [39] and Greenplum [21] are recent projects that use MapReduce to process user-defined functions (UDF).

Recently, there have been interesting studies that apply MQO to MapReduce frameworks for unstructured data; for example MRShare [40] processes a batch of input queries as a single query. The optimal grouping of queries for execution is defined as an optimization problem based on MapReduce cost model. The experimental results reported for MRShare demonstrate its effectiveness. In spite of some initial MQO studies to reduce the execution time of MapReduce-based single queries [41], to our knowledge there is no study similar to ours that is related to the MQO of Hadoop Hive by using *insert query* statements.

SharedHive system architecture

In this section, we briefly present the architecture of SharedHive which is a modified version of Hadoop Hive with a new MQO component inserted on top of the *Driver* component of Hive (see Figure 2). Inputs to the *driver* which contains compiler, optimizer and executer are pre-processed by the added Multiple Query Optimizer component which analyzes incoming queries and produces a set of merged HiveQL *insert queries*. Finally, the remaining queries that don't have any correlation with others are appended at the end of the correlated query sets. The system catalog and relational database structure (relations, attributes, partitions, etc.) are stored and maintained by *Metastore*. Once a HiveQL statement is submitted, it is maintained by *Driver* which controls the execution of tasks in order to answer the query. Compiler parses the query string and transforms the parse tree to a logical plan. Optimizer performs several passes over the logical plan and rewrites it. The physical plan generator creates a physical plan from the logical plan.

HiveQL statements are submitted via the Command Line Interface (CLI), the Web User Interface or the thrift interface. Normally, the query is directed to the driver component in conventional Hive architecture. In SharedHive, the MQO component (located after the client interface) receives the incoming queries before the driver component. The set of incoming queries are inspected, their common tables and intermediate common joins are detected, and merged to obtain a new set of HiveQL queries that answer all the incoming queries.

The details of this process are explained in the next Section.

The new MQO component passes the new set of merged queries to the compiler component of Hive driver that produces a logical plan using information from the Metastore and optimizes this plan using a single rule-based optimizer. The execution engine receives a directed acyclic graph (DAG) of MapReduce and associated HDFS tasks, then executes them in accordance with the dependencies of the tasks. The new MQO component does not require any major changes in the system architecture of Hadoop Hive and can be easily integrated into Hive.

Sharing scan and computation tasks of HiveQL queries

In order to benefit from the common scan/join tasks of the input queries and reduce the number (i.e. total amount) of redundant tasks, SharedHive merges *input queries* into a new set of HiveQL *insert queries* and produces answers to each query as a separate HDFS file.

The problem of merging a set of queries can be formally described as:

Input: A set of HiveQL queries $Q=\{q_1,...,q_n\}$.
Output: A set of merged HiveQL queries $Q'=\{q'_1,...,q'_m\}$, where $m \leq n$.

Rewrite/combine the given input queries in such a way that the total execution time of query set Q' is less than the total execution time of query set Q. If the execution time of query q_i is represented with t_i then

$$\sum_{i=1}^{m}(t'_i) \leq \sum_{i=1}^{n}(t_i)$$

Given q'_i is the merged *insert query* corresponding to queries q_j and q_k then all of the output tuples and columns required by both queries must be produced by query q'_i preserving the predicate attributes of q_j and q_k.

The existing architecture of Hive produces several jobs that run in parallel to answer a query. The *insert queries* merged by SharedHive can combine the scan and/or intermediate join operations of the input queries in a new set of *insert queries* and gain performance increases by reducing the number of MapReduce tasks and the sizes of read/written HDFS files.

Unlike the traditional SQL statements, HiveQL join query statements are written in the FROM part of the query [15] such as

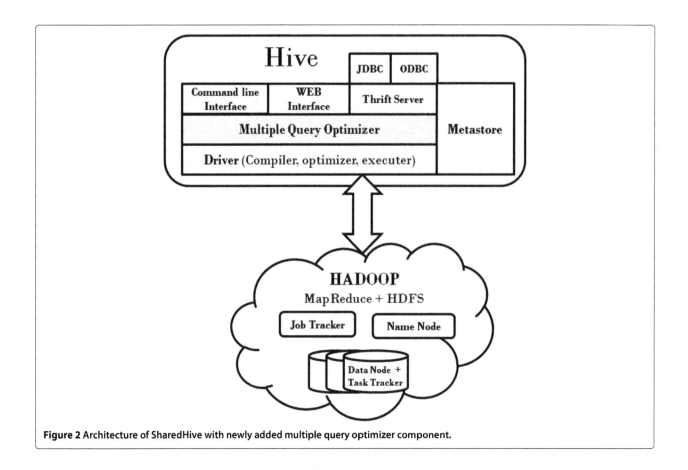

Figure 2 Architecture of SharedHive with newly added multiple query optimizer component.

SELECT SUM (L_EXTENDEDPRICE)
FROM LINEITEM L JOIN PART P ON P.P_PARTKEY = L.L_PARTKEY;

instead of
SELECT SUM (L_EXTENDEDPRICE)
FROM LINEITEM L, PART P
WHERE L.L_PARTKEY = P.P_PARTKEY;

The example below shows how a merged HiveQL *insert query* for TPC-H queries *Q1* and *Q6* is constructed.
Merging TPC-H Queries *Q1* and *Q6* :
Query *Q1*
CREATE EXTERNAL TABLE LINEITEM
(L_ORDERKEY INT ,..., L_COMMENT STRING)
CREATE TABLE q1_pricing_summary_report
(L_RETURNFLAG STRING ,..., COUNT_ORDER INT);
INSERT OVERWRITE TABLE q1_pricing_summary_report
    SELECT L_RETURNFLAG ,..., COUNT(*)
    FROM LINEITEM
    WHERE L_SHIPDATE ≤ '1998-09-02'
    GROUP BY L_RETURNFLAG, L_LINESTATUS
    ORDER BY L_RETURNFLAG, L_LINESTATUS;
Query *Q6*
CREATE EXTERNAL TABLE LINEITEM
(L_ORDERKEY INT ,..., L_COMMENT STRING)
CREATE TABLE q6_forecast_revenue_change (REVENUE DOUBLE);
INSERT OVERWRITE TABLE q6_forecast_revenue_change
    SELECT SUM(...) AS REVENUE
    FROM LINEITEM
    WHERE L_SHIPDATE ≥ '1994-01-01 AND

L_SHIPDATE < '1995-01-01' **AND**
L_DISCOUNT ≥ 0.05 **AND**
L_DISCOUNT ≤ 0.07 **AND** L_QUANTITY < 24;
Merged *insert query* for (*Q1+Q6*)
CREATE EXTERNAL TABLE LINEITEM
(L_ORDERKEY INT ,..., L_COMMENT STRING)
CREATE TABLE q1_pricing_summary_report
(L_RETURNFLAG STRING ,..., COUNT_ORDER INT);
CREATE TABLE q6_forecast_revenue_change(REVENUE DOUBLE);
FROM LINEITEM
INSERT OVERWRITE TABLE q1_pricing_summary_report
    SELECT L_RETURNFLAG ,..., COUNT(*)
    WHERE L_SHIPDATE ≤ '1998-09-02'
    GROUP BY L_RETURNFLAG, L_LINESTATUS
    ORDER BY L_RETURNFLAG, L_LINESTATUS
INSERT OVERWRITE TABLE q6_forecast_revenue_change
    SELECT SUM(...) AS REVENUE
    WHERE L_SHIPDATE ≥ '1994-01-01
    AND L_SHIPDATE < '1995-01-01' **AND** L_DISCOUNT ≥ 0.05
    AND L_DISCOUNT ≤ 0.07 **AND** L_QUANTITY < 24;

The underlying SQL-to-Mapreduce translator of Hive uses *one operation to one job* model [22] and opens a new job for each operation (table scan, join, group by, etc.) in a SQL statement. Significant performance increases can be obtained by reducing the number of MapReduce tasks of these jobs. Figure 3 presents MapReduce tasks of merged *insert query* (*Q1+Q6*) that reduces the scan operations.

Algorithm 1: Generating set of merged HiveQL queries.

1 **Input** $Q_{in} = (q_1,...,q_n)$; // HiveQL queries

2 **Output** $Q_{out} = (q'_1,...,q'_m)$, where ($m<=n$); // merged HiveQL queries

3 $Q_{out}:= \{\}$ //initial empty list of merged queries

4 //q_{miq} is a **merged insert query**;

5 **for** $q_i \in Q_{in}$ **do**

6   **if** $\exists q_{miq} \in Q_{out}$ such that $isFullyCorrelated(q_{miq}, q_i)$ **then**

7          $MergeWithFullyCorrelatedInsertQuery(q_{miq}, q_i)$;

8          $Q_{in} = Q_{in} - \{q_i\}$;

9   **else if** $\exists q_j \in \{Q_{in} - q_i\}$ such that $isFullyCorrelated(q_i, q_j)$ **then**

10         $Q_{out} = Q_{out} \cup MergedInsertQuery(q_i, q_j)$;

11         $Q_{in} = Q_{in} - \{q_i, q_j\}$;

12

13   **else if** $\exists q_{miq} \in Q_{out}$ such that $isPartiallyCorrelated(q_{miq}, q_i)$ **then**

14         $MergeWithQuery(q_{miq}, q_i)$;

15         $Q_{in} = Q_{in} - \{q_i\}$;

16

17   **else**

18   **if** $\exists q_j \in \{Q_{in} - q_i\}$ such that $isPartiallyCorrelated(q_i, q_j)$ **then**

19             $Q_{out} = Q_{out} \cup MergedInsertQuery(q_i, q_j)$;

20             $Q_{in} = Q_{in} - \{q_i, q_j\}$;

21 $MergeRemainingNonCorrelatedQueries(Q_{out}, Q_{in})$;

In the Appendix, three merged queries are presented to explain the merging process of HiveQL queries that share common input and output parts. The first one merges two *Q1* queries that have different selection predicates, the second one merges two fully-correlated queries, *Q14* and *Q19*, that share a common join operation and the third one merges two partially correlated queries *Q1* and *Q18* [42].

HiveQL statements have a preprocessing overhead for MapReduce tasks that will be executed to complete a query and this causes high latencies that could cause short running queries to take longer time on Hive [43]. In addition to the emerging opportunities of using common table scan and join operations, SharedHive intends to decrease the preprocessing period of uncorrelated query MapReduce tasks.

In the merging process of SharedHive, each query is classified according to the shared tables and/or join operations in the FROM clause of HiveQL statements. The input queries are inserted into a data structure that maintains the groups of similar queries according to the largest sharing opportunity they have with other queries.

While grouping the queries, the highest precedence is given to (a) queries with fully-correlated FROM expressions, (b) queries with partially-correlated FROM expressions and (c) queries that have no correlation with the other queries (which are appended to the end of the set of merged queries) (see Algorithm 1). With this approach, the common scan/join tasks in merged *insert queries* are not executed repeatedly [15]. After the merging process, the optimized set of *insert queries* are passed to the query execution layer of Hive.

Experimental setup and results

In this section, experimental setup and the performance evaluation of the merged HiveQL *insert queries* are presented. TPC-H is chosen as our benchmark database and related decision support queries because they process high amounts of data [44]. We believe this is a good match for our experiments since Hadoop is also designed to process large amounts of data. 11 query sets are prepared from standard TPC-H queries to experimentally analyze performance of SharedHive under different workload scenarios. These query sets define three correlation categories for merged queries (uncorrelated, partially correlated, and fully correlated). Uncorrelated queries have nothing in common, partially-correlated queries share at least one table and zero or more join operations. Fully-correlated queries have exactly the same list of the tables/joins (where conditions have different selection predicates). Table 1 gives the selected set of queries and their correlation levels. Query sets 8 and 9 use single queries that are submitted several times with different selection predicates. Query set 8 executes no join operation so that it presents the performance gains of SharedHive with intensive scan sharing, whereas query set 9 includes common join operations that require communication between datanodes. Query sets 10 and 11 include queries that produce several merged insert queries.

Three different TPC-H decision support databases with sizes 1GB, 100GB and 1TB are used. Similar experimental settings are used in previous studies [22,40].

The experiments are performed on a private Cloud server, 4U DELL PowerEdge R910 having 32 (64 with Hyper Threading) cores. Each core is Intel Xeon E7-4820 with 2.0GHz processing power. The server has 128GB DDR3 1600MHz virtualized memory and Broadcom Nextreme II 5709 1Gbps NICs. Operating system of the physical server is Windows Server 2012 Standard Edition. 20 Linux CentOS 6.4 virtual machines are installed on this server as guest operating systems. Each virtual machine has two 2.0GHz processors, 2GB RAM and 250GB disk storage. An additional master node is used

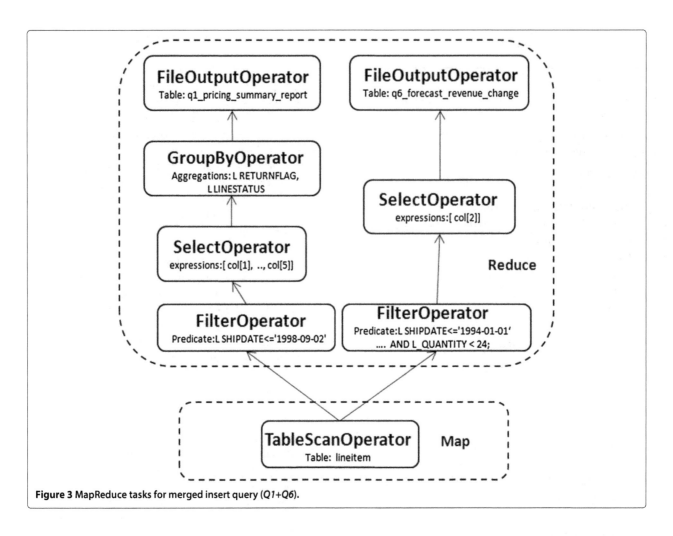

Figure 3 MapReduce tasks for merged insert query (*Q1+Q6*).

as NameNode/JobTracker (4 processors, 8GB RAM and 500GB disk storage). The latest stabilized versions of Hadoop, release 1.2.1 and Hive version 0.12.0 are used [1,11]. The splitsize of the files (HDFS block size) is 64MB, replication number is 2, maximum number of

map tasks is 2, maximum number of reduce tasks is 2 and map output compression is disabled during the experiments.

In order to remove noise in performance measurements, the Cloud server is only dedicated to our experiment during the performance evaluation. Therefore, we believe that performance interference from external factors such as network congestion or OS-level contention on shared resources are minimized as much as possible. We observe that there were only negligible changes in the response time of the queries when we repeated our experiments three times.

Table 2 presents the response times of TPC-H queries (*Q1, Q3, Q6, Q11, Q12, Q14, Q17, Q18, Q19, Q22*) with 1GB, 100GB and 1TB database sizes. These results constitute baselines to compare the results of the merged HiveQL queries with single execution performance of Hive.

Tables 3 and 4 show the performance increases for the selected HiveQL query sets given in Table 1 that are merged and run to observe the effect of SharedHive on total response times. The percentage values show the

Table 1 Sets of selected TPC-H queries and their correlation levels

Set number	TPC-H Query name	Correlation level
1	Q11,Q12	none
2	Q17,Q22	none
3	Q1,Q17	partial
4	Q1,Q18	partial
5	Q6,Q17	partial
6	Q1,Q6	full
7	Q14,Q19	full
8	Multiple *Q1s*	full
9	Multiple *Q3s*	full
10	Q1,Q14,Q18	mixed
11	Q1,Q3,Q11,Q14,Q17,Q19	mixed

Table 2 Execution times (sec.) of single TPC-H queries

Query name	1GB	100GB	1TB
Q1	66	381	3,668
Q3	150	655	7,286
Q6	37	220	1,836
Q11	140	243	1,196
Q12	91	434	4,214
Q14	65	330	3,036
Q17	126	949	9,064
Q18	186	1,159	13,922
Q19	73	674	6,564
Q22	146	385	2,014

reduction of the response time. Significant performance increases can be seen easily.

Although uncorrelated queries have nothing in common, their total execution times are observed to reduce by 0.2%-6.9% due to the improvement in HIVE query preprocessing overheads. Merging uncorrelated queries does not increase the performance when the database size reaches terabyte scale. The reductions in total execution times of partially correlated queries is higher than uncorrelated query sets (between 1.5%-20.8%). The highest benefits are observed in the fully correlated query sets (between 9.9%-39.9%). For query set 8 (single Q1 query submitted 8 times) the total query execution time is reduced from 26,716 to 3,985 seconds (85.1% reduction). The performance of mixed query sets depends on the correlation level of the queries they contain. Mixed query sets 10 and 11 execute their queries with 9.9% and 15.5% less execution times, respectively. During these experiments, the size of the intermediate tables that are written to the disks is considered carefully by SharedHive. If predicted overhead of writing intermediate results is larger than the expected improvement in response time, then queries are

not merged. SharedHive is observed to reduce the number of MapReduce tasks and the sizes of read/written HDFS files as well. The results given in Table 5 present the effect of SharedHive for the number of MapReduce tasks and the sizes of read/written files of the given *insert queries* (having different correlation levels). As the correlation level of queries increases the number of MapReduce tasks and the sizes of read/written data also decreases substantially.

The optimization time of SharedHive on analyzing and merging the queries is observed to be small. This is because of the small number of input queries and executing Algorithm 1 on them requires only examination of their FROM clauses which are parsed to identify similar expressions and rewriting the merged HiveQL query. This optimization does not take more than a few milliseconds.

In the last phase of our experiments, SharedHive is run on five different cluster sizes to observe its scalability with increasing number of datanodes. First, the merged *insert query* (Q14+Q19) is executed on the cluster using three different database sizes (1GB, 10GB and 100GB). It is observed that increasing the number of datanodes in the cluster improves the performance of the merged query reducing execution times by 29%, 81% and 88% in the database instances when the number of datanodes is increased from 1 to 20 (see Figure 4).

MQO component of SharedHive is an extension to Hive and welcomes any performance increase that is achieved on the HDFS layer either due to increase in the number of datanodes or balanced distribution of data files.

Comparison with other MapReduce-based MQO systems

SharedHive can perform the execution of the selected/correlated queries in shorter times than Hive by reducing the number of MapReduce tasks and the sizes of the files read/written by the tasks. The correlation detection mechanism of SharedHive is simple and does not find the number common rows and/or columns of

Table 3 Execution times of sequential and merged queries in seconds

Query names	Correlation	Execution time (sec.) Hive/SharedHive (reduction %)		
		1GB	100GB	1TB
11,12 (set 1)	none	231/215 (6.9%)	676/666 (1.5%)	5,410/5,386 (0.4%)
17,22 (set 2)	none	272/262 (3.7%)	1,382/1.323 (4,3%)	11,078/11,060 (0.2%)
1,17 (set 3)	partial	192/185 (3.6%)	1,330/1,134 (14.7%)	12,300/11,386 (7.4%)
1,18 (set 4)	partial	252/248 (1.6%)	1,540/1,396 (9.4%)	17,499/16,324 (6.7%)
6,17 (set 5)	partial	163/160 (1.8%)	1,169/1,042 (10.9%)	10,430/8,636 (17.2%)
1,6 (set 6)	full	103/90 (12.6%)	601/436 (27.5%)	5,057/3,936 (22.2%)
14,19 (set 7)	full	138/83 (39.9%)	1,004/789 (21.9%)	8,989/7,178 (20.1%)
1,14,18 (set 10)	mixed	317/299 (5.7%)	1,870/1,689 (9.7%)	20,425/18,590 (9.0%)
1,3,11,14,17,19 (set 11)	mixed	620/524 (15.5%)	3,232/2,830 (12.4%)	30,069/26,024 (13.5%)

Table 4 Execution times of sequential and merged query sets (8 and 9) in seconds

Query name	# of submitted queries	Execution time (sec.) Hive/SharedHive (reduction %)		
		1GB	100GB	1TB
	2	123/70 (44.9%)	756/430 (43.1%)	6,833/3,843 (43.8%)
Q1 (set 8)	4	227/77 (66.1%)	1,435/442 (69.2%)	13,365/3,928 (70.6%)
	8	444/79 (82.2%)	2,894/458 (84.2%)	26,716/3,985 (85.1%)
	2	246/176 (28.5%)	1,334/999 (25.1%)	15,546/14,316 (7.9%)
Q3 (set 9)	4	470/307 (34.7%)	2,626/1,333 (49.2%)	27,712/14,645 (47.2%)
	8	957/503 (47.4%)	5,486/1,466 (73.3%)	56,112/15,615 (72.2%)

queries with complex algorithms as in [19,29]. The execution time performance gains are observed to be within the range of %1.5-85.1% in accordance with the correlation level of the queries. For repeatedly issued similar queries that have different predicates, SharedHive performs well. SharedHive benefits from underlying HDFS architecture therefore, its scalability is preserved and better performance is obtained when additional datanodes are introduced to Hadoop. The query results obtained by SharedHive have been compared with those of Hive and verified to be the same.

MRShare [40] is a recent MQO system developed for benefitting from multiple queries containing similar MapReduce tasks. It transforms a batch of queries into a new batch that will be executed more efficiently by merging jobs into groups and evaluating each group as a single query. MRShare optimizes queries that work on the same input table and does not consider sharing of join operations. However, SharedHive can merge queries containing joins into a new set of *insert queries*. MRShare shares scan tasks by creating a single job for multiple jobs and does not use temporary files (as it is done by SharedHive).

YSmart [22] is a correlation-aware MQO system similar to SharedHive. It detects and removes redundant MapReduce tasks of single complex queries but does not optimize multiple queries. The developers of YSmart present experimental results that significantly outperform conventional Hive for single queries. SharedHive does not provide any performance increase for single queries unless they

are submitted several times (with different predicates). SharedHive works in the application layer of Hive by merging the query level operations, whereas MRShare and YSmart explore and eliminate redundant tasks in the MapReduce layer.

Apache Pig is the most mature MapReduce-based platform that supports a large number of sharing mechanisms among multiple queries [37]. Complex tasks consisting of multiple interrelated data transformations are explicitly encoded as data flow sequences; however, its query language, Pig Latin, is not compatible with standard SQL statements like SharedHive.

Conclusions and future work

In this study, we propose a multiple query optimization (MQO) framework, SharedHive, for improving the performance of MapReduce-based data warehouse Hadoop Hive queries. To our knowledge, this is the first work that aims at improving the performance of Hive with MQO techniques. In SharedHive, we detect common tasks of correlated TPC-H HiveQL queries and merge them into a new set of global Hive *insert queries*. With this approach, it has been experimentally shown that significant performance improvements can be achieved by reducing the number of MapReduce tasks and the total sizes of read/written files.

As future work, we plan to incorporate MQO functionality at MapReduce layer, similar to YSmart, into SharedHive. In this way, it will be possible to eliminate even more redundant MapReduce tasks in queries and improve

Table 5 Comparing the number of MapReduce tasks and the sizes of read/written HDFS files by Hive and SharedHive for different correlation level 100GB TPC-H data warehouse queries

Query set (correlation level)	# Map tasks		# Reduce tasks		Read (GB)		Written (GB)	
	Hive	S.Hive	Hive	S.Hive	Hive	S.Hive	Hive	S.Hive
11,12 (set 1) (none)	463	463	116	116	123	123	20	20
6,17 (set 5) (partial)	1,568	663	326	89	51,561	51,561	504,975	34,806
14,19 (set 7) (full)	668	334	280	84	356	171	168	2
1,3,11,14,17,19 (set 11) (mixed)	2,149	1,150	452	288	636	404	291	206

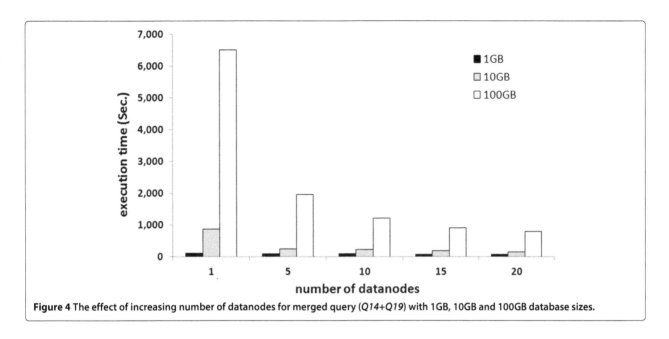

Figure 4 The effect of increasing number of datanodes for merged query (*Q14+Q19*) with 1GB, 10GB and 100GB database sizes.

the overall performance of naïve rule-based Hive query optimizer even further.

Appendix

A. Merging two *Q1* queries that have different select predicates

First query
```
SELECT L_RETURNFLAG ,..., COUNT(*)
FROM LINEITEM
WHERE L_SHIPDATE ≤ '1998-09-04'
GROUP BY L_RETURNFLAG, L_LINESTATUS
ORDER BY L_RETURNFLAG, L_LINESTATUS;
```
Second query
```
SELECT L_RETURNFLAG ,..., COUNT(*)
FROM LINEITEM
WHERE L_SHIPDATE > '1992-05-12'
GROUP BY L_RETURNFLAG, L_LINESTATUS
ORDER BY L_RETURNFLAG, L_LINESTATUS;
```

Merged Query
```
FROM
  (SELECT L_RETURNFLAG,...,COUNT(*), L_SHIPDATE
FROM LINEITEM
WHERE L_SHIPDATE ≤ '1998-09-04' OR L_SHIPDATE>
  '1992-05-12'
GROUP BY L_RETURNFLAG, L_LINESTATUS,
  L_SHIPDATE
ORDER BY L_RETURNFLAG, L_LINESTATUS,
  L_SHIPDATE) temp
INSERT OVERWRITE TABLE q1_pricing_summary_
report_1
  SELECT temp.L_RETURNFLAG ,..., COUNT(*)
  WHERE temp.L_SHIPDATE ≤ '1998-09-04'
  GROUP BY L_RETURNFLAG, L_LINESTATUS
  ORDER BY L_RETURNFLAG, L_LINESTATUS
INSERT OVERWRITE TABLE q1_pricing_summary_
report_2
  SELECT temp.L_RETURNFLAG ,..., COUNT(*)
  WHERE temp.L_SHIPDATE > '1992-05-12'
  GROUP BY L_RETURNFLAG, L_LINESTATUS
  ORDER BY L_RETURNFLAG, L_LINESTATUS;
```

B. Merging queries *Q14* and *Q19* (Fully correlated **FROM** clauses)
Query *Q14*
```
SELECT ...
FROM LINEITEM L JOIN PART P ON L.L_PARTKEY =
  P.P_PARTKEY
AND L.L_SHIPDATE ≥ '1995-09-01' AND
  L.L_SHIPDATE <'1995-10-01';
```
Query *Q19*
```
SELECT ...
FROM
LINEITEM L JOIN PART P ON L.L_PARTKEY =
  P.P_PARTKEY ;
WHERE ... ;
```

Merged Query (*Q14* + *Q19*)
```
FROM LINEITEM L JOIN PART P ON L.L_PARTKEY =
  P.P_PARTKEY
INSERT OVERWRITE TABLE q14_promotion_effect
  SELECT ...
  WHERE L.L_SHIPDATE ≥ '1995-09-01' AND
    L.L_SHIPDATE < '1995-10-01'
  INSERT OVERWRITE TABLE q19_discounted_revenue
  SELECT ...
  WHERE ...;
```

C. Merging queries *Q1* and *Q18* (Partially correlated **FROM** clauses)
Query *Q1*
```
SELECT L_RETURNFLAG ,..., COUNT(*)
FROM LINEITEM
WHERE L_SHIPDATE ≤ '1998-09-02'
GROUP BY L_RETURNFLAG, L_LINESTATUS
ORDER BY L_RETURNFLAG, L_LINESTATUS;
```

Query *Q18*
```
INSERT OVERWRITE TABLE Q18_TMP
SELECT L_ORDERKEY, SUM(L_QUANTITY) AS
  T_SUM_QUANTITY
FROM LINEITEM
WHERE L_SHIPDATE≤'1993-01-01'
GROUP BY L_ORDERKEY;
```

```
INSERT OVERWRITE TABLE Q18_LARGE_VOLUME_
  CUSTOMER
SELECT C_NAME ,..., SUM(L_QUANTITY)
FROM CUSTOMER C JOIN ORDERS O
ON C.C_CUSKEY = O.O_CUSKEY JOIN Q18_TMP T ON
O.O_ORDERKEY = T.L_ORDERKEY AND T.T_SUM_
  QUANTITY > 300
JOIN LINEITEM L ON O.O_ORDERKEY =
  L.L_ORDERKEY
GROUP BY C_NAME, C_CUSKEY, O_ORDERKEY,
  O_ORDERDATE,O_TOTALPRICE
ORDER BY O_TOTALPRICE DESC, O_ORDERDATE;
```

Merged Query (*Q1 + Q18*)

```
FROM LINEITEM

SELECT L_RETURNFLAG ,..., COUNT(*)
WHERE L_SHIPDATE ≤ '1998-09-02'
GROUP BY L_RETURNFLAG, L_LINESTATUS
ORDER BY L_RETURNFLAG, L_LINESTATUS

INSERT OVERWRITE TABLE Q18_TMP
SELECT L_ORDERKEY, SUM(L_QUANTITY) AS
  T_SUM_QUANTITY
WHERE L_SHIPDATE≤'1993-01-01'
GROUP BY L_ORDERKEY;

INSERT OVERWRITE TABLE Q18_LARGE_VOLUME_
  CUSTOMER
SELECT C_NAME ,..., SUM(L_QUANTITY)
FROM CUSTOMER C JOIN ORDERS O
ON C.C_CUSKEY = O.O_CUSKEY JOIN Q18_TMP T ON
O.O_ORDERKEY = T.L_ORDERKEY AND
  T.T_SUM_QUANTITY > 300
JOIN LINEITEM L ON O.O_ORDERKEY =
  L.L_ORDERKEY
GROUP BY C_NAME, C_CUSKEY, O_ORDERKEY,
  O_ORDERDATE, O_TOTALPRICE
ORDER BY O_TOTALPRICE DESC, O_ORDERDATE;
```

Abbreviations

HDFS: Hadoop distributed file system; RDBMS: Relational database management system; SQL: Structured query language; QL: Query language; MQO: Multiple-query optimization; UDF: User-defined functions; CLI: Command line interface; DAG: Directed acyclic graph.

Competing interests

The authors declare that they have no competing interests.

Authors' contributions

TD designed the algorithm for merging the (fully, partially correlated) queries of Hive and executed the experiments. SO implemented the new Multiple Query Optimization component and added it to Hive framework. MAB prepared the mathematical formulation of Multiple Query optimization process for Hive and drafted the manuscript. MSC prepared the Hadoop/Hive experimental setup. AC coordinated the whole study and prepared the related work section. All authors read and approved the final manuscript.

Acknowledgements

We sincerely thank all the researchers in our references section for the inspiration they provide.

Author details

[1] Middle East Technical University Computer Engineering Department, Cankaya, Ankara, Turkey. [2] Microsoft Research Redmond, One Microsoft Way, Redmond, Washington 98052, USA. [3] Hacettepe University Computer Engineering Department, Cankaya, Ankara, Turkey.

References

1. Apache Hadoop. http://hadoop.apache.org/. Last Accessed 1 February 2014
2. Dean J, Ghemawat S (2008) MapReduce: simplified data processing on large clusters. Commun ACM 51(1):107–113
3. Condie T, Conway N, Alvaro P, Hellerstein JM, Elmeleegy K, Sears R (2010) MapReduce online In: Proceedings of the 7th, USENIX conference on Networked systems design and implementation, April 28–30, San Jose, California, pp 21–21
4. Stonebraker M, Abadi D, DeWitt DJ, Madden S, Paulson E, Pavlo A, Rasin A (2010) MapReduce and parallel DBMSs: friends or foes? Commun ACM 53(1):64–71
5. DeWitt D, Stonebraker M (2008) MapReduce: A major step backwards. The Database Column, 1
6. He Y, Lee R, Huai Y, Shao Z, Jain N, Zhang X, Xu Z (2011) Rcfile: A fast and space-efficient data placement structure in mapreduce-based warehouse systems In: Proceedings of the 2011 IEEE 27th International, Conference on Data Engineering, April 11-16, pp 1199–1208
7. Kang U, Tsourakakis CE, Faloutsos C (2011) Pegasus: mining peta-scale graphs. Knowl Inf Syst 27(2):303–325
8. Grolinger K, Higashino WA, Tiwari A, Capretz MA (2013) Data management in cloud environments: NoSQL and NewSQL data stores. J Cloud Comput: Adv Syst Appl 2(1):22
9. Bayir MA, Toroslu IH, Cosar A, Fidan G (2009) Smart miner: a new framework for mining large scale web usage data In: Proceedings of the 18th international conference on World wide web. ACM, pp 161–170
10. Abouzeid A, Bajda-Pawlikowski K, Abadi D, Silberschatz A, Rasin A (2009) HadoopDB: an architectural hybrid of MapReduce and DBMS technologies for analytical workloads. Proc VLDB 2(1):922–933
11. Hadoop Hive project. http://hadoop.apache.org/hive/. Last Accessed 4 January 2014
12. Dai W, Bassiouni M (2013) An improved task assignment scheme for Hadoop running in the clouds. J Cloud Comput: Adv Syst Appl 2(1):1–16
13. Issa J, Figueira S (2012) Hadoop and memcached: performance and power characterization and analysis. J Cloud Comput: Adv Sys Appl 1(1):1–20
14. Ordonez C, Song IY, Garcia-Alvarado C (2010) Relational versus non-relational database systems for data warehousing In: Proceedings of the ACM 13th international workshop on Data warehousing and OLAP, October 30–30, Toronto, ON, Canada
15. Thusoo A, Sarma JS, Jain N, Shao Z, Chakka P, Zhang N, Murthy R (2010) Hive-a petabyte scale data warehouse using hadoop In: Proceedings of ICDE, pp 996–1005
16. Sellis TK (1988) Multiple-query optimization. ACM Trans Database Syst (TODS) 13(1):23–52
17. Bayir MA, Toroslu IH, Cosar A (2007) Genetic algorithm for the multiple-query optimization problem. IEEE Trans Syst Man Cybernet Part C Appl Rev 37(1):147–153
18. Cosar A, Lim EP, Srivastava J (1993) Multiple query optimization with depth-first branch-and-bound and dynamic query ordering In: Proceedings of the second international conference on, Information and knowledge management. ACM, pp 433–438
19. Zhou J, Larson PA, Freytag JC, Lehner W (2007) Efficient exploitation of similar subexpressions for query processing In: Proceedings of the 2007 ACM SIGMOD international conference on Management of data. ACM, pp 533–544
20. Chaiken R, Jenkins B n, Larson PÅ, Ramsey B, Shakibn D, Weaver S, Zhou J (2008) SCOPE: easy and efficient parallel processing of massive data sets. Proc VLDB 1(2):1265–1276
21. Cohen J, Dolan B, Dunlap M, Hellerstein JM, Welton C (2009) MAD skills: new analysis practices for big data. Proc VLDB 2(2):1481–1492
22. Lee R, Luo T, Huai Y, Wang F, He Y, Zhang X (2011) Ysmart: Yet another sql-to-mapreduce translator In: Distributed Computing Systems (ICDCS), 2011 31st International, Conference on. IEEE, pp 25–36
23. Finkelstein S (1982) Common expression analysis in database applications In: Proceedings of the 1982 ACM SIGMOD international conference on, Management of data. ACM, pp 235–245

24. Roy P, Seshadri S, Sudarshan S, Bhobe S (2000) Efficient and extensible algorithms for multi query optimization. ACM SIGMOD Rec 29(2):249–260

25. Giannikis G, Alonso G, Kossmann D (2012) SharedDB: killing one thousand queries with one stone. Prof VLDB 5(6):526–537

26. Chen F, Dunham MH (1998) Common subexpression processing in multiple-query processing. IEEE Trans Knowl Data Eng 10(3):493–499

27. Mehta M, DeWitt DJ (1995) Managing intra-operator parallelism in parallel database systems In: VLDB vol 95, pp 382–394

28. Beynon M, Chang C, Catalyurek U, Kurc T, Sussman A, Andrade H, Ferreira R, Saltz J (2002) Processing large-scale multi-dimensional data in parallel and distributed environments. Parallel Comput 28(5):827–859

29. Chen G, Wu Y, Liu J, Yang G, Zheng W (2011) Optimization of sub-query processing in distributed data integration systems. J Netw Comput Appl 34(4):1035–1042

30. Lee R, Zhou M, Liao H (2007) Request Window: an approach to improve throughput of RDBMS-based data integration system by utilizing data sharing across concurrent distributed queries In: Proceedings of the 33rd international conference on, Very large data bases. VLDB Endowment, pp 1219–1230

31. Harizopoulos S, Shkapenyuk V, Ailamaki A (2005) QPipe: a simultaneously pipelined relational query engine In: Proceedings of the 2005 ACM SIGMOD international conference on Management of data. ACM, pp 383–394

32. Le W, Kementsietsidis A, Duan S, Li F (2012) Scalable multi-query optimization for SPARQL In: Data Engineering (ICDE), 2012 IEEE 28th International Conference on. IEEE, pp 666–677

33. Silva YN, Larson PA, Zhou J (2012) Exploiting common subexpressions for cloud query processing In: Data Engineering (ICDE), 2012 IEEE 28th International Conference on. IEEE, pp 1337–1348

34. Wang X, Olston C, Sarma AD, Burns R (2011) CoScan: cooperative scan sharing in the cloud In: Proceedings of the 2nd ACM Symposium on Cloud Computing. ACM, p 11

35. Wolf J, Balmin A, Rajan D, Hildrum K, Khandekar R, Parekh S, Wu K-L, Vernica R (2012) On the optimization of schedules for MapReduce workloads in the presence of shared scans. VLDB J 21(5):589–609

36. Ferrera P, De Prado I, Palacios E, Fernandez-Marquez JL, Serugendo GDM (2013) Tuple MapReduce and Pangool: an associated implementation. Knowl Inf Syst:1–27. doi:10.1007/s10115-013-0705-z

37. Apache Pig. http://pig.apache.org/. Last Accessed 1 February 2014

38. Bajda-Pawlikowski K, Abadi DJ, Silberschatz A, Paulson E (2011) Efficient processing of data warehousing queries in a split execution environment In: Proceedings of the 2011 ACM SIGMOD International Conference on Management of data. ACM, pp 1165–1176

39. Friedman E, Pawlowski P, Cieslewicz J (2009) SQL/MapReduce: a practical approach to self-describing, polymorphic, and parallelizable user-defined functions. Proc VLDB 2(2):1402–1413

40. Nykiel T, Potamias M, Mishra C, Kollios G, Koudas N (2010) MRShare: sharing across multiple queries in mapreduce. Proc VLDB 3(1–2):494–505

41. Gruenheid A, Omiecinski E, Mark L (2011) Query optimization using column statistics in hive In: Proceedings of the 15th, Symposium on International Database Engineering & Applications. ACM, pp 97–105

42. Chaudhuri S, Shim K (1994) Including group-by in query optimization In: VLDB vol. 94, pp 354–366

43. Jiang D, Tung AK, Chen G (2011) Map-join-reduce: toward scalable and efficient data analysis on large clusters. Knowl Data Eng IEEE Trans 23(9):1299–1311

44. Running TPC-H queries on Hive. http://issues.apache.org/jira/browse/HIVE-600. Last Accessed 1 January 2014

7

Architecture-based integrated management of diverse cloud resources

Xing Chen[1,2], Ying Zhang[3,4], Gang Huang[3,4], Xianghan Zheng[1,2]*, Wenzhong Guo[1,2] and Chunming Rong[5]

Abstract

Cloud management faces with great challenges, due to the diversity of Cloud resources and ever-changing management requirements. For constructing a management system to satisfy a specific management requirement, a redevelopment solution based on existing management systems is usually more practicable than developing the system from scratch. However, the difficulty and workload of redevelopment are also very high. As the architecture-based runtime model is causally connected with the corresponding running system automatically, constructing an integrated Cloud management system based on the architecture-based runtime models of Cloud resources can benefit from the model-specific natures, and thus reduce the development workload. In this paper, we present an architecture-based approach to managing diverse Cloud resources. First, manageability of Cloud resources is abstracted as runtime models, which could automatically and immediately propagate any observable runtime changes of target resources to corresponding architecture models, and vice versa. Second, a customized model is constructed according to the personalized management requirement and the synchronization between the customized model and Cloud resource runtime models is ensured through model transformation. Thus, all the management tasks could be carried out through executing programs on the customized model. The experiment on a real-world cloud demonstrates the feasibility, effectiveness and benefits of the new approach to integrated management of Cloud resources

Keywords: Cloud management; Software architecture; Models at runtime

Introduction

Cloud computing is a model for enabling ubiquitous, convenient, on-demand network access to a shared pool of configurable computing resources that can be rapidly provisioned and released with minimal management effort or service provider interaction [1]. They always allocate virtual machine (VM)-based computing resources on demand through the virtualization technology, and deploy different kinds of fundamental software onto virtual machines, which are finally provided in a service-oriented style. Nowadays, more and more software applications are built or migrated to run in a cloud, with the goal of reducing IT costs and complexities. This trend brings unprecedented challenges to system management of Cloud, which mainly comes from the following two aspects:

* Correspondence: xianghan.zheng@fzu.edu.cn
[1]College of Mathematics and Computer Science, Fuzhou University, Fuzhou 350116, China
[2]Fujian Provincial Key Laboratory of Networking Computing and Intelligent Information Processing (Fuzhou University), Fuzhou 350116, China
Full list of author information is available at the end of the article

First, the virtualization not only makes the physical resources easier to share and control but also increases the complexity of management [2]. For instance, there are different kinds of Cloud resources, which include CPU, memory, storage, network, virtual machines and different types of software, such as web servers and application servers. All these resources have to be managed together.

Second, there are kinds of personalized management requirements. In some scenarios, administrators need to manage different kinds of resources together; while in other scenarios, administrators have to manage Cloud resources in appropriate styles [2]. For instance, a 3-tier JEE (Java Enterprise Edition) application typically has to use the web server, EJB server and DB server. These servers have different management mechanisms. An EJB server should comply with JMX management specification and rely on the JMX API, while a DB server is usually managed through the SQL-like scripts. In addition, the EJB server could usually sustain running of several applications simultaneously. What's more, all of the platforms are in a resource sharing and competing environment [3].

Administrators have to carefully coordinate each part to make the whole system work correctly and effectively.

Actually, Cloud management is the execution of a group of management tasks, from the view of system implementation. A management task is a group of management operations on one or more kinds of Cloud resources. A management operation is an invocation of a management interface provided by Cloud resources themselves or a third-party management service. Due to the specificity and large scale of Cloud, management tasks of different Clouds are not the same. For instance, Amazon EC2 [4] mainly manages infrastructure level Cloud resources such as virtual machines, while Google App Engine [5] manages platform-level Cloud resources such as operating systems execution environment. To satisfy the personalized management requirements, Cloud administrators usually conduct redevelopment based on the existing management systems. However, the redevelopment is usually implemented in general purpose programming languages like Java and C/C++, which can bring enough power and flexibility but also cause high programming efforts and costs. For instance, the existing VM and middleware platforms have already provided adequate proprietary APIs (e.g., JMX) to be used by monitoring and executing related code. Administrators first have to be familiar with these APIs and then build programs upon them. Such a work is not easy due to diverse resources and personalized requirements. In a management program, proper APIs have to be chosen for use and different types of APIs (e.g., JMX and scripts) have to be made interoperable with each other. Such "boring" work is not the core of management logics compared with analyzing and planning related code, but it has to be done to make the whole program run effectively. During this procedure, the irrelevant APIs as well as the collected low-level data can sometimes make administrators exhausted and frustrated. Furthermore, the programs are built on the code that directly connects with runtime systems, so they are not easy for reuse. Administrators have to write many different programs to manage different cloud applications and their platforms, even their management mechanisms are the same.

The fundamental challenge faced by the development of management tasks is the conceptual gap between the problem and the implementation domains. To bridge the gap, using approaches that require extensive handcraft implementations such as hard-coding in general purpose programming languages like Java will give rise to the programming complexity. Software architecture acts as a bridge between requirements and implementations [6]. It describes the gross structure of a software system with a collection of managed elements and it has been used to reduce the complexity and cost mainly resulted from the difficulties faced by understanding the large-scale and complex software system [7]. It is a natural idea to understand management tasks through modeling the architecture of the system. Current researches in the area of model driven engineering (MDE) also support systematic transformation of problem-level abstractions to software implementations [8].

To address the issues above, we try to leverage architecture-based runtime model for the management of diverse Cloud resources. An architecture-based runtime model is a causally connected self-representation of the associated system that emphasizes the structure, behavior, and goals of the system from a problem space perspective [9,10]. It has been broadly adopted in the runtime management of software systems [11-13]. With the help of runtime models, administrators can obtain a better understanding of their systems and write model-level programs for management. We have developed a model-based runtime management tool called SM@RT (Supporting Model AT Run Time [14-16]), which provides the synchronization engine between a runtime model and its corresponding running system. SM@RT makes any state of the running system reflected to the runtime model, as well as any change to the runtime model applied to the running system in an on-the-fly fashion.

In this paper, we present an architecture-based approach to the integrated management of diverse Cloud resources. First, we construct the architecture-based runtime model of each kind of Cloud resource (Cloud resource runtime model) automatically based on its architecture meta-model and management interfaces. Second, we define a customized model which satisfies the specific management requirement, and describe mapping relationships between the customized model and Cloud resource runtime models. Then any operation on the customized model is transformed to one on Cloud resource runtime models automatically. Finally, management tasks are carried out through executing operating programs on the customized model, which could benefit from many model-centric analyzing or planning methods and mechanisms such as model checkers [17]. The whole approach only needs to define a group of meta-models and mapping rules, thus greatly reduces the workload of hand coding. As an additional contribution, we apply the runtime model to a real Cloud system, which is a practical evaluation on architecture-based integrated management of diverse Cloud resources.

The rest of this paper is organized as follows: Section II gives a motivating example of the architecture-based approach to managing diverse Cloud resources. Section III presents the construction of Cloud resource runtime models. Section IV describes the construction of the customized model. Section V illustrates a real case study and reports the evaluation. Section VI discusses the related works. Section VII concludes this paper and indicates our future work.

Motivating example

In order to satisfy personalized requirements, Cloud administrators conduct redevelopment based on existing management systems. However, it may result in several difficulties of integrated management in general approach. For instance, management scenarios may consist of different types of resources which need to be managed collaboratively. Administrators have to be familiar with the APIs and then build programs upon them. While conducting redevelopment, they have to choose proper APIs for use and make different types of APIs interpretable with each other, as shown in Figure 1.

Such code fragments are not the core of management logics, but it has to be developed to make the whole management program run effectively. Many similar code fragments are required for a simple task. As shown in Figure 1, the code fragment for fetching the value of the "maxThreads" attribute in a JOnAS (a popular open

source Java application server) through JMX API is more than 20 LOC (Line of Code). During this procedure, the irrelevant APIs as well as the collected low-level data can sometimes make administrators exhausted and frustrated. Furthermore, as programs are built on the code that directly connect with the running systems, they are not easy for reuse. Administrators have to write different programs to satisfy similar requirements even their management objectives are the same.

When using our approach, the procedure becomes much simpler and shorter. Figure 2 shows an overview of the runtime model based approach to integrated management of Cloud resources. The architecture-based runtime models can shield administrators from the relatively low-level details of redevelopment.

There are two steps in our approach. First, we construct runtime models of Cloud resources. The Cloud resource runtime model is abstracted from the software

```
1.   /*
2.    * JAVA: To get the value of the maxThreads of a JOnAS
3.    * through the JMX.
4.    */
5.   public int getMaxThreads(String port)
6.   {
7.       //To prepare to invoke the interface
8.       String objName = "jonas:type=Connector,port=" + port;
9.       String attributeName = "maxThreads";
10.      MBeanServerConnection mbeanServerConn = null;
11.      try
12.      {
13.          JMXServiceURL connURL = new JMXServiceURL(
14.          "service:jmx:rmi://localhost/jndi/rmi://localhost
15.          :1099/jrmpconnector_jonas");
16.          JMXConnector connector = JMXConnectorFactory.
17.          newJMXConnector(connURL, null);
18.          connector.connect(null);
19.          mbeanServerConn = connector.getMBeanServerConnection();
20.      }
         ...
41.      //To invoke the specific management interface
42.      try
43.      {
44.          attributeValue = (Integer) mbeanServerConn.
45.          getAttribute(obj, attributeName);
46.      }
47.      catch (AttributeNotFoundException e)
48.      {
         ...
```

Figure 1 Example of invoking management interfaces.

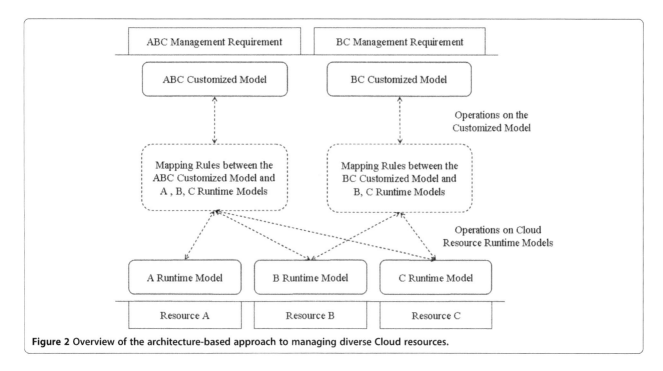

Figure 2 Overview of the architecture-based approach to managing diverse Cloud resources.

architecture of this kind of resources and the correct synchronization between the runtime model and the running system is ensured, which shields the heterogeneity of management interfaces. Second, according to the specific management style, we construct a customized model and ensure its correct synchronization with Cloud resource runtime models through model transformation. In our approach, we only need to define a group of meta-models, mapping rules and model-level programs, so the workload of hand coding can be greatly reduced.

Construction of cloud resource runtime models

There are many different kinds of resources in Cloud. For example, there are virtual machine platforms such as Xen, VMware and KVM, operating systems such as Windows and Linux, application servers such as JOnAS, JBoss and WebLogic, web servers such as Apache, IIS [18] and Nginx [19], database servers such as MySQL, SQL server and Oracle. We construct their runtime models in order to manage them in a unified manner. The runtime model is abstracted from their software architecture. It is done easily with the help of SM@RT (The source code of SM@RT can be downloaded from [16]), which is proposed in our previous work [14,15].

SM@RT consists of a domain-specific modeling language (called SM@RT language) and a code generator (called SM@RT generator) to support model-based runtime system management. The SM@RT language allows developers to specify: (1) the structure of the running system by a UML-compliant meta-model; (2) how to manipulate the system's elements by an access model.

With these two models, the SM@RT generator can automatically generate the synchronization engine to reflect the running system to the runtime model. The synchronization engine not only enables any states of the system to be monitored by the runtime model, but also any changes to the runtime model to be applied on the running system. Thus we can manage the resources through operations on the runtime models, and these operations will finally propagate to the underlying cloud resources. For instance, in Figure 3, the synchronization engine builds a model element in the runtime model for the running JOnAS platform. When the model element of JOnAS is deleted, the synchronization engine is able to detect this change, identify which platform this removed element stands for and finally invoke the script to shut down the JOnAS platform. Due to page limitation, the details of the runtime model construction with SM@RT can be found in [20-22].

Construction of the customized model

There are different management requirements in Cloud environment due to diverse Cloud resources and management styles. Different types of resources usually need to run collaboratively to support the Cloud application and the resources should be managed in an appropriate management style. In our approach, administrators just need to construct a customized model and define a set of mapping rules, in order to satisfy a specific management requirement. The customized model is abstracted from the software architecture of the required management system. The correct synchronization between the customized model and Cloud resource runtime models

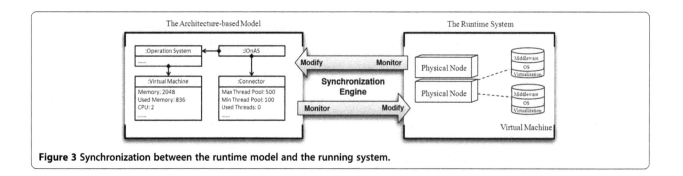

Figure 3 Synchronization between the runtime model and the running system.

is ensured through model operation transformation, which is completed automatically according to the mapping rules.

Mapping rules definition

Mapping rules are used to describe mapping relationships between the customized model and Cloud resource runtime models. Every element in the customized model is related with one in Cloud resource runtime models. As shown in Figure 4, there are three types of basic mapping relationships between model elements. Any other mapping relationship can be demonstrated as a combination of them.

One-to-one mapping relationship

One element in the customized model is related to a certain element in Cloud resource runtime models. Particularly, the attributes of elements in the customized model are also corresponding to the ones of related elements in Cloud resource runtime models. For instance, the *Flavor* element in the customized model and the *MachineType* element in Cloud resource runtime models both represent the configuration of virtual machine. The *id, name, memoryMb, imageSpaceGb* and *guestCpus* attributes of the *Flavor* element are related to the *id, name, ram, disk* and *vcpus* attributes of the *Machine-Type* element.

Many-to-one mapping relationship

One type of element in Cloud resource runtime models is related to two or more types of elements in the customized model. Particularly, the attributes of a certain type of the element in Cloud resource runtime models are related to the attributes of two or more types of elements in the customized model. For instance, *Image* and *Kernel* elements in the customized model are both used to describe the information about the type of virtual machine. In Cloud resource runtime models, all the related information is described in the *Image* element. However, in the customized model, there is not any attribute of the *Image* element, related to the *kernelDescription* attribute of the *Image* element in Cloud resource runtime

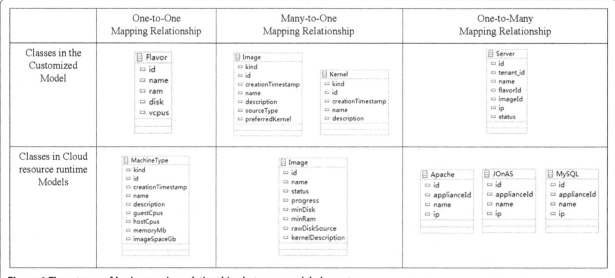

Figure 4 Three types of basic mapping relationships between model elements.

models. The related attribute is in the *Kernel* element, which is indicated by the *preferredKernel* attribute of the *Image* element in the customized model.

One-to-many mapping relationship

One type of elements in the customized model is related to two or more types of elements in Cloud resource runtime models. For instance, *Server* elements in the customized model represent virtual machines, and *Apache*, *JOnAS* and *MySQL* elements in Cloud resource runtime models represent virtual machines with software deployed. During model transformation, any Server element is mapped to one of *Apache*, *JOnAS* and *MySQL* elements, according to its *imageId* attribute.

As shown in Table 1, we have defined some keywords and presented the method to describe mapping relationships between the customized model and Cloud resource runtime models.

1. Helper: The "helper" tag is used to describe the mapping relationship between elements. There are usually three attributes in the "helper" tag, the *key* attribute, the *value* attribute and the *type* attribute. The *value* attribute describes the target element in the customized model and the *key* attribute describes the target element in Cloud resource runtime models. The *type* attribute describes the type of the mapping relationship. When its value is "basic", it is a one-to-one mapping relationship or a many-to-one mapping relationship. When its value is "multi", it is a one-to-many mapping relationship. The "helper" tag is used to describe the mapping relationship between elements. Elements often have attributes or other elements, so the "helper" tag usually nests "helper" tags, "mapper" tags and "query" tags.

2. Mapper: The "mapper" tag is used to describe the mapping relationship between attributes of elements. There are usually two attributes in the "mapper" tag, the *key* and *value* attributes. The *value* attribute describes the target attribute in the customized model and the *key* attribute describes the target attribute in Cloud resource runtime models. The element, which the attributes belong to, is defined in the outer "helper" tag.

3. Query: The "query" tag is used to describe the mapping relationship between attributes of elements. There are usually four attributes in the "query" tag. The *key* and *value* attributes in the "query" tag are similar with the ones in "mapper" tag. But the element, which the attribute belongs to, is defined by the node and condition attributes; the *node* attribute describes the type of the target element and the *condition* attribute describes the constraint that the target element should follow. The "query" tag is usually used in the descriptions of many-to-one mapping relationships between elements.

Based on the key words above, we could define the mapping rules between elements, according to their mapping relationships. As shown in Figure 5, there are three cases of basic mapping relationships between elements.

One-to-one mapping relationship

The first case is to describe the One-to-One mapping relationship between *Flavor* elements in the customized model and *MachineType* elements in Cloud resource runtime models. The "helper" tag is used to describe this mapping relationship. The value of the *key* attribute is "machineType" and the value of the *value* attribute is "flavor". The "mapper" tags are used to describe the mapping relationships between the attributes of *Flavor* and *MachineType* elements.

Many-to-one mapping relationship

The second case is to describe the Many-to-One mapping relationship between *Image*, *Kernel* elements in the customized model and *Image* elements in Cloud resource runtime models. The "helper" tag is used to describe this mapping relationship. The "mapper" tag is for describing the mapping relationships between the attributes of *Image* elements in the models above. The "query" tag is to describe the mapping relationship between *description* attributes of *Kernel* elements in the customized model and *kernelDescription* attributes of *Image* elements in Cloud resource runtime models. The related *Kernel* element is indicated by the *preferredKernel* attribute of *Image* element in the customized model.

Table 1 Keywords used to describe mapping relationships

Keywords	Descriptions	Keywords	Descriptions
Helper	Mapping Rules between Elements	**Type**	Types of Mapping Relationships
Mapper	Mapping Rules between Attributes	**Query**	Mapping Rules between Attributes
Key	Elements or Attributes in the Objective Model	**Value**	Elements or Attributes in the Source Model
Condition	Preconditions	**Node**	Types of Elements

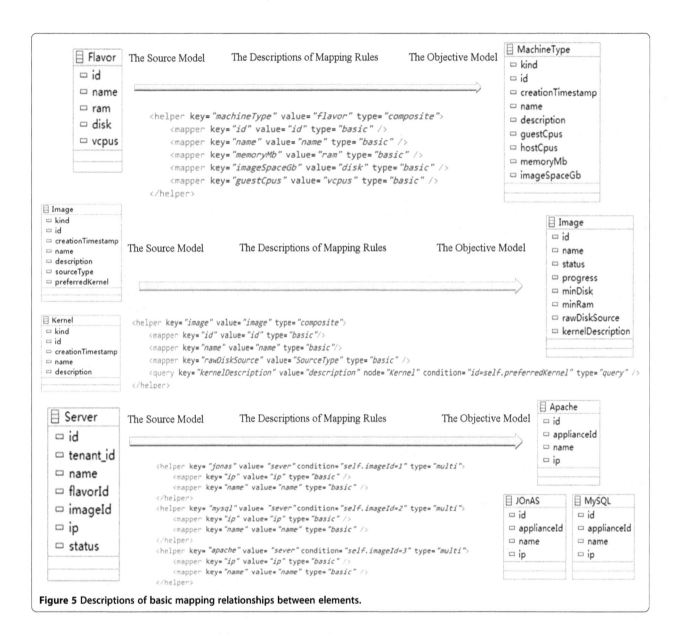

Figure 5 Descriptions of basic mapping relationships between elements.

One-to-many mapping relationship

The third case is to describe the One-to-Many mapping relationship between *Server* elements in the customized model and *Apache, JOnAS, MySQL* elements in Cloud resource runtime models. The "helper" tag is used to describe the One-to-Many mapping relationship, so the value of its *type* attribute is "multi". The *condition* attribute in the "helper" tag is to describe the mapping precondition. For instance, if the value of the *imageId* attribute of the Server element is "1", the *Server* element is mapped to the *JOnAS* element.

Model operation transformation

Model operations are aimed to monitor some system parameters or execute some management tasks. There are five basic types of model operations, including "Get", "Set", "List", "Add" and "Remove". In order to ensure the correct synchronization between the models, operations on the customized model need to be transformed to ones on Cloud resource models, as shown in Figure 2.

We define the description and execution effect of each type of basic model operation, as shown in Figure 6. When Cloud administrators operate on the customized model, an operation file will be generated automatically, which is described in the form of "action" tag. If the type of operation is "Get" or "List", the result file is required, which is describe in the form of "return" tag. Particularly, the *condition* attribute of the operation or result tag usually describes the identification of objective element, such as "id = f9764071".

List	Description	```<action node="TypeS" type=" List"> <query node="TypeF" condition="Constraint" /> </action> <ruturn> <node="TypeS" condition="Constraint1" /> <node="TypeS" condition="Constraint2" /> ...... </return>```
	Post Condition	$\exists$ TypeS s1, s2... $\exists$ TypeF f, s1, s2... $\in$ f $\wedge$ f in condition of Constraint
	Illustration	Find the "TypeF" element which satisfies the constraints and list "TypeS" elements which are its child nodes.
Get	Description	```<action key="KEY" type="get"> <query node="Type" condition="Constraint" /> </action> <return key="KEY" value="VALUE" />```
	Post Condition	$\exists$ Type n, n in condition of Constraint $\wedge$ prop $\in$ n.properties
	Illustration	Find the "Type" element which satisfies the constraints and get the value of its "KEY".
Add	Description	```<action node="TypeS" type="add"> <query node="TypeF" condition="Constraint" /> <set key="" value="" /> <set key="" value="" /> </action>```
	Post Condition	$\exists$ TypeS s, $\exists$ TypeF f, s $\in$ f $\wedge$ f in condition of Constraint $\wedge$ props $\subseteq$ s.properties
	Illustration	Find the "TypeF" element which satisfies the constraints and add a "TypeS" element as its child node.
Set	Description	```<action key="KEY" value="VALUE" type="set"> <query node="Type" condition="Constraint" /> </action>```
	Post Condition	$\exists$ Type n, n in condition of Constraint $\wedge$ prop $\in$ n.properties
	Illustration	Find the "Type" element which satisfies the constraints and set the value of its "KEY" attribute to "VALUE".
Remove	Description	`<action node="Type" condition="Constraint" type="remove" />`
	Post Condition	$\forall$ Type n, n not in condition of Constraint
	Illustration	Find the "Type" element which satisfies the constraints and remove it.

Figure 6 Basic Types of Model Operations.

As shown in Figure 5, there are three types of basic mapping relationships between model elements. We have defined the model operation transformation rules, as shown in Table 2. Then the operations on the element in the customized model can be transformed to the operations on the related element in Cloud resource runtime models automatically, according to the mapping relationships.

One-to-one mapping relationship

For instance, *A* elements in the customized model are mapped to *B* elements in Cloud resource runtime model. Thus, operations to add, remove and list *A* elements are mapped to the same operations on related *B* elements.

The operation to get or set the value of *A*'s attribute is mapped to the same operation on the related attribute too.

Many-to-one mapping relationship

For instance, *A* elements in the customized model are mapped to *B* elements in Cloud resource runtime model, but some attributes of *B* element are related to ones of *C* element in the customized model too. Thus, the operation to get or set the value of the attribute of *A* or *C* element is mapped to the same operation on the related attribute of *B* element. The operation to add, remove or list *A* elements is also mapped to the same operation on related *B* elements. In addition, when a

Table 2 Mapping rules of model operation transformation

	One-to-one	Many-to-one	One-to-many
	Mapping rule	Mapping rule	Mapping rule
Example	A -> B	A -> B	A -> B or C
	A1.a1 -> B1.b1	A1.a1 -> B1.b1	A1.a1 -> B1.b1
		C1.c1 -> B1.b2	A2.a1 -> C1.c1
Get	Get A1.a1 -> Get B1.b1	Get A1.a1 -> Get B1.b1	Get A1.a1 -> Get B1.b1
		Get C1.c1 -> Get B1.b2	Get A2.a1 -> Get C1.c1
Set	Set A1.a1 -> Set B1.b1	Set A1.a1 -> Set B1.b1	Set A1.a1 -> Set B1.b1
		Set C1.c1 -> Set B1.b2	Set A2.a1 -> Set C1.c1
List	List*A -> List*B	List*A -> List*B	List*A -> List*B and List*C
	Get A.properties -> Get B.properties	Get A.properties -> Get B.properties	Get A.properties -> Get B.properties or Get C.properties
Add	Add*A -> Add*B	Add*A -> Add*B	Add*A -> Add*B or Add*C
	Set A.properties -> Set B.properties	Set A.properties -> Get C.properties and Set B.properties	Set A.properties -> Set B.properties or Set C.properties
Remove	Remove*A -> Remove*B	Remove*A -> Remove*B	Remove*A -> Remove*B or Remove*C

B element is created, the initial values of properties come from both of *A* and *C* elements.

One-to-many mapping relationship

For instance, *A* elements in the customized model are mapped to *B* or *C* elements in Cloud resource runtime models. Thus, the operations are mapped to the same ones on the related elements or attributes. Particularly, the operation to list *A* elements is mapped to the operation to list all of related *B* and *C* elements.

Case study

In a Cloud environment, the hardware and software resources of virtual machines need to be managed together in order to optimize allocation of resources. However, to the best of our knowledge, there is currently no open source product to satisfy the requirement above. There are many Cloud management systems provide solutions to manage different kinds of Cloud resources. For instance, OpenStack [23] is an open source product which is used to manage Cloud infrastructure. Hyperic [24] is an open source product which is used to manage different kinds of software including web servers, application servers, database servers, and so on.

In order to validate the feasibility and efficiency of our approach, we implement a prototype for integrated management of the hardware and software resources of virtual machines based on OpenStack and Hyperic. Then we conduct some experiments on the prototype to make an evaluation.

Construction of cloud resource runtime models

OpenStack is used to manage the entire life cycle of virtual machines. The management elements in OpenStack include *Project, Server, Flavor, Image* and so on, as shown in Figure 7. The virtual machine (the *Server* element) is the basic unit of resource allocation, each of which is included in a project. The resources of infrastructure are divided into several projects. The configuration of virtual machine contains the image, which describes the file system of virtual machine, and the flavor, which describes the hardware resource of virtual machine. The *Images* element contains a list of images which are related to the project. The *Image* element is regarded as one type of image (For instance, web server image and DB server image). The *Flavors* element contains a list of flavors which are related to the project. The *Flavor* element describes one type of hardware resource configuration (such as tiny-flavor: CPU 1G, Memory 512 M; large-flavor: CPU 4G, memory 8G).

Hyperic provide management interfaces of middleware software products, which is based on the agents (the *Agent* element) deployed on each managed node. Due to the large number of management interfaces, the model of Hyperic in this case only contains the main management interfaces of Apache, JOnAS and MySQL, as shown in Figure 7. The attributes of *Apache, JOnAS* and *MySQL* elements represent the metrics and configurations of middleware platforms.

Given the architecture-based meta-models, we also need to identify the changes enabled by the models [22]. There are hundreds of management interfaces in OpenStack and Hyperic, so we can model them into the Access Models [14] through specifying how to invoke the APIs to manipulate each type of elements in the models. For instance, Figure 8 provides several management operations about the virtual machine. For each operation we detail the management operation names, the

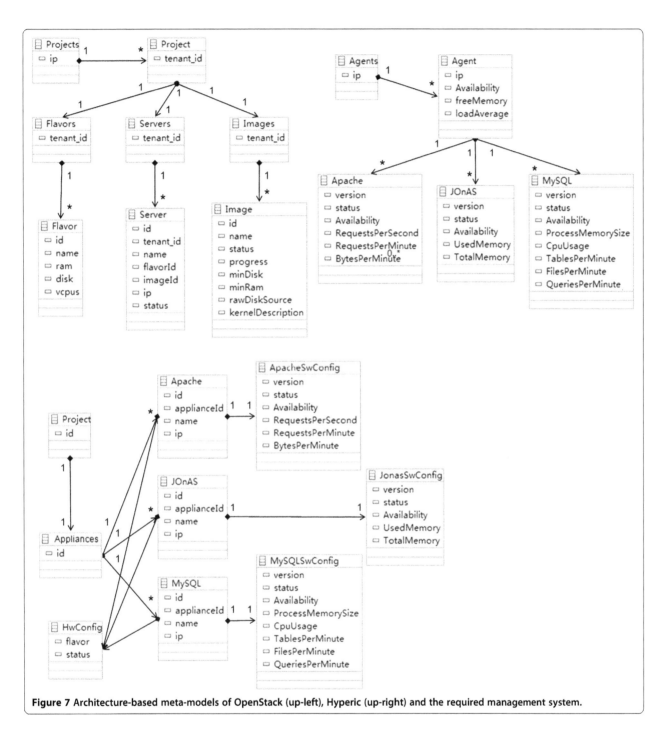

Figure 7 Architecture-based meta-models of OpenStack (up-left), Hyperic (up-right) and the required management system.

required arguments and the changes enabled by the operation. As shown in Figure 8, all types of manipulations of model elements are summarized and management operations are also classified.

Based on architecture-based meta-models and Access Models, the correct synchronization between runtime models and management systems can be guaranteed by the SM@RT tool. Thus, administrators are capable to manage the hardware and software resource at an architecture level separately.

Construction of the customized model

According to the management requirement above, the virtual machine and the software deployed can be regarded as an appliance [25], which is the basic managed unit. Several appliances compose a project that provides the infrastructure and software resources to a distributed application system. We construct a customized model, according to this management style. Figure 7 shows the main elements in the customized model. The *Project* element contains an *Appliances* element, which is regarded as a list of appliances.

Name	Argument	Post Condition
CreateAVM	Node rn, Image ri, Property[] props	∃ VM rv, rv ∈ rn.vms ∧ rv instanceof ri ∧ props ⊆ rv.properties
ShutdownAVM	Node rn, VM rv	rv ∉ rn.vms
MigrateAVM	Node rnI, VM rv, Node rnO	rv ∉ rnI.vms ∧ rv ∈ rnO.vms
PauseAVM	Node rn, VM rv	rv ∈ rn.vms ∧ rv.state = STOPED
UnpauseAVM	Node rn, VM rv	rv ∈ rn.vms ∧ rv.state = STARTED
ConfPProp	RuntimeUnit ru, Property[] props	props ⊆ ru.properties

Name	Meta element	Parameter	Description		Internal Changes	Manipulation
Get	Property(1)	-	Get the value of the property		CreateAVM	Add
Set	Property(1)	newValue	Set the property as newValue		ShutdownAVM	Remove
List	Property(*)	-	Get a list of values of this property		MigrateAVM	Auxiliary
Add	Property(*)	toAdd	Add toAdd into the value list of this property		PauseAVM	Set
Remove	Property(*)	toRemove	Remove toRemove from the list of this property		UnpauseAVM	Set
Lookfor	Class	Condition	Find an element according to condition		ConfPProp	Set
Identify	Class	Other	Check if this element equals to other			
Auxiliary	Package	-	User-defined auxiliary operations			

Figure 8 Definitions of runtime changes.

The *Appliances* element contains a list of *Apache* elements, a list of *JOnAS* elements and a list of *MySQL* elements, which are all regarded as appliances. The elements of each appliance contain configurations of the hardware and software resources. For instance, the *Apache* element contains an *ApacheSwConfig* element and an *HwConfig* element. Therefore, management tasks could be described as the sequences of operations on the customized model.

In order to ensure the correct synchronization between the customized model and Cloud resource runtime models, we define the mapping rules between them according to their mapping relationships, as shown in Figure 9.

The key challenge is to describe the mapping from *Apache*, *JOnAS* and *MySQL* elements in the customized model to *Server* and *Agent* elements in runtime models of *OpenStack* and *Hyperic*. We take the *Apache* element for an example.

1. The *Apache* element is mapped to the *Server* element in the OpenStack model. It is a one-to-one mapping relationship. The *id, applicanceId, name* and *ip* attributes of *Apache* element are mapped to the *id, tenant_id, name* and *ip* attributes of *Server* element. The *flavor* and *status* attributes of *HwConfig* element, are mapped to the *flavorId* and *status* attributes of *Server* element. In addition, the *Apache* element in the customized model represents the appliance with Apache platform deployed and the id of the certain type of virtual machine image is "6ebf952c". So the *imageId* attribute of the related *Server* element in the OpenStack runtime model should be "6ebf952c" too.
2. The *Apache* element in the customized model is mapped to the *Agent* element in the Hyperic model. It is a one-to-one mapping relationship.

The *Apache* element in the customized model contains the *ApacheSwConfig* element, which describes the configurations of Apache instance, as the same as the *Apache* element in the Hyperic model. So the *ApacheSwConfig* element in the customized model is mapped to the *Apache* element in the Hyperic model. The attributes of *ApacheSwConfig* element are also mapped to the ones of *Apache* element.

According to the mapping rules, the operations on the element in the customized model can be mapped to the operations on the related element in runtime models. Figure 10 shows an example of model operation transformation. The original operation is to create an *Apache* element and it is described as follows:

1. Query: Find the *Appliances* element whose id is "f9764071".
2. Add: Create an *Apache* element.
3. Set: Assign property values of the *Apache* element.

The original operation is mapped to the operation to create a *Server* element in the OpenStack runtime model. Model operation transformation is executed instruction-by-instruction. For instance, the action to query the *Appliances* node is mapped to the action to query the *Servers* node, whose tenant_id is "f9764071". The action to add an *Apache* node is mapped to the action to add a *Server* node. The actions to set the property values are mapped to the actions to set the values of related attributes too. According to the mapping relationships, the *imageId* attribute of related *Server* element should be "6ebf952c", so there is an extra action to assign the property value.

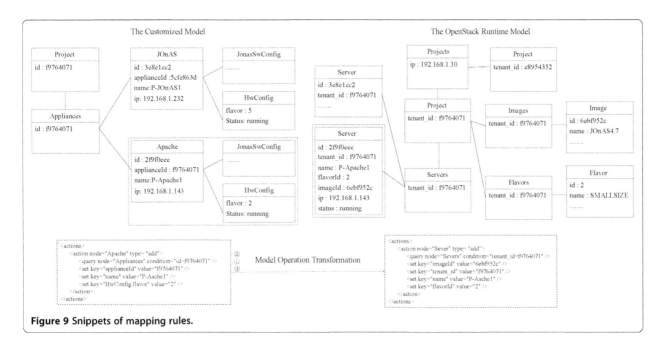

Figure 9 Snippets of mapping rules.

The generated operation file is transferred to the OpenStack runtime model. When the operation is executed, changes of the runtime model will be applied on the running system.

Evaluation

We evaluate our approach from three aspects.

1) Development of the architecture-based tool for integrated management of the hardware and software resources

For constructing Cloud resource runtime models, we just need to define the architecture-based meta-models and the Access Models on the Eclipse Modeling Framework (EMF) [26]. The runtime model will be generated automatically by our SM@RT tool. Construction of Cloud resource runtime models is one-off work, so it is acceptable for Cloud administrators. The existing forms of models and model operations are documents in XML format, and the process of model operation transformation is fulfilled in XML format based on mapping rules.

We have developed an architecture-based tool for integrated management of the hardware and software resources of virtual machines, as shown in Figure 11. Every *Appliance* element stands for a virtual machine with software deployed and these elements compose the runtime model of the running system. Administrators can manage the resources at an architecture level and the operations are transformed to the invocations of management interfaces of underlying Cloud resources. Particularly, we just reuse and reorganize management interfaces provided by OpenStack and Hyperic, instead of modifying underlying systems. We manage a cloud infrastructure, which consists of 15 physical servers and

supports about 100 appliances, through our runtime model based tool. It has been proved that management tasks could be fulfilled exactly by the tool. Furthermore, complex management tasks could be carried out through executing operating programs on the customized model, which may benefit from existing model-centric analyzing or planning methods and mechanisms.

2) Comparison of programming difficulty between general languages and model languages

According to our previous work [22], for the same management tasks, the programs are simpler to write in model languages like QVT [27], compared with in general languages like Java. With the help of the architecture-based model, Cloud administrators can focus on the logics of management tasks without handling different types of low-level management interfaces. In addition, model languages usually provide model operations such as "select" and "sum", which makes it simpler to do programming.

3) Comparison of performance between management interfaces and the runtime model

To evaluate the performance of our approach, we develop Java and QVT programs to execute two groups of management tasks, respectively based on the management interfaces or the runtime model. The first group of management tasks is to query properties of the appliances, and the second group of management tasks is to create a set of appliances, as shown in Table 3. The execution time of Java programs is less than QVT ones. The main reason is that the two sets of programs are based on the same APIs and there are some extra

```
<helper key="Project" value="Project" type="composite">
    <mapper key="tenant_id" value="id" type="basic" />
    <helper key="Servers" value="Appliances" type="composite">
        <mapper key="tenant_id" value="id" type="basic" />
        <helper key="Server" value="Apache" type="composite">                    ①
            <mapper key="imageId" value="" 6ebf952c"" type="basic" />
            <mapper key="id" value="id" type="basic" />
            <mapper key="tenant_id" value="applianceId" type="basic" />
            <mapper key="name" value="name" type="basic" />
            <mapper key="ip" value="ip" type="basic" />
            <mapper key="flavorId" value="HwConfig.flavor" type="basic" />
            <mapper key="status" value="HwConfig.status" type="basic" />
        </helper>
        <helper key="Server" value="JOnAS" type="composite">
            ......
        </helper>
        ......
    </helper>
    ......
</helper>
......
<helper key="Agent" value="Apache" type="composite">                              ②
    <mapper key="ip" value="ip" type="basic" />
    <helper key="Apache" value="ApacheSwConfig" type="composite">
        <mapper key="version" value="version" type="basic" />
        <mapper key="status" value="status" type="basic" />
        <mapper key="Availability" value="Availability" type="basic" />
        <mapper key="RequestsPerSecond" value="RequestsPerSecond" type="basic" />
        <mapper key="RequestsPerMinute" value="RequestsPerMinute" type="basic" />
        <mapper key="BytesPerMinute" value=" BytesPerMinute" type="basic" />
    </helper>
</helper>
<helper key="Agent" value="JOnAS" type="composite">
    ......
</helper>
......
```

Figure 10 Example of model operation transformation.

operations in the runtime model based approach, which are aimed to ensure synchronization between the architecture-based models and the underlying systems. However, the difference is small and completely acceptable for Cloud management.

Related work

There are many management systems, which are used to manage different types of Cloud resources. For instance, Eucalyptus [28] and OpenStack help administrators manage infrastructure level Cloud resources, while Tivoli [29] and Hyperic help administrators manage platform-level Cloud resources. However, most of these systems lack of efficient mechanisms to adjust or extend their management interfaces for personalized requirements.

There are some research works which try to integrate existing management functions based on service-oriented architecture. A solution to system management in a distributed environment is proposed in the work [30], which encapsulates management functions into RESTful services and makes them subscribed by administrators. In our previous work [31,32], a "Management as a Service (MaaS)" solution is proposed from the reuse point of view. However, management services are not so good as system parameters for reflecting the states of running systems, and service subscription and composition are also more complicated, which may lead to extra difficulties in Cloud management.

Runtime models have been widely used in different systems to support self-repair [33], dynamic adaption [34], data manipulation [35], etc. We have made lots of research in the area of model driven engineering. For a given meta-model and a given set of management interfaces, SM@RT [14,15] can automatically generate the code for mapping models to interfaces with good enough runtime performance. In addition, for the situation of incomplete formalized of modeling languages, our previous work [36] has provided an MOF meta-model extension mechanism with support for upward compatibility and automatically generates a model transformation for model integration, and the work

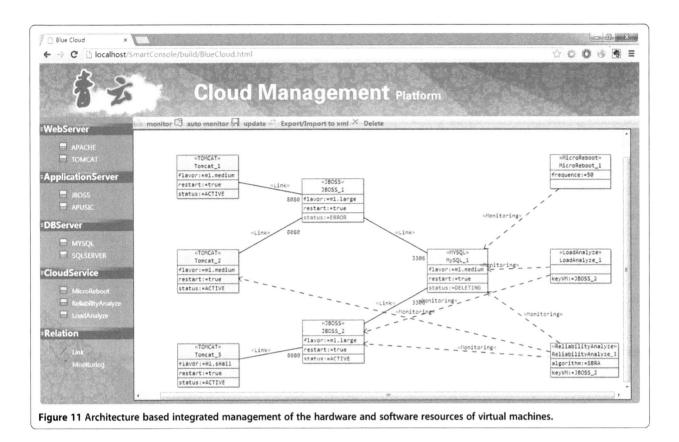

Figure 11 Architecture based integrated management of the hardware and software resources of virtual machines.

implemented on architecture-level fault tolerance [37] can also compensate for this to a degree. We have tried to construct the runtime model of a real-world Cloud and develop management programs in a modeling language [22,38]. The approach in this paper is built on our previous works. In addition, the approach is not intrusive, that is, neither instructs non-manageable systems nor extends inadequate APIs. Therefore, it is a general-purpose approach and is capable to interwork with other similar works like Pi-ADL [39].

Table 3 Comparison of performance between management interfaces and the runtime model

Management tasks	The number of the appliance	Management interfaces	Runtime model
		Execution time (second)	Execution time (second)
Monitoring	5	1.2	2.6
	20	4.2	8.5
	100	20	37
Executing	1	0.2	0.5
	5	1.0	1.7
	20	4.0	6.1

Conclusion and future work

Due to the diversity of Cloud resources and personalized management requirements, Cloud management is faced with huge challenges. To satisfy a new management requirement, the most common way is conducting re-development based on existing management systems. However, the difficulty and workload of redevelopment are very high. This paper proposed an architecture-based approach to integrated management of diverse Cloud resources. For a new management requirement , we construct runtime models of Cloud resources and the customized model which satisfies the requirement. The operations on the customized model are mapped to the ones on Cloud resource runtime models through model operation transformation. Thus, administrators could focus on the core of management logics and all the management tasks could be carried out through executing operating programs on the customized model, which greatly reduces the workload of hand coding.

As future work, we plan to give more support for administrators to manage Cloud resources. On one hand, we plan to perform further analysis such as model checking to ensure a deeper correctness and completeness of the generated causal link between the runtime model and underlying systems. On the other hand, we also plan to add some more advanced management functions with the help of model techniques to ease management tasks of Cloud.

Competing interests
The authors declare that they have no competing interests.

Authors' contributions
XC and YZ carried out the Cloud management studies, participated in the study and drafted the manuscript. GH participated in the design of the study and performed the statistical analysis. XZ and CR conceived of the study, and participated in its design and coordination and helped to draft the manuscript. WG participated in paper revision and made many suggestions. All authors read and approved the final manuscript.

Acknowledgements
This work was supported by the National Basic Research Program (973) of China under Grant No. 2011CB302604, the National Natural Science Foundation of China under Grant No. 61121063, the Technology Innovation Platform Project of Fujian Province under Grant No. 2009 J1007 and the Research Program of Fuzhou University under Grant No. 022543.

Author details
[1]College of Mathematics and Computer Science, Fuzhou University, Fuzhou 350116, China. [2]Fujian Provincial Key Laboratory of Networking Computing and Intelligent Information Processing (Fuzhou University), Fuzhou 350116, China. [3]Key Laboratory of High Confidence Software Technologies (Ministry of Education), Beijing 100871, China. [4]School of Electronics Engineering and Computer Science, Peking University, Beijing 100871, China. [5]Department of Computer Science and Electronic Engineering, University of Stavanger, Stavanger 4036, Norway.

References
1. Mell P, Grance T (2009) The NIST definition of cloud computing. Special publication 800-145. U.S. Department of Commerce. In: National Institute of Standards and Technology.
2. Kotsovinos E, Stanley M (2010) Virtualization: Blessing or Curse? Managing Virtualization at a large scale is fraught with hidden challenges. Comm ACM 54(1):61–65
3. Zhang Y, Huang G, Liu X, Mei H (2010) Integrating Resource Consumption and Allocation for Infrastructure Resources on-Demand. In: Proc. of the 3rd International Conference on Cloud Computing. IEEE Computer Society, Washington, pp 75–82
4. Amazon Amazon EC2. http://aws.amazon.com/ec2/
5. Google Google App Engine. https://appengine.google.com/
6. Garlan D (2000) Software Architecture: A Roadmap. In: Proc. of the 22nd International Conference on Software Engineering, Future of Software Engineering Track. ACM, New York, pp 91–101
7. Hong M, Junrong S (2006) Progress of research on software architecture. J Software 17(6):1257–1275, in Chinese with English abstract). http://www.jos.org.cn/1000-9825/17/1257.htm
8. France R, Rumpe B (2007) Model-driven Development of Complex Software: A Research Roadmap. In: Proc. of the 29th International Conference on Software Engineering, Future of Software Engineering Trac. IEEE Computer Society, Washington, pp 37–54
9. Bencomo N, Blair G, France R (2006) Summary of the Workshop Models@run.time at MoDELS 2006. In: Lecture Notes in Computer Science, Satellite Events at the MoDELS 2006 Conference. Springer, Heidelberg, pp 226–230
10. Blair G, Bencomo N, France R (2009) Models@ run.time. Comput 42(10):22–27
11. Huang G, Mei H, Yang F (2006) Runtime recovery and manipulation of software architecture of component-based systems. Automated Software Eng 13(2):257–281
12. Occello A, AM DP, Riveill M (2008) A Runtime Model for Monitoring Software Adaptation Safety and its Concretisation as a Service. Models@ runtime 8:67–76
13. Wu Y, Huang G, Song H, Zhang Y (2012) Model driven configuration of fault tolerance solutions for component-based software system. In: Proc. of the 15th International Conference on Model Driven Engineering Languages and Systems. Springer, Heidelberg, pp 514–530
14. Huang G, Song H, Mei H (2009) SM@RT: Applying Architecture-based Runtime Management of Internetware Systems. Int J Software Informa 3(4):439–464
15. Song H, Huang G, Chauvel F, Xiong Y, Hu Z, Sun Y, Mei H (2011) Supporting Runtime Software Architecture: A Bidirectional-Transformation-Based Approach. J Syst Software 84(5):711–723
16. Peking University SM@RT: Supporting Models at Run-Time. http://code.google.com/p/smatrt/
17. Rushby JM (1995) Model Checking and Other Ways of Automating Formal Methods. In: Position paper for panel on Model Checking for Concurrent Programs. Software Quality Week, San Francisco
18. Microsoft Internet Information Services. http://www.iis.net/
19. Igor Sysoev Nginx. http://nginx.org/en/index.html
20. Song H, Xiong Y, Chauvel F, Huang G, Hu Z, Mei H (2009) Generating Synchronization Engines between Running Systems and Their Model-Based Views. In: Models in Software Engineering (the MoDELS Workshops). Springer, Heidelberg, pp 140–154
21. Song H, Huang G, Xiong Y, Chauvel F, Sun Y, Hong M (2010) Inferring Meta-Models for Runtime System Data from the Clients of Management APIs. In: Proc. of the 13rd International Conference on Model Driven Engineering Languages and Systems. Springer, Heidelberg, pp 168–182
22. Huang G, Chen X, Zhang Y, Zhang X (2012) Towards architecture-based management of platforms in the cloud. Frontiers Comput Sci 6(4):388–397
23. OpenStack The Open Source Cloud Operating System. http://www.openstack.org/
24. SpringSource Hyperic. http://www.hyperic.com/
25. Kecskemeti G, Terstyanszky G, Kacsuk P, Neméth Z (2011) An approach for virtual appliance distribution for service deployment. Future Generation Comput Syst 27(3):280–289
26. Eclipse Eclipse Modeling Framework. http://www.eclipse.org/modeling/emf/
27. Object Management Group Meta Object Facility (MOF) 2.0 Query/View/Transformation (QVT). http://www.omg.org/spec/QVT
28. Nurmi D, Wolski R, Grzegorczyk C, Obertelli G, Soman S, Youseff L, Zagorodnov Z (2009) The Eucalyptus Open-Source Cloud-Computing System. In: Proc. of the 9th IEEE/ACM International Symposium on Cluster Computing and the Grid. IEEE Computer Society, Washington, pp 124–131
29. IBM IBM Tivoli Software. http://www-01.ibm.com/software/tivoli/
30. Ludwig H, Laredo J, Bhattacharya K (2009) Rest-based management of loosely coupled services. In: Proc. of the 18th International Conference on World Wide Web. ACM, New York, pp 931–940
31. Chen X, Liu X, Zhang X, Liu Z, Huang G (2010) Service Encapsulation for Middleware Management Interfaces. In: Proc. of the 5th International Symposium on Service Oriented System Engineering. IEEE Computer Society, Washington, pp 272–279
32. Chen X, Liu X, Fang F, Zhang X, Huang G (2010) Management as a Service: An Empirical Case Study in the Internetware Cloud. In: Proc. of the 7th IEEE International Conference on E-Business Engineering. IEEE Computer Society, Washington, pp 470–473
33. Sicard S, Boyer F, de Palma N (2008) Using components for architecture-based management: the self-repair case. In: Proc. of the 30th International Conference on Software Engineering. ACM, New York, pp 101–110
34. Morin B, Barais O, Nain G, Jezequel JM (2009) Taming dynamically adaptive systems using models and aspects. In: Proc. of the 31st International Conference on Software Engineering. IEEE Computer Society, Washington, pp 122–132
35. MoDisco Project. http://www.eclipse.org/gmt/modisco/
36. Chen X, Huang G, Chauvel F, Sun Y, Mei H (2010) Integrating MOF-Compliant Analysis Results. Int J Software Informat 4(4):383–400
37. Junguo L, Xiangping C, Gang H, Hong M, Franck C (2009) Selecting Fault Tolerant Styles for Third-Party Components with Model Checking Support. In: Proc. of the 12th International Symposium on Component-Based Software Engineering. Springer, Heidelberg, pp 69–86
38. Xiaodong Z, Xing C, Ying Z, Yihan W, Wei Y, Gang H, Qiang L (2013) Runtime Model Based Management of Diverse Cloud Resources. In: Proc. of the 16th International Conference on Model Driven Engineering Languages and Systems. Springer, Heidelberg, pp 572–588
39. Flavio O (2008) Dynamic Software Architectures: Formally Modelling Structure and Behaviour with Pi-ADL. In: Proc. Of the 3rd International Conference on Software Engineering Advances. IEEE Computer Society, Washington, pp 352–359

8

Towards full network virtualization in horizontal IaaS federation: security issues

Anant V Nimkar[*] and Soumya K Ghosh

Abstract

Horizontal IaaS federation exploits datacenter for federation of IaaS provider by supplying virtual nodes (e.g. virtual machines, virtual switches, and virtual routers) and virtual links. Today's datacenters for cloud computing do not supply full network virtualization in terms of user-level network management and user-agreed network topology. The datacenters lack the basic security services required for the collocation of tenants' virtual networks. The network virtualization research projects from academia and industry support full network virtualization but lack the basic security services required for the collocation of tenants' virtual networks. This paper investigates the security issues in four areas namely, (a) monolithic IaaS cloud, (b) network virtualization research projects, (c) datacenter network virtualization and (d) virtual resources to incorporate full network virtualization environment in horizontal IaaS federation. Further, it presents the security related qualitative comparisons of datacenters, network virtualization research projects and virtual resources to incorporate full network virtualization in horizontal IaaS federation.

Keywords: Cloud computing; Security; Horizontal federation; IaaS

Introduction

The development of cloud computing as conjectured by Celesti et al. [1] is divided into three stages: i) monolithic cloud, ii) vertical federation, and iii) horizontal federation. In the first stage, the full-fledged cloud services are provided by the cloud provider. All the services are proprietary and hence all the granular services (e.g. a storage service, computing service etc.) needs to be taken from a single cloud provider. In the vertical federation, most of the cloud providers leverage cloud services from another provider. Currently, the second stage is in transition. The future stage will be the horizontal IaaS federation where cloud providers federate to borrow virtual resources (e.g. virtual machines, virtual nodes and virtual links) from another cloud provider to gain economics of scale. The cloud federation may be economically profitable, since the datacenter utilization is only 5% to 20% of its peak time [2]. This under-utilization can be used by another cloud provider in the federation. The cloud federation also solves the problem of service provider lock-in, unavailability of the particular service provider, heterogeneous environment unavailability etc. [3].

The monolithic IaaS cloud has three limitations namely (a) maximum number of VLANs are limited to 4K because of 12 bits *VLAN ID* in 802.1Q Ethernet Header [4], (b) no user-agreed network topology at granular level configured and (c) the router gives connectivity between clouds (i.e. a single *route table* is used to manage all networks of a user), or cloud and the Internet. We will use the term *minimal network virtualization* for the three aforementioned limitations in the monolithic IaaS cloud. The IBM's TVDc is an example of vertical federation which supports minimal network virtualization [5,6]. In contrast to the minimal network virtualization, the *full network virtualization* is an environment in which the connectivity of virtual machines is provided using instances of physical network components (e.g. router and switch). It also will facilitate transparent network management of virtual network at a granular level (i.e. virtual switch, virtual router etc.).

Informally, the horizontal IaaS federation provides a federated IaaS cloud service of virtual servers using full network virtualization out of the datacenter. The transparent network virtualization in horizontal IaaS federation facilitates the network isolation, flexibility in network management, user-level network policy control [7] along

---

*Correspondence: anantn@sit.iitkgp.ernet.in
School of Information Technology, IIT Kharagpur, Kharagpur, India

with the advantages of cloud federation mentioned earlier. The full network virtualization in horizontal IaaS federation also provides separation of duties (infrastructure provider and service provider etc.), inter-operability between network owners, and portability. Few topology-aware scientific and commercial applications which can be deployed in horizontal IaaS federation are explored in [8] and [9].

There are two major challenges in the development of horizontal IaaS federation. First, the datacenters and virtual resources lack *full network virtualization* required for the horizontal IaaS federation. The second obstacle in the development is the lack of security provision required for the collocation of tenants' virtual networks on the datacenter. The obstacles demand analysis of the existing network virtualization technologies in different domains for security provision.

In this paper, we have investigated potential areas of network virtualization environment (NVE): a) generic network virtualization, b) the datacenter network virtualization, c) network virtualization in monolithic cloud and d) network virtualization in virtual resources. We use the term *generic network virtualization* to denote the research projects for testing future generation networks from academia and industry. First, we give a qualitative comparison of monolithic cloud designs, datacenters, network virtualization projects and virtual resources related to security issues. We also give limitations of aforesaid areas to incorporate full network virtualization and security services required for horizontal IaaS federation. Finally, an insight in research directions on security issues is given for the development of horizontal IaaS federation.

The rest of this paper is organized as follows. We first formally re-define *horizontal IaaS federation* for the inclusion of full server and network virtualization in Section 'Horizontal IaaS federation'. A hypothetical example of horizontal IaaS federation is also given in Section 'Horizontal IaaS federation' to illustrate the reasons for the investigation of network virtualization security. Section 'Horizontal IaaS federation security issues' explores the domains for security of horizontal IaaS federation and also gives a list of security requirements for horizontal IaaS federation. Section 'Monolithic IaaS NVE security' presents NVE security issues of monolithic cloud and vertical federation. Section 'Datacenter NVE security' and 'Generic NVE security' give security issues of datacenter and generic NVE respectively. The security issues of virtual resources related to NVE are presented in Section 'Virtual resources security'. Finally, a discussion on research directions for security in horizontal IaaS federation and concluding remarks are presented in Section 'Research directions' and Section 'Conclusions' respectively.

Horizontal IaaS federation

In horizontal IaaS federation, the service provider gives service to another cloud called *home cloud*, and the service borrower takes service from another cloud called *foreign cloud*. The *home cloud* borrows virtual resources from the *foreign cloud* either because of virtualization infrastructure saturation in *home cloud*, or the economics of scale in cloud federation [10]. The three-phase cross federation [1,10] and mobile-agent based cloud federation [3] are examples of the horizontal IaaS federation in which a *home cloud* rents virtual machines from *foreign clouds* without considering full network virtualization.

The horizontal IaaS federation should provide full network virtualization to its clients to gain advantages mentioned earlier. The existing work on horizontal IaaS federation [1,3,10] incorporates full server virtualization and minimal network virtualization while the application of network virtualization in various domains [11,12] concentrates on one of the two virtualizations. So, we first investigate the roles in the full server and network virtualization; and then formally re-define it for the inclusion of full server and network virtualization.

The network virtualization supports existence of multiple virtual network infrastructures on the top of physical network infrastructure. The NVE has two roles: *service provider (SeP)* and *infrastructure provider (InP)*. The InP owns physical infrastructure and SeP borrows/owns virtual infrastructure. Figure 1 shows an example of network virtualization environment. The network topology in plain line rectangle shows the physical infrastructure of InP. The network topologies in single-dot-dash and double-dot-dash line rectangles shows the virtual resources of SePs. The virtual nodes are installed on the physical resources. e.g. the virtual nodes, K1 and K2 are installed on the physical node K. The virtual link may be mapped to any path reachable between two nodes by some virtual network placement algorithm.

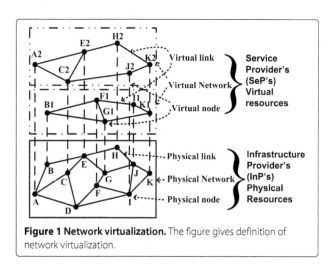

Figure 1 Network virtualization. The figure gives definition of network virtualization.

The current *horizontal IaaS federation* ecosystem has three key components: Cloud coordinators, Brokers, and an Exchange [13]. The cloud coordinators handle the datacenters for exporting market-based cloud services. A cloud coordinator can be cloud provider or consumer in the federation. A Cloud Broker is a mediator between cloud providers and cloud consumers for the federation. A cloud exchange performs match making services for the cloud users.

The *horizontal IaaS federation* with full server and network virtualization must consider at least two roles (viz. network service provider and infrastructure provider) from network virtualization and three roles (viz. a cloud provider, cloud consumer and a broker) from the current *horizontal IaaS federation* ecosystem. So the *horizontal IaaS federation ecosystem* must have four roles namely service provider (SeP), infrastructure provider (InP), broker (Br) and user to incorporate full network virtualization. The horizontal IaaS federation can be formally defined as:

Definition: *horizontal IaaS federation* The federated cloud service of virtual infrastructures of a set of virtual nodes (e.g. virtual switches, virtual routers), virtual links and virtual machines from a set of InPs (a virtual network infrastructure provider) and SePs (a IaaS cloud service provider) with transparent full server and network virtualization.

We will use the term *federation* to mean horizontal IaaS federation for the sake of brevity from now onward in the paper. We illustrate this definition with the following example. The hypothetical example presented in Figure 2 is inspired by the theoretical development of *federation* in *InterCloud* [13] and *open-flow* based network virtualization for cloud [14]. The IaaS cloud provider can be

InP, or InP as well as SeP in the *federation* as shown in Figure 2. The figure shows a federation of three IaaS cloud providers ({InP-1, SeP-1}, {InP-2} and {SeP-3, InP-3}) and three users (User-1, User-2 and User-3). The plain-line rectangles are InP providers. The bottom topologies of plain-line rectangles are physical infrastructure of the InPs. The home cloud {InP-1, SeP-1} has a cloud user, User-1. The home cloud {InP-3, SeP-3} has two cloud users, User-2 and User-3. The home cloud {InP-1, SeP-1} provides a virtual network {VN-A,VN-F} by borrowing a virtual network {VN-F} from foreign cloud {InP-3} to User-1. The home cloud {InP-3,SeP-3} provides virtual networks {VN-C,VN-D,VN-G} and {VN-B,VN-E} by borrowing the virtual networks {VN-C,VN-D} and {VN-B} to User-3 and User-2 respectively. The virtual machines are not shown in Figure 2 as the present work is concerned about virtual network infrastructure.

The virtual nodes and links are created by their respective InPs on receiving request from SePs. The virtual resources are managed by the users of SePs. The double-dot-dash and single-dot-dash line polygons show the boundary of SeP-1 and SeP-2 control respectively. The management of virtual resources is done by their respective users. In a nutshell, the various functions like virtual resource management, control and configuration are cooperatively performed by the three roles of the federation, so it is necessary to consider various security issues for proper functioning of the *federation*.

Horizontal IaaS federation security issues

To incorporate full network virtualization in *federation* ecosystem, the security issues of all constituents in the ecosystem must be investigated. The two components, *Brokers* and *an Exchange* out of three components of federation system are very similar to any brokered architecture [13] where the service/resources are leased using some kind of negotiation between service consumer and provider through the *Brokers* and *an Exchange*. So, the investigation of these two components are omitted.

Vaquero et al. [15] surveyed monolithic IaaS security issues related to virtual machines but it did not address the security issues related to network virtualization. In [7,11], the authors investigated *generic network virtualization* without security concerns. Bari et al. [12] reported the survey of datacenter network virtualization without security issues. In a nutshell, none of the existing work have concentrated on the security issues in network virtualization environment. We mainly focus on NVE security issues in monolithic IaaS cloud (Section 'Monolithic IaaS NVE security'), datacenter network (Section 'Datacenter NVE security'), generic network virtualization (Section 'Generic NVE security') and virtual resources (Section 'Virtual resources security') to incorporate full network virtualization in the federation.

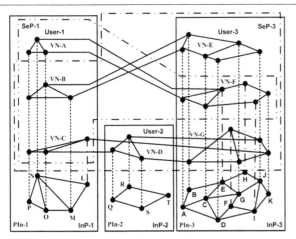

Figure 2 Horizontal IaaS federation. The figure shows an example of horizontal IaaS federation and boundary of security control.

A detailed discussion on the security requirements of *federation* ecosystem is beyond the scope of current investigation. A few security requirements of the federation are already explored in the constituents of federation ecosystem in the literature: (a) cloud security requirements [16], (b) network virtualization security requirements [17], (c) *cloud security alliance V3.0* [18], and (d) web security survey [19]. So we use following security requirements which are derived and extended from the literature [16-19].

- **R1** - Layered network architecture in which physical resources are controlled by InPs and virtual resources are transparently controlled by SePs.
- **R2** - Provide transparent view of virtual network infrastructure with a clear SLA (service level agreement) between SePs, InPs and cloud users.
- **R3** - Autonomous local identity management for physical resources used by InP.
- **R4** - Cooperative global identity management for virtual resources used by SeP and cloud users.
- **R5** - A brokered architecture between Br, InPs, SePs and cloud users for the collaboration of local and global identity management.
- **R6** - An access control mechanism to create, destroy virtual resources out of physical resources after the negotiation between InPs, SePs and cloud users.
- **R7** - An access control mechanism to manage and use virtual resources as per SLA between InPs, SePs and cloud users.
- **R8** - Intra-InP routing protocol with source authentication, operational confidentiality for cloud users within a InP.
- **R9** - Inter-InP routing protocol with source authentication, operational confidentiality and least information disclosure among InPs.
- **R10** - Tight collaboration among SePs and InPs in terms of fault handling, configuration, accounting, performance monitoring, trust negotiation and QoS.

Monolithic IaaS NVE security

As monolithic IaaS clouds are proprietary and a few technical documents are publicly available, so only two designs have been selected for the investigation of NVE security. Amazon *Elastic Cloud 2* (EC2) [20-22] and *GoGrid* [23] are the representatives of the most popular and a randomly selected IaaS cloud provider respectively.

The first representative, EC2 provides minimal network virtualization using either a software or hardware gateway to facilitate the communication between VPCs or virtual machines. A software gateway uses *route tables* as *software virtual router* while hardware gateway uses hardware router. Cisco integrated service routers and Juniper J-series are examples of software virtual routers. RTX 3000 is an example of hardware router. The EC2 uses *security groups* to provide the basic security services among the users. A *security group* acts as a virtual firewall to control the traffic allowed that is allowed into a group of virtual machines instances.

The second representative, GoGrid offers limited network service using a private switch to each private cloud. GoGrid also makes use of hardware firewall to protect the servers of private clouds. Xu et al. [24] proposed secured *wide area network* virtualization for virtual private cloud using tunnelling.

Datacenter NVE security

Cloud computing exploits datacenter for the provision of large data storage and network services with highly redundant data network and backup power supplies. We have thoroughly gone through the literature to find the limitation of NVE and its security services in the datacenters. The main aim of NVE provided in current datacenter is high utilization of its resources and not for any kind of network virtualization provision to its user. Md Faizaul Bari et al. [12] reported the survey of datacenter network virtualization without any security features. The first four datacenters (i.e., CloudNAS, Diverter, VICTOR and SEC2) provide security services in terms of *security components* and *security implementations* as shown in Table 1. The security implementation can be tunnelling, anti-spoofing, policy enforcement and visibility filters. The security components can be FE (Fowarding Element), CC (Central Controller), DPI or IDS. The CloudNAS supports full network virtualization but optional confidentiality and authentication using tunnelling.

The Diverter provisions network virtualization on the top of customized layer-3 network addressing. Each host has triplet ⟨f:s:h⟩ address where f is farm of hosts, s is subnet identifier and h is a particular host. The layer-3 triplet addresses are transparent to the tenants. Each host also runs VNET as distributed router in OS kernel-space. The VNET implements anti-spoofing and visibility filters to provide security services to tenants. The anti-spoofing filter prevents a VM impersonation by another VM. The visibility filter contains all network visibility rules to enforce separation between virtual machines. The tenants can use optional tunnelling for confidentiality.

The SEC2 and VICTOR have some common features. The network infrastructure of SEC2 as well as VICTOR is organized in two levels: a core domain and edge domains. An edge domain consists of physical hosts and switches. The core domain is made of a set of customized layer 2 switch called as Forwarding Element (FE) and Central Controller (CC). Central Controller (CC) controls the operation of FEs. FE performs two functions namely, (a) address lookup and mapping and (b) policy enforcement. The security service of SEC2 is made available through tunnelling or FEs. FEs can implement firewalls, NAT and

Table 1 Datacenter network virtualization security

Datacenter	Features	Security components	Network virtualization	Security implementation
CloudNAS [25]	Network Specification and embedding	Middlebox (Deep Packet Insepction - DPI or IDS)	Full NVE	Optional tunnelling
Diverter [26]	Multi-tenant virtual networks	VNET	Layer-3 distributed virtual routing	Anti-spoofing and visibility filters
VICTOR [27]	Dynamic VM migration	FE and CC	Set of distributed FEs	Policy enforcement
SEC2 [4]	Multi-tenancy network isolation	FE and CC	Set of distributed FEs	Policy enforcement, VPLS and MPLS
Gatekeeper [28]	Bandwidth performance isolation	-	Set of vNIC	-
NetShare [29]	Bandwidth guarantees and high utilization	-	Topology-driven	-
NetLord [30]	Flexible network abstraction	-	L2 and L3 encapsulation	-
Oktopus [31]	Virtual network abstractions provision	-	Assumption - physical mapping to virtual and oversubscribed cluster	-
PortLand [32]	VM migration, automatic switch configuration	-	L2 switching using hierarchical Pseudo MAC	-
SPAIN [33]	Multipath forwarding	-	Datacenter topology-driven	-
VL2 [34]	Performance isolation	-	AA(Application) and LA(Local) addressing	-

middleboxes. The remaining seven datacenters proposals have different aims but do not provide any security features as summarized in Table 1.

Generic NVE security

The existence of virtual network on the top of physical network may appear at any layers of OSI reference model. Consequently, there are mainly four types of network virtualization: (a) virtual local area network (VLAN), (b) virtual private network (VPN), (c) active and programmable network, and (d) overlay networks [11]. Some of the surveyed network virtualization projects using aforementioned types are not useful for the investigation of security issues. So we used three filtering criteria for the survey. The first, VLAN and VPN inherently provides security features to network virtualization environment using segmentation, isolation, tunnelling, IPSec and VLAN. Second, the main aim of some network virtualization projects (e.g. AKARI, CABO, 4WARD, Triology, and Clean-slate) is the design of next generation network. They are long-term projects; and are evolving and extending from another network virtualization projects like GENI and VINI. Third, the research in old network virtualization projects namely Genesis (is from Active and programmable network type) has been stopped. So the

network virtualization projects for security investigation after applying the three filtering criteria are GENI, Planet-Lab, UCLP, VINI and X-bone.

As per the security requirements of full network virtualization in *federation* given in Section 'Horizontal IaaS federation', we surveyed the network virtualization projects by classifying them under five categories: (a) identity management for resources, (b) authentication and trust management, (c) resource access control, (d) routing security issues; and (e) other security issues.

Identity management for resources

The digital identities for virtual resources in network virtualization environment give a provision of dynamic connectivity between virtual resources. An identity management for resources in network virtualization provides mechanisms for managing and gaining access to the resource's identity and information across organizational boundaries to SePs and InPs. Yuan et al. [35] classified the identity management models in three categories — isolated, centralized and federated — by considering various attributes. We will consider only four attributes — *the number of InPs, the number of SeP, user control over identity*, and *identities' storage* — as per the requirements, **R4** and **R5**. Table 2 shows the comparison of

Table 2 Identity management for resources: comparison

Project	No. of InPs	No. of SePs	User control	Identity storage
GENI [36]	Many	One	Yes	Decentralized
PlanetLab [37]	Many	One	Yes	Centralized
UCLP [38]	Many	Many	No	Decentralized
X-bone [39]	One	One	No	Centralized
NouVeau [40]	Many	Many	-	Decentralized

GENI, PlanetLab, UCLP, X-Bone and NouVeau using four attributes mentioned earlier. The roles from the projects are mapped to InP, SeP and cloud user so that it is easier to compare the projects.

The GENI have InPs (called as *Aggregates*) and SePs (called as research organizations). The users of research organization (i.e., SeP users) are called principal. The principal may be a researcher, principal investigator (which is an administrator) and slice admin. The virtual network instance is called slice and consists of objects. The GENI defines identifiers called GENI Global Identifiers (GGID) for all principal and objects in the system. The GENI uses X.509 certificate to represent GGID for authentication. In federated GENI system, an identity of an object in SeP is a union of identities stored across multiple InPs. The database of identity name-space is stored at the research organization's site and allows control by the principal.

The PlanetLab has three main roles: an owner, a user and PLC (PlanetLab Consortium). The owner (i.e., InP) supply physical nodes to create VMs. A service is installed on PlanetLab by a researcher (i.e., SeP). The PLC is a centralized entity and has mainly two functions: (a) manages physical resource and (b) maintains trust among owners and researchers. A slice is a collection of VMs. Each slice is uniquely identified by the hierarchical name where each level has the responsibility to manage and control the resources at that level. The PLC acts as slice authority and maintains state of all slices in the system.

The UCLP is the most promising project for *federation* in which the identities of virtual resources (e.g. LightPath, End2End object) is managed by *UCLP Admins* (SePs) and the identities of physical resources are managed by *network owners* (InPs). The UCLP end users cannot control UCLP virtual resources. The UCLP uses decentralized JavaSpace storage for the identities at InPs' sites. The overlay manager (SeP as well as InP) in X-bone manages the identity of virtual nodes at central repository. The X-bone user cannot control the identity of the virtual resources. The *NouVeau* is an identity management for a abstract network virtualization model and is similar to UCLP. It is based on three main principles: separation of identity and location, local autonomy, and global identifier space. It also requires special entities called controller and adapters for the managements of identities in SePs and InPs.

Authentication and trust management

A typical identity management has any of the three types of trust relationship between the service provider (SP) and identity provider (IdP) - pairwise, brokered and community trust models [41,42]. In network virtualization, SeP or InP may play a role as IdP and SP. The identity management may have any of the three trust relationships between SePs and/or InPs in network virtualization depending on the number of InPs and SePs. The PlanetLab, UCLP and X-bone uses PKI infrastructure (i.e., community trust) for authentication and trust management between SePs and InPs.

GENI uses a brokered trust model in which four entities namely clearinghouse, aggregates, research organization and researcher form a bilateral automatic trust negotiation [43-45] between them. The GENI is a decentralized system in which most of the times, a requester may not be from the same security domain (InP) for the authorization of resources. So, it uses attribute-based access control (ABAC) in which a request may be granted based on the characteristic of the requester's attributes. The negotiator contacts access mediator (i.e., GENI clearinghouse) to start bilateral negotiation (i.e., *automatic trust negotiation*). The negotiation is a sequence of credential exchange starting from non-sensitive credentials between negotiators. After successful negotiation, the request is granted to access the resource.

Resource access control

The authorization decision of an entity in a closed and open system about the resources is treated differently. So we divide the access control mechanism in two parts: local access control for a closed system and a global access control for the open system. The local access control performs the local authorization decision about the physical resources. The global access control performs the authorization decision of distributed virtual resources. We will compare three projects from academics and industry to know the status of resource access control in the network virtualization environment. Table 3 shows the access control mechanism used by the different projects.

The network *slices* of GENI are created out of physical network of *aggregates*. The aggregates are strangers to each other, so the GENI uses ABAC in which automatic trust negotiation is performed by exchanging

Table 3 Resource access control for network virtualization projects

Project	Physical resources	Virtual resources
GENI [36]	-	ABAC [43]
UCLP [38,46]	Switch management	MAC & DAC
X-bone [39]	ACL	ACL

sensitive credentials. ABAC authorizes the access to virtual resources using attribute *acknowledgement* (ACK) policies and *trust-target graph* (TTG) protocol. The ACK policy and TTG protocol perform attribute disclosure and resource access decisions respectively using directed graph.

The UCLP satisfies some requirements of **R6** and **R7** for physical and virtual network resources. The resource access control for UCLP physical resources is either implemented in the UCLP system, or an intermediate system between the UCLP and switch management. The UCLP system may use *mandatory access control* (MAC) or *discretionary access control* (DAC) for UCLP virtual resources. The UCLP supports three approaches for access control of UCLP virtual resources. The three approaches are traditional DAC, generic authorization-based distributed DAC and attributed-based distributed DAC. The first method performs all the evaluation of access and enforcement of policy in a centralized manner. The second method stores authorization information in different domains and performs the authorization process in multiple domains. The third method uses certificate-based system for authorization. The traditional DAC cannot make authorization of users in other domains. The second method is difficult to realize while the third approach is the easiest to implement.

X-bone system uses very simple access control mechanism for the authorization using ACL (access control list). It maintains the list of permission on the virtual resources for each user in the system. X-bone first checks the ACL for applicable entry to decide whether the requested operation is authorized based on subject and object identities.

Routing security issues

The user's virtual infrastructure of the SeP may be installed on an InP or a set of InPs in the *federation*. Similarly, the InP also collocates virtual networks from different SePs. The nature of the routing protocol used within InP and among InPs are totally different as per the security requirements, **R8** and **R9**. The routing protocol within InP for a set of SePs must provide *hop integrity*, *origin authentication* and *path validation*. The first three parameters are necessary for users' collocation of virtual networks in a InP. The fourth parameter provides least information disclosure and operational confidentiality of the virtual network installed on multiple InPs. The *hop integrity* of a routing protocol refers to the confidentiality between peers. The *origin authentication* is the authentication of a router. The *path validation* refers to the validity and authenticity of a received topological path. The *number of tenants* affects information leakage on the same physical network infrastructure. The routing protocol among InPs must provide control over the *information disclosure* and *routing basis*. The *routing basis* shows the

significance of name-space and/or identity used in the routing protocol. Table 4 shows the comparison of routing protocols for all the parameters mentioned above. We have mainly focussed our investigation on the protocols which gives some security features and upcoming virtual network routing.

The three variants of BGP namely S-BGP, IRV, and So-BGP provide security services in terms of - *PKI, address attestation* (a statement of delegation of identity), a special SECURITY message, or *IRV–Identity Request Server* with no provision for *information disclosure*. The minimum disclosure routing (MDR), routing on flat label (ROFL) and secure virtual trust routing (SVTR) are the upcoming routing protocols for virtual network in the field of *federation*. The MDR gives the minimum disclosure and operational confidentiality through the extension of Secure Multi-party Computation (SMC). The SMC reveals secret information among multiple parties using their individual secrets. The nodes of ROFL routing guarantees origin authentication and path validation using self-certification and access control mechanism respectively. SVTR is the only protocol that gives provision for multi-tenant collocation using *hop integrity*.

Basic security services

The network virtualization projects have components to perform the specific functions related to either management or security services. Any data traffic — plain or protocol related — transferred in the projects may provide basic security services like authentication, confidentiality etc. Table 5 shows the data traffic among the component(s) and/or resource(s) of the projects. We will use the convention - "Authentication | Confidentiality | Protocol" for brevity to describe the basic security services. The values for the convention are: A for Authentication, S for Confidentiality, $\sim$ for negation, * for all available protocols for data transmission. The communication between the components of GENI, PlanetLab and UCLP is secured and authenticated while X-bone does not use authenticated communication. All projects do not provide secured communication between the resources while GENI provides authenticated data transfer between them. X-bone does not provide authenticated communication between resources and components while all other projects provide authenticated communication. All projects provide secured data transfer either optional or compulsory.

Virtual resources security

The virtual resources for network virtualization in monolithic cloud are fully or partially implemented as software. We specifically focussed on virtual resources namely virtual routers, virtual switches and virtual links. Sections 'Virtual routers', 'Virtual switches', 'Virtual links' and 'Virtual resource migration' gives the detailed survey

Table 4 Routing security issues for horizontal IaaS federation

Routing protocol	Hop integrity	Origin authentication	Path validation	Information disclosure	Routing basis	No. of tenants
MDR [47]	IPSec	-	-	YES (SMC)	Location & identity	Single
ROFL [48]	-	Self certification	ACM	-	Flat-label	Single
SVTR [49]	Secured	-	-	NO (Privacy of attributes)	Flow-level	Multiple
S-BGP [50]	PKI	Address attestation	Address attestation	-	Location & identity	Single
IRV [51]	Secure transport	Source attestation	IRV server	-	Location & identity	Single
So-BGP [52]	SECURITY message	SECURITY message	SECURITY message	-	Location & identity	Single

of virtual resources in monolithic IaaS cloud and generic network virtualization.

Virtual routers

The virtualization of software routers called *virtual software routers* exploits processing power out of physical router or commodity hardware using NICs or NetFPGA. Juniper's *intelligent logical router* on the top of M-Series and T-Series routers are examples of virtual software routers [53]. The *intelligent logical router* supports customized policy control, protocol assignment, configuration but no on-the-fly configuration and administration. It also does not support source authentication. Most of *virtual software routers* from monolithic cloud including Amazon EC2 use *route tables*. The *route table* maintains network filtering policy and are managed by VPC network administrator. The EC2 also uses *security groups* which offer secured virtual network isolation among cloud users.

The router has two modules: *control plane* and *data plane*. The control plane performs the function of routing and maintains routing table. The data plane performs the function of packet forwarding. All the router architectures using the combination of data and control plane proposed by Pisa et al. concentrates on performance in terms of delay [54]. The VROOM [55,56] router architecture also concentrates on the performance in terms of delay using control plane virtualization. Table 6 classifies the literature in two areas. First six literatures give the proposal of the router. The remaining gives the performance evaluation of *virtual software routers*. It is found that all *virtual software routers* provide physical or logical isolation to improve the performance but no specific security services. Some software routers on commodity

hardware are implemented with general-purpose workstations [57-62]. The proposals for router design aim at low-cost and moderate-performance solutions and have no security provision.

Virtual switches

The virtual switches can be broadly divided into *hypervisor-based* or *hardware-based* depending on the location of the implementation of virtual switches. The hypervisor-based virtual switches are typically written entirely in software. The hardware-based virtual switch is partly implemented on special hardware like NIC, NetF-PGA etc. The basis of hypervisor-based virtual switch is Open vSwitch [71]. Open vSwitch resides within the management domain of hypervisor (e.g. Domain-0 in Xen) and provides connectivity between virtual machines and physical interfaces. Open vSwitch uses VLANs and GRE tunnels for secured virtual network and virtual path respectively. It also supports basic ACL.

Hardware-based virtual switch eliminates some limitations (like CPU or memory usage) of software-based virtual switch. Two hardware-based virtual switch implementations are *Virtual Ethernet Port Aggregator* (VEPA) [72] and VNTag [73]. The Virtual Ethernet Port Aggregator (VEPA) is a standardization led by HP Extreme, IBM, Brocade and Juniper etc. The VEPA allows traffic of VM to exit and re-enter the same port to enable switching among VMs. The VEPA has *MACSec* scheme to provision a secure connection between VEPA and bridges.

Tseng et al. [74] proposed the integration of open-source hypervisor with software-based virtual switch and aims at secure network environment among VMs.

Table 5 Basic security services of network virtualization projects

Project	Resource-Component	Component-Component	Resource-Resources
GENI [36]	A | ~S | SSL	A | S | SSL	A | ~S | *
PlanetLab [37]	A | S | SSL	A | S | SSL	~A | ~S | *
UCLP [38]	A | S | (SSL/JINI)	A | S | (SSL & JINI)	~A | ~S | *
X-bone [39]	~A | (S/~S) | (UDP/UDP-S/TCP/TCP-SSL)	~A | S | (UDP-S/TCP-SSL)	~A | ~S | *

* indicates all available protocols for data transmission.

Table 6 Commodity and physical virtual routers' control plane properties

Hardware type	Virtualization type	Control plane (Routing table)	Performance	Isolation	Migration	Flexibility
Commodity-Intel IXP2400 [58]	Pattern tables	L3VR and L3/4VR	×	✓	-	✓
Commodity-Click [63]	Trie braiding	Shared trie	✓	-	-	-
Commodity-FPGA [64]	Hybrid DS	TCAM/SRAM	-	✓	-	-
Commodity [65]	PEARL	NetFPGA & TCAM	✓	✓	-	✓
Commodity-NetFPGA [56]	VROOM	Software & hardware	✓	✓	✓	✓
Simulation [66]	-	Trie braiding	-	-	×	×
Commodity [67]	Container-based	Guest OS	Evaluation(OpenVZ,LinuxNamespace) (OpenVZ,LinuxNamespace)	-	-	-
Commodity [68]	Hypervisor-based	Guest OS	Evaluation(SR,VSR)	-	-	-
Commodity [69]	Hypervisor-based	Guest OS	Evaluation(1,2,4 flows)	-	-	-
Commodity [70]	Container-based	Application	✓	×	×	×
	Hypervisor-based	Guest OS	✓	×	×	×
	Hypervisor-NIC mapping	Guest OS	✓	✓	×	×
	Hypervisor-Host OS	Guest OS	×	✓	✓	✓

× indicates the property doesn't exist for the router.
√ indicates the property exist for the router.

Luo et al. [75] proposed hardware-based virtual switch using special NIC to provide network connectivity among VMs in the datacenter.

Virtual links

The virtual links can be created using either *signalling protocol* or *encapsulation*. The virtual link setup protocol (VLSP) is an example of signalling protocol to create the virtual links. The encapsulation-based virtual link creation in the literature are *Virtual Tunnel (VTun), Layer Two Tunnelling Protocol - V3 (L2TPV3), Generic Routing Encapsulation (GRE)* and *IP in IP Tunnelling (IIP)*.

Roland Bless et al. [76] proposed VLSP to create authenticated and secured virtual link using NSIS authorization [77] and secured signalling [78] protocols. It also provides QoS as per user's requirement for link creation. The L2TPV3 [79] encapsulation protocol creates tunnel between nodes at layer 2. It does not inherently provide authentication and encryption but IPSec can be used for security provision. The VTun is a virtual link implementation over various kinds of tunnels (e.g. Ethernet, serial tunnel, pipe tunnel) and; provides security services like authentication, compression and encryption etc. [80]. The GRE [81] encapsulation protocol is used to create a virtual link between two nodes using an additional header in the packet called *delivery header* without any security features. The IIP [82] link creation protocol has a packet format consisting of the outer header, security header, original header and IP payload. The security header adds optional security services using IPSec.

Virtual resource migration

As network virtualization is new emerging field, there is few literature on some important field like the migration of virtual router and link etc. Chen et al. uses VROOM [56] router architecture to provide energy-saving IP-WDM network architecture [83] by the process of virtual router migration. All the router architecture proposals and their migration methods using the combination of data and control plane proposed by Pisa et al. concentrates on performance in terms of delay [54]. The full virtual network migration including virtual machines is proposed by Keller et al [84]. All the literature concentrate on virtual resource migration without any security concerns. The virtual link migration suggested by Pisa et al does not provide any security services.

Research directions

All domains surveyed in the paper lacks network virtualization and/or its security provision. Most of network virtualization projects are meant for scientific purpose where the performance is major concern so the focus of the projects are collocation of SePs' networks on InPs' physical network without any security concerns. Similarly, datacenters do not exploit full network virtualization and facilitates minimum security services in terms of VLAN or VPN technology. The virtual resources lack very basic level of security services. As a result of aforementioned shortcomings, we will discuss NVE security issues for *federation* and give few research directions. The research directions are classified as: (a) router architecture (b) datacenter NVE security, (c) resource identity management, (d) resource access control and (e) intra-InP and inter-InP routing.

Router architecture

All the router architectures using the combination of data and control plane concentrates on performance in terms of delay. The control plane as well as data plane virtualization allows best-effort memory utilization but may promote confidentiality threat due to the collocation of multiple SePs' virtual routers on the same physical router. The *software virtual routers* on commodity as well as physical router lacks source authentication, remote configuration using SeP's access control as shown in Table 6. The source authentication, remote configuration and access control mechanism are basic requirements (**R6-R10**) to perform inter-InP and intra-InP routing by the *software virtual routers*. By adding the above functionality, we pose few research questions like: What will be the impact on router performance in terms of packet-delay? What is the maximum number of tenants' virtual software routers that can coexist on a physical router without degrading the performance? How the router virtualization handles intra-InP and inter-InP routing by considering the collocation of tenants' virtual networks? How the virtual router migration be handle by this architecture?

Datacenter NVE security

The most promising datacenter network virtualization architecture for the *federation* is SEC2 [4] which supports basic security services like source authentication, transparent network management etc., but does not support full network virtualization (requirements **R1** and **R2**). The network isolation among customers of CloudNAS can be compromised if hypervisors, switches, or middleboxes are compromised [4]. The customized devices like FEs or CCs may expose MAC address of host and VM [30]. No datacenter supports federation of virtual resources (requirement **R10**), full NVE (requirements **R1-R2**) and resource access control (requirements **R6** and **R7**). All datacenter network virtualization projects support minimum security services using VLAN, L2/L3 addressing or special routing devices (e.g. FE, CC etc.) as shown in Table 1. The datacenter also do not permit *transparent network management* (requirement **R2**), user-level policy control and resource access control (requirements **R6** and **R7**) required for the *federation*.

Resource identity management

Table 2 shows that there is no identity management which provides the feature of multiple InPs and SePs (requirement **R5**), user's control over identities (requirement **R4**) and decentralized storage. We used the generic term *user control* to mean various operations on virtual

resources e.g., creation of virtual link, configuration of virtual resource etc. The UCLP project shows some potential towards the design of an identity management for *federation* but lacks users' control over identities (requirement **R4**). The *federation* requires federated identity management, so a trust between InPs and/or SePs must be established to gain the control over the requested resources automatically on-the-fly. So, the *federation* needs the identity management with automated trust negotiation (requirement **R10**). We must also address the following research question related to resource identity management: How to map heterogeneous address space of resources in datacenters to local and global identity namespace?

Resource access control

The trivial resource access control for horizontal IaaS federation requires user-controlled access control mechanism (requirement **R7**) at virtual infrastructure and *mandatory access control* (requirement **R6**) at physical infrastructure. The GENI does not provide any kind of resource access control over the physical resources while virtual resources are managed in terms of *Trust-Target Graph* protocol of ABAC (requirement **R7**). The UCLP provisions MAC or DAC at virtual infrastructure level but it does not fulfil the requirement at physical level. X-bone uses ACL, a simplest access control management of resources. Some research questions related to resource access control are: Where should be the placement of resource access controls in physical resources? If the location of access control is in *control plane* of physical resource; and distributed among InPs and SePs, how would they interact? What would be *bandwidth-delay product* performance of physical as well as virtual network infrastructures after deploying resource access controls?

Intra-InP and Inter-InP routing

Keller et al. [85] and Fukushima et al. [47] open up theoretical research directions for intra-InP and inter-InP routing respectively. The inter-InP routing should not disclose routing information to InPs other than intended InPs (i.e *minimum disclosure*) and also provide operational confidentiality in routing process. MDR offers both *minimum disclosure* and operational confidentiality among InPs but does not provide other properties mentioned in Table 4. The intra-InP and inter-InP routing should possess the security requirements, **R6** and **R7** with the consideration of tenants' virtual network collocation. We pose the following research questions for routing process in the *federation* by including aforementioned security requirements: How the router maintains *routing table* using intra-InP and inter-InP routing? How the information (i.e., packets) of different virtual networks of cloud users are separated? How the router will forward the packets of different virtual networks without exposing or compromising?

Conclusions

With the motivation of adding full network virtualization in horizontal IaaS federation, we investigated network virtualization security in four areas: monolithic IaaS cloud, generic network virtualization, datacenter network virtualization and virtual resources. We presented the qualitative comparisons of *generic network virtualization projects*, datacenters, routing protocols and virtual resources from aforementioned areas. Our qualitative comparisons show the following important insights related to network virtualization and security issues in horizontal IaaS federation. The monolithic IaaS clouds do not support full network virtualization but give minimal network virtualization to offer the connectivity of virtual networks or virtual machines. The simple security services are offered in terms of VLAN, VPN or tunnelling for the collocation of multiple tenants in monolithic IaaS clouds. The datacenters lack both full network virtualization and basic security services for the horizontal IaaS federation. The network virtualization projects offer full network virtualization but partial security provisions in terms of one or more services of identity management, resource access control and trust management. The router architectures mostly focus on the performance of virtual software routers and do not add any security features for the collocation of tenants networks. The virtual switches cannot have more than 4K VLANs. This paper shows that the virtual links can be created using either signalling protocol or encapsulation. The encapsulation-based virtual link has an extra overhead of encapsulation on the top of L2/L3 protocols but give *hop integrity* security service. The signalling-based virtual link offers various security services like *origin authentication, hop integrity* and *path validation*. The research challenges mentioned in Section 'Research directions' are crucial to the success of horizontal IaaS federation in cloud computing.

Competing interests
The authors declare that they have no competing interests.

Authors' contributions
All the listed authors made substantive intellectual contributions to the research work and manuscript. AVN formally defined the network virtualization for horizontal IaaS federation. He and SKG investigated the domains presented in the manuscript. SKG was responsible for the overall technical approach and edited the paper. Both authors read and approved the final manuscript.

References
1. Celesti A, Tusa F, Villari M, Puliafito A (2010) How to enhance cloud architectures to enable cross-federation. In: Cloud Computing (CLOUD), 2010 IEEE 3rd international conference on. IEEE, Miami, pp 337–345
2. Armbrust M, Fox A, Griffith R, Joseph AD, Katz R, Konwinski A, Lee G, Patterson D, Rabkin A, Stoica I, Zaharia M (2010) A view of cloud computing. Commun ACM 53(4): 50–58. http://doi.acm.org/10.1145/1721654.1721672
3. Zhang Z, Zhang X (2009) Realization of open cloud computing federation based on mobile agent. In: Intelligent computing and intelligent systems, 2009. ICIS 2009. IEEE international conference on, Volume 3. IEEE, Shanghai, pp 642–646
4. Hao F, Lakshman TV, Mukherjee S, Song H (2010) Secure cloud computing with a virtualized network infrastructure. In: Proceedings of the 2nd USENIX conference on Hot topics in cloud computing, HotCloud'10. USENIX Association, Berkeley, pp 16–16. http://dl.acm.org/citation.cfm?id=1863103.1863119
5. Berger S, Cáceres R, Goldman K, Pendarakis D, Perez R, Rao JR, Rom E, Sailer R, Schildhauer W, Srinivasan D, Tal S, Valdez E (2009) Security for the cloud infrastructure: trusted virtual data center implementation. IBM J Res Dev 53(4): 560–571. http://dl.acm.org/citation.cfm?id=1850659.1850665
6. Berger S, Cáceres R, Pendarakis D, Sailer R, Valdez E, Perez R, Schildhauer W, Srinivasan D (2008) TVDc: managing security in the trusted virtual datacenter. SIGOPS Oper Syst Rev 42: 40–47. http://doi.acm.org/10.1145/1341312.1341321
7. Chowdhury N, Boutaba R (2009) Network virtualization: state of the art and research challenges. Commun Mag IEEE 47(7): 20–26
8. Fan P, Chen Z, Wang J, Zheng Z, Lyu M (2012) Topology-aware deployment of scientific applications in cloud computing. In: Cloud Computing (CLOUD), 2012 IEEE 5th international conference on. IEEE, Honolulu, pp 319–326
9. Chae Y, Merugu S, Zegura E, Bhattacharjee S (2000) Exposing the network: support for topology-sensitive applications. In: Open Architectures and Network Programming, 2000. Proceedings. OPENARCH 2000. 2000 IEEE Third Conference on. IEEE, Tel, Aviv, pp 65–74
10. Celesti A, Tusa F, Villari M, Puliafito A (2010) Three-phase cross-cloud federation model: the cloud SSO authentication. In: Advances in Future Internet (AFIN), 2010 second international conference on. IEEE, Venice, pp 94–101
11. Chowdhury NMK, Boutaba R (2010) A survey of network virtualization. Comput Netw 54(5): 862–876. http://dx.doi.org/10.1016/j.comnet.2009.10.017
12. Bari M, Boutaba R, Esteves R, Granville L, Podlesny M, Rabbani M, Zhang Q, Zhani M (2012) Data center network virtualization: a survey. Commun Surv Tutorials, IEEE PP(99): 1–20
13. Buyya R, Ranjan R, Calheiros RN (2010) InterCloud: utility-oriented federation of cloud computing environments for scaling of application services. In: Proceedings of the 10th international conference on algorithms and architectures for parallel processing - Volume Part I, ICA3PP'10. Springer-Verlag, Berlin, Heidelberg, pp 13–31. http://dx.doi.org/10.1007/978-3-642-13119-6_2
14. Matias J, Jacob E, Sanchez D, Demchenko Y (2011) An OpenFlow based network virtualization framework for the cloud. In: Cloud Computing Technology and Science (CloudCom), 2011 IEEE Third International Conference on. IEEE, Athens, pp 672–678
15. Vaquero LM, Rodero-Merino L, Morán D (2011) Locking the sky: a survey on IaaS cloud security. Computing 91: 93–118. http://dx.doi.org/10.1007/s00607-010-0140-x
16. Iankoulova I, Daneva M (2012) Cloud computing security requirements: A systematic review. In: Research Challenges in Information Science (RCIS), 2012 sixth international conference on, pp 1–7
17. Natarajan S, Wolf T (2012) Security issues in network virtualization for the future Internet. In: Computing, Networking and Communications (ICNC), 2012 international conference on, pp 537–543
18. Security Guidance for Critical Areas of Focus in Cloud Computing V3.0, Cloud Security Alliance. Tech. rep. 2011. https://cloudsecurityalliance.org/guidance/csaguide.v3.0.pdf
19. Rubin A, Geer JDE (1998) A survey of Web security. Computer 31(9): 34–41
20. Onisick J (2012) Access Layer Network Virtualization: VN-Tag and VEPA. http://wikibon.org/wiki/v/Edge_Virtual_Bridging
21. Amazon Virtual Private Cloud Network - Administrator Guide. Tech. rep. 2012. http://awsdocs.s3.amazonaws.com/VPC/latest/vpc-nag.pdf
22. Amazon Virtual Private Cloud - User Guide. Tech. rep. 2012. http://awsdocs.s3.amazonaws.com/VPC/latest/vpc-ug.pdf
23. GoGrid - Getting Started Guide L-20121018. Tech. rep. 2012. http://storage.pardot.com/3442/103057/WP_Getting_Started_L_20121018.pdf

24. Xu Z, Di S, Zhang W, Cheng L, Wang CL (2011) WAVNet: Wide-area network virtualization technique for virtual private cloud. In: Parallel Processing (ICPP), 2011 international conference on, pp 285–294

25. Benson T, Akella A, Shaikh A, Sahu S (2011) CloudNaaS: a cloud networking platform for enterprise applications. In: Proceedings of the 2nd ACM symposium on cloud computing, SOCC '11. ACM, New York, pp 8:1–8:13. http://doi.acm.org/10.1145/2038916.2038924

26. Edwards A, Fischer A, Lain A (2009) Diverter: a new approach to networking within virtualized infrastructures. In: Proceedings of the 1st ACM workshop on Research on enterprise networking, WREN '09. ACM, New York, pp 103–110. http://doi.acm.org/10.1145/1592681.1592698

27. Hao F, Lakshman TV, Mukherjee S, Song H (2010) Enhancing dynamic cloud-based services using network virtualization. SIGCOMM Comput Commun Rev 40: 67–74. http://doi.acm.org/10.1145/1672308.1672322

28. Rodrigues H, Santos JR, Turner Y, Soares P, Guedes D (2011) Gatekeeper: supporting bandwidth guarantees for multi-tenant datacenter networks. In: Proceedings of the 3rd conference on I/O virtualization, WIOV'11. USENIX Association, Berkeley, pp 6–6. http://dl.acm.org/citation.cfm?id=2001555.2001561

29. Lam T, Vahdat A, Radhakrishnan S, Varghese G (2010) NetShare: Virtualizing Data Center Networks across Services. Tech. rep., Microsoft Research Lab. http://research.microsoft.com/apps/video/dl.aspx?id=132892

30. Mudigonda J, Yalagandula P, Mogul J, Stiekes B, Pouffary Y (2011) NetLord: a scalable multi-tenant network architecture for virtualized datacenters. SIGCOMM Comput Commun Rev 41(4): 62–73. http://doi.acm.org/10.1145/2043164.2018444

31. Ballani H, Costa P, Karagiannis T, Rowstron A (2011) Towards predictable datacenter networks. SIGCOMM Comput Commun Rev 41(4): 242–253. http://doi.acm.org/10.1145/2043164.2018465

32. Niranjan Mysore R, Pamboris A, Farrington N, Huang N, Miri P, Radhakrishnan S, Subramanya V, Vahdat A (2009) PortLand: a scalable fault-tolerant layer 2 data center network fabric. SIGCOMM Comput Commun Rev 39(4): 39–50. http://doi.acm.org/10.1145/1594977.1592575

33. Mudigonda J, Yalagandula P, Al-Fares M, Mogul JC (2010) SPAIN: COTS data-center Ethernet for multipathing over arbitrary topologies. In: Proceedings of the 7th USENIX conference on Networked systems design and implementation, NSDI'10. USENIX Association, Berkeley, pp 18–18. http://dl.acm.org/citation.cfm?id=1855711.1855729

34. Greenberg A, Hamilton JR, Jain N, Kandula S, Kim C, Lahiri P, Maltz DA, Patel P, Sengupta S (2009) VL2: a scalable and flexible data center network. SIGCOMM Comput Commun Rev 39(4): 51–62. http://doi.acm.org/10.1145/1594977.1592576

35. Cao Y, Yang L (2010) A survey of identity management technology. In: Information Theory and Information Security (ICITIS), 2010 IEEE international conference on. IEEE, Beijing, pp 287–293

36. GENI Security Architecture, Global Environment for Network Innovations. Tech. rep. http://groups.geni.net/geni/attachment/wiki/GENISecurity/GENI-SEC-ARCH-0.4.pdf

37. Peterson L, Roscoe T, Muir S, Klingaman A (2006) PlanetLab architecture: an overview. Tech. rep., PlanetLab Consortium

38. Hulsebosch B, Groote R, Snijders J (2009) Secure user-controlled lightpath provisioning with user-controlled identity management. In: Proceedings of the 3rd international conference on autonomous infrastructure, management and security: scalability of networks and services, AIMS '09. Springer-Verlag, Berlin, Heidelberg, pp 1–14. http://dx.doi.org/10.1007/978-3-642-02627-0_1

39. Clem J, MacAlpine T, Badgett B (2003) X-Bone: Automated System for Deployment and Management of Network Overlays Security Assessment Report. Tech. rep., Information Design Assurance Red Team, Sandia National Laboratories, P. O. Box 5800, Albuquerque, NM 87185-0784, 2003. http://www.isi.edu/xbone/pubs/xbone_security_assessment.pdf

40. Chowdhury N, Zaheer FE, Boutaba R (2009) iMark: An identity management framework for network virtualization environment. In: Integrated Network Management, 2009. IM '09. IFIP/IEEE International Symposium on. IEEE, Long Island, pp 335–342

41. Bhargav-Spantzel A, Squicciarini A, Bertino E (2007) Trust negotiation in identity management. Secur Privacy, IEEE 5(2): 55–63

42. Zhang P, Durresi A, Barolli L (2011) Survey of trust management on various networks. In: Complex, Intelligent and Software Intensive Systems

(CISIS), 2011 international conference on. IEEE Computer Society, Seoul, pp 219–226

43. Winsborough W, Jacobs J (2003) Automated trust negotiation technology with attribute-based access control. In: DARPA Information Survivability Conference and Exposition, 2003. Proceedings, Volume 2. IEEE Computer Society, Los Alamitos, pp 60–62

44. Li N, Winsborough W (2002) Towards practical automated trust negotiation. In: Proceedings of the 3rd international workshop on policies for distributed systems and networks (POLICY'02), POLICY '02. IEEE Computer Society, Washington, p 92. http://dl.acm.org/citation.cfm?id=863632.883493

45. Winsborough WH, Li N (2002) Protecting sensitive attributes in automated trust negotiation. In: Proceedings of the 2002 ACM workshop on Privacy in the Electronic Society, WPES '02. ACM, NY, pp 41–51. http://doi.acm.org/10.1145/644527.644532

46. Chen J (2004) UCLP Security. Tech. rep., School of Information Technology and Engineering University of Ottawa. www.uclp.ca/files/uclp1.x/Report-UCLP-Security.pdf

47. Fukushima M, Hasegawa T, Hasegawa T, Nakao A (2011) Minimum disclosure routing for network virtualization. In: Computer communications workshops (INFOCOM WKSHPS), 2011 IEEE Conference on. IEEE, Shanghai, pp 858–863

48. Caesar M, Condie T, Kannan J, Lakshminarayanan K, Stoica I (2006) ROFL: routing on flat labels. SIGCOMM Comput Commun Rev 36(4): 363–374. http://doi.acm.org/10.1145/1151659.1159955

49. Huang D, Ata S, Medhi D (2010) Establishing secure virtual trust routing and provisioning domains for future internet. In: Global telecommunications conference (GLOBECOM 2010), 2010 IEEE. IEEE, Miami, pp 1–6

50. Kent S, Lynn C, Seo K (2000) Secure Border Gateway Protocol (S-BGP). Selected Areas Commun, IEEE J 18(4): 582–592

51. Goodell G, Aiello W, Griffin T, Ioannidis J, McDaniel P, Rubin A (2003) Working around BGP: an incremental approach to improving security and accuracy of interdomain routing. In: In Proc. NDSS. Internet Society, San Diego

52. Ng J (2002) Extensions to BGP to Support Secure Origin BGP (soBGP). Tech. rep., IETF. http://tools.ietf.org/pdf/draft-ng-sobgp-bgp-extensions-00.txt

53. Kolon M (2004) Intelligent Logical Router Service. Tech. rep., Juniper Networks. http://netscreen.com/solutions/literature/white_papers/200097.pdf

54. Pisa P, Fernandes N, Carvalho H, Moreira M, Campista M, Costa L, Duarte O (2010) OpenFlow and Xen-Based Virtual Network Migration. In: Pont A, Pujolle G, Raghavan S (eds) Communications: wireless in developing countries and networks of the future, Volume 327 of IFIP advances in information and communication technology. Springer, Berlin, Heidelberg, pp 170–181. http://dx.doi.org/10.1007/978-3-642-15476-8_17

55. Layer 3 Virtual Switching - Integrated Virtual Routing with Multi-Layer Switching. Tech. rep., Extreme Networks, Inc 2006. http://www.extremenetworks.com/libraries/whitepapers/WPL3Virtual_1185.pdf

56. Wang Y, Keller E, Biskeborn B, van der Merwe J, Rexford J (2008) Virtual routers on the move: live router migration as a network-management primitive. SIGCOMM Comput Commun Rev 38(4): 231–242. http://doi.acm.org/10.1145/1402946.1402985

57. Rus A, Barabas M, Boanea G, Dobrota V (2010) Implementation of QoS-Aware virtual routers. In: Electronics and Telecommunications (ISETC), 2010 9th International Symposium on, pp 161–164

58. Comer D, Martynov M (2006) Building experimental virtual routers with network processors. In: Testbeds and Research Infrastructures for the Development of Networks and Communities, 2006. TRIDENTCOM 2006. 2nd International Conference on. IEEE, Barcelona, pp 9–230

59. Bianco A, Birke R, Bolognesi D, Finochietto J, Galante G, Mellia M, Prashant M, Neri F (2005) Click vs. Linux: two efficient open-source IP network stacks for software routers. In: High performance switching and routing, 2005. HPSR. 2005 workshop on. IEEE, Hong Kong, pp 18–23

60. Dobrescu M, Egi N, Argyraki K, Chun BG, Fall K, Iannaccone G, Knies A, Manesh M, Ratnasamy S (2009) RouteBricks: exploiting parallelism to scale software routers. In: Proceedings of the ACM SIGOPS 22nd symposium on Operating systems principles, SOSP '09. ACM, New York, pp 15–28

61. Karlin S, Peterson L (2001) VERA: an extensible router architecture. In: Open architectures and network programming proceedings, 2001 IEEE, pp 3–14

62. Spalink T, Karlin S, Peterson L, Gottlieb Y (2011) Building a robust software-based router using network processors. SIGOPS Oper Syst Rev 35(5): 216–229. http://doi.acm.org/10.1145/502059.502056

63. Fu J, Rexford J (2008) Efficient IP-address lookup with a shared forwarding table for multiple virtual routers. In: Proceedings of the 2008 ACM CoNEXT Conference, CoNEXT '08. ACM, New York, pp 21:1–21:12. http://doi.acm.org/10.1145/1544012.1544033

64. Erdem O, Le H, Prasanna V, Bazlamacci C (2011) Hybrid data structure for IP lookup in virtual routers using FPGAs. In: Application-Specific Systems, Architectures and Processors (ASAP), 2011 IEEE international conference on. IEEE, Santa Monica, pp 95–102

65. Xie G, He P, Guan H, Li Z, Xie Y, Luo L, Zhang J, Wang Y, Salamatian K (2011) PEARL: a programmable virtual router platform. Commun Mag, IEEE 49(7): 71–77

66. Song H, Kodialam M, Hao F, Lakshman T (2010) Building scalable virtual routers with trie braiding. In: INFOCOM, 2010 proceedings IEEE. IEEE, San Diego, pp 1–9

67. Rathore M, Hidell M, Sjodin P (2010) Performance evaluation of open virtual routers. In: GLOBECOM workshops (GC Wkshps), 2010 IEEE. IEEE, Miami, pp 288–293

68. Rojas-Cessa R, Salehin K, Egoh K (2011) Experimental performance evaluation of a virtual software router. In: Local Metropolitan Area Networks (LANMAN), 2011 18th IEEE Workshop on. IEEE, Chapel Hill, pp 1–2

69. Rojas-Cessa R, Salehin K, Egoh K (2012) Evaluation of switching performance of a virtual software router. In: Sarnoff symposium (SARNOFF), 2012 35th IEEE. IEEE, Newark, pp 1–5

70. Bourguiba M, Haddadou K, Pujolle G (2010) Evaluating the forwarding plane performance of the commodity hardware virtual routers. In: Communications and Networking (ComNet), 2010 second international conference on. IEEE, Tozeur, pp 1–8

71. Pfaff B, Koponen T, Amidon K, Casado M, Pettit J, Shenker S (2009) Extending networking into the virtualization layer. In: 8th ACM Workshop on Hot Topics in Networks (HotNets-VIII). ACM SIGCOMM, NY

72. Congdon P (2008) Virtual Ethernet Port Aggregator Standards Body Discussion. http://www.ieee802.org/1/files/public/docs2008/new-congdon-vepa-1108-v01.pdf

73. Pelissier J (2008) VNTag 101. http://www.ieee802.org/1/files/public/docs2009/new-pelissier-vntag-seminar-0508.pdf

74. Tseng HM, Lee HL, Hu JW, Liu TL, Chang JG, Huang WC (2011) Network virtualization with cloud virtual switch. In: Parallel and Distributed Systems (ICPADS), 2011 IEEE 17th international conference on. IEEE, Tainan, pp 998–1003

75. Luo Y (2010) Network I/O virtualization for cloud computing. IT Prof 12(5): 36–41

76. Bless R, Rohricht M, Werle C (2011) Authenticated setup of virtual links with quality-of-service guarantees. In: Computer Communications and Networks (ICCCN), 2011 proceedings of 20th international conference on. IEEE, Maui, pp 1–8

77. Manner J, Tschofenig H, Bless R, Stiemerling M (2001) Authorization for NSIS Signaling Layer Protocols. RFC5981. Internet Engineering Task Force. https://tools.ietf.org/html/rfc5981

78. Bless R, Röhricht M (2009) Secure signaling in next generation networks with NSIS. In: Proceedings of the 2009 IEEE international conference on Communications, ICC'09. IEEE Press, Piscataway, pp 2156–2161. http://dl.acm.org/citation.cfm?id=1817271.1817673

79. Lau J, Townsley M, Goyret I (2005) Layer Two Tunneling Protocol - Version 3 (L2TPv3). RFC3931. Internet Engineering Task Force. http://www.ietf.org/rfc/rfc3931.txt

80. VTun - Virtual Tunnels over TCP/IP networks. Tech. rep. http://vtun.sourceforge.net/tun/

81. Farinacci D, Li T, Hanks S, Meyer D, Traina P (2000) Generic Routing Encapsulation (GRE). RFC2784. Internet Engineering Task Force. www.ietf.org/rfc/rfc2784.txt

82. Simpson W (1995) IP in IP Tunneling. RFC1853. Internet Engineering Task Force. http://www.ietf.org/rfc/rfc1853.txt

83. Chen X, Phillips C (2012) Virtual router migration and infrastructure sleeping for energy management of IP over WDM networks. In: Telecommunications and Multimedia (TEMU), 2012 International Conference on, pp 31–36

84. Keller E, Ghorbani S, Caesar M, Rexford J (2012) Live migration of an entire network (and its hosts). In: Proceedings of the 11th ACM Workshop on Hot Topics in Networks, HotNets-XI. ACM, New York, pp 109–114. http://doi.acm.org/10.1145/2390231.2390250

85. Keller E, Lee RB, Rexford J (2009) Accountability in hosted virtual networks. In: Proceedings of the 1st ACM workshop on Virtualized infrastructure systems and architectures, VISA '09. ACM, New York, pp 29–36. http://doi.acm.org/10.1145/1592648.1592654

Fine-grained preemption analysis for latency investigation across virtual machines

Mohamad Gebai*, Francis Giraldeau and Michel R Dagenais

Abstract

This paper studies the preemption between programs running in different virtual machines on the same computer. One of the current monitoring methods consist of updating the average steal time through collaboration with the hypervisor. However, the average is insufficient to diagnose abnormal latencies in time-sensitive applications. Moreover, the added latency is not directly visible from the virtual machine point of view. The main challenge is to recover the cause of preemption of a task running in a virtual machine, whether it is a task on the host computer or in another virtual machine.

We propose a new method to study thread preemption crossing virtual machines boundaries using kernel tracing. The host computer and each monitored virtual machine are traced simultaneously. We developed an efficient and portable trace synchronization method, which is required to account for time offset and drift that occur within each virtual machine. We then devised an algorithm to recover the root cause of preemption between threads at every level. The algorithm successfully detected interactions between multiple competing threads in distinct virtual machines on a multi-core machine.

Keywords: Virtual machine; Tracing; KVM; LTTng; Performance; CPU

Introduction

Cloud environments present advantages of increased flexibility and reduced maintenance cost through resource sharing and server consolidation [1]. However, virtual machines (VMs, or guests) on the same host computer may compete for shared resources, introducing undesirable latency. Previous study found that jitter impacts response time of programs on popular commercial cloud environment [2]. In cloud environments, virtual machines have the illusion of absolute and exclusive control over the physical resources. However, the host's resources are more often than not overcommitted, whereas they appear to guest operating systems as being more available than they actually are [3]. As a result, virtual machines on the same host computer may interfere with each other without their knowledge, inducing invisible yet real latency.

The diagnosis is more complex when the guest is isolated from its external environment and an additional virtualization layer is introduced. It is therefore necessary

*Correspondence: mohamad.gebai@polymtl.ca
Department of Computer and Software Engineering, Polytechnique Montreal, 2900 Boulevard Edouard-Montpetit, Montreal, QC H3T 1J4, Canada

to have powerful and efficient tools to diagnose the root cause of unexpected delays at low granularity when they occur in a virtualized environment. To our knowledge, no such tool was available.

This study focuses on processor multiplexing across virtual machines. In particular, we are interested in automatically identifying the root cause of task preemption crossing virtual machines boundaries. The approach we propose is based on kernel tracing, which is an effective and efficient way to investigate latency problems [4]. The method we propose consists of aggregating kernel traces recorded simultaneously on the host and each virtual machine. However, more often than not, timekeeping is a task left to each of the operating systems. In such cases, timestamps from different traces are not issued using the same clock reference. As a result, trace merging without an appropriate synchronization method to account for clock differences would produce incoherent results.

The challenge is to consider the system as a whole, while preserving virtual machine isolation. Flexibility and portability constraints are also important for practical considerations. The approach should be independent from the underlying architecture and the operating system to account for portability, whereas flexibility requires independence from the hypervisor and the tracer.

Three main contributions are presented in this paper. First, we propose an approach for trace synchronization. At the trace merging step, we propose an algorithm that modifies timestamps of the guests' traces to bring them back to the same timespan as the host. Secondly, we implemented an analysis program that transforms aggregated kernel traces to a graphical view that shows the states of the virtual machines and their respective virtual CPUs (vCPUs) through time while taking into consideration virtualization and its impact. Thirdly, we implemented an additional analysis program that presents the interactions of threads across different systems. Such an analysis can be performed by recovering the execution flow centered around a particular thread.

The rest of this paper is structured as follows: Section 'Related work' goes through different approaches currently used for virtual machine monitoring. Section 'Problem statement and definitions' introduces the required concepts in virtualization and tracing, and states the problem addressed by this paper. Section 'Trace synchronization' explains our approach for trace synchronization at the aggregation step. Each of sections 'Multi-level trace analysis' and 'Execution flow recovery' introduces an analysis module and its inner working. Section 'Use cases' shows some representative use cases and their analysis results. Section 'Flexibility and portability' reiterates over flexibility and portability. Section 'Conclusion' concludes.

Related work

On Linux kernels supporting paravirtualization, `top` reports a metric specific to virtual machines, named *steal time*. This metric shows the percentage of time for which a vCPU of the VM is preempted on the host. While this information can give a general idea or a hint of overcommitment of the CPU, it does not report the actual impact on the running threads nor the source cause of preemption. Additionally, this approach is specific for Linux paravirtualized systems and thus limits portability. Moreover, `top` adds significant overhead as it gathers information by reading entries in the `proc` pseudo-filesystem, and offline analysis or replay of the execution flow are not possible.

Perf has been extended to support profiling and tracing specifically for KVM. Using its "kvm" subcommand, one can use Perf to get runtime statistics and metrics about each virtual machine. Common metrics include the number of traps caught by the hypervisor, their cause and the time to process each of them. The information reported by Perf also includes CPU time for the guest kernel, host kernel and the hypervisor, which are good indicators about the overhead introduced by virtualization. Perf also reports information about the Performance Monitoring

Unit (PMU), which is a set of counters that keep track of particular events such as cache misses, TLB misses, CPU cycles, etc. However, these performance counters aren't available for virtual machines. In [5], an approach for PMU virtualization is proposed, which are then used to monitor the runtime behavior of virtual machines in more detail. In [6] and [7], the authors also use Perf for virtual machine profiling and resource utilization. Such methods may also require exporting the symbol table of the guest kernel to the host to resolve. While it is possible to detect performance degradation due to resource sharing among virtual machines, the analysis doesn't cover detailed fine-grained information about the root causes of preemption. However, the interactions between the virtual machines through the usage of shared resources are essential to understand performance degradations and easily pinpoint their cause in order to remedy them. Finally, the approach using `perf kvm` is dependent on both the operating system and the hypervisor, which doesn't meet the portability requirement.

Shao et al. use an approach based on tracing within Xen to generate useful metrics for virtual machines [8]. Based on scheduling events, latency due to virtual CPU preemption can be easily calculated. Other metrics of interest are also presented such as the wake-to-schedule time. However, these metrics are mostly useful for analyzing Xen's scheduler itself. Such an analysis would be less relevant in the case of KVM (or some other hypervisors) as it is a an "extension" to the Linux kernel via loadable kernel modules and thus uses its scheduler. Moreover, the impact of the applications running inside the virtual machines on the system as a whole can not be retrieved from Xen traces. Differently put, perturbations caused by userspace applications across different virtual machines cannot be analyzed or quantified using solely Xen traces.

As for trace synchronization, previous studies [8,9] have used the TSC (TimeStamp Counter) as a common time reference to approach timekeeping and clock drift issues among VMs. The TSC is a CPU register on x86 architectures which counts CPU cycles since the boot of the system (uptime). When read from a virtualized system, the TSC is usually automatically offset in hardware to reflect the uptime of the guest operating system. The value of the offset is specified by the `TSC_OFFSET` field in the Virtual Machine Control Structure (VMCS). Each VM has its own `TSC_OFFSET` value, and reading the TSC from different systems always returns a coherent value with respect to their respective uptime. Once traces are recorded on different systems, converting guest TSC values to host TSC values comes down to subtracting the value of `TSC_OFFSET` from each timestamp. However, the TSC offset may have to be adjusted during the execution of the VM upon certain events, such as virtual machine migration. As a result, `TSC_OFFSET` adjustments have to be tracked down by the tracer at run-time. If tracing is not enabled before the creation of the virtual machine, the initial value of the TSC offset can-not be obtained, unless explicitly requested by the tracer. Additionally, this approach does not allow for the possi-bility of lost events since a TSC adjustment event could be lost. In any manner, even if the TSC isn't virtualized and is unique across all systems, synchronization using the TSC does not meet our requirement of portability, as it is an x86-specific register. Moreover, TSC offsetting is spe-cific to hardware-assisted virtualization, thus it cannot be used with other virtualization methods, which does not meet our flexibility requirement. Finally, the TSC register only counts CPU cycles since boot time, which is not as meaningful as an absolute wall clock time, especially on computers with a non-constant TSC where the conversion from TSC to real time would be an additional challenge (CPU flag `constant_tsc` can be queried to verify this property).

Problem statement and definitions
Addressed problem and motivation
We noticed that one of the main limitations of current approaches for virtual machine monitoring is the lack of a general approach, which takes into account in-depth anal-ysis of all the involved systems. Most of the monitoring tools are designed to be centered either around the hyper-visor or the guest OS. In the former case, only an analysis from the host point of view, abstracted by the virtualiza-tion layer, is possible. In the latter case, the analysis is too restricted inside the guest OS and doesn't consider the outside environment for detecting the root causes of performance degradations.

As mentioned in section 'Introduction', investigating latency problems in virtualized systems is a non-trivial task. The isolation of virtual machines from their envi-ronments imposes limits on the scope of traditional anal-ysis tools. Moreover, the virtualization layer itself adds overhead due to the involvement of the hypervisor for privileged operations [10]. Furthermore, the assumption of exclusive access to the hardware layer by each vir-tual machine inevitably induces hidden latency due to the overcommitment of resources, particularly the CPU. As a result, the CPU becomes a scarce resource, which has to be shared among running VMs. As we presented in the previous section, there is no obvious way for a VM to detect runtime perturbation caused by the "outside world". While a guest OS may perceive one of its processes taking full use of the CPU for a certain amount of time, this might not be effectively the case on the actual hardware. Indeed, when a process is allocated a limited amount of vCPU time in a guest OS, it might get deprived of this resource by the host's scheduler which might elect a different VM for execution at any moment. Analyzing preemption across

virtual machines boundaries (inter-VM) allows the user to detect such perturbations and take actions to remedy them.

In this paper, we explain how we used kernel traces recorded in each VM and on the host simultaneously to investigate such problems. As we present in section 'Use cases', the tools resulting from our study help the users to easily find the latency cause due to CPU sharing among virtual machines, as well as the actual threads that affect the completion time of a certain workload. How-ever, merging distributed traces is a problem in itself as each operating system is solely responsible for its own timekeeping. The next sections present prerquisites in order to understand all of the parts used in our final solution.

Hypervisor
CPU vendors introduced extensions at the hardware level which allow for efficient architecture virtualization and overcome design issues, as presented in [10] for x86. On Intel hardware, this CPU extension is called VMX (Virtual Mahine eXtension), while AMD-V is its counterpart from AMD. On hardware-assisted virtualization, the CPU tran-sits between non-root and root modes. On Intel CPUs, these modes are respectively called VMX non-root and VMX-root. The former is entered using the `vmentry` instruction by the hypervisor, giving control to the VM's native code. The later is reached when the VM executes an instruction that triggers a trap, called `vmexit`. A trap is usually a sensitive instruction such as writing to a priv-ileged register, and allows the hypervisor to take control of the execution and react to the trapped instruction, usu-ally through emulation. `Vmexit` can be thought of as a *reaction*, as opposed to `vmentry` which is an actual instruction. Moreover, a data structure called VMCS (Vir-tual Machine Control Structure) [11] contains runtime information about a virtual machine. This data structure is used as an interaction mechanism between the VM and the hypervisor [12] (i.e. between non-root and root modes), as well as a way to define behavioral elements, such as enabling or disabling hardware TSC offsetting.

The software that interacts with these hardware exten-sions is called a hypervisor. KVM [13] is an example of such software and is included in Linux as a loadable kernel module. Its role is to exploit and manage the vir-tualization capabilities of the hardware, and provide easy access to these capabilities to any userspace component via the `ioctl` interface. As a result, many userspace emu-lators can be built atop KVM without reimplementing hardware-specific functionalities. We use QEMU as this userspace component that interacts with KVM to take advantage of hardware assistance. Moreover, as KVM is an extension to the Linux kernel, it can take advantage of its basic functionalities, such as the scheduling, NUMA node management, and even its tracing infrastructure. Thus, KVM is instrumented with tracepoints which can be traced using any kernel tracer. In QEMU/KVM, each virtual machine is a QEMU process, and each of its virtual CPUs (vCPUs) is emulated by a separate thread that belongs to that process.

In this article, the terms hypervisor and VMM (Virtual Machine Monitor) will be used interchangeably. The same applies for the terms VM, guest system and virtualized system.

Trace indexing

We implemented our trace analysis algorithm using the Trace Compass trace viewer (previously TMF - Tracing and Monitoring Framework) [14]. Trace Compass is a Free and Open tool for viewing traces in different graphical views. Views are usually designed for specific kind of analyses. The most common views in Trace Compass are the Control Flow view and the Resource view. The former shows the states of all threads on a system throughout the tracing session (Running, Idle, Preempted, Blocked), whereas the latter shows the states of different resources such as the CPU and IRQ lines. This project resulted in two additional views integrated to Trace Compass, which can be used for Virtual Machine runtime analysis of inter-VM preemption.

Trace Compass indexes the trace using a State History Tree (SHT) [15]. The SHT represents the state of the whole system, and is updated at each event to define time intervals [16]. This index allows efficient stabbing queries, returning the complete state of the system at a given time. A node of the tree is a key-value pair, where the key is a path component, and the value is an attribute associated with a duration, that gets updated as the trace is being processed. The rules, by which attributes are updated, are established by our algorithm presented in section 'Multi-level trace analysis'.

Our algorithm requires kernel traces from all systems in the setup, i.e., the host and guests operating systems. Events from these traces are then merged and sorted by chronological order for processing. Trace Compass reads the trace one event at a time and modifies the SHT attributes. Figure 1 shows a part of our SHT. For instance, the path "/Virtual Machines/Ubuntu/CPUs/CPU0/Current Thread" contains the thread ID executing on CPU 0 of the VM named "Ubuntu". When a scheduling event such as *sched_switch* from the VM's trace is processed, the value of the attribute is changed from the TID of the former thread to the latter's. Similarly, the attribute at path "/Host/Threads/Thread 1234/Status" holds the status of the thread whose TID is 1234 on the host. This attribute may be modified when a context switch event involving the thread 1234 is being processed.

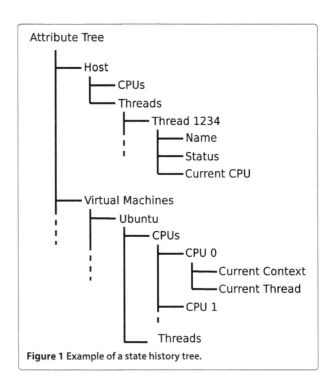

Figure 1 Example of a state history tree.

Relevant tracepoints

In this study, we use LTTng as a kernel tracer. LTTng was designed for high throughput tracing while reducing as much as possible its impact on the traced system [17]. We now introduce the key tracepoints for our analysis. We present their significance, as well as the content of their respective payload. This section is complementary to section 'Multi-level trace analysis' which explains how these tracepoints are used to update the SHT.

The `sched_switch` tracepoint indicates a context switch on the CPU which recorded the event. Useful payload fields are the names and the TIDs (Thread Identifiers) of the former and new threads involved in the context switch. Since all events are timestamped using the system's time at the nanosecond scale, the amount of time spent on each CPU by a specific thread is easily computed by subtracting the timestamps of the `sched_switch` events involving a particular thread.

Tracepoint `sched_migrate_task` indicates the migration of a thread from one CPU to another. Its payload holds the TID of the migrated task, as well as the origin and the destination CPU identifiers. Tracepoint `sched_process_fork` indicates the creation of a new process, and exposes the names, PIDs (Process Identifiers) and TIDs of the newly created process as well as its parent's. Its complementary event, `sched_process_exit`, records the end of life of a thread. The payload contains the name and TID of the process.

VMX mode transitions by KVM can be tracked by enabling the `kvm_entry` and `kvm_exit` events. Tracepoint `kvm_entry` indicates a transition from root to non-root modes, and thus the beginning of the execution of the VM's native code. On the other hand, tracepoint `kvm_exit` indicates the opposite transition, which interrupts the execution of the VM and gives control to KVM. Elapsed time between consecutive `kvm_exit` and `kvm_entry` events represents overhead introduced by the hypervisor.

Trace synchronization
System timekeeping
LTTng uses the monotonic clock of the kernel for timestamping events, rather than the raw TSC. It avoids architecture-dependent limitations inherent to the TSC, such as TSC synchronization between cores and nonconstant TSC on variable frequency CPUs. Even in the case of an ideal TSC (invariant and synchronized between cores), the value is based on the processor frequency, and thus needs to be scaled, or translated, for the user. Moreover, the TSC is an x86-specific register and using it as a clock source does not meet our requirement of portability. However, it is worth mentionning that the monotonic clock internally scales the TSC to nanoseconds and applies an offset to represent the current time, as shown in Equation 1:

$$t = T + f(TSC) \tag{1}$$

where T is a coarse-grained value updated on system timer interrupts. For a finer timekeeping, T needs to be adjusted using the TSC to account for the elapsed time since the last update (last timer interrupt). This is done using function $f()$, which translates the TSC to an actual time value that can be used for fine-grained timekeeping.

In addition, the monotonic clock guarantees total ordering, even in the case of modification of the system's wall clock time while tracing, and therefore is an ideal source for event timestamps.

Although the TSC is paced at the same rate across the different virtual systems, the offset values T of each system are not, and thus are subject to drifting apart as time goes by. In fact, modern tickless operating systems disable timer interrupts on idle processors to reduce energy consumption. As a result, the update period of T is variable, which may contribute to increase the time difference between systems. Furthermore, virtual machines may be set to different timezones, introducing even more incoherent timestamping when traces are merged together, which would make them appear as being recorded at different moments. As a result, high precision timestamping and clock drifting do not allow for simple clock offsetting

to ensure coherency between traces, and require a specific synchronization method. The next section presents our approach to ensure coherent trace merging.

Event matching
We use the fully incremental convex hull synchronization algorithm to achieve offline trace synchronization, introduced by [18] for distributed traces synchronization. Each guest trace is processed individually and synchronized according to the host's trace whose timeline is taken as a reference. This approach is based on event matching between two traces. In order to use the synchronization algorithm, an event a from one trace must be associated to another complement event b from the other. Each couple of events $\{a, b\}$ must respect the following equation:

$$a_{T_1} \xrightarrow{k} b_{T_2} \tag{2}$$

More formaly, the following requirements have to be met:

1. Causality: a must (quickly) trigger b;
2. Bijection: a and b must share a common and unique key k in their payloads;
3. Every event b must be matched to at most one event a (one-to-one). Unmatched events b are ignored.

The key k is used to ensure a one-to-one relation between a and b. A lower delay between events a and b results in a more precise synchronization scheme. A synchronization formula is then derived by the algorithm which is a function of clocks offset and time drift. This formula is then applied to all timestamps of the guest's trace, bringing them to the same timebase as the host. By using the relation "a triggers b", a lower bound is imposed on the timestamps of events b as they cannot appear before their matching event a. Events between two consecutive events b are then adjusted to respect this constraint. With that being said, an upper bound has to be imposed as well to events b. To set an upper bound on events b, we use the same matching approach in the opposite direction between systems. If a is an event in the guest OS that triggers b on the host, then an event c on the host that triggers an event d on the guest is needed. Figure 2 shows events a, d, b, c from the original traces correctly reordered as a, b, c, d after synchronization. The next section explains how we used and adapted this method for virtual machines.

Implementation in virtualized systems
Previous section 'Event matching' explained the theory of the fully incremental convex hull algorithm for trace synchronization. However, the requirements for this algorithm are not directly met in the case of virtual machines. Originally, the algorithm was built based on TCP packet exchange events, where `send` and `receive` events are

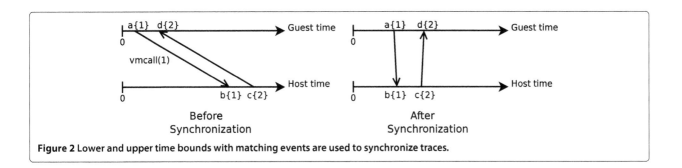

Figure 2 Lower and upper time bounds with matching events are used to synchronize traces.

respectively a and b: send triggers receive and the TCP packet number is the key k. In Cloud environments, virtual machines do not necessarily exchange TCP packets with each other or with the host, as VMs are usually provided to different clients. As a result, we need to customize the setup of the virtual machines to generate events both in the VMs and on the host that would respect the requirements established earlier. This section introduces our approach to obtain events that can be used to achieve trace synchronization.

We added tracepoints to the kernel through a loadable module for flexibility, so no modification to kernel code would be required to perform trace synchronization. Upon loading, this module registers a probe to the system timer's interrupt. In other words, every time the system timer issues an interrupt to the CPU, our synchronization routine will be invoked. The synchronization routine can be summed up as follows:

- Guest: Trigger hypercall (event a)
- Host: Acknowledge hypercall (event b)
- Host: Give control back to the VM (event c)
- Guest: Acknowledge control (event d)

The first pair of events (a, b) can be simulated by issuing a hypercall. When executing the vmcall instruction from the guest OS (event a), a trap is generated by the CPU and control is given to the hypervisor, which in turn acknowledges the trap (event b). A counter X is passed to the host OS as a parameter to the hypercall. This parameter will serve as the shared key required by the synchronization algorithm. As a result, events a and b are both recorded in a short period of time on the guest and host OS respectively, both holding the same value X as their payload.

Simulating the pair of events (c, d) is not as trivial since different constraints are imposed on the host-to-guest communication, as no mechanism of parameter transmission is easily accessible. Implementing shared memory between the guest and host is too intrusive as it would add too much complexity to both systems, and would probably require modification to both kernels. However, the trap

generated by the hypercall is virtually invisible to the guest OS, which continues execution "normally" after involvement from the hypervisor. We can take advantage of this property to simulate a parameter transmission when the hypercall handling returns. Event c is recorded on the host right before it finishes the synchronization routine and gives control back to the VM. Event d is recorded on the guest right after the hypercall, which effectively is as soon as the guest OS resumes execution. This model simulates property (1) as c indicates that the host is giving control to the VM and d represents its acknowledgement. Both these events hold $X + 1$ in their payloads to respect the one-to-one relationship.

The downside of this approach is the overhead introduced by the hypercall. Table 1 shows overhead measurements added by the hypercall, with and without tracing. However, registering to the system timer interrupt takes advantage of tickless kernels as they aim to reduce energy consumption by disabling interrupts on idle CPUs. In other words, the synchronization routine is not invoked on idle virtual machines, which otherwise would trigger a costly context switch on the host for no actual work.

Once traces are generated on both systems, the fully incremental convex hull algorithm is applied, which derives a synchronization function applied on all of the guest's timestamps. This approach is resistant to clock drifts as the convex hull algorithm considers this issue and compensates for it in the generated formula. Additionally, it does not require TSC_OFFSET tracking or any other architecture-specific configuration.

Synchronization results

To show the results of our trace synchronization algorithm, we traced simultaneously a running virtual

Table 1 Overhead induced by the hypercall

	Time (ns)		
	Without tracing	With tracing	Relative
One synchronization tracepoint	102	153	50.0%
Hypercall round-trip	5168	5565	7.7%

machine and its host. We then merged the traces recorded from both systems and used Trace Compass to view the result.

We show in Figure 3 the state of threads on different systems (the color legend is shown in Table 2). Thread qemu:Debian with TID 7030 serves as a virtual CPU of the VM as seen from the host. Events from the host's trace are used to recreate its state. Thread wk-pulse is a periodic CPU workload (in a pulse-like manner) running inside the VM. Therefore, events from the VM's trace are used to show its state. We can already expect that the vCPU of the virtual machine will follow a pulse-like pattern, as the guest system is mostly idle. On Figure 3, the staggered start of wk-pulse indicates a time gap of about 6 seconds between the host's and guest's clocks. We then used our synchronization algorithm to correct the guest trace's timestamps and reused the same view in Trace Compass to view the result, as shown in Figure 4. We clearly see that wk-pulse is running on vCPU qemu:Debian because of their simultaneous state transitions. It is worth mentioning that the states of threads qemu:Debian and wk-pulse are computed independently from each other, yet they appear almost in perfect sync after applying the synchronization formula.

Multi-level trace analysis

This section presents how the state of each virtual CPU of a VM is recovered and rebuilt by analyzing the merged traces. The purpose of the analysis is to show the state of the vCPU throughout the trace as seen from the host. Our module parses the resulting trace and updates the attributes of the state system after each processed event. Moreover, we want to show the impact of preemption on the threads running within a VM. This analysis is useful as it shows the effective running time and execution of a thread compared to what is visible to the guest operating system. A vCPU at any time can be in one of the following states: VMM, RUNNING, IDLE or PREEMPTED. The state attribute of each vCPU can be found in the state system at path "/Virtual Machines/VM Name/CPUs/vCPU ID/Status. Figure 5 is a FSM (finite state machine) that shows transitions between these states. All of the events that trigger transitions originate from the host. Although not included in Figure 5, events from the virtual machines' traces are used to rebuild the states of the threads running on each vCPU within a VM. These threads can be found

in the state system at paths "/Virtual Machines/ VM Name/Threads/TID/Status". Following section 'Virtual CPU states' explains these states as well as the transitions by which they can be reached.

For clarity, we introduce the term pCPU which designates a physical CPU, as opposing to a vCPU which is in reality a QEMU thread emulating the CPU of a VM.

Virtual CPU states
VMM

State VMM represents the state when a QEMU thread is running hypervisor code instead of virtual machine code. In other words, it represents participation or involvement from the VMM, as to provide emulation, inject an interrupt into the guest's OS, or any other instruction requiring the external help of KVM. As explained in section 'Hypervisor', CPU transitions between non-root and root are instrumented with tracepoints kvm_entry and kvm_exit respectively. When a kvm_exit event is reached, the vCPU's state is set to VMM (transition 2). On the other hand, it leaves this state on a kvm_entry event, returning to the state it was in prior to the 's involvement (transition 1). This state serves as an intermediate between any two states, as hypervisor cooperation is required for QEMU threads scheduling.

We also noticed that this state is reached everytime a QEMU thread is involved in a context switch, i.e., when a vCPU is scheduled out of a pCPU. Interestingly, when a QEMU thread is selected by the scheduler to run again, it first executes in the VMM state before explicitly invoking the vmentry instruction to give control to the guest's OS. This procedure is required because KVM needs to execute specific operations related to the Virtual Machine Control Structure of the VM. KVM uses Linux's notifier chains to "register" on context switches involving a vCPU. When a vCPU reaches this state, its current thread's status is set to PROCESS_VIRT_PREEMPTED, which designates wasted time due to the virtualization layer (we see it as preemption to execute hypervisor code, the thread is marked as "virtually preempted").

RUNNING

RUNNING shows execution of the VM's code. When in this state, a virtual CPU is considered as running without any involvement from the hypervisor, and instructions dedicated to a specific vCPU are running directly on one of

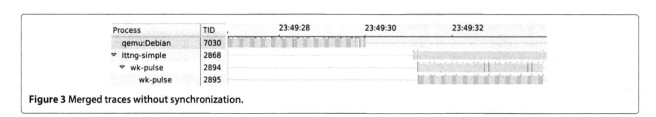
Figure 3 Merged traces without synchronization.

Table 2 Virtual Machine Analysis Color legend

Color	State
Green	Running
Yellow	Blocked
Orange	Preempted
Grayed out green	PROCESS_VIRT_PREEMPT

the host's pCPUs. For this state to be reached, two conditions must be satisfied. First, the QEMU thread emulating a vCPU must be in a running state on the host operating system. Secondly, in the guest operating system, the CPU associated with the specified QEMU thread must be in the running state as well, meaning that any process other than the idle task (swapper) is executing on the CPU.

IDLE

IDLE represents a state when a vCPU is not executing any code, and thus voluntarily yields the physical CPU. This state is reached when the QEMU thread emulating a vCPU is scheduled out of a pCPU, and if no thread other than the idle task is scheduled to run on this vCPU in the guest OS (transition 4). On Linux, the purpose of swapper (the idle task) is to invoke the scheduler to choose potential threads ready for execution, or to halt the CPU in case no thread is ready to run. The vCPU goes out of this state as soon as the thread emulating it gets scheduled back on the host (transition 3).

PREEMPTED

PREEMPTED is the state that indicates direct latency to the execution of a virtual machine. This state is reached when a vCPU is scheduled out of the pCPU by the host's scheduler (transition 5), while the vCPU was effectively serving a thread. Note that the running process on the vCPU stays in the PROCESS_VIRT_PREEMPTED state, which indicates that the vCPU on which the thread is running was preempted on the host operating system. Usually, this kind of information is not visible to a virtual machine, though it directly impacts the completion time of a task by introducing delays throughout the execution. As a result, a task may seem to complete in much longer than the effective time during which it was running. When scheduled back in (transition 6), the vCPU passes by the VMM state

again to finally reach the RUNNING state and resume VM code execution.

Illustrative example

We launched a thread that computes a Fibonacci sum on what appeared to be an idle virtual machine. The computer used was an Intel i7 (Nehalem) with 4 hyper-threaded cores (8 logical CPUs), 8 GB of RAM, 1 TB HDD, and running Debian GNU/Linux. Using top, no CPU-intensive thread was reported in the VM, and the *steal time* column showed a 0% vCPU preemption. Figure 6 shows the state of the Fibonacci task (thread fibo) as seen from the guest operating system. This view shows a monopoly of the CPU and a 100% utilization by the fibo task for the whole duration of the trace. This state has been reconstructed by processing only the trace recorded on the guest.

Figure 7 shows the result of our analysis module for the same experiment, after the host's and guest's traces merging and synchronization. We notice that vCPU 0 of the "Debian" VM is constantly transitioning between states RUNNING (green) and PREEMPTED (purple). With proper zooming, we can see VMM state as an intermediate for every transition. These transitions have direct repercussions on the execution of the fibo task, which is in turn moving between states RUNNING (green) and PROCESS_VIRT_PREEMPTED (grayed out green). With a quick look at the graphical view, we can see that the Fibonacci sum could potentially execute approximately twice as fast on a fully available pCPU, or less loaded host system.

The reason why top reported a 0% vCPU preemption (steal time), before starting the Fibonacci task, is because the vCPU was mostly idle. As a result, when it asks for CPU time, its request is immediately answered by the host's scheduler as it has the "highest priority" due to its idle nature. We can see that using such a tool to measure resource availability can actually be misleading. The only way to detect vCPU preemption using top would be to actively monitor the steal time while running the Fibonacci task.

Execution flow recovery

We now reach the second part of the analysis, which is to reconstruct the execution flow for a specific task of one of the virtual machines. The execution flow with regard to

Process	TID	23:49:27	23:49:28	23:49:29
▽ lttng-simple	2868			
▽ wk-pulse	2894			
wk-pulse	2895			
qemu:Debian	7030			

Figure 4 Merged traces with synchronization.

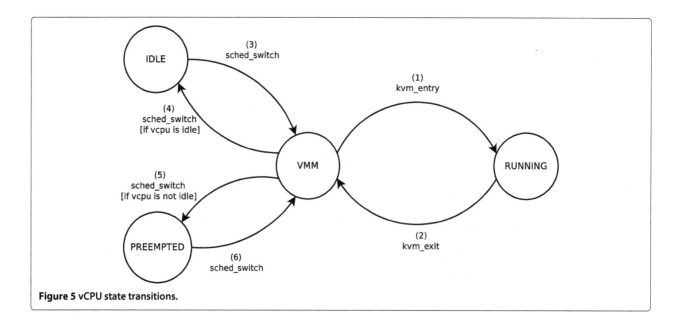

Figure 5 vCPU state transitions.

a certain task A is defined as the ordered set of execution intervals of all the tasks affecting the completion time of A. The purpose of the execution flow is to show detailed information about the execution of a certain thread as well as its interactions with other threads.

In the scenario shown in Figure 8, the execution flow is computed with regard to task A. The timeline shows the start and the end of the lifespan of this task, thus the analysis is time-bounded. In this example, it is clear that task A yields the CPU to allow execution of other tasks B and C. The scheduler then selects A after a certain amount of time, letting it complete its execution. Therefore, the completion of A was affected by the execution of B and C. When flattened, the execution intervals of all the threads form one continuous execution interval which represents a busy CPU for the duration of the trace. Although this kind of information could be vaguely suspected from top-like tools, this level of detailed information is necessary for an advanced analysis of latency sources.

For a task executing inside a virtual machine, the computation of the execution flow should be adjusted to take into consideration interactions between different operating systems through the usage of shared resources. The objective of such an analysis is to provide detailed information not only about the execution of a certain task, but also about its interactions with other threads, whether

they belong to the same VM, the host, or even a different VM. With such information, major causes of overhead can be easily tracked down by the host's administrator, and adjustments can be made to resolve the issues. Recovering the execution flow comes down to tracking all preemption events involving A. Causes of preemption can be within the same operating system and thus easier to investigate, or from a different system making them almost completely hidden. In this section, we show that the execution flow recovery can be computed simply by querying the state system for key attributes modifications, without having to read the trace again.

Implementation

In this section, we call *A* the thread around which we want to recover the execution flow. The first step of the algorithm is to find all the entries involved in the execution flow according to task *A*. In Figure 8, each of tasks A, B and C represents an entry. First, all the threads of all the systems are inserted as entries in the execution flow. This list of all the threads across systems can be recovered by parsing through attributes "/Virtual Machines/*/Threads/*" and "/Host/Threads/*" in the SHT. The second step of the algorithm is to compute the execution intervals of each entry with regard to task A. As a final step,

Process	TID	02:53:49.200	02:53:49.400	02:53:49.600	02:53:49.800
▽ lttng-simple	2970				
▽ fibo_wrapper	2993				
fibo	2995				

Figure 6 View of Fibonacci experiment with traditional analysis.

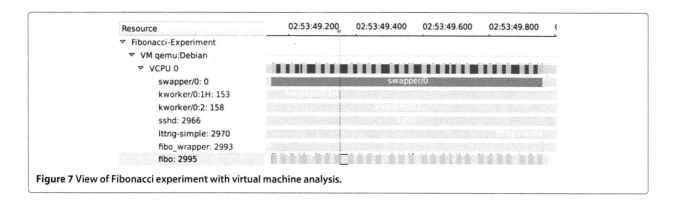

Figure 7 View of Fibonacci experiment with virtual machine analysis.

we remove the entries that have minimal or no impact on the analyzed thread according to a minimal impact threshold. The selection of the threshold doesn't affect the computing time of the algorihtm, as it is performed only after the whole algorithm has executed and all the durations have been computed. The impact of each thread can be measured using Equation 3, as explained in section 'Investigation of execution anomalies'.

To respect the relationship of affiliation between a thread and its system (host or VM), entries are stored in a tree-like structure with a depth of 2, where each node on the first level represents a system, and its children on the second level represent its threads.

As mentioned earlier, the execution flow can be represented with an ordered list of intervals, where each interval contains a start time, end time, a state, and the TID of the thread executing for the said interval. Algorithms 1 and 2 explain how this list can be built, recovering the execution flow with regard to task A.

Algorithm 1 is used to insert all intervals of A holding the "RUNNING" state. As a first step, we query the SHT to retrieve all modifications to the "Status" attribute of thread A. The SHT returns a list of intervals for different values of this attribute. Algorithm 1 parses this list

and each interval holding the "RUNNING" state is directly inserted in the result list. However, for each interval holding the "PREEMPTED" value, a separate function is invoked to find which thread is preempting A. This function is shown in Algorithm 2.

Algorithm 1: Recovering the execution flow: inserting intervals in the RUNNING state

---

Input: StateHistoryTree s
List *result*; // the list of execution intervals
StatusIntervals *intervals* = Query status intervals of A from s;
for *each interval in intervals* **do**
    currentPCpu = Query current pCPU of A;
    if *interval.state == RUNNING* **then**
        result.insert(*interval*);
    else
        result.insertAll(**resolve**(s, *interval*, currentPCpu));
    end
end
return *result*;

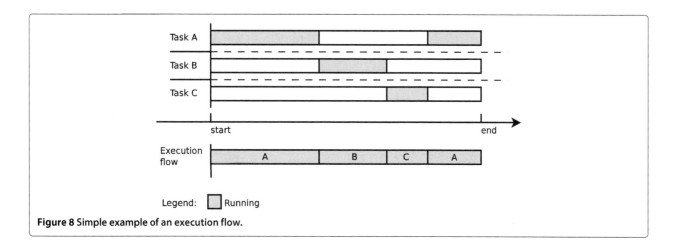

Figure 8 Simple example of an execution flow.

The `resolve` function requires an interval as well as a pCPU Id as input values. The work done by this routine is to find which threads are running on the pCPU for the duration of the interval. In the case where the running thread is the vCPU of another VM, this function will then query the state system to get the running thread inside this VM. Once the running thread preempting *A* is deduced, it is returned to Algorithm 1 which will insert it in the `result` list.

Algorithm 2: Function `resolve()`: Querying the state history tree to get the running threads while `A` is preempted

---

Input: *interval*
Input: *pCpu*
Output: *outList*
start = *interval*.start;
end = *interval*.end;
ThreadIntervals = Query "Current Thread" intervals of *pCpu* between *start* and *end*;
for *each interval t in ThreadIntervals* **do**
    if *t.tid is a vCPU* **then**
        intervals = Query "Current Thread" intervals of *t* between *t.start* and *t.end*
        outList.addAll(intervals);
    else
        outList.add(*t*);
    end
end
/* All intervals inserted in *outList* are in *RUNNING* state */
return *outList*;

Finally, in the `result` list returned by Algorithm 1, each interval "interval" of the list respects the following rules:

$$prevInterval.end = interval.start - 1$$
$$interval.end + 1 = nextInterval.start$$

Where `prevInterval` and `nextInterval` are respectively the previous and next intervals of `interval` in the ordered list `result` from Algorithm 1.

Use cases

This section shows how our work can be used in real-life cases to investigate latency in virtual machines. We start with a follow-up on the Fibonacci example introduced earlier (section 'Follow-up on the Fibonacci Case'). We then present different use cases that show either how to investigate a known issue (section 'Investigation of execution anomalies'), or a general analysis to verify normal execution of the system as a whole (Investigating a residual timer).

Follow-up on the Fibonacci Case

Figure 7 showed that the Fibonacci took longer to execute due to preemption of the vCPU on which it was running. We follow-up on the matter by recovering the execution flow of the experiment. Figure 9 shows the result; we can see that the preemption is due to a single CPU-intensive process on the host called `burnP6`.

Investigation of execution anomalies

We now show a use case of a performance issue which can be easily tracked down using our graphical views. We developed a CPU-intensive task, named `critical_task` which computes for approximately 280 ms. A script spawns a `critical_task` thread in a periodic fashion, asynchronously every second (without waiting for completion). We traced the host and the guest operating systems simultaneously. Figure 10 shows only the guest's trace over 7 seconds, for 7 `critical_task` threads. We can see the rate of thread forking at one thread per second. However, executions 3, 4, 5 and slightly 6 (threads 3523, 3525, 3527 and 3529) show abnormal computing duration although they appear as running (green) without interruption.

We then merged and synchronized kernel traces, and used our first graphical view to analyze the execution, as shown in Figures 11, 12 and 13. In Figure 11, the vCPU 0 line shows transitions between states IDLE (gray) and RUNNING (green) which indicates that the VM is mostly idle, except when `critical_task` threads are spawned. Additionally, still by looking at the vCPU 0 line, we can clearly see vCPU preemption (purple) for executions 2, 3, 4 and 5. These vCPU preemptions translate into unexpected latency on threads 3523, 3525, 3527 and 3529, as shown by their respective lines in the view

Resource	Duration	02:53:49.200	02:53:49.400	02:53:49.600	02:53:49.800
fibo: 2995	0.420946				
▷ VM qemu:Debian	0.001044				
▽ Host: Host	0.402527				
burnP6: 4692	0.402467				

Figure 9 Execution flow recovery of previous Fibonacci experience.

Figure 10 Execution of a periodic task as perceived by the VM. In some cases, the execution inexplicably takes longer to compute although the task appears as running.

(greyed out green). This is an indicator that the VM is not allocated enough CPU time by the host's scheduler, which is time slicing the pCPU more or less equally among the host processes. We also notice that vCPU0 of the VM Ubuntu woke up from the IDE state into the RUNNING state for this period of time, which might be the reason for the latencies on the critical tasks running in VM Debian. Figure 12 shows the state of two vCPUs of different virtual machines, respectively Debian and Ubuntu. For simplicity reasons, the Figure shows only the timeframe for the lifespan of critical_task with PID 3525. The Figure suggests that these two vCPUs are complimentary in their execution, as when one of them is running, the other one is preempted. This is a strong indicator of a shared resource between these two vCPUs. Moreover, the Figure also shows that both vCPUs are simultaneously being preempted for small amounts of time, which suggests that another thread, outside of the scope of these VMs, is also competing over the same resource. Figure 13 is a magnified view of Figure 11 over the lifespan of critical_task 3525, showing how the preemption of vCPU0 is perturbating its execution.

Finally, as a last step, we recovered the execution flow to investigate the source of this latency. The result is shown in Figure 14. The execution flow is centered

around thread 3525, which seems to be the execution of the critical_task with the most latency. For clarity reasons, we only show a part of the lifespan of the critical_task. The view shows that the pCPU is shared amongst three operating systems: Debian (the VM in which the critical tasks are running), Ubuntu (which is another virtual machine) and the host. We notice that threads burnP6 from the host and cc from the Debian VM both strongly preempt the critical task, which explains its excessive duration. The "Duration" column shows the duration of the preemption of each process for the lifespan of thread 3525. For system entries (non-leaf nodes), the "Duration" number indicates the sum of all their threads, ie. the time for which the whole system preempted the analyzed task.

We can see that the critical task ran for 274 ms (as expected, however it was over a longer period), the Ubuntu virtual machine ran for 270 ms and the host ran for 260 ms. These numbers indicate approximately a 33% usage of the CPU for each system, which indicates that the pCPU is strongly shared amongst them. Moreover, we see that process irq/46-iwlwifi executes for 296 us, indicating heavy network usage and packet processing.

For each thread T, the proportion of time for which it preempted A is computed using Equation 3, where T_{out} is

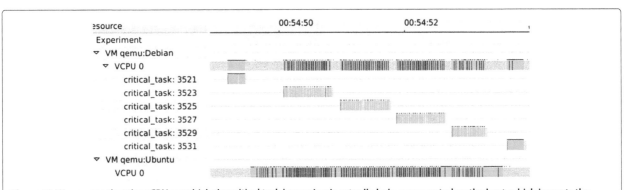

Figure 11 We can see that the vCPU on which the critical task is running is actually being preempted on the host, which impacts the execution of the running thread.

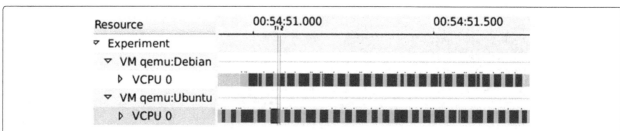

Figure 12 vCPU0 of Debian and vCPU1 of Ubuntu are taking turns in exection, which indicates competition over a shared resource. The figure also shows some timeframes in which both vCPUs are preempted, most probably by a different thread on the host system.

the timestamp indicating a scheduling out and T_{in} is the timsetamp indicating a scheduling in.

$$D(T) = \frac{\sum_{A.start}^{A.end} T_{out} - \sum_{A.start}^{A.end} T_{in}}{A.end - A.start} \qquad (3)$$

Investigating a residual timer

We now present a use case that helped us investigate an unexpected operating systems problem. Figure 15 shows the result of our analysis for a workload similar to the one presented in the previous use case (section 'Investigation of execution anomalies'). We first see that the analyzed task is sharing the CPU with threads cc from the VM "Ubuntu" and burnP6 from the host. However, for the second half of the analysis, the ciritcal task is being preempted by swapper, the idle task, from "Ubuntu". Such a behavior seems problematic as control is taken away from the analyzed thread to serve an idle thread. With a quick look at the trace when swapper is scheduled, we noticed events indicating the expiration of a timer. It turns out that a periodic timer was scheduled in the virtual machine, which would require CPU time for a very short period to acknowledge each timer expiration. This behavior introduces significant overhead as context switches are somewhat costly on the host system. We clearly see the use of such an analysis specifically for virtualized systems. While acknowledging an expired timer on an idle physical machine only consumes a few CPU cycles and little energy, it is much more costly in a virtualized system since it generates a context switch on the host. To sum up this example, we saw how a "forgotten" timer in one virtual

machine can affect the execution of others. Such a problem can be easily fixed by the system administrator once it is located.

Flexibility and portability

Throughout this project, we set different constraints to ensure for a portable and flexible solution to our initial problem. First, we used the State History Tree as an abstraction for the traces. The SHT not only delivers performance enhancement for event querying in the trace [15], but allows to dissociate the analysis step from the trace itself. In other words, multiple trace parsers can be used to handle the kernel traces, regardless of the operating system on which they were recorded, or the tracer used, as long as the trace format is open. As long as the backend used for trace representation is the SHT, and given that the required events are reported in the trace, our proposed algorithms will produce the expected results, which accounts for both portability (independant from the OS) and flexibility (independant from the tracers and trace formats). It is worth mentioning that although we used LTTng as a kernel tracer for this project, any other kernel tracer could have been potentially used as long as a trace parser is available.

Moreover, as we explained in previous sections, although a TSC-based approach for trace synchronisation is potentially simpler to use under certain conditions, the TSC is an x86-specific CPU register. Using a higher-level algorithm such as the fully incremental convex hull algorithm provides portability to the synchronisation solution. And, although using hypercalls as a communication

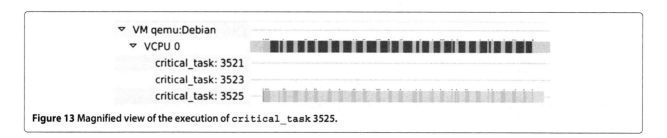

Figure 13 Magnified view of the execution of critical_task 3525.

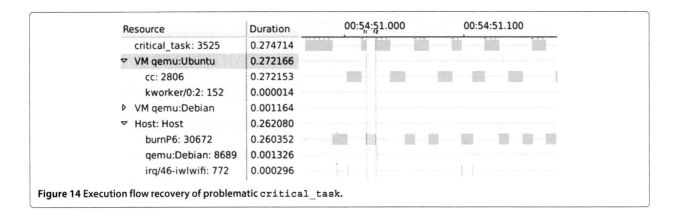

Figure 14 Execution flow recovery of problematic `critical_task`.

mechanism between the host and its guests is specific to hardware virtualization, any pair of events across systems with a causality relation can be a potential replacement, such as network packets exchange.

Finally, it is worth mentioning that the only KVM-specific tracepoints are `kvm_entry` and `kvm_exit`, which represent VMX mode transitions. Since these transitions are common to all hypervisors supporting hardware-assisted virtualization, our approach is therefore not specific to KVM. And, although these tracepoints are already included in Linux's source tree, they can be added in any hypervisor by simply instrumenting all calls to `vmentry` and `vmexit` instructions which requires very little effort, thus allowing this model to be used with any hypervisor. Moreover, if the administrator chooses not to instrument these transitions, little information would be lost, as the only state lost in Figure 5 would be VMM. Preemption and execution recovery would still be possible with little analysis precision lost (hypervisor involvement would account as effective CPU time instead of overhead due to virtualization). Furthermore, kernel traces generated from other operating systems can be used as well with minimal effort. As long as the events required to cover the FSM presented in section

'Multi-level trace analysis' are available, the model can be ported by simply specifying the names of these events. Moreover, in the case of microcomputers without hardware virtualization, the synchronization approach could potentially be extended to any other type of communication between the guest and the host, such as a TCP packet exchange. The rest of the analysis is based on the state system built, and thus does not depend on the details of the underlying traces.

Conclusion

Cloud computing and virtualization are evolving at a rapid pace. These emerging technologies created a need for analysis tools that can live up to the technological advance. In this paper, we showed that kernel tracing can be used to analyze the execution of virtual machines under such conditions. We first proposed an approach to resolve the problem of clock drift and offset between operating systems. We then showed how the merged traces can be processed to rebuild the state of the virtual machines, as well as their vCPUs, throughout the trace. Finally, we explained how the execution flow with regard to a certain thread can be rebuilt for an in-depth analysis of its execution and interactions with other systems. All

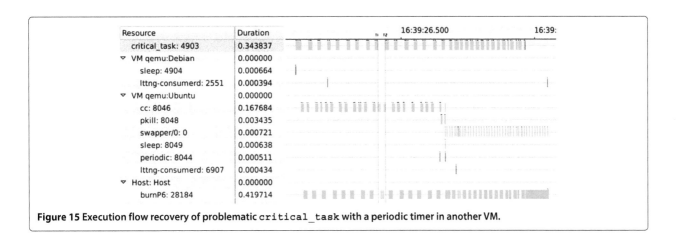

Figure 15 Execution flow recovery of problematic `critical_task` with a periodic timer in another VM.

the solutions proposed in this paper were designed with requirements of portability and flexibility in mind. As a result, all the approaches explained are portable across operating systems, computer architectures, and complementary software (tracer and hypervisor).

Competing interests
The authors declare that they have no competing interests.

Authors' contributions
MG built the state of the art of the field, defined the objectives of this research, did the analysis of the current virtual machine monitoring tools and their limitations, did research on the synchronization algorithms and developed an algorithm specific for virtual machines. He also implemented the analysis tool presented in this paper, as well as most of the experiments. FG contributed to the implementations of the analysis tool and the synchronization algorithms, provided general input to the study and oriented the experiments. He also participated in the writing of this article. MRD initiated and supervised this research, lead and approved its scientific contribution, provided general input, reviewed the article and issued his approval for the final version.

Acknowledgements
The authors would like to thank Ericsson for their input to this study as well as for funding this research project. We also thank Geneviève Bastien for her help in the Open Source project Trace Compass and Naser Ezzati Jivan for reviewing this paper.

References
1. Padala P, Zhu X, Wang Z, Singhal S, Shin K (2007) Performance evaluation of virtualization technologies for server consolidation. HP Labs Technical Report HPL-2007-59
2. Barker SK, Shenoy P (2010) Empirical evaluation of latency-sensitive application performance in the cloud. In: Proceedings of the 1st annual ACM SIGMM conference on Multimedia systems (MMSys'10). ACM, Scottsdale, AZ, USA. pp 35–46
3. Bueso D, Heymann E, Senar MA (2012) Towards efficient working set estimations in virtual machines. Jornadas Sarteco:1. Elx, Spain
4. Fournier P-M, Dagenais MR (2010) Analyzing blocking to debug performance problems on multi-core systems. ACM SIGOPS Oper Syst Rev 44(2):77–87
5. Du J, Sehrawat N, Zwaenepoel W (2011) Performance profiling of virtual machines. In: In Proceedings of the 7th ACM SIGPLAN/SIGOPS international conference on Virtual execution environments (VEE '11). ACM, New York, NY, USA Vol. 46. pp 3–14
6. Anand A, Dhingra M, Lakshmi J, Nandy SK (2012) Resource usage monitoring for kvm based virtual machines. In: Proceedings of 18th annual International Conference on Advanced Computing and Communications (ADCOM 2012). IEEE, Bangalore, India. pp 66–70
7. Khandual A (2012) Performance monitoring in linux kvm cloud environment. In: Cloud Computing in Emerging Markets (CCEM), 2012 IEEE International Conference on. IEEE, Bangalore, India. pp 1–6
8. Shao Z, He L, Lu Z, Jin H (2013) Vsa: an offline scheduling analyzer for xen virtual machine monitor. Future Generation Comput Syst 29(8):2067–2076
9. Yunomae Y (2013) Integrated trace using virtio-trace for a virtualization environment. In: LinuxCon North America/CloudOpen North America, New Orleans, LA. Keynote presentation
10. Agesen O, Garthwaite A, Sheldon J, Subrahmanyam P (2010) The evolution of an x86 virtual machine monitor. ACM SIGOPS Oper Syst Rev 44(4):3–18
11. Intel Corporation (2013) Intel® 64 and IA-32 Architectures Software Developer's Manual. Number 325462-045US
12. Fisher-Ogden J (2006) Hardware support for efficient virtualization. University of California, San Diego, Tech. Rep
13. Kivity A, Kamay Y, Laor D, Lublin U, Liguori A (2007) kvm: the linux virtual machine monitor. In: Proceedings of the Linux Symposium, Ottawa Vol. 1. pp 225–230
14. Toupin D (2011) Using tracing to diagnose or monitor systems. IEEE Softw 28(1):87–91
15. Montplaisir-Gonçalves A, Ezzati-Jivan N, Wininger F, Dagenais M (2013) State history tree: an incremental disk-based data structure for very large interval data. In: Social Computing (SocialCom), 2013 International Conference on. IEEE. pp 716–724
16. Montplaisir A, Ezzati-Jivan N, Wininger F, Dagenais M (2013) Efficient model to query and visualize the system states extracted from trace data. In: Runtime Verification. Springer, Berlin Heidelberg. pp 219–234
17. Desnoyers M, Dagenais MR (2012) Lockless multi-core high-throughput buffering scheme for kernel tracing. ACM SIGOPS Oper Syst Rev 46(3):65–81
18. Jabbarifar M, Dagenais M, Shameli-Sendi A (2014) Online incremental clock synchronization. J Netw Syst Manage:1–15

10

A framework for cloud-based context-aware information services for citizens in smart cities

Zaheer Khan[1*], Saad Liaquat Kiani[2] and Kamran Soomro[1]

Abstract

Background: In the context of smart cities, public participation and citizen science are key ingredients for informed and intelligent planning decisions and policy-making. However, citizens face a practical challenge in formulating coherent information sets from the large volumes of data available to them. These large data volumes materialise due to the increased utilisation of information and communication technologies in urban settings and local authorities' reliance on such technologies to govern urban settlements efficiently. To encourage effective public participation in urban governance of smart cities, the public needs to be facilitated with the right contextual information about the characteristics and processes of their urban surroundings in order to contribute to the aspects of urban governance that affect them such as socio-economic activities, quality of life, citizens well-being etc. The cities on the other hand face challenges in terms of crowd sourcing with quality data collection and standardisation, services inter-operability, provisioning of computational and data storage infrastructure.

Focus: In this paper, we highlight the issues that give rise to these multi-faceted challenges for citizens and public administrations of smart cities, identify the artefacts and stakeholders involved at both ends of the spectrum (data/service producers and consumers) and propose a conceptual framework to address these challenges. Based upon this conceptual framework, we present a Cloud-based architecture for context-aware citizen services for smart cities and discuss the components of the architecture through a common smart city scenario. A proof of concept implementation of the proposed architecture is also presented and evaluated. The results show the effectiveness of the cloud-based infrastructure for the development of a contextual service for citizens.

Keywords: Smart cities; Citizen services; Context-awareness; Cloud computing; Public awareness; Decision-making

Introduction

A smart city [1-4] attempts to make the best use of innovative ICT solutions to manage urban issues related to mobility, people, economy, security, public health, environment and resource management, etc. With continuous increase in urban population, the need to plan and implement smart city solutions for better urban governance is becoming more evident. These solutions are driven, on the one hand, by innovations in ICT and, on the other hand, to increase the capability and capacity of cities to mitigate environmental, social inclusion, economic growth and sustainable development challenges. In this respect, citizens' science or public participation provides

a key input for informed and intelligent planning decision and policy-making. However, the challenge here is to facilitate public in acquiring the right contextual information in order to be more productive, innovative and be able to make appropriate decisions which impact on their well being, in particular, and economic and environmental sustainability in general. Meeting such a challenge requires contemporary ICT solutions, such as using Cloud computing. Use of elastic Cloud resources enable these solutions to store and process significant amount of data and produce intelligent contextual information with high quality of service. However, processing, utilising and visualising contextual information in a Cloud environment require tailored mechanisms for user profiling and contextual segregation of data that could be used in different applications of a smart city.

Smart cities include several applications where socio-technical interaction between citizens and pervasive

*Correspondence: zaheer2.khan@uwe.ac.uk
[1] Centre for Complex Cooperative Systems, Faculty of Environment And Technology, University of the West of England, Coldharbour Lane, BS16 1QY Bristol, UK
Full list of author information is available at the end of the article

devices a.k.a. Internet of Things (IoT) is often needed [5-7]. A continuous monitoring of these interactions can provide: i) evidence based urban planning, policy-making and collaborative decision making support, and ii) raise situational and environmental awareness that can eventually result in behavioural change based on the information of citizens daily life usage of these interconnected devices. Furthermore, these IoT can also facilitate environmental data gathering in order to mitigate environmental challenges. For instance, environmental sensors can pervasively collect data from the environment e.g. noise and air quality. Similarly, citizens can participate in environmental data collection and dissemination using smart phones or through social networking sites, resulting in promoting the concept of citizen science. Other crowd sourcing applications can be highly useful in emergency response (e.g. flood, accident), traffic management (e.g. gridlock on a busy motorway), quality of life surveys etc. However, such monitoring, citizen's engagement, information processing, visualisation and decision making require sufficient computing infrastructures and attached resources for data storage and real-time processing.

The need for such resources becomes more evident when a city is considered as a single unit dealing collectively with challenges related to environment, socio-economic, security, health and well-being of citizens, education and public services. These multi-spectrum challenges necessitate cross-thematic data harmonisation, integration and coordination between various departmental boundaries in order to monitor and model future smart cities. For instance, cities face challenges of urbanisation, and it is expected that by 2020 up to 80% of population will be living in cities [8], that puts enormous pressure on the limited municipal resources. It also becomes challenging for ICT to manage such monitoring, support smart planning and facilitate better governance for socio-economic growth and sustainable urban development. Such a system requires large storage and processing power in order to capture, store, process and generate required necessary real-time information to end users. Cloud computing [9] has the potential to manage this monitoring challenge and can provide the necessary storage and computing facilities at comparable costs [10]. For example, Komninos et al. [11] review technologies for smart cities by introducing a short to long-term roadmap towards smart cities. In addition to Cloud computing, other complementary technologies include future internet, analysis and visualisation tools, sensors, RFIDs, semantic web, linked data and ontologies for smart cities [11].

Figure 1 illustrates an information perspective within smart cities. It highlights the dependencies between citizens, data, ICT tools, utilisation and provisioning of

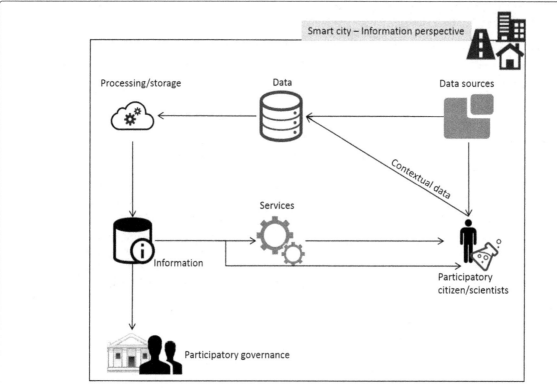

Figure 1 Smart cities - Information perspective. The dependencies between citizens, data, ICT tools, utilisation and provisioning of municipal services in order to support participatory governance.

municipal services, and effectively supporting participatory governance. Figure 2 illustrates a number of pertinent smart cities issues that affect sustainable development of the city. With respect to public participation, citizens can perform two roles: i) act as information recipients for better awareness of their surroundings, and ii) data collectors. As information recipients, context-aware information availability can help citizens to make informed decisions in their daily life. For example, knowing the air quality at a specific location can be useful for taking necessary precautions for citizens with respiratory issues. As data collectors, participatory sensing can help in collecting environmental or other data (e.g. quality of surroundings such as offices and parks) that otherwise is either difficult or expensive to collect and manage. Citizens may not need to collect the data all the time and at different locations (e.g. when travelling) and only need to receive information that is more related to their profile and situational needs. Such a requirement, on the one hand, reduces the amount of data to be captured and processed. On the other hand, new filtering and computational services need to be developed in order to fulfil this requirement. In this regard, smart city based context-aware services [12] for citizens can help them to better use their environment by getting awareness about their surroundings and

available services. However, using Clouds and developing context-aware user services for participatory monitoring to support better decision making is not straightforward and raises several research, development, deployment and adoption related challenges such as user profiling and security, data and information segregation, processing and storage.

In this paper, we discuss related issues of data and computation infrastructure and context-awareness and present related work in the 'Context-awareness, data and computational infrastructure requirements' section. Thereafter in the section 'Conceptual framework for cloud-based context-aware services', we propose a conceptual framework that provides a roadmap establishing the basis for the development of an integrated Cloud-based architecture for context-aware user services, which is then elaborated further in the section titled 'Proposed architecture'. Furthermore, we showcase a hypothetical example using Bristol Open Data [13] in order to walk-through the proposed Cloud based architecture for smart cities in the section 'Use case and discussion'. In 'Proof of the concept', we present a proof of concept implementation of the proposed architecture along with evaluation and discussion. Finally, we conclude in the 'Conclusion and future work' section.

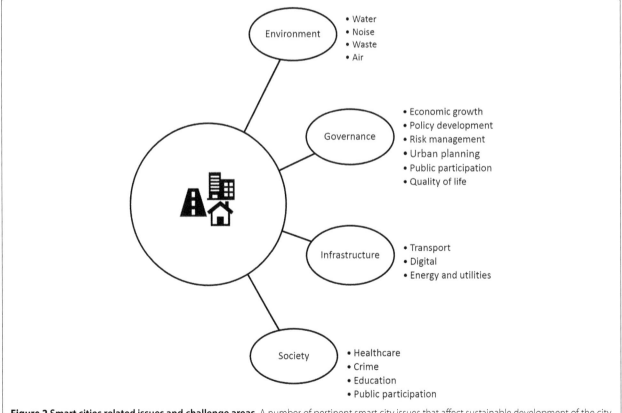

Figure 2 Smart cities related issues and challenge areas. A number of pertinent smart city issues that affect sustainable development of the city.

Context-awareness, data and computational infrastructure requirements

As discussed earlier, communication and information services provided by ICT bring smart aspect to the management of cities by transforming data into useful knowledge and actionable information. The challenge in realisation of smart cities through ICT lies in the integration of data from disparate sources and processing into useful information delivered through services, consumed by citizens and public administrations. This challenge has different dimensions including the collection of huge amounts of data, the aggregation of data in various formats, relevance of such data to practical problems and scenarios, analysis of the data to deduce useful information and visualisation, and management of the historic and ever-increasing sets of such data. Addressing these challenges require a multipronged approach involving standardisation of data formats, data harmonisation mechanisms, computational processing and storage infrastructure and mechanisms to ascertain contextual relevance of the data with its consumers.

The sources of data related to urban environments continue to increase, ranging from data gathering services and sensing platforms deployed by administrative authorities to data gathered by/from the citizens through participatory and opportunistic sensing mechanisms. However, the absence of a common and standardised platform for collection, storage and utilisation of such data for collection, analysis and dissemination of such data severely curtails the prospects of information and services that can be developed and benefit the smart city themed infrastructures. Hence the foremost requirement for realising holistic smart city related information services by and for wide-spectrum entities (citizens, governments, private enterprises) is to agree and utilise common, standard and inter-operable data formats.

An important qualitative provisioning of ICT for smart cities is the inclusive governance by informed citizens through participation i.e. an aspect of citizen science that allows their participation in information collection as well as information utilisation. Citizens are likely to be better informed and engaged if the services they consume relate to their social and environmental context. Context-awareness, which is an established discipline in the computer science and human-computer interaction domains, is thus pertinent to the employment of ICT in smart cities. However, integration of such contextual information is not straightforward due to a number of factors. These include the availability of relevant contextual information, heterogeneity of information that is available, inter-linking different types of context from possibly different sources, aggregating independently sourced contextual information to infer higher-order context about citizens and environments.

The provisioning of context-aware services also depends on the seamless integration of data collection, processing and dissemination systems whose challenges we have discussed in the earlier sections. Such technology integration to develop comprehensive smart city platforms is one of the primary objectives of the European Innovation Partnership that is endeavouring to catalyse progress in this area [14]. Situation and contextual association of data to their pertinent environmental and human artefacts exists and not only in the raw state of the data (e.g. when it is collected by a sensor node), but also continues to associate as data are aggregated and synthesised into higher level information sets (e.g. by combining multiple data values and inferring higher complex informational concepts about the environment). Therefore, any data formats, data collection mechanisms and information processing steps should continue to retain and extend contextual characteristics of aggregated data as it moves vertically from raw state towards its manifestation as complex, serviceable information.

The requirements of data collection, aggregation, representation formats and contextual annotation hint towards another requirement of a resourceful and scalable computational infrastructure. Cloud computing – based on the concepts of converged infrastructure and shared services – can be utilised to address some of the challenges in this domain, primarily those related to the collection, storage and processing of the urban domain data. Cloud computing is ideally placed to provide infrastructural support for meeting the smart city domain challenge through its key characteristics of reliability, scalability, performance and cost effectiveness. Most importantly, utilising a cloud computing infrastructure for smart city related data collection, processing and service delivery can remove the burden of computational infrastructure management and administration from a single entity (e.g. a city government). It also reduces the risk of increasing heterogeneity, which is likely to set in when different stakeholders utilise their own computation infrastructure for data collection and processing related activities. There is an industry-wide push towards providing Cloud-based smart city solutions [15] and we are beginning to see prototype implementations at various early adopter cities [16].

Recently there has been considerable interest in context-awareness in clouds. Hyun and Soo have proposed a framework for enabling context-aware mobile services [17]. The framework enables providing better services to users that fit their current context. Saad et al. [18] have investigated caching strategies in context-aware clouds. Their solution takes advantage of the inherent temporal dimension in context data to improve the accuracy of context-based systems. Other endeavours attempt to investigate energy conservation in context-aware clouds

[19]. In a cloud-based setting data is vulnerable to cyber attacks. As more and more users are storing sensitive data online, privacy becomes a legitimate concern in these settings. Hamza et al. investigate privacy concerns in cloud-based user data by utilising their sharing context [20]. Paelke et al. have proposed a solution that gathers geo-referenced contextual information from public sources such as Wikipedia [21]. This information is rendered as a tag-cloud and presented to users to increase their awareness about their spatial context. In short, utilising context in cloud-based systems is an active research area with many interested parties.

The issues and requirements discussed above are spread across a range of areas and addressing these holistically requires a bottom up approach that considers the individual artefacts affected by these issues. These artefacts, e.g. data/process models, context models, services, infrastructure, and their subcomponents may have different objectives, roles, stakeholder association and utility. In order to develop a computational architecture for enabling citizen participation in smart cities and delivering contextual information services, we need to categorise and understand these artefacts, their characteristics and inter-relationships. We describe a conceptual framework in the following section to elaborate this point further.

Conceptual framework for cloud-based context-aware services

The motivation behind introducing the framework is to develop a roadmap for the development of cloud-based context aware services for citizens of smart cities. The framework attempts to establish the what, why, how and who characteristics of the relevant artefacts and associated components or procedures. The artefacts are the main building blocks for the development of cloud-based context aware services architecture (discussed later). The artefacts include process models, data models, contextual models, citizen participation, application thematic models, cyberspace infrastructure, management aspects and service federation. The description (i.e. what), goals and objectives (i.e. why) of these artefacts briefly explain their purpose. In addition, various standards and technologies are identified to exemplify how these artefacts can be operationalised and who can be the potential stakeholders. The framework, explained in Table 1, also briefly describes the usefulness of the artefacts.

The framework is generic in a sense that various artefacts, components, standards and technologies can be applied (as platform-as-a-service or software-as-a-service model) depending on the need of different applications. Also, it is flexible to accommodate new artefacts and procedures and include new technologies and standards for various stakeholders. For example, the contextual

models artefact consists of three components structuring and profiling, context exchange and context management. These components contribute in developing user preference profiles, structuring and managing contextual information and associated actions to provide necessary information to end users. In the next section, we attempt to operationalise the above framework by developing a layered architecture using different framework artefacts.

Proposed architecture

Khan et al. [10] presented the capabilities required in a Cloud environment to acquire integrated intelligence for urban management systems. These capabilities provide a sound foundation to respond to smart cities requirements by developing a context-aware component in a Cloud environment. Here we apply the proposed framework and adopt the Cloud-based layered architecture proposed in [10]. The layered architecture is extended by introducing context-aware capabilities to respond to requirements of access to contextual information by citizens as well as data provision on demand basis, as depicted in Figure 3. The proposed architecture can be used to build either a platform-as-a-service or a software-as-a-service solution. For example, when it is used to build modelling service, then it becomes a platform-as-a-service solution on top of which other services can be built. When it is used to build a service that interacts directly with users, for example through visualisation, then it becomes a software-as-a-service solution. In 'Proof of the concept' section we present it as a software-as-a-service model.

The architecture depicted in Figure 3 consists primarily of five horizontal and two vertical layers. In our bottom up approach, the Platform Integration, Thematic and Data Acquisition and Analysis layers output generic data, which can be tailored to specific smart cities related application needs in the top three layers. One of the design principles here is to introduce context-aware components at different layers of the architecture in order to continually coordinate the vertical flow of data and retain or associate contextual information. Below we walkthrough the above architecture with the objective that how each layer contributes towards providing contextual information to end users for various purposes.

1. The *Platform Integration* layer constitutes a collection of hardware and software components providing the necessary computational infrastructure e.g. a hybrid public and private cloud instances that ensures cross-platform accessibility of data. In addition to the physical computational hardware and virtual Cloud resources, this layer also provides the integration of hardware and software sensors that form the data sources in this architecture. OGC's

Table 1 Context-aware citizen services framework for smart cities

Components or Procedures	Description (e.g. What?)	Goals/Objectives (e.g. Why?)	Operationalisation (e.g. How?)	Stakeholders (e.g. Who?)	Usefulness
			Process Models		
Data Processes	Processes related to data collection & acquisition, cleansing and filtering, harmonisation and integration	To ensure high quality raw data is collected and transformed into application specific target data model	Apache Solr, Appache Cassandra, (Geo-)SPARQL and RDF query languages, ISO 19100 series of standards, OGC PUCK protocol, OpenGIS Simple Feature Implementation specs (CORBA, OLE/COM)	**Data custodians** e.g. city administrations, local agencies including security, environment, energy, transport, and economic development, office of national statistics, Eurostat, etc. **Business organisations** e.g. insurance companies, utility services etc. **General Public** e.g. citizens, NGOs	Refinement of data and usability for variety of applications to get cross-disciplinary information intelligence
Service Processes	Process related to thematic service discovery, service chaining and/or workflow composition	To discover and connect with required utility services	UDDI, (CSW-)ebRIM, OGC OWS standards - WCS (metadata discovery), CSW (discovery), WMS (view), WFS (download), GeoAPI	**Service consumers** e.g. business organisations, public administrations, general public, etc. **Service producers** e.g. IT research industry, SMEs, statistical and IT experts etc	Service oriented approach supports process agility by using service plug-n-play feature
Analytical Processes	Analysis algorithms, statistical models, reasoning	To identify and use existing and new algorithms (machine learning, data mining etc) and models to analyse application specific data and generate required output	Hadoop MapReduce, RapidMiner, R, OGC WPS		Knowledge generation can support decision making
Security Processes	Authorisation, Anonymity, Encryption	To ensure that proper information security measures are applied	ISO/IEC 10181-4:1997 - Security Framework for Open System, GeoXACML	**Cyber security providers** e.g. SMEs. **Beneficiaries** e.g. general public.	Provides increased privacy and establishes trust on the system
User Interaction Processes	Visualisation, Simulation, Interactivity	To facilitate end users by providing intuitive GUI to interact with applications	Lynx Browser, OGC OpenLS, OGC Web 3D Service, WMS, OpenGIS SLD, OGC WMTS	**Social scientists**, e.g. experts in socio-technical aspects. **SMEs** e.g. IT developers, etc.. **End users** e.g. general public, etc.	Increases application usability and intuitiveness
Resource management Processes	Resource utilisation, virtualisation, performance and reliability	To ensure that system resources are utilised to their maximum potential	Public, private and hybrid cloud infrastructure e.g. IBM Smart City Control Centre	**IT Administrators**	Results in efficient resource utilisation that can contribute towards green computing
Organisational Processes	Business organisation and institutional processes	Aligning the information processing with business processes	BPMN, BPEL	**Organisations** e.g. Met Office, Disaster management authority, Tourism development, Public transport authority, Energy distributor, etc.	Ability to adopt organisational processes can result wider adoption

Table 1 Context-aware citizen services framework for smart cities *(Continued)*

Data Models					
Data Management	Standards and management of data and metadata	Structured (SQL/NoSQL based) and non-structured data management, Relational, Object-oriented, Cube, Spatial	OpenGIS specification based MySQL, NuoDB, Oracle, MS SQL Server, PostgreSQL - PostGIS, Apache Cassandra, CouchDB, MongoDB, SimpleDB, DynamoDB	**Data modellers and administrators** e.g. IT experts	Ability to store, retrieve, update and manage data
Metadata and Data structure		data and metadata models, Adoption of data and metadata standards such as ISO 19000, Dublin Core etc	Dublin Core, DBLP, OSI metadata standards - 19115, JSON, OGC NetCDF, EO metadata profile, CityGML, OGC TJS	**Data providers and custodians** e.g. city administrations, environmental agencies, office of national statistics, Eurostat, etc. **General Public** e.g. citizens.	Increases understanding and promotes reusability of data models
Contextual Models					
Structuring and Profiling	User profiles and preferences	To structure context information that can be reused for specific users and environments			Personalisation of information enhances usability
Context Exchange	Understandable context description for reusability purposes	To enable exchange context information between various services and components	ContextML, OGC Context standard, KML standard, OWL, RDF, OGC Web Map Context Document, Context casting	**Social scientists. IT experts. End users** e.g. general public, etc.	Exchanging context between various services helps to improve context-aware information processing and provision
Context Management	Context entity and relationship model	To manage context data model and associated actions for specific circumstances and environments			Structured management of context models enhances reusability and improves application performance
Citizen Participation					
Information provision	Awareness raising, Information provision, communication	To provide contextually related information to citizens and enable them to participate in decision making processes	Web 2.0/3.0, WS-Notification	**End users** e.g. general public, local business organisations, etc.	Contextual information for better decisions
Data collection	Crowd sourcing, Citizen science, Public participation and engagement		OGC SWE, SOS, SensorML, OpenLS, GeoSMS		Supporting participatory sensing and bottom-up democracy
Behavioural Change models	Behavioural changes of individuals or evolving business processes	To identify changes in behaviour of users due to environmental awareness	Interventions, policies, Study Protocol		Healthy and environment friendly behaviour change and better work productivity
Application Thematic Models					
Thematic Applications	Environment, Energy, Mobility, Security, Urban etc	To use collected data for specific application thematic domains		**Application domain experts** e.g. energy, transport, planning, health etc.	Application specific as well as cross-disciplinary integrated knowledge generation for better environmental and urban planning

Table 1 Context-aware citizen services framework for smart cities (Continued)

Cyber-space Infrastructure				
Hardware and software	Cloud infrastructure, Sensors, RFIDs, Storage, Processing H/W, IoTs, software frameworks	To apply related hardware and software technologies	OpenStack, Apache Cassandra	**IT experts and developers. SMEs** e.g. sensors web, wireless ad-hoc networks, cloud infrastructure, service provision etc.	Use of contemporary technology for information management
Management Aspects				
System Management	Flow of Info, auditing and pricing, security	To ensure that all components are well integrated and support flow of information and an appropriate cost model is developed	WebMethods, Oracle BPM Suite, OpenText	**IT Administrators**	Enabling sustainable business model
Service Federation				
System of systems	Application integration	Applying standards and developing wrappers/adaptors to enable flow of information between multiple applications and systems	Corba, Web Services	**IT experts and developers. SMEs. Research and Academia, Application domain experts**	Enabling inter-cloud information and resource exchange
Interoperability	Standards, service wrappers		W3C web standards, OASIS RM-ODP, OGC services		

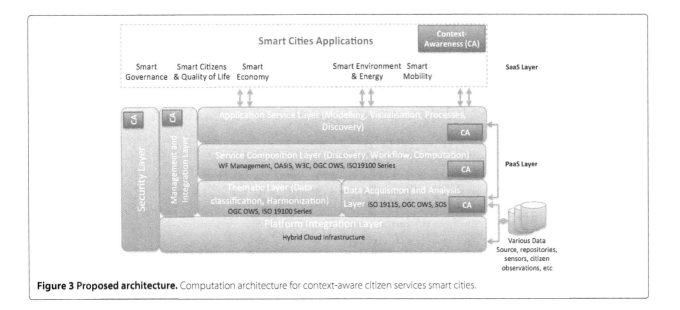

Figure 3 Proposed architecture. Computation architecture for context-aware citizen services smart cities.

Sensor Observation Service [22], which provides the standardised APIs for managing deployed sensors and retrieving observation data is a suitable candidate for this role. The standard also includes provisions for specifying sensor metadata, both for existing and new sensors and can thus provide the necessary building blocks for acquiring contextual information about the sensors.

2. The *Data Acquisition and Analysis* layer allows collection of environmental data from various sources including remote database repositories, sensor nets, and citizens' observations, e.g. using smart phones, in the Cloud environment. This layer also ensures the quality of data acquired and identifies the need for necessary data cleansing. A context-aware component is introduced here to filter out unrelated data and to perform quality check and harmonisation only to contextually related data. With respect to the sensed data format, Open GIS Sensor Modelling Language [22] is an established standard that caters for simple, aggregated and derived data concepts and supports multiple encodings (text, XML) as well. Other features that enable harvesting of contextual data from sensed observations include ability to encompass measurements about composite physical and non-physical processes, phenomena, temporal concepts and metadata information.

3. The *Thematic* layer classifies the acquired data into application specific thematic categories and performs data harmonisation and updates the data/service catalogues for further use of the data. The thematic categorisation of data, that is already contextually annotated, can help in its efficient and appropriate

utilisation by services and applications in the higher layers of the proposed architecture.

4. The *Service Composition* layer is required to design and specify service workflows, identify data sources, and link necessary processing components to enact the workflows that can constitute context-aware, citizen-specific services. Furthermore, necessary analytical analysis of the workflow outputs can be performed in this layer. This layer also ensures that the provenance of data and specific processes is maintained that can be utilised for analysis by different expert systems in the application layer. The context-aware component in this layer helps to utilise contextually related services for workflow composition and information generation.

5. The *Application Service* layer uses the outcomes from the service composition layer in application domain specific tools such as simulations, smart phone apps and visual maps to perform contextual analysis for decision-making. Further, this layer enables stakeholders to use existing tools and develop new application domain specific components and services (at SaaS level) to satisfy contextual information needs of end users. User context can be modelled in a simple, extensible and machine readable context representation formats e.g. a civil address context snippet related to a person is shown in ContextML [23] format in Figure 4. This layer also supports participatory sensing applications for collection of new data from end users. For example, reporting of micro-criminalities in a neighbourhood using smart phone application.

6. The *Management and Integration* layer is used to automate the flow of filtered data and information

```
<contextML> <ctxEls> <ctxEl>
    <contextProvider id="CAddrCP" v="1.0" />
    <entity id="3P31-Frenhay-UWE" type="room" />
    <scope>civilAddress</scope>
    <timestamp>...</timestamp>
    <expires>...</expires>
    <dataPart>
     <parS>
      <parA n="civilAddress">
       <par type="streetAdress">3P31, Frenchay Campus, Coldharbour Lane,
         University of the West of England, Bristol, BS16 1QY, UK</par>
       <par n="name">3P31</par>
       <par n="street">Coldharbour Lane</par>
       <par n="adminCode">BS16 1QY</par>
       <par n="locality">Frenchay Campus</par>
       <par n="adminUnit">Univeristy of the West of England</par>
       <par n="city">Bristol</par>
       <par n="countryCode">UK</par>
      </parA>
      <parA n="geographicalAddress">
       <par n="latitude"></par>
       <par n="longitude"></par>
      </parA>
     </parS>
    </dataPart>
   </ctxEl> </ctxEls> </contextML>
```

Figure 4 ContextML. ContextML encoded data for a person's civil address.

between the horizontal layers. It ensures that processed outputs from one layer to another are contextually related and syntactically correct. It also aims to handle change management that occurs at different layers and to reduce the extent to which the layered architecture requires management overhead.

7. The *Security* layer ensures the necessary authentication, authorisation and auditing for the use of data and services by legitimate users. Further, it ensures secure personalisation of end users services based on pre-defined preferences for processing and retrieval of contextual information from a Cloud environment.

Use case and discussion

The following discussion showcases a smart city scenario that can benefit from the architecture we have presented in the preceding section. Our premise rests on the importance of smart city solutions for urban governance that involves citizens' participation for their general wellbeing, city planning and decision-making. We consider citizens not as mere consumers of services offered in smart cities but highlight their inclusive role by acting as collectors

of data that informs the development and utilisation of such services. The issue in any such scenario is that the amount of data resulting from the efforts of public agencies that collect such data and contributions from citizens will overwhelm a conventional computing system due to initial and continually increasing storage and processing requirements and compromise quality of service. A Cloud computing based infrastructure that is designed with smart city themed services is well placed to address such issues.

Consider a local city government that maintains a collection of various parameters that reflect the quality of life in the region. These parameters may include general census information and population statistics, labour market profile, crime statistics, traffic, energy and water quality statistics, etc. Occurrence of crime is a critical indicator of the quality of life in a neighbourhood and affects the socio-economic outlook of the region significantly. Research has shown that in addition to the actual occurrence of crime, the perceived fear of crime is also a significant element that affects the quality of life measurement of a region [24,25]. Coupled with the fact that a proportion of crimes (or micro-crimes) go unreported

[26], and hence are not reflected in the regional quality of life records. We can present the use case where citizens, through our proposed architecture, can supplement the authoritative data by collection/submission of regional micro-crime statistics. This data then can be used to deliver informative services to the citizen for various purposes e.g. prototype scenario in next section.

1. *Data sources and Platform Integration Layer*

    (a) One of the major sources of data is through Open Data Initiative e.g. UK Open Data [27]. Many city councils and public agencies have started to publish data in both raw and processed, visual format. For example, crime and safety data profile of a local authority e.g. Bristol city council (Bristol Open Data initiative [13]) is a collection of related statistical indicators and can be downloaded as well as viewed in an online visual atlas. Such data is useful for various stakeholders in making decisions such as buying a house in a specific area. However, the aggregated data here is covered at ward scale and hence makes it difficult to associate individual aspects of crimes and safety to a specific spatial coordinates such as smaller streets. The following option (b) complements data collection by associating different events and citizens' perception to specific locations. The data storage and processing in performed in a cloud-based infrastructure to dynamically scale resource provisioning for citizens queries.

    (b) User reported micro (and/or macro) security events or crimes e.g. through a desktop based visual interactive map or smartphone based application using GPS coordinates.

2. *Data Acquisition and Analysis Layer*

    (a) The local authority collected data is imported into data repositories. The import process can be automated if data is in a standardised format e.g. compliant to Open Geospatial Consortium (OGC) OWS [28] and ISO 19000 Series on geospatial data standards [29]. Otherwise manual extraction, transformation and loading (ETL) process and conversion to standardised formats needs to be carried out.

    (b) Citizen submitted data, through smartphone or desktop-based applications is also imported at this layer. A significant difference from local authority data is that this submission can benefit from collection of user context at the time of submission e.g. location, time of submission, proximity to reported crime, relevance to supported crime (observer, witness) etc. This context awareness augmentation can be built into the data submission tools used by the citizens. However, this approach may require additional data quality checks to improve accuracy and precision of the spatial data captured by citizens. Also, privacy concerns must be dealt by security layer.

3. *Thematic Layer*: The available data is harmonised and classified into specific thematic areas e.g. Crime & Safety class, 'Bristol' locality, temporal validity of 2001–2012 are examples of expected classification parameters. The INSPIRE data specifications[a] play a major role in harmonising spatial data and reusing at various spatial scales.

4. *Service Composition Layer*

    (a) The collection, classification and harmonisation of the aggregated data at the lower layers provide a platform for utilising the data into workflow definitions for service composition. For example, administrators can specify the data fields which can serve as querying parameters for analysis or trigger points that can be used for generating notifications. For the use case being discussed here, these fields can be correlated with user context (through a user profile maintained in the 'Management' layer) such that applications can compare user preferences and specified parameters e.g. crimes and offensives related to dog attacks, during the evenings, within the past year.

    (b) Similarly, further data aggregation and analysis that can be carried out by using other data sources stored in the lower layers to generate datasets of higher complexity and granularity e.g. aggregating a crime profile with a 'Child wellbeing' profile [2] to link crimes or offences that can affect children including road accidents, dog attacks, fights, etc.

5. *Application Service Layer*: The services and applications at this layer build upon the data collected and aggregated with user context information in the lower layers. Exemplar application include dissemination of the collected data to users in novel, interactive formats including visualisations, analysis services, periodic reports and automated

triggers/notifications based on user context e.g. a user who frequents evening walks on a particular track may receive notifications of past and/or recent crimes in the vicinity of the track.

Proof of the concept

As a proof of concept we simulate a cloud-based implementation of selected components of the proposed framework. The purpose is to demonstrate the effectiveness of cloud-based infrastructures to meet Quality-of-Service (QoS) requirements in an urban environment. Based on the above use case, consider the scenario where a user is passing through an area in Bristol. The user would like to buy a flat in this area or start a small business. Such a user would be interested in information about the quality of life situation in that area (e.g. crime and safety, dog attacks, anti-social behaviour etc.). For this purpose, he opens up UrbanAwareness, a smart phone app provided by the City Council for just such purposes. The user selects Crime and Safety from the list of choices available and the app sends a query to the Council's servers along with contextual information; more specifically the coordinates of the user along with the data type preference. Moreover, the user also chooses to restrict the geographical radius about which information is presented to him. This radial preference is also sent by the app as part of the contextual information. For this simulation, we have chosen to focus on the Broadmead area of Bristol City Centre.

The contextual query

The query is encoded in ContextML [23] and sent to the contextual service where it is processed and the results returned to the user. A sample contextual query is shown in Listing 1.

In addition to the location and the radius preference of the user, it also contains a timestamp and an expiry limit for the information. This ensures that the location information is considered invalid after a reasonable amount of time as the user may be moving around.

Processing the queries

Processing the query involves retrieving all data pertaining to the city centre from the database. The data consists of reported incidents along with their description, location and date of occurrence. The incidents are filtered according to the user's preferences. In this case the Vincenty distance [30] from the user's location to the location of each reported incident is calculated. All incidents that occurred outside of the user's preferred radius are filtered. The remaining incidents are sent back to the mobile app, where they are visualised on a map and presented to the user.

Calculating the Vincenty distance between two points is a compute-intensive task. From the contextual service provider's point-of-view, there may be many users issuing similar queries at the same time. For example, in a medium-sized city of 400,000 to 1 million inhabitants, it is not unreasonable to expect that 20,000 or more people may be using the UrbanAwareness app at any given time. Such a high volume of concurrent queries can easily overload any desktop system, degrading the QoS. This is evidenced by the results shown in Figure 5. This figure depicts high execution times of such queries on a single compute node. In order to maintain an acceptable QoS, it may be desirable for the local council to process the queries concurrently on a cloud infrastructure. This prototype explores the efficacy of using such an infrastructure. The methodology adopted involves measuring the net execution time when multiple concurrent queries

Listing 1 Sample ContextML query

```
<contextML>
  <ctxEls>
    <ctxEl>
      <entity id="john" type="username" />
      <scope>location</scope>
      <timestamp>2014-02-08T16:21:20+01:00</timestamp>
      <expires>2014-02-08T16:26:20+01:00</expires>
      <dataPart>
        <par n="latitude">52.281571</par>
        <par n="longitude">8.024918</par>
        <par n="radius">0.5</par>
      </dataPart>
    </ctxEl>
  </ctxEls>
</contextML>
```

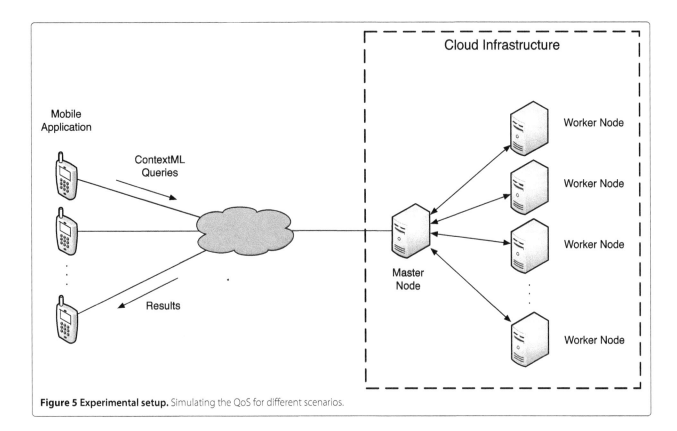

Figure 5 Experimental setup. Simulating the QoS for different scenarios.

are issued and processed for an urban environment. A mapping between various stages in the prototype application to specific layers in the proposed architecture is shown in Table 2. The prototype, therefore, comprises a cloud-based software-as-a-service.

Experimental setup

The experimental setup is shown Figure 6. The mobile application sends a query to the cloud infrastructure via the internet. The infrastructure consists of a single *master node* that also acts as the *scheduler*. This node is responsible for receiving queries from the mobile applications and dispatching them to the *worker nodes*. It is also responsible for receiving the results and communicating them back to the mobile applications. For these experiments actual crime data from the UK Police website[b] (http://www.police.uk/avon-and-somerset/BC192/crime/+osm1Dh/stats/) was used; in

particular, data about all reported incidents within 1 mile of the Broadmead area. To simulate the cloud infrastructure, the SimGrid toolkit was used [31]. It allows users to simulate execution of various kinds of jobs on distributed cloud infrastructures. The infrastructure itself is described in terms of its *topology*, *network connectivity* and *computing power*. To accurately simulate execution, a job is described using its *computing* and *data* requirements. The unit for computing power in SimGrid is Floating-Point Operations (FLOPS) and for data size is bytes. The parameters shown in Table 3 were used for the cloud infrastructure configuration.

To estimate the FLOPS required by a typical query of the previously-discussed nature, a sample query was implemented. This query took the user context, queried a database for reported criminal incidents and filtered the results based on the radial distance preference specified by the user. The FLOPS required by the application were then calculated using the following formula:

$$\mathcal{F} = R \times F \times C \times \phi$$

where $\mathcal{F}$ = FLOPS required by query

R = Runtime of query

F = CPU frequency in GHz

C = No of CPU cores

ϕ = CPU FLOPS per cycle per core

Table 2 Mapping the prototype to the proposed architecture

Prototype stage	Architecture layer
User interface	Application service layer
Crime statistics retrieval	Data acquisition and analysis layer
Data filtering	Service composition layer
Simulated cloud infrastructure	Platform integration later

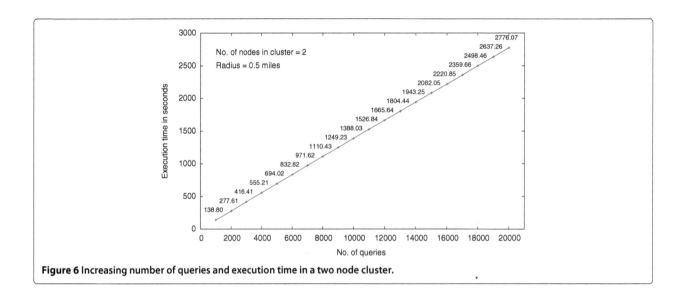

Figure 6 Increasing number of queries and execution time in a two node cluster.

The prototype query was executed on a quad-core 2.2 GHz processor using the Sandy Bridge architecture [32]. To simplify the calculation, the query process was bound to a single CPU core. To the best of our knowledge, a CPU with the Sandy Bridge technology can perform 8 FLOPS per cycle per core. Based on this and the observed runtime of the query, it was calculated that each query requires approximately 11 GFLOPS to be executed when the user radius preference was set to 0.5 miles and approximately 13 GFLOPS for a radius preference of 1 mile. The numbers of required GFLOPS will significantly increase with larger sample area.

Results

Using the aforementioned experimental setup, two sets of experiments were conducted. For both sets a simple Round-Robin scheduler was implemented [33]. In one set, the number of queries being executed on the cloud infrastructure were varied and the results are shown in Figures 7 and 8. For this set of experiments, a virtual cluster of 20 nodes was used. As can be seen, there is a significant increase in execution time as the number of queries increases. Such a delay in getting results significantly deteriorates the QoS for users who may consider it unacceptable. In the other set the number of queries remained constant (20000) while the number of nodes in the infrastructure were varied. The results for this are shown in Figures 9 and 10. In this case a sharp decline in execution time is observable at first as the number of nodes is doubled. However, the rate of decline decreases as computing power increases. This is due to the fact that as the number of nodes increases in the cluster, the cost of scheduling the queries for execution also increases. At a critical point (approximately at about 150 nodes), the time taken by the scheduler to schedule the first round of queries becomes greater than the time taken to execute a query. Therefore, at this point increasing worker nodes becomes meaningless since most of them sit idle for most of the time. Compared to these results, the relationship between total execution time and number of queries in the first set of experiments is linear because the number of nodes does not change. Thus, the scheduling time for the cluster remains constant, eliminating its influence.

Based on the aforementioned results, it can be argued that a utility-based computing model is well-suited for such applications in which demand ebbs and flows with time. Such a model is used in clouds, where resources are provisioned as they are needed and utilised elsewhere when they are not. This way resources are utilised efficiently. Moreover, it is also possible to dynamically decommission and recommission resources as required, saving both energy and money. Clouds have the added benefit that they are invisible to the user. Given all these benefits, clouds are an attractive option for organisations wishing to employ distributed processing resources for similar urban applications.

Table 3 Configuration parameters for simulated cloud infrastructure

Parameter	Value	Justification
Computing power	80 GFLOPS per machine	Approximately equivalent to a Quad-core 2.5 GHz Sandy Bridge CPU
Internet connectivity between machines	1 Gbps	Arbitrarily chosen value
Topology	Master-slave architecture	Represents typical cluster architectures
Network latency	50 ms	Arbitrarily chosen value

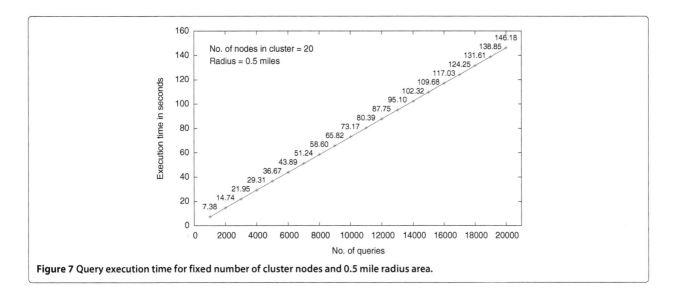

Figure 7 Query execution time for fixed number of cluster nodes and 0.5 mile radius area.

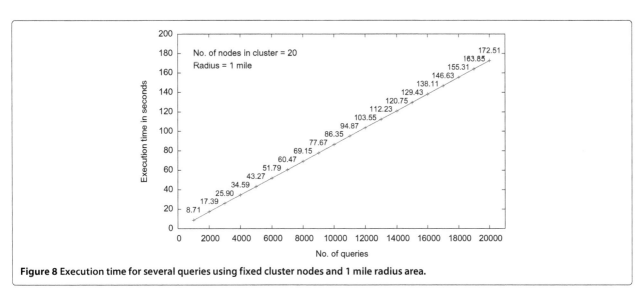

Figure 8 Execution time for several queries using fixed cluster nodes and 1 mile radius area.

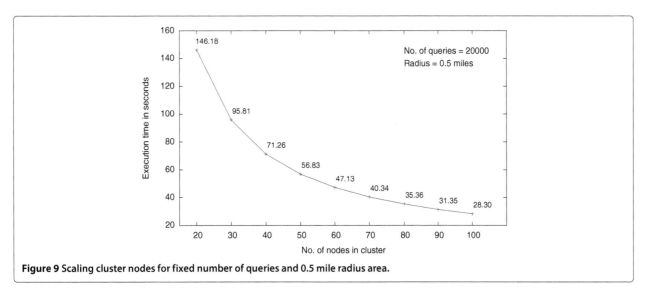

Figure 9 Scaling cluster nodes for fixed number of queries and 0.5 mile radius area.

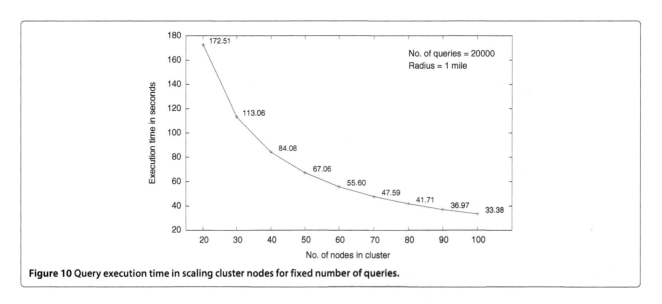

Figure 10 Query execution time in scaling cluster nodes for fixed number of queries.

Conclusion and future work

In this paper we have briefly presented a smart cities perspective and argued that it necessitates myriad of complex interactions between its different applications to generate intelligent information for smart urban governance. Further, we have proposed that Cloud computing can provide a suitable computing infrastructure for data storage and processing needs of smart cities applications. We also emphasise that, on one hand, end users e.g. citizens can collect data from their environment and, on the other hand, should be able to access contextual information from a smart cities based integrated information system with reasonable quality of service. The contextual information presents necessary information to end users based on their predefined preferences but it requires additional processing for contextual data preparation and information visualisation. In this regard, we have proposed a cloud based context-aware service framework and architecture. The context-aware components enable data processing in a specific application context and facilitate application layer to correlate information based on end users preferences.

The use case indicates that citizens' participation for quality of life and in particular crimes and safety related data collection can provide precise location information but is subject to data quality checks for accuracy tolerance. This capability of the proposed system can be utilised to raise awareness about crime and safety situation of specific places but can also help in collecting data from citizens using smart phones and/or web-based interfaces. However, much concentration would be required to ensure data security and digital citizens' privacy issues and QoS. Our proof-of-concept implementation of the proposed architecture indicates the effectiveness of cloud-based infrastructure for context-aware citizen services in smart cities. The prototype results show that in order to meet increasing number of user queries cloud-based dynamic resource provisioning can satisfy required QoS requirement. This is true especially when more citizens participate and/or area of interest for querying is enlarged (e.g. 1 to 10 miles). Our future work aims to develop a participatory application for data collection using sensors and smart phones and information provisioning using an open cloud-based infrastructure.

Endnotes

[a]INSPIRE Themes - Annexes: http://inspire.jrc.ec. europa.eu/index.cfm/pageid/2/list/7.

[b]Contains public sector information licensed under the Open Government Licence v2.0. (http://www. nationalarchives.gov.uk/doc/open-government-licence/ version/2/).

Competing interests
The authors declare that they have no competing interests.

Authors' contributions
ZK and SLK carried out the research in identifying the scope of this research. ZK developed the case for smart cities and citizen participation and SLK integrated context-based information development. ZK introduced the generic contextual framework and SLK applied it to the proposed architecture. Both applied the proposed architecture on a smart city use case. KS and ZK derived a scenario for prototype application. KS designed, described, implemented and evaluated the proof-of-concept implementation. He also presented and analysed the results of the evaluation. All authors read and approved the final manuscript.

Author details
[1]Centre for Complex Cooperative Systems, Faculty of Environment And Technology, University of the West of England, Coldharbour Lane, BS16 1QY Bristol, UK. [2]Department of Computer Science and Creative Technologies, Faculty of Environment And Technology, University of the West of England, Coldharbour Lane, BS16 1QY Bristol, UK.

References

1. Khan Z, Kiani SL (2012) A cloud-based architecture for citizen services in smart cities. In: Proceedings of the 2012 IEEE/ACM fifth international conference on utility and cloud computing. IEEE Computer Society, Washington, DC. pp 315–320
2. Ludlow D, Khan Z (2012) Participatory democracy and the governance of smart cities. In: Proceedings of the 26th annual AESOP congress, Ankara, Turkey
3. Suciu G, Vulpe A, Halunga S, Fratu O, Todoran G, Suciu V (2013) Smart cities built on resilient cloud computing and secure internet of things. In: Control Systems and Computer Science (CSCS), 2013 19th international conference on. IEEE. pp 513–518. http://ieeexplore.ieee.org/xpl/articleDetails.jsp?arnumber=6569312
4. Naphade M, Banavar G, Harrison C, Paraszczak J, Morris R (2011) Smarter cities and their innovation challenges. Computer 44(6):32–39
5. Mitton N, Papavassiliou S, Puliafito A, Trivedi KS (2012) Combining cloud and sensors in a smart city environment. EURASIP J Wireless Commun Netw 1:1–10
6. Gubbi J, Buyya R, Marusic S, Palaniswami M (2013) Internet of things (iot): a vision, architectural elements, and future directions. Future Generat Comput Syst 29(7):1645–1660. Elsevier Science Publishers B. V. Amsterdam, The Netherlands
7. Bandyopadhyay D, Sen J (2011) Internet of things: applications and challenges in technology and standardization. Wireless Pers Comm 58(1):49–69
8. European Environment Agency (2006) Urban sprawl in Europe, the ignored challenge. Technical report, ISBN: 92-9167-887-2, EEA and OPOCE. European Commission. http://www.eea.europa.eu/publications/eea_report_2006_10
9. Furht B, Escalante A (2010) Handbook of cloud computing. Springer, New York
10. Khan Z, Ludlow D, McClatchey R, Anjum A (2012) An architecture for integrated intelligence in urban management using cloud computing. J Cloud Comput 1(1):1–14
11. Komninos N, Schaffers H, Pallot M (2011) Developing a policy roadmap for smart cities and the future internet. In: eChallenges E-2011 conference proceedings, Paul Cunningham and Miriam Cunningham (Eds). IIMC International Information Management Corporation Ltd 2011. http://www.urenio.org/wp-content/uploads/2008/11/2011-eChallenges_ref_196-Roadmap-for-Smart-Cities-Publised.pdf
12. Meier R, Lee D (2011) Context-aware pervasive services for smart cities. Ubiquitous developments in ambient computing and intelligence: human-centered applications. IGI Global, pp 1–6. http://www.igi-global.com/book/ubiquitous-developments-ambient-computing-intelligence/45968
13. Bristol City Council GIS Support team (2014) Bristol data profiles. http://profiles.bristol.gov.uk. Accessed 06 Sept 2014
14. European Innovation Partnership (2012) Communication from the commission - smart cities and communities. Technical Report C (2012). 4701 final, European Commission. http://ec.europa.eu/energy/technology/initiatives/doc/2012_4701_smart_cities_en.pdf
15. Naccarati F, Hobson S (2011) IBM Smarter City Solutions on Cloud. http://public.dhe.ibm.com/common/ssi/ecm/en/giw03021usen/GIW03021USEN.PDF. Accessed 06 Sept 2014
16. IBM (2012) IBM Intelligent Operations Center for Smarter Cities. http://public.dhe.ibm.com/common/ssi/ecm/en/gvs03044usen/GVS03044USEN.PDF. Accessed 06 Sept 2014
17. La HJ, Kim SD (2010) A conceptual framework for provisioning context-aware mobile cloud services. In: Cloud Computing (CLOUD), 2010 IEEE 3rd international conference on. IEEE. pp 466–473. http://ieeexplore.ieee.org/xpl/articleDetails.jsp?arnumber=5557960
18. Kiani S, Anjum A, Antonopoulos N, Munir K, McClatchey R (2012) Context caches in the clouds. J Cloud Comput Adv Syst Appl 1(1):7
19. Kiani S, Anjum A, Antonopoulos N, Knappmeyer M (2014) Context-aware service utilisation in the clouds and energy conservation. J Ambient Intell Humanized Comput 5(1):111–131
20. Harkous H, Rahman R, Aberer K (2014) C3P: Context-Aware Crowdsourced Cloud Privacy. In: 14th Privacy Enhancing Technologies Symposium (PETS 2014). Springer International Publishing, Switzerland
21. Paelke V, Dahinden T, Eggert D, Mondzech J (2012) Location based context awareness through tag-cloud visualizations. Adv Geo-Spatial Inf Sci 10:265
22. Botts M, Percivall G, Reed C, Davidson J (2008) OGC® sensor web enablement: overview and high level architecture. In: GeoSensor Networks. Springer, New York. pp 175–190
23. Knappmeyer M, Kiani SL, Frà C, Moltchanov B, Baker N (2010) ContextML: a light-weight context representation and context management schema. In: Wireless Pervasive Computing (ISWPC), 2010 5th IEEE International Symposium On. IEEE, Modena, Italy. pp 367–372. http://ieeexplore.ieee.org/xpl/articleDetails.jsp?arnumber=5483753
24. Van Dijk J, Manchin R, van Kesteren J, Nevala S, Hideg G (2005) The burden of crime in the EU, A Comparative Analysis of the European Survey of Crime and Safety, EUICS Report. Gallup Europe:126. http://vorige.nrc.nl/redactie/binnenland/Misdaad.pdf
25. Keller W, Weinrich M (2004) Insecurities in European cities: crime-related fears within the context of new anxieties and community-based crime prevention. Final report HPSE-CT-2001-00052. DG Research, European Commission. Office for Official Publications of the European Communities, Luxembourg. p 152. http://cordis.europa.eu/documents/documentlibrary/100124091EN6.pdf
26. Nyiri Z (2005) Crime and security in European capitals. European Union International Crime Survey (EU ICS) Consortium. Research papers, Gallup Europe. pages 7
27. Shadbolt N, O'Hara K, Berners-Lee T, Gibbins N, Glasser H, Hall W, Schraefel MC (2012) Linked open government data: lessons from data.gov. uk. IEEE Intell Syst 27(3):16–24
28. Open Geospatial Consortium Inc. (2014) OGC Web Services Common Standard. http://www.opengeospatial.org/. Accessed 06 Sept 2014
29. Zarazaga-Soria FJ, Muro-Medrano PR (2005) Geographic information metadata for spatial data infrastructures: resources, interoperability and information retrieval. Springer, New York
30. Vincenty T (1975) Direct and inverse solutions of geodesics on the ellipsoid with application of nested equations. Surv Rev 23(176):88–93
31. Casanova H (2001) SimGrid: a toolkit for the simulation of application scheduling. In: cluster computing and the grid, 2001. Proceedings. First IEEE/ACM international symposium on. IEEE. pp 430–437. http://ieeexplore.ieee.org/xpl/articleDetails.jsp?arnumber=923223
32. Yuffe M, Knoll E, Mehalel M, Shor J, Kurts T (2011) A fully integrated multi-cpu, gpu and memory controller 32nm processor. In: Solid-State Circuits Conference digest of technical papers (ISSCC) 2011. IEEE. pp 264–266. http://ieeexplore.ieee.org/xpl/articleDetails.jsp?arnumber=5746311
33. Rasmussen RV, Trick MA (2008) Round robin scheduling – a survey. Eur J Oper Res 188(3):617–636

11

The design of a redundant array of independent net-storages for improved confidentiality in cloud computing

Martin Gilje Jaatun[1*], Gansen Zhao[2], Athanasios V Vasilakos[3], Åsmund Ahlmann Nyre[1], Stian Alapnes[4] and Yong Tang[2]

Abstract

This article describes how a Redundant Array of Independent Net-storages (RAIN) can be deployed for confidentiality control in Cloud Computing. The RAIN approach splits data into segments and distributes segments between multiple storage providers; by keeping the distribution of segments and the relationships between the distributed segments private, the original data cannot be re-assembled by an observer. As long as each segment is small enough, an individual segment discloses no meaningful information to others, and hence RAIN is able to ensure the confidentiality of data stored in the clouds. We describe the inter-cloud communication protocol, and present a formal model, security analysis, and simulation results.

1 Introduction

Security concerns are frequently cited [1,2] as one of the major obstacles to cloud computing adoption. In a traditional outsourcing scenario, technical and organizational security mechanisms contribute to protect a customer's data, but the most important factor is that the customer establishes a trust relationship with the provider. This implies that the customer acknowledges that if the provider is evil, the customer's data may be used improperly [3].

One aspect of Cloud Computing can be described as "outsourcing on steroids"; where both storage and processing is handled by one or several external providers, and where the provider(s) may be in a different jurisdiction than the customer. Not knowing where your data is physically located may be uncomfortable to the customer, and personal data may even be illegal to export from some jurisdictions [4]. Just like with traditional offshoring, settling disputes is more challenging when the provider may be on a different continent, which is all the more reason to limit the degree to which the customer has to trust the provider. This is the "need to know" principle in a nutshell

- if the provider does not need to read the information, why should it be allowed to?

In this article, we explore a Cloud Computing scenario where the dependency on *trust* will be reduced through a divide-and-conquer approach, where each actor gets access to sufficiently small units of data so as to minimize confidentiality concerns. In a way, our approach is the opposite of the aggregation problem in database security [5] – we *de-aggregate* the sensitive data.

The remainder of the article is structured as follows: In Section 2 we outline the background for our contribution. In Section 3 we sketch our solution, and detail the protocol between the various actors further in Section 4. We present a formal model in Section 5, and provide a security analysis in Section 6. We discuss implementation considerations in Section 4.6 and present simulation results in Section 7. We discuss our contribution in Section 8, outline further work in Section 9, and offer our conclusions in Section 10.

2 Background

Cloud computing provides on-demand services delivered via the Internet, and has many positive characteristics such as convenience, rapid deployment, cost-efficiency,

*Correspondence: martin.g.jaatun@sintef.no
[1] SINTEF ICT, Trondheim, Norway
Full list of author information is available at the end of the article

and so on. However, we have shown [6] that such off-premises services cause clients to be worried about the confidentiality, integrity and availability of their data.

In previous work [7], we identified five deployment models of cloud services designed to ease users' security concerns:

- **The Separation Model** separates storage of data from processing of data, at different providers.
- **The Availability Model** ensures that there are at least two providers for each of the data storage and processing tasks, and defines a replication service to ensure that the data stored at the various storage providers remains consistent at all times.
- **The Migration Model** defines a cloud data migration service to migrate data from on storage provider to another.
- **The Tunnel Model** defines a data tunneling service between a data processing service and a data storage service, introducing a layer of separation where a data processing service is oblivious of the location (or even identity) of a data storage service.
- **The Cryptography Model** extends the tunnel model by encrypting the content to be sent to the storage provider, thus ensuring that the stored data is not intelligible to the storage provider.

By use of these deployment models, we have shown [1] that through duplication and separation of duty, we can alleviate availability and integrity concerns, and to some extent also confidentiality by implementing encrypted storage. However, even with encrypted storage, we still have to trust the encryption provider with *all* our data. Furthermore, if the data needs to be processed in the cloud, the cloud processing provider in general also needs to have access.

The main motivation for confidentiality control in the cloud is currently various privacy-related legislation forbidding the export of sensitive data out of a given jurisdiction, e.g. the Privacy legislation in the EU [4]. The current solution to this problem has been to sidestep it: By offering geolocalized cloud services, where a customer may request the cloud provider to ensure that the sensitive data is only stored and processed on systems that are physically located in a geographically defined area, e.g., within the borders of the European Union. However, this is rapidly becoming a moot point, since cloud service providers typically run global operations, and although data might physically reside in one jurisdiction, it will in principle be accessible from anywhere in the world.

Although misappropriation of data by cloud providers has not been documented, Jensen et al. [8] show that current cloud implementations may be vulnerable to attack, and the first examples of Cloud compromises have surfaced [9]. Ristenpart et al. [10] demonstrate that even supposedly secret information such as where a given virtual machine is running may be inferred by an attacker, highlighting another attack path. Furthermore, insider malfeasors can be a challenge for any organization, and an incident at Google shows they are as vulnerable as anyone [11].

Krautheim [12] proposes to achieve cloud security through the introduction of Trusted Platform Modules (TPM) in all datacenter equipment. It is not clear, however, how the user could verify that a TPM is indeed present in any given cloud infrastructure. You might argue that the cloud provider could assert, and have an auditor confirm that they are using a TPM, but this is really not much better than today's situation where providers are asserting that they will treat your data properly, and all their certifications is a testament to them staying true to their words.

2.1 Previous work on security through splitting data

The Free Haven project [13] describes a collaborative distributed storage system, where participants are allowed to store (or publish) data by offering to store data for others, in the same general fashion of peer-to-peer file sharing. The Free Haven project does not provide a new solution for the anonymous communications channel, but uses a set of anonymous remailers as a basis. The Free Haven project makes no assumptions on the participants being honest, but uses a reputation system to identify non-cooperative (or dishonest) nodes.

The OceanStore [14] system is also based on distributed storage, but is not concerned with ensuring anonymity of the individual users.

The ShareMind framework [15,16] offers distributed privacy-preserving[a] computations, based on the principles of secure multiparty computations. Sharemind is not focused on (anonymous) storage; the current prototype solution is based on distributing data from one source among three nodes referred to as *data miners*, and is only secure as long as the three miners do not collude.

2.2 A brief introduction to Botnets

A *botnet* is a collection of compromised computers (*bots*) which are controlled by a human *botmaster*, often through a convoluted hierarchy of subnodes to evade detection and disclosure of the network and its owner. This is illustrated in Figure 1, inspired by by Wang et al. [17].

A traditional C&C (Command & Control) botnet is created by infecting regular PCs with malware that opens up a backdoor. Furthermore, the infected hosts actively poll a shared communication medium (typically: An Internet Relay Chat channel) for instructions. When correctly tagged instructions are observed on the shared medium,

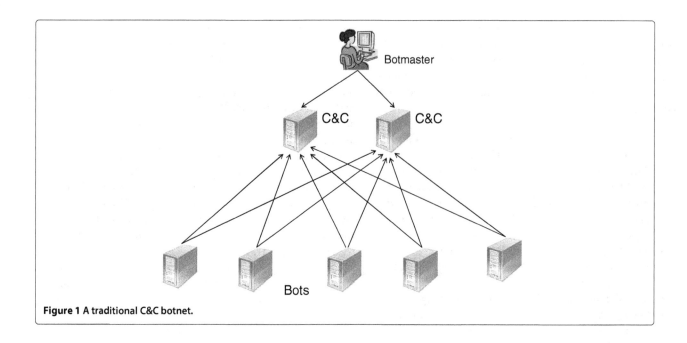

Figure 1 A traditional C&C botnet.

the infected host obeys without verifying (or even knowing) the identity of the issuer.

Botnets are used for mundane tasks such as sending unsolicited commercial email (spam) and performing Distributed Denial of Service (DDoS) attacks, but could in theory be used for any task that is amenable to distributed computing on nodes with modest processing and memory resources. In the following, we will show that we can exploit some properties of a botnet, not by infecting Cloud nodes, but by running autonomous agents as legitimate processes on Cloud processing providers.

3 Approach

We have extended the deployment models [1] with a new concept where data is split up and kept by several independent (non-colluding) storage providers in a Redundant Array of Independent Net-storages (RAIN) [6], in such a manner that a single chunk does not compromise confidentiality [18]. The data can then be stored using one or several cloud storage providers (duplicated, according to the deployment models).

3.1 Assumptions

The RAIN solution makes the following security assumptions:

1. We have a file (or dataset) that has been divided into small chunks
2. A provider will not be able to link two different chunks of the same dataset, should it gain access to them
3. The cloud service providers can be classified as "Honest but curious", i.e., we expect them to carry out

the protocol faithfully, but they may try to access the information either through collusion or other means.

4. There are enough simultaneous users to make anonymity feasible[b]
5. We have a lightweight authentication mechanism which can be used to regulate access to a data item
6. The C&C node has a list of "honest" Cloud Processing providers, and their public keys
7. The C&C node maintains a record of all data IDs
8. The C&C node maintains a record of all nonces generated by legitimate users and itself, for as long as a data ID is active
9. The user maintains a log of any outstanding requests sent to the C&C node, and will reject any unsolicited responses
10. The C&C node maintains a log of any outstanding requests sent to cloud processing providers, and will reject any unsolicited responses

The adversarial model is less powerful than Dolev-Yao, in that we assume that an adversary can observe all traffic, and possibly insert traffic, but not in general *delete* traffic (e.g. does not carry the message).

3.2 Using Botnets for non-nefarious purposes

We propose to organize the various elements in our distributed cloud architecture as a traditional multi-tier Command & Control (C&C) botnet, e.g. as described by Wang et al. [17].

We implement the shared medium as a cloud multicast service which can be freely accessed by anyone. To prevent tracing, we employ an approach similar to Onion Routing [19] when issuing commands from the C&C node.

We introduce a new type of cloud service provider which assumes the role of the botnet C&C node, and which is in charge of assembling the information and presenting it. This keeps all processing in the cloud, but leaves us with the problem that we have to trust this provider with our information. The resulting configuration is conceptually illustrated in Figure 2a.

The key property of the solution is that all the subnodes (cloud processing providers) and leaf nodes (cloud storage providers) only get to observe a small subset of a user's data, and that these nodes are prevented from associating a given piece of data with a specific user, or with other pieces of the same dataset. Ultimately, it will be like breaking open a large number of jigsaw-puzzles and distributing the pieces among storage providers – a single provider will not be able to determine where the pieces come from, or even if they are part of the same puzzle. Note that we do not propose to make the cloud processing provider work with encrypted data; the confidentiality control is achieved through the de-aggregation of information, and hiding the relationships between the processing providers. Also note that assuming the volume of such "botnet computations" is large enough (i.e., many enough users employ this technique), it is also possible to re-use providers, since it will not be possible for a provider to relate two different processing tasks with each other. Note that requiring a certain number of users is not unusual in similar applications, e.g., the TOR designers [19] make the same assumption regarding TOR's ability to provide privacy for its users.

For the truly paranoid, it could be possible to introduce uncertainties by routinely accessing bogus data, but although the user will know which data is real, and which is bogus, this will introduce the need for some "intelligence" on the client (to separate the wheat from the chaff), and we find ourselves transported to the alternative solution presented in Section 3.8.

3.3 A revival for autonomous mobile agents

Mobile agents [20] have already been suggested as a viable paradigm for services in Cloud Computing [21-23]. Many traditional security concerns with mobile agents are related to security of the host platform [24], but in a cloud setting these are mostly alleviated through the virtualization strategies employed. As will be detailed below, the mobile agent paradigm is a very good fit for the intermediate nodes in our design.

3.4 Example 1 – digital image

To illustrate the concept, we will in the following consider the storing of bitmap images in the cloud. Figure 3a shows a 480X480 image. The image is sliced into a 10X5 grid, of 48X98 pixels each. For our purposes, a single slice of the picture does not reveal much useful information to the observer, and this information can be stored unencrypted as long as it is not possible to combine it with the other slices.

The C&C node performs the slicing of the image, and randomly distributes the slices among (say) 10 subnodes. Each subnode then stores the slices independently

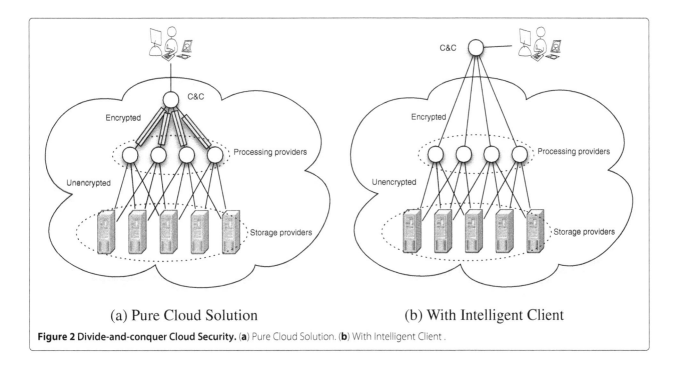

(a) Pure Cloud Solution   (b) With Intelligent Client

Figure 2 Divide-and-conquer Cloud Security. (a) Pure Cloud Solution. **(b)** With Intelligent Client .

(a) Original Lena Image   (b) Randomly Segmented Lena
                                           Image

Figure 3 Segmentation and Randonmization. (a) Original Lena Image. **(b)** Randomly Segmented Lena Image.

using as many cloud storage providers as available (ideally one for each slice, but even for this small example we would probably be hard pressed to find 50 independent providers). To prevent observability, the subnodes may use an encrypted tunnel to transfer the data to the storage providers.

It is the responsibility of the C&C node to keep track of which subnode has received which slices, but also to record the location. When the image is to be retrieved, the user will instruct the C&C node to fetch all the slices.

Admittedly, this is a toy example, with all the real processing being performed by the C&C node – the real challenge comes when it is required to perform complicated processing on each subnode. This will also introduce the need for more sophisticated "slicing" of data.

Note that, without the proper knowledge of the distribution of the slices, it is very unlikely that the original image can be reconstructed. Given all the slices, it is still not easy to reconstruct the original image, if the number of slices is large enough. Figure 3b is an example of the reconstructed image without knowledge of the slices' order. The reconstructed image does not look much like the original image. If the image is sliced into even smaller slices, the reconstructed image would be even more different from the original image.

3.5   Example 2 – electronic document
The need to permutate the different slices becomes more evident if we consider the example of an online document stored in the Cloud. The naïve solution might be to let every N character be stored at each cloud storage provider, but if the number of providers is as low as three, the risk of a single provider inferring the missing characters is too

high for our liking. However, if there is a sufficiently high number of users in total, and the cloud provides cannot differentiate between the users, even this solution may provide adequate security.

Updating a stored document will currently require storing everything anew as if it were a new document, since there are no relationships between the various slices. A possible future extension could be to allow the C&C node to keep track of changes, and only add new data. Note that although the previous example used contiguous image regions as slices (see Figure 3b), this is merely for illustration; both a document and an image could be sliced, e.g., by selecting every n^{th} byte.

3.6   Criteria
Since we perform the slicing and distribution of data in order to achieve data confidentiality, it is important that the slicing and distribution processes adhere to the following criteria:

- Data must be sliced into segments small enough such that each segment bears no meaningful information to malicious entities. With data sliced in this way, malicious entities may be able to access an individual data segment, but the access to the data segment should not compromise the confidentiality of the data as a whole.
- Data segments must be distributed in a random manner, such that it is not possible to establish the relationships between data segments without knowledge of the original data. The relationships between data segments are kept secret by the data owner.

With the above two criteria strictly enforced, the proposed approach would be able to ensure the confidentiality of data. This is achieved without encrypting the data.

3.7 Minimal data unit for processing

In the presented example, the minimal data unit that can be handled by a cloud processing provider is the entire image (e.g. for image manipulation). A similar situation is reasonable to expect for documents, whereas database operations may only need access to a limited number of records, not the whole database.

3.8 Alternative solution

If we are unwilling to trust the C&C provider described in the previous section, an alternative solution is place this functionality on the client, i.e. running on the user's own infrastructure, as figure 2b.

This solution requires a certain amount of computing power present on the client side in order to (re-)assemble all the different pieces of information produced by the cloud processing provides, and may thus not necessarily be considered a pure cloud solution.

4 Protocol

In the following we describe the protocol [25] to be used in RAIN in greater detail. The scheme is dependent on creating a small mix-net [26] in the cloud, and creating a collection of autonomous cloud processing agents explained below (see Figure 4). The autonomous agents will retain a one-to-one relationship with a cloud storage provider. Each agent will have a unique ID that is known

to the C&C node, but this knowledge should in principle not allow the C&C node to locate the agent. Furthermore, we need to create a cloud service that can serve as a broadcast medium similar to an IRC channel; for simplicity we will call this the IRC node.

4.1 Protocol for storing data

First, we will describe briefly the main thrust of the protocol, with more details in the following subsections.

Let D be a piece of data to be split and stored in the clouds. The user U will send D to the C&C node, encrypted with that node's public key:

$$U \rightarrow C\&C : \{store-full, auth, ID_D, D\}_{K_{C\&C}}$$

Here, "auth" is an authentication token used to verify the user's rights to the dataset[c]. If this message is replayed, it will be ignored; the only way to re-use a data ID is to first delete the data-set that uses it.

The C&C node performs the split [18] such that H can be represented as $H = < D_s, R_s >$ where

- $D_s = \{d_i | i = 1, ..., n\}$
- $R_s = \{< d_i, d_{i+1} > | i = 1, ..., n-1\}$.

Here, R_s specifies how the segments are related to each other; this knowledge is necessary for reassembly. The reulting sequence H can thus be written $H = (d_1, d_2, ..., d_n)$. We need to assign a unique ID (or pseudonym) to each data item, which we in the following refer to as ID_{di}.

The C&C node then distributes H among the cloud storage providers by assigning their respective identifiers

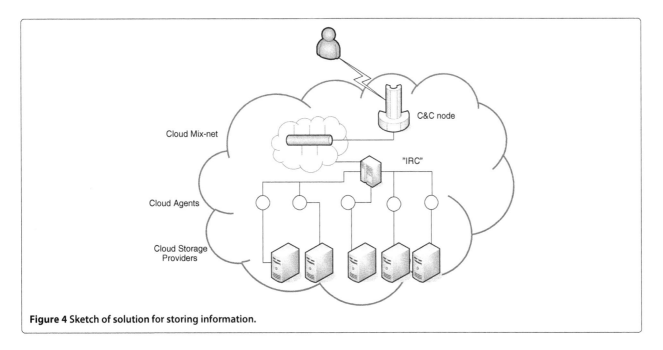

Figure 4 Sketch of solution for storing information.

$(CS_x, \ldots, CS_y)$ to the corresponding d_i, this through the mix-net (see section 4.2 for details) to IRC:

$$\forall i | C\&C \rightarrow IRC : mix(\{CS_j, store-part, auth, ID_{di}, d_i\})$$

The C&C node needs to maintain a table mapping which data items have been sent to which cloud storage service. Furthermore, it is important that the pseudonyms are unique within a given C&C provider, but created in such a manner that it cannot be determined that two different pseudonyms refer to data items from the same file. As mentioned in Section 3.1, we're assuming that the traffic volume will contribute to hide which items belong to which datasets, so although we are effectively broadcasting the mapping tables, this should not matter: An adversary can tell that the data item with pseudonym X is stored with cloud storage service Y, but this information is of little use if there is no way to tie the pseudonym to a dataset (or user). Furthermore, due to the use of the mix-net, the identity of the cloud storage provider is effectively a pseudonym as well.

The IRC node then publishes this information on its broadcast medium, where all the autonomous agents are listening. When an autonomous agent sees its own ID, it copies the associated d_i and stores this at its associated cloud storage provider.

4.2   Mix-net in the cloud

Chaum's original mix-net idea [26] has been employed with some success in the TOR network [19,27]. In the following, we will describe a simplified scheme tailored to the task at hand.

We assume we have a set of n autonomous agents $m_1, m_2, \ldots, m_n$. The agents are running as cloud web services, and their addresses and public keys are known to the C&C node.

By a slight paraphrasing of Chaum [26] we have that when using a single mixer node m_1, communication from Bob to Alice via m_1 occurs as follows:

$$B \rightarrow m_1 : \{R_m, m_1, A, \{R_a, A, store, d_i, CS_j\}_{K_A}\}_{K_m 1}$$

$$m_1 \rightarrow A : \{R_a, A, store, d_i, CS_j\}_{K_A}$$

Here, R_a and R_m are nonces that are discarded upon decryption, and d_i is the item of data to be sent. The only purpose of the nonce here is to prevent repeated sending of identical plaintexts from generating the same ciphertext. The parameter CS_j identifies the storage agent, which is effectively a pseudonym for the Cloud storage provider below. By recursively applying the scheme above, it is possible to extend it to an arbitrary number of mixer nodes.

In our case, the sender is the C&C node, and the final recipient is always the IRC node. The sole purpose of the mix-net is thus to hide the identity of the C&C node from the IRC node. Naturally, this only makes sense if there are multiple C&C nodes in the system as a whole. In the protocol descriptions, we will use the notation $mix(\ldots)$ to indicate that a message is sent through the mix-net.

4.3   IRC node

The IRC node receives a large amount of data items from multiple C&C nodes, and for each data item, the parameter CS_j identifies which *storage agent* should handle the item. The CRC then simply sends the following to *all* storage agents, using a fixed multicast address *Rain*:

$$\forall i | IRC \rightarrow Rain : CS_j, store-irc, auth, ID_{di}, d_i$$

The multicast traffic is UDP-based, and there is thus no acknowledgment or retransmission at the transport level. Although not explicitly shown here, an important feature is then that each data item must be sent to *multiple* storage agents; this redundancy both ensures duplication of storage, and introduces error tolerance in case of bit errors in the transmission.

4.3.1   Storage agent

Each storage agent subscribes to the *Rain* multicast address, and thus receives all the data items, but discards all messages that are not addressed to it. Note that the Storage agent ID (CS_j) can be viewed as a pseudonym, since it is never used as a return address in any way, and can thus not be directly linked to the storage agent.

The storage agents need to maintain a record of data items and associated IDs; the IDs are not actually revealed to the cloud storage providers. However, the storage agents are not anonymous to the cloud storage providers, i.e., the cloud storage providers can log the real addresses of the storage agents, but they do not know their pseudonyms.

4.4   Data retrieval

The user may ask the C&C to retrieve a dataset:

$$U \rightarrow C\&C : \{retrieve-full, auth, ID_D\}_{K_{C\&C}}$$

When asked to retrieve a dataset, the C&C node will need to ask each storage service via the IRC to return their respective data items:

$$\forall i | C\&C \rightarrow IRC : mix(\{CS_j, retrieve-part, ID_{di}\})$$

Note that we do not need to authenticate when retrieving individual data items in order to fulfill any security claims made by RAIN.

Unfortunately, simply running the storage process in reverse by asking for the data does not work, since an observer then quickly could make the link between storage agent pseudonym and its address. Instead, when we need to retrieve a data set, the C&C will instruct the IRC node to issue a "call for data items", listing the IDs of the data items. In order to complicate traffic analysis, the IRC node will also ask for some[d] bogus IDs; these will simply be discarded.

The storage agents that find matching data item IDs in their records, will retrieve these from the storage providers. In addition, they will also retrieve some other random data which will be discarded. Storage agents who don't find any data they have stored in the list will periodically retrieve random data, and send this on as explained below.

The retrieved data is then sent back to the IRC node, but this time via the mix-net. The IRC node then sends each data item back to the C&C node, again via the mix-net. This operation is dependent on the C&C node providing the IRC node with an anonymous return address [26].

Each storage agent[e] responds with its piece of the puzzle, and the IRC node forwards everything to the C&C node:

$$\forall i | IRC \rightarrow C\&C : mix(\{CS_j, return-part, ID_{di}, d_i\})$$

The C&C node then re-assembles the data, and either returns it to the user:

$$C\&C \rightarrow U : \{U, return-full, ID_D, D\}_{K_U}$$

or sends it off to be processed as explained in the next section.

The complete picture is illustrated in Figure 5.

4.5 Processing data in the cloud
When the user wants to do something with the data, it will tell the C&C node:

$$U \rightarrow C\&C : \{process-cnc, operation, auth, ID_D, N_u\}_{K_{C\&C}}$$

Here, "operation" identifies what should be done, ID_D identifies the dataset, and N_u is a nonce chosen by the user.

The data will first have to be retrieved and re-assembled as explained above. The C&C node then selects an appropriate number of cloud processing providers, depending on the type of data and what is to be done with it. If the data is, e.g., a digital image, and the user wants to manipulate it using a Cloud-based image editor, then the complete data set typically needs to be sent to a single processing provider.

$$C\&C \rightarrow CP_j :$$

$$\{\{CP_j, process-cp, operation, D, K_{PC}, N_c\}_{K_{CP_j}}\}_{mix}$$

The data, the nonce chosen by the C&C node, a symmetric key K_{PC} for encrypting the response, and the rest is encrypted with the public key of the cloud processing provider, and sent through the mix-net.

$$CP_j \rightarrow C\&C : mix(\{\{result-cnc, D_{result}, N_c\}_{K_{PC}}\})$$

Note that since the C&C node keeps track of requests to processing providers, the operations are idempotent; replayed responses are ignored, and in case of response failures, a new request will be sent, canceling the former.

The result is returned to the user:

$$C\&C \rightarrow U : \{U, result-user, D_{result}, N_u\}_{K_U}$$

Again, the user will reject any spurious responses with a nonce that doesn't match that of an outstanding request.

If the result is a change in the dataset, it will either have to be re-stored or delivered to the user, depending on the user's wishes. If data items need to be updated or deleted, the authentication mechanism comes into play again. In

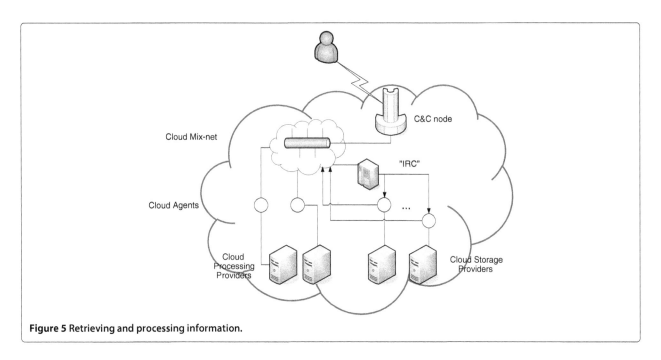

Figure 5 Retrieving and processing information.

any case, a confirmation is sent to the user, closing the outstanding request.

An example of an editing operation is shown in Figure 6. In this case, an image of a rodent (Figure 6a) is to be modified to become a feline (Figure 6d). This example also highlights an optimization opportunity; Figure 6b and 6c identify the modified areas of the image, and on completion only these parts need to be re-stored. The exact mechanisms of how to determine which parts have been changed are beyond the scope of this article, however.

4.6   Implementation considerations

Space does not permit a full implementation specification, but in the following we will illustrate in a little more detail how the actual storage and retrieval process may be realized from the C&C node's point of view.

Although we do not go into specifics here, it is clear that the actual splitting must depend on the type of document. The process is illustrated in Figure 7. A user (or a client running e.g. in a cloud environment) initiates writing of content to the system. The user can configure which storage providers to use for certain file types or content. Part of the config contains information on how each of the storage providers can be used, i.e. description on how to access, write and read content. Typically this can be a proprietary web API. Based on the selection of storage providers available and the content type a recipe is generated. The recipe states the size of blocks the original file is to be split into and a sequence for writing the blocks

to the various storage providers. Based on the recipe the content is divided in blocks that each is stored at a storage provider. The recipe is stored, and using the recipe, the content can be retrieved from the storage providers and assembled. The fileID is returned to the initiating part.

The retrieval process is illustrated in Figure 8. A user (or a client running e.g. in a cloud environment) initiates reading of content from the system. The recipe is retrieved based on the fileID. Based on the recipe the file is read from storage providers and assembled. The assembled file is returned to the initiating party.

5   Formal model

We recall from Section 4 that D is a piece of data to be split and stored on a cloud, and *split* is a function that splits D into a sequence H of smaller segments such that $H = (d_1, d_2, ..., d_n)$ where n is the number of segments D shall be split into.

The above process can be denoted as follows.

$$H = split(D) \tag{1}$$
$$= (d_1, d_2, ..., d_n) \tag{2}$$

Recall that H can be represented as $H = <D_s, R_s>$ where

- $D_s = \{d_i | i = 1, ..., n\}$
- $R_s = \{<d_i, d_{i+1}> | i = 1, ..., n-1\}$.

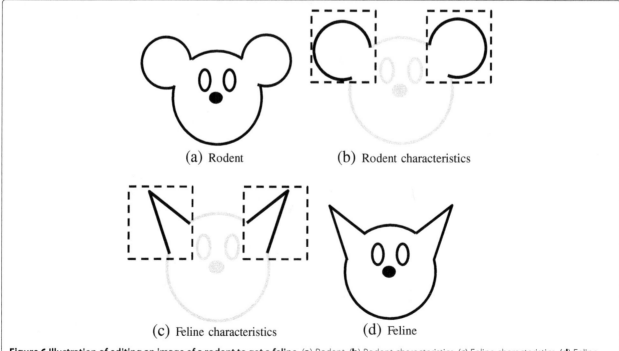

(a) Rodent

(b) Rodent characteristics

(c) Feline characteristics

(d) Feline

Figure 6 Illustration of editing an image of a rodent to get a feline. (a) Rodent. **(b)** Rodent characteristics. **(c)** Feline characteristics. **(d)** Feline.

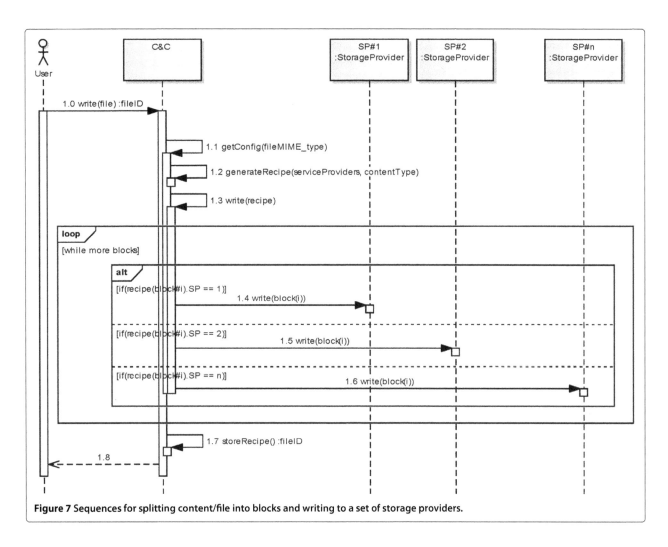

Figure 7 Sequences for splitting content/file into blocks and writing to a set of storage providers.

Note that D_s is the set of all segments D is split into. R_s is the set of relations between the segments in D_s, specifying the order of the segments.

The split data is then distributed to different service providers. In general, the dividing of the data is to control the length of each segment to avoid having too much information in a single segment. The permutation of the original data is to diffuse the data in a way that the new presentation conveys very limited information on the original data. Combining the division and permutation could greatly reduce the amount of information carried by a single segment.

5.1 Data segmentation

The criteria stated in section 3 mandate that the data segmentation must make sure that each data segment bears no sensitive information of the original data. The segmentation does not mandate the size of each segment as the size has not direct relationship with the information of the segment bears. Commonly, the bigger a piece of segment, the more information it may bear. Thus a bigger segment is more likely to bear sensitive information.

The criteria do not impose any restriction on the way the original data is segmented. A most simple way to segment data is a sequential segmentation, by which the original data is treated as a binary stream and is divided into multiple substreams in their original order, as illustrated by Figure 9. An alternative way to segment the original data is to pick bytes from random positions of the original data and put them into different segments. Figure 10 shows a case of data segmentation based on the random segmentation approach. The segmentation process is in fact a permutation of the original data, followed by dividing of the permutated data.

The data segmentation is in fact the implementation of the function *split*, where

$$H = split(D) \tag{3}$$
$$= (d_1, d_2, \ldots, d_n) \tag{4}$$

Assuming that e is the maximum amount of information that could be tolerated to be disclosed by any single segment, and *inf* be the function that evaluates the amount of information disclosed.

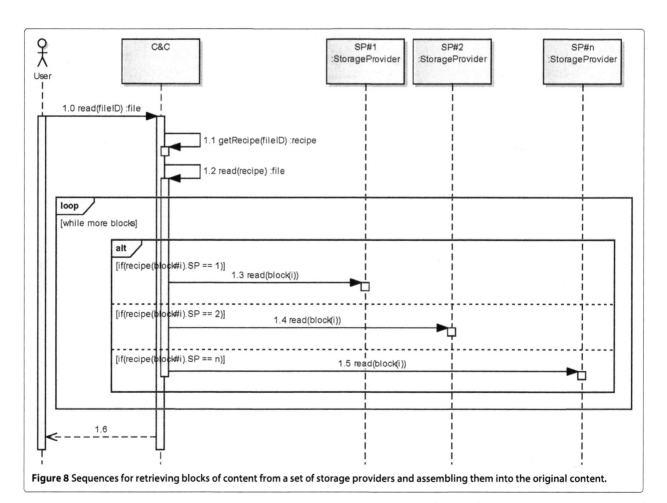

Figure 8 Sequences for retrieving blocks of content from a set of storage providers and assembling them into the original content.

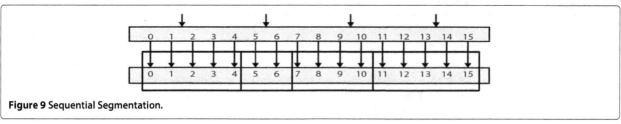

Figure 9 Sequential Segmentation.

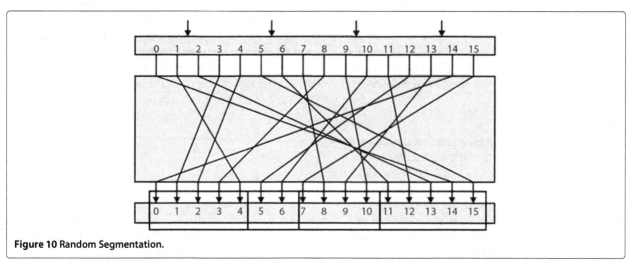

Figure 10 Random Segmentation.

The *split* funciton must make sure that the following holds.

$$\forall d_i \in D, inf(d_i) \leq e \qquad (5)$$

Assuming that E is the maximum amount of inforomation that could be tolerated to be disclosed by the whole set of segments, and INF be the function that evaluates the amount of information disclosed by a set of segments, where

$$INF(D_s) = inf(d_1) \times INF(D_s - \{d_1\}) \qquad (6)$$
$$= \times_{i=1}^{n} inf(d_i) \qquad (7)$$

$\times$ be an operator for calculating the sum of two disclosure degrees.

The *split* funciton must make sure that the following holds.

$$INF(D_s) \leq E$$

5.2 Randomize distribution

Once the original data is transformed into segments, the segments need to be stored on different cloud storage services. This is performed by the segment distribution process, which needs to make sure that the distribution is random to avoid tracking of the segments. Otherwise, segments can be identified by malicious users with limited cost.

Let M be the set of cloud providers that are providing cloud storage services. $\forall m_i \in M, \exists D_i \subseteq D_S$ such that $\forall d_j \in D_i$ then d_j is stored in m_i, where

$$\bigcup_{i=1}^{n} D_i = D \qquad (8)$$
$$D_j \bigcap D_i = \oslash \qquad (9)$$

The distribution process is to generate the set $D_D \subset D_S^*$, where $D_D = \{D_i | i = 1, \ldots, n, D_i$ is the set of segments kept on $m_i\}$. This process can be denoted by a function *dist*, where

$$D_D = dist(D_S, M) \qquad (10)$$

Note that D_D is the set of segment sets, specifying the set of segments on each storage server.

An ideal distribution would be a complete random distribution of the segments over the available cloud storage services. A possible way to achieve random distribution is to have the *dist* function randomly pick a cloud storage service for each segment, such that

$$p(d_i \in D_j) \leq \frac{|D_S|}{|M|} \qquad (11)$$

where $p(d_i \in D_j)$ denote the possibility that $d_i \in D_j$ holds, $|D_S|$ and $|M|$ represent the number of elements in the set D_S and M respectively.

5.3 Data re-assembling

The re-assembling of the original data requires two pieces of information.

1. The segment distribution information. The segment distribution information allows the picking of related segments from all the cloud storage services. This process is to generate either D_S out from all the segments kept on M without any secret information.
2. The order relations of the segments, R_S. With R_S, the picked data segments, D_S, can be permutated back to the original order to construct the original data.

6 Security analysis

Malicious users can either collect individual data segments or re-assemble the complete data to compromise the data confidentiality.

6.1 Compromization by a single data segment

Malicious users can randomly pick up individual data segments if they have excessive access privilege to the cloud storage services. Any individual data segment that is picked by a malicious user should disclose no information on the original data, according to the criteria of data segmentation. Therefore, it is not possible for malicious users to compromise the confidentiality by any single data segments.

6.2 Compromization by re-assembling

Malicious users can also re-assemble the original data. The re-assembling consists of a few steps as follows.

1. Picking all related data segments.
2. Permuting the data segments.

Picking all the related data segments requires a malicious user to have excessive access privileges to access all the involved cloud storage services, and also requires that the malicious user to pick up all the data segments from all the involved cloud storage services.

Suppose that for each $m_i \in M$, where M is the set of all the cloud storage services, the set of all data segments stored by the cloud storage service m_i is N_i.

The number of data segments stored in M is *TotalSegs* where

$$TotalSegs = \sum_{i-1}^{|M|} |N_i| \qquad (12)$$

To be able to re-assemble the original data, a malicious user must be able to pick all the segments and permutate the segments into the right order.

If the malicious user does not know the number of segments the original data has been split into, the total number of possible re-assembled data is *NumOfAllReassembled*, where

$$Num\ Of\ All\ Reassembled = \sum_{i=1}^{U} P^i_{TotalSegs} \qquad (13)$$

$$= \sum_{i=1}^{U} P^i_{\sum_{i-1}^{|M|}|N_i|} \qquad (14)$$

Where R is the upper limit of the number of segments that a data is likely to be split into.

If the malicious user knows, s, the number of segments the original data has been split into, the total number of possible re-assembled data is *NumOfReassembled*, where

$$Num\ Of\ Reassembled = \sum_{i=1}^{s} P^i_{TotalSegs} \qquad (15)$$

$$= \sum_{i=1}^{s} P^i_{\sum_{i-1}^{|M|}|N_i|} \qquad (16)$$

Both cases require a large amount of computation to brute-force search the complete space. Hence it is not trivial for a malicious user to compromise the data confidentiality by re-assembling the original data.

From a complexity point of view, assuming that there are in total n pieces of data stored in the cloud, let a malicious user try to illegally access a file, which has been split into k pieces and kept in the cloud. The malicious user must first re-assemble the whole file, taking two steps.

1. Step 1: All k pieces must be retrieved corrected out from the n pieces. The probability to retrieve the correct pieces is as follows.

$$p_1 = \frac{1}{C_n^k} = \frac{k!}{n*(n-1)*\cdots*(n-k+1)}$$

2. Step 2: Re-order all the k pieces into the correct order, given the k pieces. The probability of putting all k pieces in the right order without any knowledge of the original data is

$$p_2 = \frac{1}{P_k^k} = \frac{1}{k!}$$

Hence, the probability of re-assembling the file correctly is

$$p = p_1 \times p_2 = \frac{k!}{n*(n-1)*\cdots*(n-k+1)} \times \frac{1}{k!}$$

$$= \frac{1}{n*(n-1)*\cdots*(n-k+1)}$$

Assuming that there is a very large number of pieces in the cloud and each file is split into small enough chunks, n

and k are both large enough to ensure that the probability p is small enough to counter attacks.

The cost for an attacker is far from only the computation complexity of re-assembling the k pieces. Due to the distributed characteristics of the proposed storage system, the system contains a very large amount of data and the data are distributed across various networks. The attacker attempting to re-assemble a file by brute force will have to have an extremely large storage space to keep all the retrieved data pieces (both the correct ones and the wrong ones), and it also has to afford the cost for the network bandwidth to transfer such an amount of data across the network.

6.3 Protocol analysis

As can be seen from Table 1, pain has been taken to avoid reusing commands that otherwise might have made it possible to replay messages from A to B as a message from B to C. This is according to Principle 1 of Abadi and Needham [28], and to some extent also Principle 3, since it ensures that every message will only be handled by the same type of actor as intended. However, full adherence with Principle 3 may be difficult to achieve in a setting of anonymous communication. The explicit naming of commands is also in accordance with Principle 10, since it allows for unambiguous encoding of each message.

Since data is sent encrypted from the C&C node to the Cloud Processing provider, it cannot be observed by an

Table 1 Summary of all protocol commands

Command	Explanation
store-full	Command from User to C&C to store a complete dataset
store-part	Command from C&C to IRC to store a piece of data
store-IRC	Command from IRC to storage agent to store a piece of data
retrieve-full	Command from User to C&C to retrieve a complete dataset
retrieve-part	Command from C&C to Cloud Storage provider to retrieve a piece of data
return-part	Cloud Storage provider is returning a piece of data
return-full	C&C node is returning a complete dataset to User
process-cnc	Command from User to C&C to perform processing operation on a dataset
process-cp	Command from C&C to Cloud Processing provider to perform processing operation on a dataset
result-cnc	Cloud Processing provider returning result of processing operation on a dataset to C&C node
result-user	C&C node returning result of processing operation on a dataset to User

adversary, who cannot determine the symmetric key used to encrypt the response, and thus cannot do a suppress-replay attack to replace the result with a bogus result. We are assuming the C&C node has verified public keys to the providers, which means only the selected provider sees the data, but as long as the relationship between user and data is kept secret, it does not really matter exactly *which* Cloud Processing provider handles the data.

By applying the Scyther tool [29], we find (unsurprisingly) that the assumption that data and session keys from the C&C node are kept confidential holds (see Listing 1), but unless the public key of the processing provider has been verified, we cannot assume that it remains confidential. Since the Scyther tool does not support verifying privacy/anonymity claims, it cannot be used to verify the full protocol.

6.4 Listing 1: Scyther code for verifying confidentiality

```
/*
 * Secrecy protocol
 *
/* Uses asymmetric encryption
*/

// PKI infrastructure

const pk: Function;
secret sk: Function;
inversekeys (pk,sk);

// The protocol description

protocol protocol0 (I,R)
{
        role I
        {
                const ni: Nonce;
                const data;
                secret sessionkey: Function;
                send_1(I,R, {ni,sessionkey}pk(R) );
                claim_i(I,Secret,ni);
                claim_i(I,Secret,sessionkey);
        }

        role R
        {
                var ni: Nonce;
                var sessionkey: Function;
                read_1(I,R, {I,ni,sessionkey}pk(R) );
        }
}

// An untrusted agent, with leaked information

const Eve: Agent;
untrusted Eve;
compromised sk(Eve);
```

Note that we have made no claims with respect to resource consumption on the cloud providers. Thus, it may be possible for a malfeasor to waste the resources of a Cloud Processing provider by replaying `process-cp` messages from the C&C node. This could be countered by having the Cloud Processing provider store all nonces N_c,

and discard all messages with non-fresh nonces, but since this does not contribute to keeping data and users anonymous, it has been omitted to avoid forcing the providers to maintain state information. However, in a possible future commercial solution, this might be solved as part of a payment solution.

7 Simulations

In this section we describe our efforts to simulate the performance of the protocol. The source code and detailed settings are available from the authors upon request.

7.1 Simulation environment

We implemented the protocol utilising a the Nessi simulation framework[30] written in the Python programming language. The main motivation for selecting a Python-based framework was the flexibility and ease of use that the programming language offers despite its obvious performance penalty as compared to other C and C++ based simulation frameworks. The Nessi Framework is not currently actively maintained and lacks a few basic elements such as support for the Internet Protocol (IP), Address Resolution Protocol (ARP) and Transport layer protocols such as TCP and UDP. The framework offer a stack consisting of everything up to and including the Data Link Layer of the OSI reference model as well as some application layer traffic generators. We therefore had to make some simplifying assumptions to cater for the fact that our protocol is designed to run on top of TCP/IP or UDP/IP.

7.2 Simulation implementation

Since our implementation aimed at demonstrating the delay and throughput of the protocol, we simplified the described protocol somewhat. The Mixnet is modelled as a number of nodes connected through a Point-to-Point (P2P) links. Each node contains three network interface cards and is randomly connected to other mixnet nodes through these cards. The Mixnet does not setup a path or route information in the network, instead we specify a *hopcount* that determines the number of times a packet should be forwarded by the network. Forwarding is done by randomly selecting one of the network interface cards attached to the host and then forwarding over the data link layer to the host connected to the other end. When the hopcount reaches zero, the mixnet node forwards the packet to the IRC-node. The IRC-node is connected to the mixnet through an Ethernet bus, and forwards packets to the agents on another Ethernet bus. By utilising the MAC-address as an application level address, our implementation circumvents the problems of not having a network layer protocol. The user and C&C are represented as Traffic generating sources attached to a mixnet-node, whereas the agents are implemented only as Traffic sinks. Hence, the protocol is only implemented in one direction.

7.3   Simulation setup

The default values of all simulation parameters are given in Table 2 and if not explicitly stated otherwise, these are the values used for all simulation runs. We have attempted to keep the values as realistic as possible, without exhausting the resource requirements of the PC running the simulations. This particularly includes memory allocation, which can be quite challenging in Python.

The Mixnet size is given in number of nodes contained in the network and is relatively small compared to what is foreseeable in the Cloud. However, it should be sufficiently large to provide meaningful data. Further, the hopcount, i.e. the number of times a packet is routed inside the mixnet, is set to half the size of the network. The packet size set to 1/10000 of the traffic source data size and the redundancy factor is set to 1. Thus, the default behaviour is not to have redundancy in packet transmission. All of these parameters are configured one at a time for the various simulation runs, except the number of network interfaces per node. This is set to 3, such that each node has a direct connection to three other nodes in the network.

The traffic source is supposed to mimic a kind of FTP-traffic generation. That is, traffic data is characterised by fairly long inter-arrival times and relatively large PDU sizes, which resembles the action of storing data quite well. The simulation time is adapted to the traffic inter-arrival time. The number of agents in the RAIN-network does not really affect the simulation at this point, since we only consider one-way traffic to the agents.

7.4   Results

In this subsection we provide the results and interpretations of our simulation runs related to *delay*, *throughput* and *queue length*.

7.4.1   Delay

Since we have chosen a traffic source that produces burst-traffic, the packet delay as measured on the agents also tend to vary greatly. Figure 11 demonstrates the periodicity of the delay function as compared to the arithmetic mean (dotted line). We measure the delay by recording the time interval between when the packet was sent and when it was received. Hence, we only consider end-to-end delay and do not compute intermediate packet delays (e.g. after k hops).

The packet delay is of course dependent on the distance it has to travel and the amount of time spent being processed and queued along the way. However, in our setup we have fixed the distances between nodes and therefore view delay as a product of changed traffic intensity. In Figure 12 demonstrates that only direct changes to the source traffic either by increasing the PDU size or replicating the packets causes significant changes to the delay. Whereas altering the hop count and packet size of the mixnet have little influence on the end-to-end packet delay. A reason for this may be that additional transmissions within the Mixnet tend to stretch the burst and thereby reduce the congestion problems occurring when to many nodes transmit simultaneously.

7.4.2   Throughput

We measure the throughput as it is seen by the agent, that is, the number of octets received by the agents within the simulation time. The computation is somewhat hampered by the lack of error handling due to missing network and transport layer protocols. However, the average queue

Table 2 Default simulation settings for the RAIN protocol

Mixnet settings

MIXNET_SIZE⋆	= 10
MIXNET_HOPCOUNT⋆	= 5
MIXNET_PACKET_SIZE⋆	= 1 kB
MIXNET_REDUNANCY_FACTOR⋆	= 1
MIXNET_LINKS_PER_NODE	= 3

Traffic source settings:

TRAFFIC_INTERARRIVAL	= 50 s
TRAFFIC_TYPE	= PoissonSource
TRAFFIC_PDU_SIZE⋆	= 10 MB
SIMULATION_TIME	= 100 s

Network characteristics:

LINK_DATA_RATE	= 100MB/s
LINK_DISTANCE	= 1000 km

Agent network settings:

AGENT_NUMBER	= 5

Items marked ⋆ are configurable and may vary.

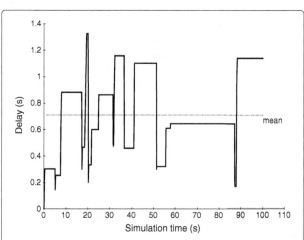

Figure 11 Packet delay on default simulation measured on the agents.

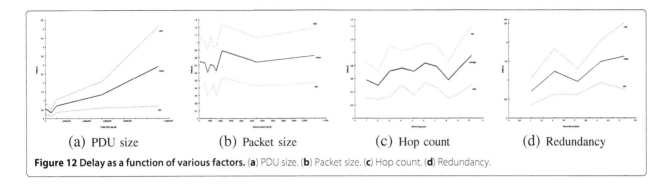

Figure 12 Delay as a function of various factors. (a) PDU size. **(b)** Packet size. **(c)** Hop count. **(d)** Redundancy.

time (see next paragraph) suggests that there are not too many packets dropped.

The throughput is dependent on the amount of inbound traffic in the network, the delay and the packet drop rate. Therefore, as can be seen in Figure 13, increasing the traffic through either PDU size, redundancy or number of nodes yields increased throughput. Note however that the increase in network size (number of nodes and traffic sources) is not proportional to the increase in throughput. Doubling the network size yields only about 50% increase in throughput. The hop count does not seemingly affect the throughput consistently. It is unclear why there is a considerable peak around the default hop count value (MIXNET_HOPCOUNT= 5).

7.4.3 Queue length

We measure the queue length on all nodes in the Mixnet at with a sampling frequency of 10/s. Any changes to the queue between these samples are not detected and hence we only provide an estimate of the queue length. Note that we measure the total queue length, i.e. the sum, on all nodes in the Mixnet. The packet delay described above is partially dependent on the queue length, such that the longer the queue, the longer the delay. However, the reason for measuring the queue length of Mixnet nodes is that are indicators for network congestion.

From Figure 14 we see that both the size of traffic source generated PDUs and the redundancy factor greatly influence the queue length. Also, the Mixnet packet size affects the queue length as larger sizes reduces the queues to a

level close to zero. The hopcount has only moderate effect on the queue, which is in line with what we discovered for packet delay and throughput. Note however, that although the average total queue length is quite small, the standard deviation is considerable, indicating that the queue may be considerable for shorter periods of time. This is expected since the traffic source we have selected, generates packets in bursts which yields a burst behaviour in the queues as well.

8 Discussion

Cloud service providers have been identified as potential targets of attack simply because of the vast amounts of data they store on behalf of their multitude of customers. In this sense, it may be in the providers' best interest to "know less" - if even the provider cannot access the customers' data directly, there is little point in attacking them.

Strictly speaking, most users would probably be happy if it were possible to impose universal usage control [31] on data submitted to providers (a sort of "reverse DRM", where end-users get to control how multi-national corporations use their data), but despite Krautheim's efforts [12], we do not believe this will be a reality in the foreseeable future. Thus, it would seem that the easiest way to control what a provider does with your information is to hide it - either through encryption (as previously proposed for the storage providers) or through separation. A brief comparison of RAIN with other such approaches is provided in Table 3.

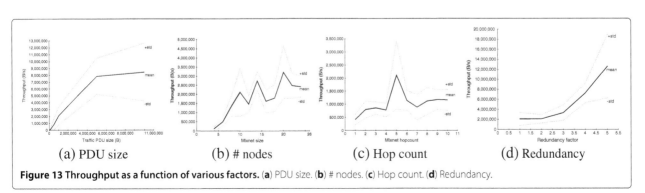

Figure 13 Throughput as a function of various factors. (a) PDU size. **(b)** # nodes. **(c)** Hop count. **(d)** Redundancy.

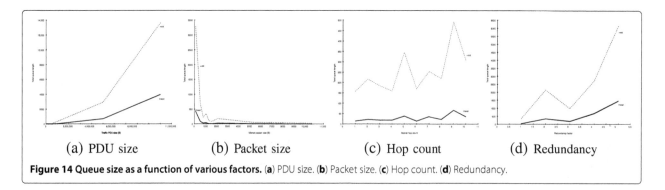

Figure 14 Queue size as a function of various factors. (**a**) PDU size. (**b**) Packet size. (**c**) Hop count. (**d**) Redundancy.

In a real-life setting, there will be cases where very small units of data carry a significant amount of sensitive information, such as blood type for patients. It will thus be imperative that not only shall it not be possible to match e.g. a blood type to an identity, but in storage it should also not be possible to determine what the data item refers to.

In this respect, our approach is different from the *k*-anonymity concept proposed by Sweeney [39], since we assume that it generally will *not* be possible for an observer to deduce what the data mean; Sweeney's concept is meant to ensure "statistical anonymity" by ensuring that at least *k* different persons have the same characteristics in any given dataset.

8.1 Searching and indexing

One major unsolved problem with our solution is related to searching and indexing. Even if it were possible to create an index to search in, where can we store it? Thus, we currently have to accept that searching is not possible without re-constructing each file first.

8.2 Business model

It's been said that everybody wants security, but nobody is willing to pay for it. This means that not only is it difficult to get funding for security measures in organizations where security is viewed as a net expense, but most users are also not willing to put up with the extra inconvenience that added security mechanisms often imply. Contrasting this with the (at least currently) free services such as Google Docs [40] that cloud providers are throwing at customers, it may be hard to imagine anybody paying money to get the same thing "more secure".

However, privacy is evidently an issue for some people, as the usage statistics of the TOR network can testify [19], and also experiments in Scandinavia have shown that many people will choose privacy if it's made available to them [41]. In general, it is dangerous to confuse the concepts of "privacy" and "confidentiality", but in our case we believe that the privacy aspects will be the major driver for people wanting to keep their data confidential.

Table 3 Comparison of RAIN with other approaches of splitting data

Approach	Summary	Misgivings
Singh et al. [32]	A scheme for *n-out-of-m* secret sharing of data [33]	Do not provide an algorithm for the actual splitting of the data to be stored.
Parakh and Kak [34]	Another *n-out-of-m* scheme	Do not discuss why their scheme should be better than e.g. the one proposed by Rabin [35].
Luna et al. [36]	Yet another *n-out-of-m* scheme, but add an additional concept of *Quality of Security* (QoSec) to rate individual storage providers.	Solution is tailored to a Grid computing scenario, not to commercial cloud operators.
RACS [37]	Prevents vendor lock-in and data loss through failures by performing striping of data (in RAID-5 fashion) across multiple cloud providers	Does not offer privacy or confidentiality.
Mnemosyne [38]	Offers steganographic storage which not only hides data, but also prevents anyone from determining that there is anything hidden in the first place.	Mnemosyne encrypts each block, and thus requires a key management system in addition to the information dispersal algorithm.
Free Haven [13]	A collaborative distributed storage system, based on peer-to-peer file sharing principles.	Does not provide a new solution for the anonymous communications channel, but uses a set of anonymous remailers as a basis.
OceanStore [14]	Provides distributed storage	Is not concerned with ensuring anonymity of the individual users.
ShareMind [16]	Offers distributed privacy-preserving computations	Is not focused on storage, only computation.

How to pay for the services anonymously has not been completely resolved. Most existing solutions such as TOR [19] and Free Haven [13] are based on volunteer or barter arrangements, where participants get free use of the service by supporting parts of it on their own systems. The payment problem is also the main obstacle for Chaum's approach [42], since he assumes the existence of a digital cash system, something which remains elusive. Still, since the cloud paradigm is oriented toward *pay per use*, we believe it will be easier to solve this in the clouds than in many other situations.

8.3 Trust

Since we place all our trust in the C&C node, it will remain as a "single point of trust" as long as it is realized as part of the cloud. It would have been desirable to strengthen this by ensuring that the C&C node provider only sees the information as we see it ourselves, preventing it from mining stored information. However, as long as the C&C node is required to keep track of all the data items (or slices, as in the example), there is nothing to prevent it from accessing this information as it pleases. Currently, only the alternative solution in Figure 2b keeps this information out of the cloud.

However, we maintain that even if we still have to trust the C&C node in the cloud, this in an improvement over handing all our data over to Google. The C&C node in effect plays the role of a Trusted Third Party, and generally does not need to have the enormous resources of the current commercial cloud providers. Thus, the C&C node could in principle be run by some small company in the user's neighbourhood, enabling a traditional trust relationship.

9 Further work

This divide-and-conquer approach may be suitable for privacy-conscious home users and small businesses, but the ultimate holy grail is absolute confidentiality in the cloud, and thus a deliverance from trust. Only then can cloud computing deliver on the dream of computing power as a utility akin to power, water and gas. A further refinement of our approach that removes the necessity to trust the C&C node is therefore a natural challenge.

We have implemented a simple proof-of-concept prototype [43], so the next step will be to implement a large-scale prototype to gauge performance impacts on typical cloud applications. One particular challenge in this respect is to determine the optimal slicing strategy for arbitrary data. It is likely that a trade-off between security and efficiency will have to be made in order to capitalize on the advantages of the Cloud Computing paradigm. The prototype will be targeted toward a "sensitive but unclassified" application, representing a realistic use case.

10 Conclusion

We have described the design of the Redundant Array of Independent Net-storages (RAIN) that achieves confidentiality in the cloud through dividing data in sufficiently small chunks. We have provided a formal model and security analysis to motivate our claims, and our simulation results indicate that the efficiency of our approach is acceptable. We believe that this may be useful for small office and home users, but experimentation and practical experience will be necessary to validate the approach.

11 Endnotes

[a]It may be a matter for debate whether the solution rather should have been referred to as *confidentiality*-preserving.

[b]This is a rather fuzzy assumption, but it is clear that if there are only two parties communicating, an adversary can trivially determine that all data observed leaving one party will arrive at the second party. This assumption of "more than a few" users is also used in, e.g., TOR [19].

[c]In the current description, we make no attempt to hide the identity of the user from the C&C node, so here we could assume that the authentication is an (as yet unspecified) conventional mechanism authenticating the user to the C&C provider. However, in the following we will use this authentication mechanism to control access to individual data items, and in this case the cloud providers should of course not know the identity of the user or other actors.

[d] The number of bogus IDs requested is configurable.

[e]It may be debatable whether it makes sense to include the provider ID in the response, but certainly the C&C node ID cannot be there, as it is supposed to be anonymous.

Competing interests
The authors declare that they have no competing interests.

Acknowledgements
This work has been supported by Telenor through the SINTEF-Telenor research agreement, by China State Key Lab of Software Engineering through grant SKLSE2010-08-22, and by China Canton-HK research project TC10-BH07-1.

Author details
[1] SINTEF ICT, Trondheim, Norway. [2] South China Normal University, Guangzhou, China. [3] University of Western Macedonia, Florina, Greece. [4] Telenor Research and Future Studies, Trondheim, Norway.

Author's contributions
MGJ initated the RAIN concept, constructed the RAIN protocol and drafted the article. GZ constructed the formal model and performed the security analysis. AVV contributed to the formal model. ÅAN performed the simulations and wrote up the results. SA provided the implementation considerations. YT contributed to the security analysis. All authors read and approved the final manuscript.

References
1.   Zhao G, Rong C, Jaatun MG, Sandnes F (2012) Reference deployment models for eliminating user concerns on cloud security. J Supercomputing 61(2): 337–352. http://dx.doi.org/10.1007/s11227-010-0460-9 [10.1007/s11227-010-0460-9]

2. Chen Y, Paxson V, Katz RH (2010) What's new about cloud computing security? Technical Report UCB/EECS-2010-5, EECS Department, University of California, Berkeley. http://www.eecs.berkeley.edu/Pubs/TechRpts/2010/EECS-2010-5.html

3. Nyre ÅA, Jaatun MG (2010) A probabilistic approach to information control. J Internet Technol 11(3): 407–416

4. European Parliament (1995) Directive 95/46/EC of the European Parliament and of the Council of 24 October 1995 on the protection of individuals with regard to the processing of personal data and on the free movement of such data

5. Hinke TH (1988) Inference aggregation detection in database management systems. In: Proceedings of the 1988 IEEE conference on, Security and privacy, SP'88. IEEE Computer Society, Washington, DC, USA, pp 96–106. http://portal.acm.org/citation.cfm?id=1949221.1949237

6. Jaatun MG, Nyre ÅA, Alapnes S, Zhao G (2011) A Farewell to, Trust: An Approach to Confidentiality Control in the Cloud. In: Proceedings of the 2nd International Conference on Wireless Communications, Vehicular Technology, Information Theory and Aerospace & Electronic Systems Technology (Wireless Vitae Chennai 2011). IEEE, Piscataway, NJ

7. Zhao G, Rong C, Jaatun MG, Sandnes F (2010) Deployment Models: Towards Eliminating Security Concerns from Cloud Computing. In: Proceedings of the International Conference on High Performance Computing & Simulation. pp 189–195

8. Jensen M, Schwenk J, Gruschka N, Iacono LL (2009) On Technical Security Issues in Cloud Computing. In: Cloud Computing, IEEE International Conference on, Volume 0. IEEE Computer Society, Los Alamitos, pp 109–116

9. Whitney L (2009) Amazon EC2 cloud service hit by botnet, outage. http://news.cnet.com/8301-1009_3-10413951-83.html

10. Ristenpart T, Tromer E, Shacham H, Savage S (2009) Hey, you, get off of my cloud: exploring information leakage in third-party compute clouds. In: Proceedings of the 16th ACM conference on Computer and communications security. ACM New York, pp 199–212

11. Chen A (2010) GCreep: Google Engineer Stalked Teens, Spied on Chats. Http://gawker.com/#!5637234/gcreep-google-engineer-stalked-teens-spied-on-chats

12. Krautheim F (2009) Private virtual infrastructure for cloud computing. In: proceedings of the Workshop on Hot Topics in Cloud Computing, HotCloud

13. Dingledine R, Freedman MJ, Molnar D (2000) The Free Haven Project: Distributed Anonymous Storage Service. In: Proceedings of the Workshop on Design Issues in Anonymity and Unobservability

14. Rhea S, Eaton P, Geels D, Weatherspoon H, Zhao B, Kubiatowicz J (2003) Pond: the OceanStore Prototype. In: Proceedings of the 2nd USENIX Conference on File and Storage Technologies (FAST '03)

15. Bogdanov D, Laur S, Willemson J (2008) Sharemind: a framework for fast privacy-preserving computations. Cryptology ePrint Archive, Report 2008/289. Http://eprint.iacr.org/

16. Cybernetica News blog - Sharemind (2008). http://research.cyber.ee/sharemind/. Http://research.cyber.ee/sharemind/, visited: Sept. 9, 2010

17. Wang P, Wu L, Aslam B, Zou CC (2009) A Systematic Study on Peer-to-Peer Botnets. In: ICCCN '09: Proceedings of the 2009 Proceedings of 18th International Conference on Computer Communications and Networks. IEEE Computer Society, Washington, pp 1–8

18. Zhao G, Jaatun MG, Vasilakos A, Nyre ÅA, Alapnes S, Ye Q, Tang Y (2011) Deliverance from Trust through a Redundant Array of Independent Net-storages in Cloud Computing. In: Proceedings of IEEE Infocom

19. Dingledine R, Mathewson N, Syverson P (2004) Tor: The second-generation onion router. In: Proceedings of the 13th conference on USENIX Security Symposium-Volume 13. USENIX Association, Cerrito, pp 21–21

20. Wooldridge M (2002) An Introduction to MultiAgent Systems. John Wiley & Sons Ltd, Chichester

21. Li X, Zhang H, Zhang Y (2009) Deploying Mobile, Computation in Cloud Service. In: Jaatun M, Zhao G, Rong C (eds) Cloud Computing, Volume 5931 of Lecture Notes in Computer Science. Springer, Berlin / Heidelberg, pp 301–311. http://dx.doi.org/10.1007/978-3-642-10665-1_27. [10.1007/978-3-642-10665-1_27]

22. Zhang Z, Zhang X (2009) Realization of open cloud computing federation based on mobile agent. In: Intelligent Computing and Intelligent Systems, 2009. ICIS 2009. IEEE International Conference on, Volume 3. pp 642–646

23. Aversa R, Di Martino B, Rak M, Venticinque S (2010) Cloud Agency: A Mobile Agent Based Cloud System. In: Complex, Intelligent and Software Intensive Systems (CISIS), 2010 International Conference on. pp 132–137

24. Borselius N (2002) Mobile agent security. Electron & Commun Eng J 14(5): 211–218

25. Jaatun MG, Zhao G, Alapnes S (2011) A Cryptographic Protocol for Communication in a Redundant Array of Independent Net-storages. In: Proceedings of the 3rd IEEE International Conference on Cloud Computing Technology and Science (CloudCom 2011)

26. Chaum DL (1981) Untraceable electronic mail, return addresses, and digital pseudonyms. Commun ACM 24: 84–90. http://doi.acm.org/10.1145/358549.358563

27. McCoy D, Bauer K, Grunwald D, Kohno T, Sicker D (2008) Shining Light in, Dark Places: Understanding the Tor Network. In: Borisov N, Goldberg I (eds) Privacy Enhancing Technologies, Volume 5134 of Lecture Notes in Computer Science. Springer, Berlin / Heidelberg, pp 63–76. http://dx.doi.org/10.1007/978-3-540-70630-4_5

28. Abadi M, Needham R (1996) Prudent engineering practice for cryptographic protocols. Software Eng, IEEE Trans 22: 6–15

29. Cremers C (2006) Scyther - Semantics and Verification of Security Protocols. Ph.D. dissertation, Eindhoven University of Technology

30. Vernez J, Ehrensberger J, Robert S (2006) Nessi: A Python Network Simulator for Fast Protocol Development. In:Computer-Aided Modeling, Analysis and Design of Communication Links and Networks, 2006 11th International, Workshop on. IEEE, Piscataway, NJ, pp 67–71

31. Park J, Sandhu R (2004) The UCON_ABC usage control model. ACM Trans Inf Syst Secur 7: 128–174

32. Singh Y, Kandah F, Zhang W (2011) A secured cost-effective multi-cloud storage in cloud computing. In: Computer Communications Workshops (INFOCOM WKSHPS), 2011 IEEE Conference on. pp 619–624

33. Shamir A (1979) How to share a secret. Commun ACM 22: 612–613. http://doi.acm.org/10.1145/359168.359176

34. Parakh A, Kak S (2009) Online data storage using implicit security. Inf Sci 179(19): 3323–3331. http://www.sciencedirect.com/science/article/pii/S0020025509002308

35. Rabin MO (1989) Efficient dispersal of information for security, load balancing, and fault tolerance. J ACM 36(2): 335–348

36. Luna J, Flouris M, Marazakis M, Bilas A (2008) Providing security to the Desktop Data Grid. In: Parallel and Distributed Processing 2008 IPDPS 2008 IEEE International Symposium on. pp 1–8. http://ieeexplore.ieee.org/xpls/abs_all.jsp?arnumber=4536443

37. Abu-Libdeh H, Princehouse L, Weatherspoon H (2010) RACS: a case for cloud storage diversity. In: Proceedings of the 1st ACM symposium on Cloud computing, SoCC '10. ACM, New York, NY, USA, pp 229–240. http://doi.acm.org/10.1145/1807128.1807165

38. Hand S, Roscoe T (2002) Mnemosyne: Peer-to-Peer Steganographic Storage. In: Revised Papers from the First International Workshop on Peer-to-Peer Systems, IPTPS '01. Springer-Verlag, London, pp 130–140. http://dl.acm.org/citation.cfm?id=646334.756802

39. Sweeney L (2002) k-anonymity: A model for protecting privacy. Int J Uncertainty, Fuzziness and Knowledge-Based Syst 10(5): 557–570

40. Google (2011) Google Docs - Online documents, spreadsheets, presentations, surveys, file storage and more. Http://docs.google.com

41. Larsen NE (2009) Privacy in The Polippix Project. In: D 7.3 PRISE Conference Proceedings: "Towards privacy enhancing security technologies - the next steps". pp 143–149

42. Chaum D (1988) The dining cryptographers problem: Unconditional sender and recipient untraceability. J Cryptology 1: 65–75. http://dx.doi.org/10.1007/BF00206326 [10.1007/BF00206326]

43. Jaatun MG, Askeland C, Salvesen AE (2012) Drizzle: The RAIN Prototype. In: "Proceedings of the 12th International Conference on Innovative Internet Community Systems"

12

Towards bandwidth guaranteed energy efficient data center networking

Ting Wang[1*], Bo Qin[1], Zhiyang Su[1], Yu Xia[1], Mounir Hamdi[1,2], Sebti Foufou[3] and Ridha Hamila[3]

Abstract

The data center network connecting the servers in a data center plays a crucial role in orchestrating the infrastructure to deliver peak performance to users. In order to meet high performance and reliability requirements, the data center network is usually constructed of a massive number of network devices and links to achieve 1:1 oversubscription for peak workload. However, traffic rarely ever hits the peak capacity in practice and the links are underutilized most of the time, which results in an enormous waste of energy. Therefore, aiming to achieve an energy proportional data center network without compromising throughput and fault tolerance too much, in this paper we propose two efficient schemes from the perspective of resource allocation, routing and flow scheduling. We mathematically formulate the energy optimization problem as a multi-commodity minimum cost flow problem, and prove its NP-hardness. Then we propose a heuristic solution with high computational efficiency by applying an AI resource abstraction technique. Additionally, we design a practical topology-based solution with the benefit of Random Packet Spraying consistent with multipath routing protocols. Both simulations and theoretical analysis have been conducted to demonstrate the feasibility and convincing performance of our frameworks.

Keywords: Energy efficiency; Data center network; Energy-aware routing; Bandwidth allocation

Introduction

The data center, as a centralized repository clustering a large number of servers, has become home to essential large-scale computation, storage and Internet-based applications which provide various services like search, social networking, e-mails, gaming, cloud computing, and so on [1,2]. In order to provide high performance service with strong reliability to users, the data center network (DCN) architectures are usually over-provisioned and constructed aggressively with large number of switches and links to achieve high-capacity and high fault tolerance [3]. However, the research [4,5] shows that, in practice the average link utilization in different data centers ranges only between 5% and 25% and varies largely between daytime and night. This reveals that most network devices and links stay idle or underutilized most of the time, but an idle device consumes up to 90% of the power consumed at full loads [6], which leads to a great waste of energy. Apart from the energy wasted due to over-richly network

*Correspondence: twangah@cse.ust.hk
[1] Hong Kong University of Science and Technology, Hong Kong SAR, China
Full list of author information is available at the end of the article

interconnections, traditional non-energy-aware routing algorithms (like shortest path routing or its variations) can also lead to poor link utilization or even congestion, which worsens the situation.

According to current research findings [7,8], the power consumed by servers and infrastructure (i.e. power distribution and cooling) accounts for over 70% of overall power, while the network consumes around 15% of the total power budget. However, as the servers become more energy proportional, the fraction of the power consumed by the network in a data center grows correspondingly higher. As illustrated in [4], suppose the servers are totally energy-proportional, when the data center is 15% utilized (servers and network), then the network will consume up to 50% of overall power. Even if the servers are not energy-proportional, with 15% traffic load, making the network proportional still can save as much as 975 KW (for a data center with 10,000 servers) [4]. Unfortunately, today's commodity network devices are not energy proportional, mainly because the components of the network devices (such as transceivers, line cards, fans, etc) are always kept on regardless of whether they have data packets to transfer or not, leading to a significant energy wastage.

Based on the above observations, this paper aims to achieve a bandwidth guaranteed energy proportional data center network, where the amount of power consumed by the network is proportional to the actual traffic workload. The key principle behind this approach is that most of time the traffic can be merged and satisfied by just a certain subset of network devices and links, and the remaining ones can be put onto sleep mode or powered off for the sake of power conservation. With this goal, we propose two efficient green frameworks from the perspective of bandwidth allocation and flow scheduling. However, the bandwidth in a data center is a scarce resource [9,10], and the energy-aware routing problem is NP-hard, which is proved in Section "Problem statement". Besides, the time complexity of dynamically computing a feasible network subset to meet the traffic demands is horrible and unmanageable due to the exponential number of nodes and routes. In order to address these critical issues, derived from Artificial Intelligence our first framework employs a resource abstraction technique named Blocking Island (BI) and some well designed heuristic algorithms to efficiently reduce the searching space and significantly decreases the computation and time complexity. This framework can be applied in any arbitrary data center network topology. In the second framework, we put forward a topology-based energy-aware algorithm by computing a network subset and adopting one recently proposed multipath routing mechanism RPS [11] for flow scheduling and packet transmission.

The primary contributions of this paper can be summarized as follows:

1.) We formulate the energy optimization problem in DCNs mathematically and prove its NP-hardness.
2.) We propose two efficient general frameworks, which provide efficient solutions from the perspective of bandwidth allocation, routing and flow scheduling.
3.) To the best of our knowledge, we are the first to employ the AI model - Blocking Island Paradigm into data centers for resource allocation to achieve power savings.
4.) We conduct extensive simulations to evaluate and demonstrate the performance of our frameworks under various network conditions and reliability requirements.

The rest of the paper is organized as follows. First we review the related research literature in Section "Related work". Then we formulate the energy optimization problem and prove its NP-hardness in Section "Problem statement". Afterwards, Blocking Island Paradigm is briefly reviewed in Section "Blocking island paradigm". Then we propose two energy-aware heuristic schemes in Section "Energy-aware heuristic schemes", followed by the evaluations and simulation results in Section "System

evaluation". Finally, Section "Conclusion" concludes the paper.

Related work

A considerable amount of investigation and research for achieving a green data center have been conducted in both academia and industry due to its great potential and benefits. Apart from the works on green/renewable resources [12-14], low-power hardware [15-18], energy-efficient network architecture [4,19-23], and network virtualization techniques (VM migration and placement optimization) [24,25], there are also many network-level proposals, which focus on traffic consolidation. The typical representatives include ElasticTree [5], and Energy-aware Routing Model [26].

ElasticTree is a network-wide energy optimizer, which consists of three logical modules – Optimizer, Routing, and Power Control. Once the Optimizer outputs a set of active components, Power Control toggles the power states of ports, linecards, and entire switches, while Routing chooses paths for all flows, then pushes routes into the network. The authors proposed three types of optimizers with different quality of solution and scalabilities. The formal method achieves the best solution but is computationally very expensive and does not scale beyond a 1000-node sized data center. The greedy bin-packer ends up with suboptimal solutions as with any greedy approach but is much faster than the formal method. Lastly, the topology aware heuristic needs the smallest amount of computation time but the quality of its solution is inferior to both the greedy and formal method.

Energy-aware Routing Model is also a network-wide approach, which aims to compute the routing for a given traffic matrix, so that as few switches are involved as possible to meet a predefined performance (throughput) threshold. The basic idea is that: Firstly, they take all switches into consideration and compute basic routing and basic throughput. Then, they gradually eliminate the switches from basic routing and recompute routing and throughput until the throughput reaches the predefined threshold. Finally, they power off the switches not involved in the routing. However, this approach suffers inefficient computation efficiency, where it takes several seconds to calculate a non-optimal power-aware routing paths for thousands of flows and takes even hours to calculate a near optimal solution, which is intolerable for a latency-sensitive data center network.

Problem statement
MCF problem description
The multi-commodity flow (MCF) problem is a network flow problem, which aims to find a feasible assignment solution for a set of flow demands between different source and destination nodes. The MCF problem can be

expressed as a linear programming problem by satisfying a series of constraints: capacity constraints, flow conservation, and demand satisfaction. This problem occurs in many contexts where multiple commodities (e.g. flow demands) share the same resources, such as transportation problems, bandwidth allocation problems, and flow scheduling problems. In the next subsection, we show that the energy-aware routing problem can also be formulated as an MCF problem.

Problem formulation

From the perspective of routing, the crucial resource to manage in a data center is the bandwidth. To describe the bandwidth allocation problem in a data center network $G = (V, E)$, we define the constraints as follows:

1. Demand completion—each traffic demand specified as a tuple (i, j, d_{ij}) should be satisfied with the required bandwidth simultaneously, with i, j, d_{ij} $(i, j \in V)$ as the source node, destination node and bandwidth request, respectively (i.e., Constraint (1));
2. Reliability requirement—each demand should be assigned FT number of backup routes (i.e., Constraint (2));
3. Capacity constraint—each link $k \in E$ has a bandwidth capacity C_k and none of the traffic demands ever exceed the link capacities (i.e., Constraint (3));
4. Flow conservation (i.e., Constraint (4)).

The objective is to find a set of optimal routing paths that minimizes the power consumption of the switches and ports involved, satisfying the above constraints. Hereby, the parameter Ω_s denotes the power consumed by the fixed overheads (like fans, linecards, and tranceivers, etc) in a switch, Ω_p represents the power consumption of a port, and α serves as a safety margin ($\alpha \in (0, 1)$ with 0.9 as default). The binary variables S_i and L_k represent whether the switch i and the link k are chosen or not (equal to 1 if chosen), $x_{ij}^{(k)}$ denotes the flow value of the demand d_{ij} that the link k carries from i to j, $R(d_{ij})$ means the number of available paths for demand d_{ij}, N_i consists of all links adjacent to the switch i, and N_i^+ (N_i^-) includes all links in N_i and carrying the flow into (out of) the switch i. Then, the MCF problem can be modeled in the following form:

$$\text{Minimize} \quad \Omega_s \sum_{i \in V} S_i + 2\Omega_p \sum_{k \in E} L_k$$

Subject to:

$$\forall i, j \in V, \quad \sum_{k \in N_i} x_{ji}^{(k)} \geq d_{ji}, \quad \sum_{k \in N_i} x_{ij}^{(k)} \geq d_{ij}, \quad (1)$$

$$\forall i, j \in V, \quad R(d_{ij}) \geq FT, \quad (2)$$

$$\forall k \in E, \quad \sum_{i \in V} \sum_{j \in V} x_{ij}^{(k)} \leq \alpha C_k, \quad (3)$$

$$\forall i, j \in V, \quad \sum_{k \in N_i^+} x_{ij}^{(k)} = \sum_{k \in N_i^-} x_{ij}^{(k)}, \quad (4)$$

$$\forall k \in E, \quad L_k \geq \frac{1}{C_k} \sum_{i \in V} \sum_{j \in V} x_{ij}^{(k)}, \quad L_k \in \{0, 1\}, \quad (5)$$

$$\forall i \in V, \quad S_i \geq \frac{1}{\sum_{k \in N_i} C_k} \sum_{i \in V} \sum_{j \in V} \sum_{k \in N_i} x_{ij}^{(k)}, S_i \in \{0, 1\}, \quad (6)$$

$$\forall i, j \in V, \quad \forall k \in E, \quad x_{ij}^{(k)} \geq 0 \quad (7)$$

Note that if we assume the optimal rounting paths are link-disjoint, we can simplify Constraint (2) as $\forall i, j \in V, \sum_{k \in N_i} Y_{ji}^{(k)} \geq FT, \sum_{k \in N_i} Y_{ij}^{(k)} \geq FT$ with $Y_{ij}^{(k)} \geq x_{ij}^{(k)}/C_k$ and $Y_{ji}^{(k)} \in \{0, 1\}$.

NP-hardness

For the MCF problem described above, we change to its corresponding decision problem (DMCF): Is there any set of routing paths such that satisfy $\Omega_s \sum_{i \in V} S_i + 2\Omega_p \sum_{k \in E} L_k \leq N$, and all constrains in MCF. To prove the DMCF problem is NP-hard, we show the classical 0-1 knapsack problem [27] can be reduced to a DMCF instance. Thus, both DMCF and MCF are NP-hard due to the equivalence of hardness.

The formal definition of the 0-1 knapsack problem is given as below. There are n kinds of items $I_1, I_2, ..., I_n$, where each item I_i has a nonnegative weight W_i and a nonnegative value V_i, and a bag with the maximum capacity as C. The 0-1 knapsack problem determines whether there exists a subset of items S ($S \subseteq [n]$) such that $\sum_{i \in S} W_i \leq C$ and $\sum_{i \in S} V_i \geq P$.

Proof. Reduction: We first construct a specific instance G of the DMCF problem. Suppose there exists a source s and a sink t in G, and only one demand ($s, t, d_{st} = P$). For each item I_i in the knapsack problem, we build a path p_i with W_i links from s to t in G, and each link k in p_i has capacity of $C_k = V_i/\alpha$. The parameters are set as $\Omega_p = 1$, $\Omega_s = 0$, $FT = 1$, and the predefined threshold of DMCF is set as $N = 2C$.

(i) The solution for the 0-1 knapsack problem exists $\Rightarrow$ The solution for the specific DMCF instance exists. Suppose there exists a subset of items S such that $\sum_{i \in S} W_i \leq C$ and $\sum_{i \in S} V_i \geq P$. Then, we can use S to construct a solution for the specific DMCF instance. For each item I_i ($i \in S$), we choose the corresponding path p_i in G, and assign a flow of size V_i to this path, i.e., $x_{st}^{(k)} = V_i$ for all links in p_i. Thus, the capacity constraint (3) holds since $x_{st}^{(k)} = V_i \geq \alpha C_k = V_i$, the flow conservation (4) holds naturally, and then the demand completion (1) is satisfied since $\sum_{k \in N_t} x_{st}^{(k)} = \sum_{k \in N_s} x_{st}^{(k)} = \sum_{i \in S} V_i \geq P = d_{st}$, and hence the reliability requirement (2) is met due to $FT = 1$. Constraint (5) means we will choose all W_i links in the path p_i, and then the total number of chosen links is $\sum_{i \in S} W_i$, leading to the value of the objective function $2\Omega_p \sum_{k \in E} L_k = 2 \sum_{i \in S} W_i \leq 2C = N$. Therefore, the found solution is indeed a solution for the specific DMCF instance.

(ii) The solution for the specific DMCF instance exists $\Rightarrow$ The solution for the 0-1 knapsack problem exists. Suppose there exists a set of S_i's and L_k's satisfying all constraint in the specific DMCF instance and $2\Omega_p \sum_{k \in E} L_k \leq N$. If a link k $(k \in N_t)$ in the path p_i has $L_k > 0$, then $x_{st}^{(k)} > 0$ by Constraint (5) and $x_{st}^{(k)} \leq \alpha C_i = V_i$ by Constraint (3). For such a p_i, we choose the corresponding item i in the 0-1 knapsack problem and form a subset of item S. Then, $\sum_{i \in S} V_i \geq \sum_{k \in N_t} x_{st}^{(k)} \geq d_{st} = P$ due to Constraint (1). On the other hand, since $x_{st}^{(k)} > 0$ $(k \in N_t)$ in p_i, the flow values of all links in p_i is equal to $x_{st}^{(k)} > 0$ due to the flow conservation. This means all W_i links in p_i have $L_k = 1$ by Constraints (5). Then, the total number of chosen links is $\sum_{i \in S} W_i = \sum_{k \in E} L_k \leq N/2\Omega_p = C$. Thus, we find the solution for the 0-1 knapsack problem. That ends the proof. $\square$

Blocking island paradigm

Derived from Artificial Intelligence, BI model provides an efficient way to represent the availability of network resources (especially bandwidth) at different levels of abstraction. The Blocking Island is defined as: *A β-Blocking Island (β-BI) for a node x is the set of all nodes of the network that can be reached from x using links with at least β available resources, including x* [28]. The key idea of BI is to abstract the original network graph into a hierarchy tree containing available bandwidth information. As shown in Figure 1, N_1 is a 50-BI for node S3.

BI has several fundamental properties which are very useful in routing decidability. Here we list some of the most important ones without proof.

- **Unicity:** Each node has one unique β-BI. If S is the β-BI for node x, then S is the β-BI for all the nodes in S.
- **Route Existence:** An unallocated demand $d_u = (x, y, \beta_u)$ can be satisfied with at least one route if and only if both the endpoints x and y are in the same β_u-BI.
- **Route Location:** The links of a route with β available bandwidth are all in the β-BI of its endpoints.
- **Inclusion:** If β_i is larger than β_j, then the β_i-BI for a node is a subset of β_j-BI for the same node.

The obtained BIs can be used to construct the Blocking Island Graph (BIG), which is a graph abstraction of the entire available network resources. The BIG can be

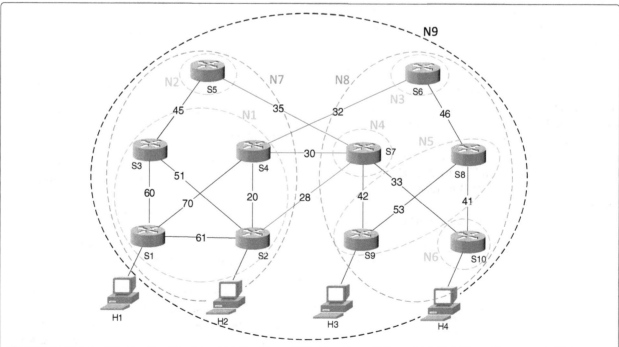

Figure 1 An example of Blocking Island Graph, in which $N_1 - N_6$ are 50-BIs, $N_7 - N_8$ are 40-BIs, and N_9 is 30-BI. The red lines are critical links between two 40-BIs. The weights on the links are their available bandwidth.

denoted as $G = (S, L)$, where S indicates the set of all different β-BIs while L denotes the critical links between BIs. Figure 1 gives an example of BIG. We can further construct a recursive decomposition of BIGs in decreasing order of demands (βs), and the lowest level has the largest β. This layered BIG structure is named as Blocking Island Hierarchy (BIH). It can be used to identify all bottlenecks, i.e. critical links, of the network. The BIH can also be viewed as an abstraction tree when taking the father-child relation into consideration. An example of BIH is illustrated in Figure 2. The leaves of the BIH tree are the network nodes, and the other vertices denote the abstract BIs. This abstraction tree can reflect the real-time state of the available network bandwidth.

Energy-aware heuristic schemes

In this section, we propose two heuristic solutions to the energy optimization problem formulated in Section "Problem statement", one of which is based on Blocking Island Paradigm while the other one is topology based. The BI based heuristic achieves bandwidth guaranteed green networks and enjoys low computation complexity with the help of Blocking Island Paradigm for resource allocation. The topology based heuristic holds the best scalability ($O(N)$) in computation time growth where N is the number of servers, but the resulting solution is not as good as the BI based solution. Comparatively, the BI based heuristic provides a more attractive and practical option.

Power conservation strategy

Most existing proposals apply device-level power conservation strategy, which intends to switch off the entire device (router/switch) including fixed overheads (like fans, linecards, transceivers, etc.) only when all ports on the device are idle. This means even if only one port has data to transfer, the device (including idle ports) should be kept alive all the time. Comparatively, in our energy-aware

heuristic schemes we apply the component-level strategy, which intends to power down the unused ports, and switch off the linecard if all the ports on this linecard are idle or disabled. If all linecards on a device are idle then to power off the entire device. Clearly, the component-level strategy achieves the most power savings.

Consequently, the total power consumption of a switch Ω_{switch} can be computed as below:

$$\Omega_{switch} = \Omega_s + N_p * \Omega_p \qquad (8)$$

where Ω_s and Ω_p are the same as described in Section "Problem statement", and N_p denotes the number of active ports on the switch.

BI-based heuristic scheme

As proved in Section "Problem statement", energy-aware bandwidth allocation and routing is an NP-hard problem with a high complexity due to the exponential number of nodes and routes. In response to this issue, we present an approach that applies the Blocking Island Paradigm to solve the problem efficiently with much lower and more manageable complexity. The BI-based Heuristic Scheme (BHS) can also be regarded as a bandwidth allocation scheme, which can help achieve a bandwidth guaranteed green data center network. Several key intuitions behind BHS can be summarized as below:

- Drawing support from BI model to guide the bandwidth allocation for the traffic demands in the most advantageous order.
- Using the energy-aware routing algorithm to compute the most beneficial routes for these allocated demands.
- Switching off devices that are not involved in the final routings for power conservation.

Bandwidth allocation mechanism

In line with the data center policy which requires fast response to the request, the *Route Existence* property of BI enables much faster decisions in determining whether a request can be satisfied just by checking whether both the endpoints are in the same β-BI, while traditional routing algorithms have to compute the routes before deciding the route's existence. For example, if we want to assign a path for a traffic demand (*H1, H3, 50*) in the network as shown in Figure 1, then we can immediately know that the route does not exist since *H1* and *H3* are not in the same 50-BI without any effort to search the whole network space and compute the routes. Moreover, if we need to find a path for (*H1, H2, 50*), then the search space can be reduced from the whole network to only {*S1, S2, S3, S4*}, which leads to a significant improvement in the efficiency of computation and bandwidth allocation. The unique β-BI for a given node x can be obtained by a simple greedy algorithm

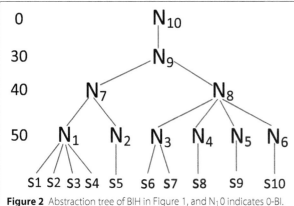

Figure 2 Abstraction tree of BIH in Figure 1, and N_10 indicates 0-BI.

(as depicted in Algorithm 1) whose complexity is linear in $O(L)$, where L denotes the number of links. Additionally, querying two nodes in the same BI experiences a complexity of just $O(1)$ since only two hashing operations are needed.

Algorithm 1 Construct β-BI

1: **function** CONSTRUCTBI($N = \{V, E\}, \beta$)
2:    $L \leftarrow \{\emptyset\}$ ▷ L: Result β-BI list
3:    **for all** v in V **do**
4:        **if** not visited(v) **then**
5:            $I \leftarrow ConstructBIFromNode(N, \beta, v)$
6:            $L \leftarrow L.Add(I)$
7:        **end if**
8:    **end for**
9:    **return** L
10: **end function**

11: **function**   CONSTRUCTBIFROMNODE(N =
    $\{V, E\}, \beta, x$)
12:    $I \leftarrow \{x\}$ ▷ I: Result β-BI
13:    $S \leftarrow$ {links incident to x and weight $\geq \beta$}   ▷ S: stack
14:    **while** $S \neq \emptyset$ **do**
15:        $l \leftarrow pop(S)$
16:        $e \leftarrow$ another endpoint of l
17:        **if** $e \notin I$ and $weight(l) \geq \beta$ **then**
18:            $I \leftarrow I \cup \{e\}$
19:            $S \leftarrow S \cup$ {links incident to e and weight $\geq \beta$}
20:        **end if**
21:    **end while**
22:    **return** I
23: **end function**

As a known NP-hard MCF problem, it cannot be guaranteed to find an assignment to satisfy all the flows for all kinds of traffic matrix all the time. How to select the next demand to allocate bandwidth has a great impact on the future allocation success ratio, and also affects the search efficiency. There are some static methods for addressing this kind of MCF problem or constraint satisfaction problem (CSP) [29], such as first-fail principle based technique, or first selecting the largest demand. However, these static techniques are not suitable to be directly applied in the data center network which requires a more dynamic and efficient bandwidth allocation mechanism. In addition, considering the data center's own particular characteristics, these traditional static techniques do not take the mean flow completion time and deadline into consideration as well. In our approach, these concerns are effectively resolved by exploiting the advantages of Blocking Island Paradigm.

The BI-based bandwidth allocation mechanism (BAM) is mainly responsible for deciding which traffic demand should be chosen to allocate with its required bandwidth. In order to achieve a higher success ratio of bandwidth allocation and higher computation efficiency, BAM selects the unallocated traffic demands strictly following the principles as below.

(i)   It firstly choose the demand of which the lowest common father (LCF) of the demand's endpoints in the BIH tree is highest. The intuition behind this principle is to first allocate the more constrained demands, which follows the fail-first principle.

(ii) If there are multiple candidate demands after the first step, then the Shortest Demand First (SDF) principle is applied, which aims to meet as many deadlines as possible and reduce the mean flow completion time. The shortest demand indicates the demand whose expected completion time is minimum (i.e. $min \left\{ \frac{flow\ size}{required\ bandwidth} \right\}$) where the *flow size* and *required bandwidth* are provided by the application layer [30,31].

(iii) In case there are still two or more satisfied demands, then the demand with the highest bandwidth requirement is preferentially selected. This criterion, apart from implying a near deadline flow, also follows the fail-first principle, where more bandwidth allocation more likely cause BI splittings and thus hinder any future allocation of other demands.

(iv) Finally, we randomly select one demand from the output of step (iii).

The demand selection rules for bandwidth allocation not only decreases the computation complexity and increases the search efficiency, but also takes the flow deadline into consideration. Moreover, they can also increase the success ratio of bandwidth allocation, which targets at simultaneously satisfying as many flows of the traffic matrix as possible. If some demands can not be allocated currently, they will be queued for a certain period until some allocated flows expire or departure so that some resources are released for further allocation.

Energy-aware routing

After selecting the most beneficial traffic demand from the traffic matrix by applying the BI-based bandwidth allocation mechanism, the energy-aware routing is designed to assign one best route for each selected demand request. However, the searching domain is too large and the valid route set is too time-consuming to be computed using a traditional routing algorithm. In order to improve the search efficiency and increase the success ratio of bandwidth allocation, several route selection criterions are carefully customized for our energy-aware routing algorithm (ERA) as follows.

(i) The traffic should be aggregated together to the greatest extent, which would allow us to conserve more energy in a tighter data center network.
(ii) The route should use as few critical links (inter-BI links) as possible, which aims to decrease the failure ratio of future allocations and also reduce the computation cost caused by splitting/merging BIs.
(iii) The route should use as few network devices as possible, which prefer to choose the shortest path.
(iv) The current allocation should impact on the future allocation as little as possible.

Guided by these rules, the ERA assigns a route for each requested demand in an efficient and dynamic way based on the current network status. Initially, ERA searches the lowest-level BI where the two endpoints of the requested demand are located, and generates a set of feasible candidate routes. For example, as shown in Figure 1 the lowest level for demand (s1, s4, 45) is 50-BI N_1. This procedure aims to meet the rule i and ii, which tries to aggregate the flows into the same subnet (lowest BI) and use as few critical links as possible. Afterwards, sort these candidate routes by the number of their induced BI splittings, and choose the route(s) that cause fewest BI splittings. This step complies with rule ii and iv, which takes the computation cost and future allocation into consideration. If there are more than one such route, then choose the shortest route which tries to meet the objective of rule iii. In case there are still multiple routes, then choose the route with the maximum number of flows which can contribute to the network traffic aggregation. Finally, we randomly choose one route or just choose the first route from the sorted candidate routes. The power-aware routing procedure terminates as long as the output of the above five procedures is unique, and allocates the best route with the required bandwidth to the current demand.

Reliability satisfaction
Admittedly, the energy conservation in the way of powering off devices sacrifices the network fault tolerance, which is an inevitable conflict between them. In order to improve the robustness of the network, we need to add additional number of available backup routes according to the reliability requirements as illustrated in Constraint (3). The selection of backup routes applies the shortest-path routing algorithm other than following the aforementioned multiple route selection rules. This strategy means to reserve as few devices as possible to meet the requirements of fault tolerance. From another perspective, as indicated in [32] the switches are fairly reliable (only 5% failure rates for ToR switches per year), hence it is not so wise to sacrifice a great deal (network resources, computation time, energy, etc.) for a small probability event. Therefore, the shortest-path routing algorithm is well suited and adequate for the backup route selection.

The whole procedure of the BI-based heuristic scheme is illustrated in Figure 3. The input includes network topology, traffic matrix with the required bandwidth and the reliability requirement. The outputs are expected to be a subset of original network topology and a set of routing paths taken by flow demands with satisfied bandwidths. Firstly, based on the network topology BHS generates multiple levels of BIs according to the current available link capacities and further constructs BIG and BIH. Then, on the basis of BIH the system computes and allocates the best routes associated with a required bandwidth to each demand, applying the bandwidth allocation mechanism and energy-aware routing algorithm. Afterwards, according to the reliability requirement, a certain number of backup routes are added to guarantee the network's fault tolerance. Finally, all the ports, linecards, or switches, that are not involved in the final routings, are put into sleep mode or switched off for the sake of energy conservation.

Analysis of complexity
As aforementioned, the complexity of constructing a β-BI is $O(L)$, where L denotes the number of links. The route searching or routing decidability experiences a complexity of $O(1)$. The Blocking Island Hierarchy (BIH) reflects the real-time state of the available network bandwidth, and it needs to be updated when the link state changes. Yet we only need to update the BIs, which are involved in allocating or deallocating bandwidths, by means of splitting or merging BIs. This means there is no need to compute the whole BIH again. The complexity of updating the BIH is $O(rl)$, where r is the number of different resource requirements (β) and l indicates the number of involved links.

Topology-based heuristic scheme
In this subsection, the topology-based heuristic scheme (THS) is described based on the multi-rooted Fat-Tree topology [33] (as shown in Figure 4), yet the idea can be extended to any other tree-like topologies. THS needs to resolve two issues:

- How many switches and ports should be sufficient to support the network traffic.
- How to distribute the traffic flows among the calculated network subset and achieve high network utilization.

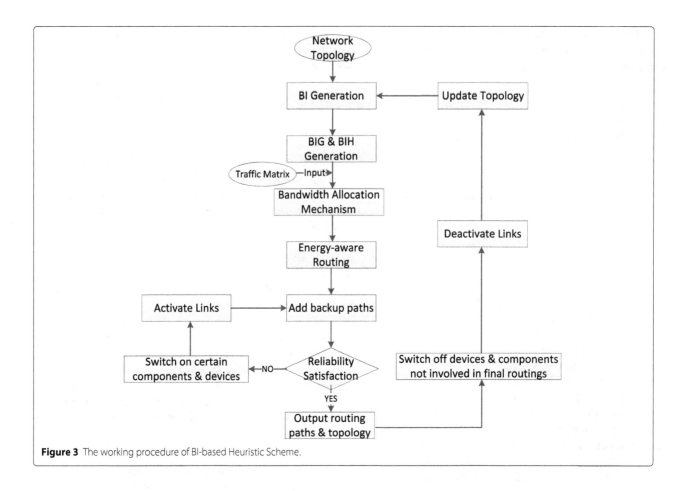

Figure 3 The working procedure of BI-based Heuristic Scheme.

Calculate the minimum network subset

In order to maximize power conservation, we need to only keep the required networking capacity available by merging the traffic flows and switch off idle devices. The minimum network subnet should be dynamically computed according to the statistics of traffic demands in runtime. The port statistics and switch status are collected by the centralized controller from OpenFlow enabled switches through the OpenFlow secure channel. It can accurately and directly obtain the statistics of the

traffic matrix by using the built-in features (bytes, packet counters, etc.) for active flows kept in OpenFlow switches. In order to deal with the single point failure of the controller, THS provides multiple controllers with different roles (OFPCR_ROLE_EQUAL ,OFPCR_ROLE_MASTER and OFPCR_ROLE_SLAVE) to guarantee the robustness of the system (the same as specified in [34]).

We assume that k-port switches are used in the Fat-Tree topology. Consequently, there are k Pods, $\frac{k}{2}$ edge/aggregation switches in each Pod, and $\frac{k^2}{2}$

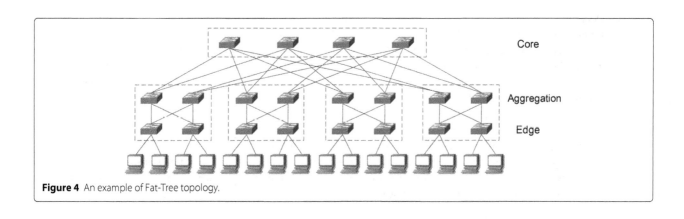

Figure 4 An example of Fat-Tree topology.

edge/aggregation switches (Equation 9) in total. The number of core switches on the network is $\frac{k^2}{4}$. Furthermore, there are $\frac{k^2}{4}$ equal-cost paths between any given pair of hosts in different Pods.

First we provide definitions of several notations used in calculating the required network subset: NS_i^{Edge} and NS_i^{Agg} denote the number of edge switches and aggregation switches in Pod i that should be activated (Equation 10 and 11), respectively, NP_i^{Edge} and NP_i^{Agg} indicate the number of active ports on each activated edge switch and aggregation switch in Pod i (Equation 13 and 14), NS^{Core} represents the number of core switches that should be turned on (Equation 12), and NP^{Core} means the number of active ports on each activated core switch (Equation 15). Besides, we define $DEdge_{ij}^{up}$, $DAgg_{ij}^{up}$ and $DCore_{ij}^{down}$ as the up-traffic of edge switch j in Pod i, the up-traffic of aggregation switch j in Pod i, and the down-traffic sending from core switch j to Pod i, respectively. Lastly, for the sake of simplicity we assume all links have the same link capacity C. Then the minimum subset of switches and ports is calculated according to the realtime traffic demands as follows:

$$NS_i^{Edge} = \frac{k}{2} \qquad (9)$$

$$T = \max \left\{ \left\lceil \frac{\sum_{j=1}^{\frac{k}{2}} DEdge_{ij}^{up}}{C * \frac{k}{2}} \right\rceil, \left\lceil \frac{\sum_{j=1}^{(\frac{k}{2})^2} DCore_{ij}^{down}}{C * \frac{k}{2}} \right\rceil, 1 \right\} \qquad (10)$$

$$NS_i^{Agg} = T \qquad (11)$$

$$NS^{Core} = \max \left\{ \max_{i \in [1,k]} \left\{ \left\lceil \frac{\sum_{j=1}^{\frac{k}{2}} DAgg_{ij}^{up}}{C * k} \right\rceil \right\}, 1 \right\} \qquad (12)$$

$$NP_i^{Edge} = \frac{k}{2} + NS_i^{Agg} \qquad (13)$$

$$NP_i^{Agg} = \frac{k}{2} + NS^{Core} \qquad (14)$$

$$NP^{Core} = k; \qquad (15)$$

The relative notations are summarized as in Table 1. Importantly, the critical switches that may cause network disconnections cannot be powered off and each server should be guaranteed reachable at any time. Hence, all edge switches (i.e. ToR switches connecting servers) should stay alive at all times as expressed in Equation 9.

Traffic distribution using multipath routing

After obtaining the capable network subset, we need to distribute the traffic flows evenly among the subset. Since the size of each flow demand varies much, so the traffics that should be able to fill the network subset cannot fully utilize the network with unexpected low throughput when single path routing is applied. As aforementioned, the Fat-Tree DCN holds many equal-cost paths between any pair of servers. Therefore, we can divide the total flow demands by the switch capacity and distribute them evenly using multipath routing algorithms by splitting each flow into multiple sub-flows. However, the existing flow-level multipath routing relying on per-flow static hashing, like ECMP-based MPTCP [35], still cannot guarantee the traffic will be evenly distributed, which would lead to substantial bandwidth loss and significant load imbalance. Against this kind of bin-packing problem, one may apply best fit decreasing (BFD) or first fit decreasing (FFD) heuristic algorithms to mitigate this issue, but still not achieve perfect network utilization and bisection bandwidth. Intuitively, the best method is to distribute all packets evenly among all equal cost paths using packet-level multipath routing.

Based on some careful studies and extensive experiments, recently A. Dixit et al. proposed a packet-level traffic splitting scheme named RPS (Random Packet Spraying) [11] for data center networks. RPS achieves near ideal load balance and network utilization, and causes little packet reordering by exploiting the symmetry of the multi-rooted tree topologies. Noticing that THS's strategy of powering off switches barely affects the symmetry of the network since we always choose the leftmost switches. Therefore, after obtaining the required subset and adding FT-redundancy, we directly borrow the packet-level RPS multipath routing scheme to spread all flows equally among multiple different equal cost shortest paths. Then

Table 1 The number of active switches and ports on the network

Devices	Number of active Switches in pod i	Total number of active Switches on the network	Uplink ports	Downlink ports	Number of active ports per Switch in pod i
Edge switch	$\frac{k}{2}$	$\frac{k^2}{2}$	NS_i^{Agg}	$\frac{k}{2}$	$NP_i^{Edge} = \frac{k}{2} + NS_i^{Agg}$
Agg switch	NS_i^{Agg}	$\sum_i NS_i^{Agg}$	NS^{Core}	$\frac{k}{2}$	$NP_i^{Agg} = \frac{k}{2} + NS^{Core}$
Core switch	/	NS^{Core}	/	/	$NP^{Core} = k$

switch off the switches and ports which are not involved in final subset and update the network topology. The whole THS procedure is depicted in detail in Algorithm 2.

Algorithm 2 Topology-based Heuristic Algorithm

Require:

1: (1) DCN topology $G = (V, E)$ using k-port switches;

2: (2) Traffic matrix $TM = \{(s, t, d_{st}); s, t \in V\}$;

3: (3) Reliability requirement $R(d_{st})\ (\geq FT)$;

Ensure:

4: (1) A set of edge switches, aggregation switches, and core switches satisfying all traffic demands;

5: (2) The updated network topology;

6: **for** $t \in [t_m, t_n]$ **do**

7:     Obtain the traffic demands of each switch on the network;

8:     **for** $i \in [1, k]$ **do**

9:         Calculate $\sum_{j=1}^{\frac{k}{2}} DEdge_{ij}^{up}$ and $\sum_{j=1}^{(\frac{k}{2})^2} DCore_{ij}^{down}$.

10:         Calculate NS_i^{Agg}, NP_i^{Edge} and NP_i^{Agg}.

11:         Activate the leftmost NS_i^{Agg} aggregation switches with NP_i^{Agg} ports on each switch in Pod i.

12:         Activate all $\frac{k}{2}$ edge switches with NP_i^{Edge} active ports on each switch.

13:     **end for**

14:     Calculate $\sum_{j=1}^{\frac{k}{2}} DAgg_{ij}^{up}$ in each Pod.

15:     Calculate NS^{Core} and activate NS^{Core} core switches.

16:     Activate redundant switches forming FT minimum spanning trees to meet the requirement of fault tolerance.

17:     Spread all traffic flows evenly into the network using RPS multipath routing algorithm.

18:     Switch off the unused switches and ports.

19:     Update the network topology $G' = (V', E')$.

20: **end for**

System evaluation

Simulation overview

In order to evaluate the performance and effectiveness of our proposed approaches (BHS and THS) to the power optimization problem, in this section we implement the blocking island paradigm and two heuristic schemes in the DCNSim simulator [36]. DCNSim can simulate several data center network topologies and compute many metrics, such as the power consumption, aggregate bottleneck throughput, network latency, average path length, fault-tolerance, and statistics of device status. Without

loss of generality, all simulations in this section are conducted based on Fat-Tree topology, and all the links are capable of bidirectional communications, where the unidirectional link bandwidth is set to be 1 GBps. The default MTU of a link is 1500 bytes, the default packet size is one MTU, and the default buffer size of each switch is 10 MTU. The default processing time for a packet at a node is 10 μs while the default propagation delay of a link is 5 μs, and the TTL of a packet is set to be 128. The time interval between two packets from the same source to the same destination is set to be 5 ms as default.

Evaluation indicator

The traditional always-on strategy is used as the base line to be compared with BHS and THS in the percentage of power savings, shown as below,

$$PEC = 100\% - \frac{P_{BHS/THS}}{P_{always-on}} * 100\%, \qquad (16)$$

where PEC denotes the percentage of energy conservation, $P_{BHS/THS}$ indicates the power consumed by BHS or THS, and $P_{always-on}$ represents the power consumed by the traditional always-on strategy.

To calculate the power consumption, we use the real power consumption data of Cisco Nexus 3048 Data Center Switch. According to its switch data sheet [37], the typical operating power consumption of a Nexus 3048 switch is 120 watts at 100% loads, and powering off one port of the switch saves around 1.5 watts. Moreover, reducing the power consumed by the network can also result in cooling power savings proportionally, though this part of power savings is not taken into any calculation in this paper.

Network traffic matrix

Aside from the power-aware routing and resource allocation mechanisms which mainly determine how much power can be conserved, the traffic pattern also has a great impact on power savings and network performance. In data center networks, there are several typical types of traffic patterns, including One-to-One, One-to-Many, and All-to-All. In this section, all the simulations are conducted by applying the All-to-All traffic pattern, which simulates the most intensive network activities and can evaluate the guaranteed performance under the most rigorous case. Furthermore, according to the findings in [38] about the characteristics of the packet-level communications, the packet inter-arrival time reveals an ON/OFF pattern and its distribution follows the Lognormal mode for OFF phase, while the distribution varies between Lognormal mode, Weibull mode and Exponential mode in different data centers during the application-sensitive ON phase. Here, the Exponential Flow Mode is applied to determine the distribution of packet inter-arrival times.

Simulation results

This subsection evaluates the overall performance of BHS and THS. The primary simulation results show that achieving 20% to 60% of power savings is feasible, and it varies under different network conditions (traffic loads, network scales, traffic patterns, etc.) and different reliability requirements.

System reliability

As aforementioned, achieving energy conservation by powering off network devices might sacrifice system's reliability, where a reasonable trade-off can be made according to the actual needs. For example, one possible way is to take $Max\{FT + \alpha * PEC\}$, where higher weight factor α gives more weight to achieving better PEC at the cost of less improvement to FT as illustrated in Figure 5. The value of α can be decided by the network administrator according to the different requirements of reliability and power savings. Figure 6 presents the simulation results of power savings by applying THS and BHS under different fault tolerance (FT) levels in a 128-server Fat-Tree topology, where the abscissa axis means the number of backup routes (in BHS) or minimum spanning trees (in THS). Several careful observations can be derived from this figure: firstly, the component-level power conservation strategy achieves more power savings than the device-level strategy using either heuristic schemes; secondly, BHS performs better than THS in power savings, and it earns more advantages for higher fault tolerance levels; thirdly, lower fault tolerance level results in more power savings, and around 55% of power savings can be achieved for $FT = 1$.

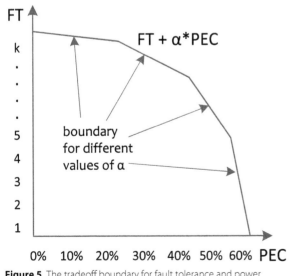

Figure 5 The tradeoff boundary for fault tolerance and power savings.

Network latency

The queuing delay, which plays a dominant role in the resulting network latency, is usually caused by the network congestion because of exceeding the network capacity. However, guaranteeing the required bandwidth for each flow's transmission could help mitigate network congestion and decrease queuing delay. Here we use the average global packet lifetime (the time from packet's generation to the arrival at its destination) to measure the overall network latency, and the always-on scheme applying two-level routing tables [33] is used as the baseline to be compared with BHS and THS. With the benefit of BI-based bandwidth allocation mechanism and carefully designed routing algorithm, BHS implements a bandwidth guaranteed network and achieves even lower network latency than the original always-on scheme using its original two-level routing, as illustrated in Figure 7. However, THS receives higher network latency without any bandwidth-guarantee mechanism. Admittedly, the packet level multipath routing algorithm applied in THS could help fill the computed network subset perfectly, but it also may incur the incast problem at the last hop, resulting in queuing delays caused by traffic collisions or even packet loss, where packet retransmission further delays the flow completion time. However, this can be mitigated by many already existing techniques dealing with incast issues and reducing flow completion time, which is beyond the scope of this paper.

Network scales

Our efficient heuristic schemes have a good scalablity enabling that the system can easily adapt to larger sized data centers with good performance. Figure 8 exhibits the performance of BHS and THS in power savings by applying component-level strategy under various network loads in 128-server, 250-server and 2000-server sized Fat-Tree DCNs. The fault tolerance level is set to be $FT = 2$. The simulation results show that both BHS and THS achieve more power savings for larger sized network and lower network load, and BHS gains a better performance than THS for all three cases. Either BHS or THS conserves no energy at full network loads.

Computation efficiency

The traditional routing algorithm suffers a bad exponential time complexity due to the huge search space. However, utilizing blocking island to guide the search and bandwidth allocation, BHS achieves a much lower computation complexity. Comparatively, THS only needs to compute the capable minimum network subset based on the sum of traffics without doing any bandwidth allocations for each particular flow, thus THS scales at roughly $O(N)$ where N is the number of servers. Figure 9 presents the time costs for computing different number

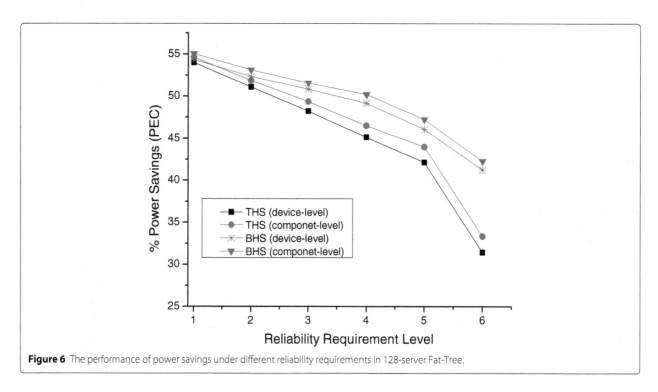

Figure 6 The performance of power savings under different reliability requirements in 128-server Fat-Tree.

of bandwidth allocation instances using BHS and basic shortest path routing (BSP) under the 3456-server sized FatTree topology (using 24-port switches). The result reveals that BHS is several times faster than BSP on average, where BHS takes 0.41 and 1.05 seconds in computing 2000 and 4000 allocation instances, respectively, while BSP costs 1.91 and 4.72 seconds correspondingly. This

further witnesses the high computation efficiency of BHS, though the maintenance of BIH may take some time.

The implementation of BHS and THS in real world scenario
We have provided theoretical analysis and simulation studies for the proposed two green schemes BHS and THS. Although the simulation conditions are very close

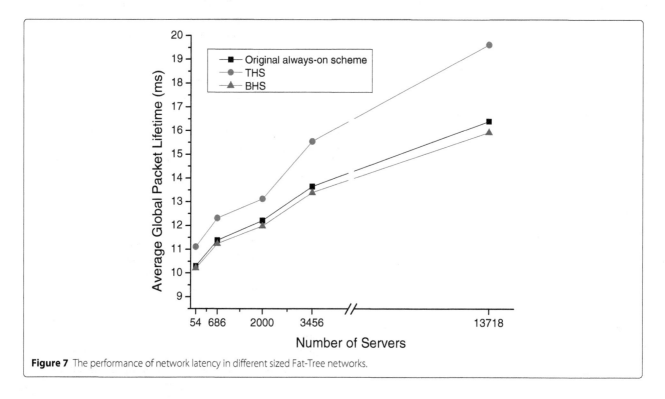

Figure 7 The performance of network latency in different sized Fat-Tree networks.

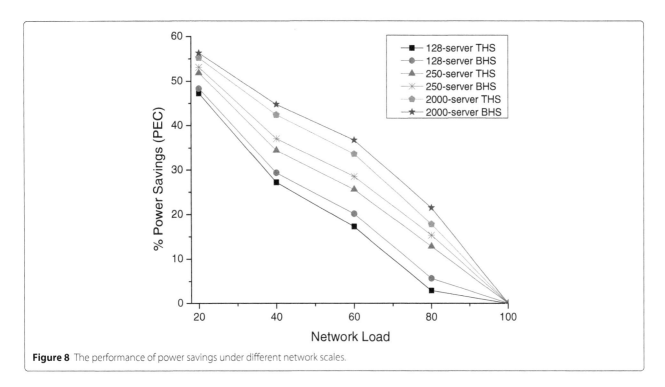

Figure 8 The performance of power savings under different network scales.

to the real world data center environments, there are still some issues needed to be considered in real world deployment of BHS and THS. Firstly, as aforementioned, the traffic patterns and packet inter-arrival time change time to time in the real world, though they may follow some disciplines (Lognormal, Exponential, Weibull, etc.) on the whole in the long run. We only simulated the Exponential flow mode according to the findings about the real world traffic characteristics in [38], and the performance of BHS and THS under other one or several mixed traffic patterns in a real world are left for further evaluation. Secondly, we also care about how the time cost in switching off/on a switch will affect the system performance in real data centers, which is actually a common concern of this research field. Another issue needed to be considered is the deployment of BHS. BHS requires a centralized controller which plays a very important role in the BI/BIG/BIH generation, bandwidth allocation and routing rules computation. How to guarantee the robustness of the centralized controller is a big concern. Besides,

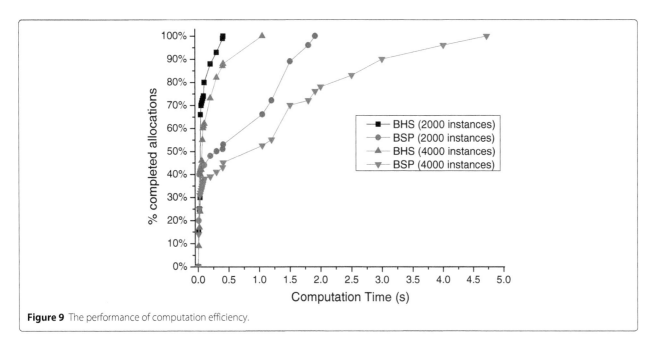

Figure 9 The performance of computation efficiency.

the choice of communication method (in-band or out-of-band) between controller and switches is also needed to be weighted. All of the mentioned issues above are difficult to be simulated in simulators, which should be considered in real world scenarios.

Conclusion

In this paper, firstly we rigorously formulated the power optimization problem in data center networks into an MCF problem, and proved its NP-hardness. In response to this NP-hard problem, inspired by an Artificial Intelligence abstraction technique, we proposed a Blocking Island based heuristic scheme (BHS) by designing an energy-aware bandwidth allocation mechanism and an energy-aware routing algorithm, which can decrease the computation complexity and increase the success ratio of bandwidth allocation. To the best of our knowledge, we are the first to employ the BI paradigm into data center networks to achieve power conservation. Furthermore, we proposed a topology-based heuristic scheme (THS), which focuses on how to compute the minimum network subset and how to distribute the traffic flows properly among the network subset. THS performs faster than BHS and holds the best scalability $(O(N))$, but the quality of the resulting solution is not as good as BHS. BHS achieves a bandwidth guaranteed data center network irrespective of network topologies with a high quality solution and low computation cost. Comparatively, BHS provides a more attractive and practical solution. The conducted simulations further confirmed their feasibility and good performance.

Competing interests
This paper is supported in part by NPRP grant from the Qatar National Research Fund and HKUST RGC Fund. Except this, the authors declare that they have no other competing interests.

Authors' contributions
Author TW proposed the idea of this paper, carefully designed two green frameworks, and drafts the manuscript. Author BQ was responsible for the problem formulation and proof of the NP-hardness of the MCP problem. Author ZS was involved in the experiments and evaluations of two frameworks. Author YX conducted a deep investigation in related works and revised the manuscript draft critically from the system design to the experiments. Author SF and RH discussed frequently with us about this research and gave us many useful and constructive suggestions to perfect the idea of this paper. Author MH supervised our research group about this research topic and given final approval of the version to be published. All authors read and approved the final manuscript.

About the Authors
Ting Wang received his Bachelor Sci. degree from University of Science and Technology Beijing, China, in 2008, and received his Master Eng. degree from Warsaw University of Technology, Poland, in 2011. From 02.2012 to 08.2012 he interned as a research assistant in the Institute of Computing Technology, Chinese Academy of Sciences. He is currently working towards the PhD degree in Hong Kong University of Science and Technology. His research interests include data center networks, cloud computing, green computing, and software defined network.
Bo Qin is currently a PhD student in Department of Computer Science and Engineering, the Hong Kong University of Science and Technology. He was a visiting PhD student at Aarhus University and University of Southern California. His research interests include spectral graph theory, algorithmic game theory and combinatorial optimization.
Zhiyang Su received his B.E. degree in computer science and technology from China University of Geosciences (Beijing) in 2009, and M.S degree in computer network and application from Peking University in 2012. Currently, he is pursuing Ph.D. degrees in Hong Kong University of Science and Technology. His research interests focus on software defined networking (SDN) and data center networking, especially on improving the performance of SDN.
Yu Xia is currently a postdoctoral fellow in Department of Computer Science and Engineering, the Hong Kong University of Science and Technology. He received the Ph.D. in computer science from Southwest Jiaotong University, China. He was a joint Ph.D student and a visiting scholar at Polytechnic Institute of New York University. His research interests include high-performance packet switches, data center networks and network architectures.
Mounir Hamdi received the B.S. degree from the University of Louisiana in 1985, and the MS and the PhD degrees from the University of Pittsburgh in 1987 and 1991, respectively. He is a Chair Professor at the Hong Kong University of Science and Technology, and was the head of department of computer science and engineering. Now he is the Dean of the College of Science, Engineering and Technology at the Hamad Bin Khalifa University, Qatar. He is an IEEE Fellow for contributions to design and analysis of high-speed packet switching. Prof. Hamdi is/was on the Editorial Board of various prestigious journals and magazines including IEEE Transactions on Communications, IEEE Communication Magazine, Computer Networks, Wireless Communications and Mobile Computing, and Parallel Computing as well as a guest editor of IEEE Communications Magazine, guest editor-in-chief of two special issues of IEEE Journal on Selected Areas of Communications, and a guest editor of Optical Networks Magazine. He has chaired more than 20 international conferences and workshops including The IEEE International High Performance Switching and Routing Conference, the IEEE GLOBECOM/ICC Optical networking workshop, the IEEE ICC High-speed Access Workshop, and the IEEE IPPS HiNets Workshop, and has been on the program committees of more than 200 international conferences and workshops. He was the Chair of IEEE Communications Society Technical Committee on Transmissions, Access and Optical Systems, and Vice-Chair of the Optical Networking Technical Committee, as well as member of the ComSoc technical activities council.
Sebti Foufou obtained a Ph.D. in computer science in 1997 from the University of Claude Bernard Lyon I, France, for a dissertation on parametric surfaces intersections. He worked with the computer science department at the University of Burgundy, France from 1998 to 2009 as an associate professor and then as a full professor. He was invited as a guest researcher at NIST Maryland, USA, in 2005-2006. He is with the computer science department at Qatar University since September 2009. His research interests concern image processing, geometric modelling, and data representations and processing for product lifecycle management.
Ridha Hamila received the Master of Science, Licentiate of Technology with distinction, and Doctor of Technology degrees from Tampere University of Technology (TUT), Department of Information Technology, Tampere, Finland, in 1996, 1999, and 2002, respectively. Dr. Ridha Hamila is currently an Associate Professor at the Department of Electrical Engineering, Qatar University. Also, he is adjunct Professor at the Department of Communications Engineering of TUT. From 1994 to 2002 he held various research and teaching positions at TUT within the Department of Information Technology, Finland. From 2002 to 2003 he was a System Specialist at Nokia research Center and Nokia Networks, Helsinki. From 2004 to 2009 he was with Etisalat University College, Emirates Telecommunications Corporation, UAE. His current research interests include mobile and broadband wireless communication systems, cellular and satellites-based positioning technologies, synchronization and DSP algorithms for flexible radio transceivers. In these areas, he has published over 60 journal and conference papers most of them in the peered reviewed IEEE publications, filed two patents, and wrote numerous confidential industrial research reports. Dr. Hamila has been involved in several past and current industrial projects Qtel, QNRF, Finnish Academy projects, TEKES, Nokia, EU research and education programs. He supervised a large number of under/graduate students and postdoctoral fellows.

Acknowledgement
We thank Mrs. Shauna Dalton who carefully revised this paper for grammar and spelling.

Author details
[1]Hong Kong University of Science and Technology, Hong Kong SAR, China.
[2]Hamad Bin Khalifa University, Doha, Qatar. [3]Qatar University, Doha, Qatar.

References
1. Ting W, Zhiyang S, Yu X, Yang L, Jogesh M, Mounir H (2014) SprintNet: A high performance server-centric network architecture for data centers. In: Communications (ICC), 2014 IEEE International Conference on. IEEE. pp 4005-4010
2. Ting W, Zhiyang S, Yu X, Yang L, Jogesh M, Mounir H (2015) Designing efficient high performance server-centric data center network architecture. Comput Netw 79:283-296
3. Ting W, Yu X, Jogesh M, Mounir H, Sebti F (2014) A general framework for performance guaranteed green data center networking. In: Global Communications Conference (GLOBECOM), 2014 IEEE. IEEE. pp 2510-2515
4. Abts D, Marty MR, Wells PM, Klausler P, Liu H (2010) Energy proportional datacenter networks. In: ACM SIGARCH Computer Architecture News. ACM Vol. 38. pp 338–347
5. Heller B, Seetharaman S, Mahadevan P, Yiakoumis Y, Sharma P, Banerjee S, McKeown N (2010) Elastictree: Saving energy in data center networks. In: NSDI Vol. 10. pp 249-264
6. Mahadevan P, Banerjee S, Sharma P, Shah A, Ranganathan P (2011) On energy efficiency for enterprise and data center networks. Commun Mag IEEE 49(8):94–100
7. Greenberg A, Hamilton J, Maltz DA, Patel P (2008) The cost of a cloud: research problems in data center networks. In: ACM SIGCOMM computer communication review 39(1):68-73
8. Pelley S, Meisner D, Wenisch TF, VanGilder JW (2009) Understanding and abstracting total data center power. In: Workshop on Energy-Efficient Design
9. Ting W, Zhiyang S, Yu X, Mounir H (2014) Rethinking the Data Center Networking: Architecture, Network Protocols, and Resource Sharing. In: Journal of IEEE Acess 2(1):1481-1496
10. Dean J, Ghemawat S (2008) Mapreduce: simplified data processing on large clusters. Commun ACM 51(1):107–113
11. Dixit A, Prakash P, Hu YC, Kompella RR (2013) On the impact of packet spraying in data center networks. In: INFOCOM, 2013 Proceedings IEEE (pp. 2130-2138). IEEE
12. Arlitt M, Bash C, Blagodurov S, Chen Y, Christian T, Gmach D, Hyser C, Kumari N, Liu Z, Marwah M, McReynolds A, Patel C, Shah A, Wang Z, Zhou R (2012) Towards the design and operation of net-zero energy data centers. In: 13th IEEE Intersociety Conference on Thermal and Thermomechanical Phenomena in Electronic Systems (ITherm)
13. Goiri Í, Le K, Nguyen TD, Guitart J, Torres J, Bianchini R (2012) Greenhadoop: leveraging green energy in data-processing frameworks. In: Proceedings of the 7th ACM european conference on Computer Systems. ACM. pp 57-70
14. Nguyen K-K, Cheriet M, Lemay M, Savoie M, Ho B (2013) Powering a data center network via renewable energy: A green testbed. Internet Comput IEEE 17(1):40-49
15. David H, Fallin C, Gorbatov E, Hanebutte UR, Mutlu O (2011) Memory power management via dynamic voltage/frequency scaling. In: Proceedings of the 8th ACM international conference on Autonomic computing. ACM. pp 31-40
16. Leverich J, Monchiero M, Talwar V, Ranganathan P, Kozyrakis C (2009) Power management of datacenter workloads using per-core power gating. Comput Architecture Lett 8(2):48–51
17. Meisner D, Gold BT, Wenisch TF (2009) Powernap: eliminating server idle power. In: ACM SIGARCH Computer Architecture News 37(1):205-216
18. Rangan KK, Wei G-Y, Brooks D (2009) Thread motion:fine-grained power management for multicore systems. In: ACM SIGARCH Computer Architecture News (Vol. 37, No. 3, pp. 302-313). ACM
19. Ting W, Zhiyang S, Yu X, Bo Q, Mounir H (2014) NovaCube: A low latency Torus-based network architecture for data centers. In Global Communications Conference (GLOBECOM), 2014 IEEE (pp. 2252-2257). IEEE
20. Abu-Libdeh H, Costa P, Rowstron A, O'Shea G, Donnelly A (2010) Symbiotic routing in future data centers. ACM SIGCOMM Comput Commun Rev 40(4):51–62
21. Hong C-Y, Caesar M, Godfrey P (2011) Pcube: Improving power efficiency in data center networks. In: Cloud Computing (CLOUD), IEEE International Conference on. IEEE. pp 65-72
22. Singla A, Singh A, Ramachandran K, Xu L, Zhang Y (2010) Proteus: a topology malleable data center network. In: Proceedings of the 9th ACM SIGCOMM Workshop on Hot Topics in Networks. ACM. p 8
23. Valancius V, Laoutaris N, Massoulié L, Diot C, Rodriguez P (2009) Greening the internet with nano data centers. In: Proceedings of the 5th international conference on, Emerging networking experiments and technologies. ACM. pp 37-48
24. Liu L, Wang Hm, Liu X, Jin X, He WB, Wang QB, Chen Y (2009) Greencloud: a new architecture for green data center. In: Proceedings of the 6th international conference industry session on Autonomic computing and communications industry session. ACM. pp 29-38
25. Mann V, Kumar A, Dutta P, Kalyanaraman S (2011) Vmflow: leveraging vm mobility to reduce network power costs in data centers. In: NETWORKING. Springer Berlin, Heidelberg. pp 198-211
26. Shang Y, Li D, Xu M (2010) Energy-aware routing in data center network. In: Proceedings of the first ACM SIGCOMM workshop on Green networking (pp. 1-8). ACM
27. Martello S, Toth P (1990) Knapsack problems: algorithms and computer implementations. John Wiley and Sons, Inc.
28. Frei C, Faltings B (1997) Simplifying network management using blocking island abstractions. Internal Note from the IMMuNe Project
29. Mackworth AK (1992) Constraint satisfaction problems. Encyclopedia of AI, 285, 293
30. Hong C-Y, Caesar M, Godfrey PB (2012) Finishing flows quickly with preemptive scheduling. ACM SIGCOMM Computer Communication Review 42(4):127-138
31. Wilson C, Ballani H, Karagiannis T, Rowtron A (2011) Better never than late: meeting deadlines in datacenter networks. In: ACM SIGCOMM Computer Communication Review (Vol. 41, No. 4, pp. 50-61). ACM
32. Bodík P, Menache I, Chowdhury M, Mani P, Maltz DA, Stoica I (2012) Surviving failures in bandwidth-constrained datacenters. In: Proceedings of the ACM SIGCOMM 2012 conference on, Applications, technologies, architectures, and protocols for computer communication. ACM. pp 431-442
33. Al-Fares Mohammad, Loukissas Alexander, Vahdat Amin (2008) A scalable, commodity data center network architecture. In: ACM SIGCOMM Computer Communication Review Vol. 38. pp 63-74
34. (2012) Openflow switch specification v1.3.0. www.opennetworking.org/images/stories/downloads/sdn-resources/onf-specifications/openflow/openflow-spec-v1.3.0.pdf
35. Ford Alan, Raiciu Costin, Handley Mark, Bonaventure Olivier and others (2011) Tcp extensions for multipath operation with multiple addresses. Internet Engineering Task Force, RFC, 6824
36. Liu Y, Muppala J (2013) DCNSim: A data center network simulator. In: Distributed Computing Systems Workshops (ICDCSW), 2013 IEEE 33rd International Conference on. IEEE. pp 214-219
37. Nexus C (2012) 3048 switch data sheet
38. Benson T, Akella A, Maltz DA (2010) Network traffic characteristics of data centers in the wild. In: Proceedings of the 10th ACM SIGCOMM conference on Internet measurement. ACM. pp 267-280

13

Towards a cloud-based integrity measurement service

John Zic[1*] and Thomas Hardjono[2]

Abstract

The aim of this paper is to propose the use of a cloud-based integrity management service coupled with a trustworthy client component – in the form of the *Trust Extension Device* (TED) platform – as a means to to increase the quality of the security evaluation of a client. Thus, in addition to performing authentication of the client (e.g. as part of Single Sign-On), the Identity Provider asks that the integrity of the client platform be computed and then be evaluated by a trustworthy and independent *Cloud-based Integrity Measurement Service* (cIMS). The TED platform has been previously developed based on the Trusted Platform Module (TPM), and allows the integrity measurement of the client environment to be conducted and reported in a secure manner. Within the SSO flow, the portable TED device performs an integrity measurement of the client platform, and sends an integrity report to the cIMS as part of the client authentication process. The cIMS validates the measurements performed by the TED device, and reports a *trust score* to the Identity Provider (IdP). The IdP takes into account the reported trust score when the IdP computes and issues a Level of Assurance (LOA) value to the client platform. In this way the Service Provider obtains a greater degree of assurance that the client's computing environment is relatively free of unrecognized and/or unauthorized components.

Introduction

Today there is a strong interest within Enterprises to move some or all their IT infrastructure and services to the cloud, with the aim among others of reducing the cost of IT operations as a whole. However, there are a number of security and privacy issues relating to cloud-based services, including the issues relating to providing access to external entities.

Two of the common cloud deployment scenarios faced by many Enterprises today are as follows:

- *Employee access to cloud-based applications*: An Enterprise seeks to make cloud-based productivity-applications available to its employees. The employees should not notice any differences between accessing the application in the cloud versus the same application running on a local machine. This scenario has a number of security implications. One implication is the need for the employee authentication status and authorization data to be

conveyed from the Enterprise to Cloud-based provider. In this scenario the Enterprise remains being the authoritative source of all employee identity. Typically employee identities and privileges are managed through the corporate directory service, which itself may or may not be in the cloud (though this is tangential to the case of the cloud-based applications scenario).

- *Enterprise with in-bound institutional customers*: Another scenario is one in which an Enterprise with its applications running in the cloud is sharing this application with another organization. Thus, consider an Enterprise-A that has as its customer another institution called Enterprise-B with its own employees. For example, Enterprise-A could be financial services company offering retirement fund (e.g. U.S. 401K) management for employees of Enterprise-B. Here Enterprise-A has customer-facing applications that are operating in the Cloud (e.g. SaaS application). A key aspect of this scenario is that Enterprise-B is the authoritative source of identity for its employees, all of whom are accessing the cloud-based application belonging to Enterprise-A. Thus, authentication and authorization data must be

*Correspondence: john.zic@csiro.au
[1] CSIRO ICT Centre, PO Box 76, Epping, NSW 1710, Australia
Full list of author information is available at the end of the article

conveyed from Enterprise-B into the cloud-based application within the domain or realm of Enterprise-A.

An additional aspect of these scenarios is that Enterprises have already invested in and deployed strong authentication infrastructure and identity management services. Many seek to extend and re-use these infrastructures to address the needs of the new cloud environment.

Parallel to the recent developments in cloud-based services is that of the development of loosely connected federated identity and authentication services in the low-value consumer space. These low-value federated identity services have been exemplified by social networks where one simple password-based login to one social network allows the user to access other social networks without needing to perform further authentications. Although Enterprises have been interested in using this model to expand their customer base, one stumbling block remains that of the low security-quality of these loosely connected federated identity services.

Partly in response to this poor security quality, several organizations have emerged with the aim of defining the so-called standard *trust frameworks* as a means to bootstrap trust among entities in the identity ecosystem [1,2]. These trust frameworks provide a foundation for entities to transact based on an agreed common legal contract, thereby overcoming the limitations and non-scalability of bilateral agreements. One common aspect of many of these trust frameworks is the use of a *Level of Assurance* (LOA) as a means to denote the quality of authentication performed by (and therefore confidence in) an identity provider. The LOA is a way to express the quality of the authentication event from the perspective of security. Thus, for example, a user wielding a hardware token in a two-factor authentication event will obtain a higher LOA value compared to a user that authenticates merely using a password. The US National Institute for Standards and Technology (NIST) has issued a publication defining a granular level of LOA values [3].

In this paper we argue that in addition to strong authentication with high LOA values, identity-based services in the cloud need to also perform access decisions based on the quality of the computing platforms or devices from which clients (e.g. employees, customers, or users) perform remote access to these cloud-based applications and services. We believe that a measured trustworthiness indicator or the so-called *trust score* of a given computing platform should be part of the authentication and authorization of that platform when it seeks access to services in the cloud. In so far as possible, the computing platform elements being measured include all softwares and firmwares, and also the hardware component identifiers [4].

We also argue that in order for new cloud-based services to be acceptable by Enterprises today, a high degree of interoperability with existing "Enterprise-grade" authentication and authorization infrastructures is required.

In this paper we propose an architecture for a *cloud-based Integrity Measurement Service* (cIMS). The cIMS performs the evaluation of the integrity measurements received about the client, and issues a trust score reflecting its evaluation against one or more predetermined profiles for client measurements. We use the classic SAML 2.0 ecosystem [5] as a means to illustrate usage of the cIMS. In this model, a client seeking access to a *Service Provider* (SP) must first be authenticated by an *Identity Provider* (IdP), who issues SAML assertions pertaining to the client. Here we extend the SAML2.0 model by having the IdP request also from the client an *integrity measurement report*. In order to satisfy the need for a high LOA level, we propose the use of a trustworthy portable computing platform, the *Trust Extension Device* (TED) to provide the client-side trusted computing environment capable of performing integrity measurements of the client-side components.

Since the NIST Recommendations [3] already point to the need of hardware tokens to achieve a Level of Assurance (LOA) Level-3 or higher, we believe that the TED device offers a flexible and portable computing environment that satisfies the NIST Requirements. We believe the TED device represents a strong token for the subscribers within the e-Authentication model defined within the NIST Recommendation.

Background: TED and integrity measurements

There has been a growing interest by commercial organisations in providing portable, trusted and secure computing platforms that may be used in the scenarios such as those outlined in the Introduction section. A number of solutions have been proposed from a variety of vendors, ranging from IronKey [6], and Gemalto [7], to the Singapore Government's DIVA [8]. Some of these solutions are strongly tamper resistant and locally tamper evident.

The Trust Extension Device (TED) was developed with similar goals of providing a portable, secure and trusted computing platform. However, its key differentiator is that it adopted and implemented the Trusted Computing Group's (TCG) [9] standards and architectures into a small, portable device. In particular, the TED provides an issuing enterprise a truly *trusted computing platform* whose root of trust and associated functionality is based on the Trusted Platform Module (TPM v1.2b [10]) cryptographic microcontroller hardware. The TPM becomes a root of trust for the TED platform, and allows the *remote validation* of its hardware and software through the use of cryptographically secure integrity measurement and attestation protocols.

In the TCG architecture, a specialised Privacy Certifying Authority service is required to participate and provide supporting validation of credentials and keys that are used by the TPM to encrypt and sign messages (including integrity measurements) between the TED and the service provider's cloud infrastructure. Together, the TED, Privacy Certifying Authority and the service provider's cloud infrastructure, develop and maintain a provable, measurable trust relationship between themselves.

It should be noted here that there are two significant points need to be addressed when implementing and ultimately deploying such a system.

First, in every TPM enabled enterprise system, the enterprise application servers need to have *complete* knowledge of the hardware and software characteristics of *all* their client computers in order to engage, and successfully complete, the integrity measurements and attestation protocol. Each variation from a standard, known environment needs to be identified, captured and maintained within the application server so that the attestation protocols can continue to operate correctly. However, the variety of software images and hardware configurations, the rate at which these change, coupled with the typically large number of computers connecting to the enterprise server makes the task of maintaining and managing this information difficult and challenging.

The TED and associated infrastructure addresses the management issue by (i) reducing the complexity of the device and associated operating system and application software, (ii) having the device issued by a controlling enterprise/authority and (iii) being sufficiently cheap and portable for a new one to be easily re-issued if required. The TED's environment (drivers, operating system and applications) was specifically designed and optimised for execution speed and offers a restricted and controlled set of applications and services. It is completely under the control of the issuer. By design, the TED cannot be altered or modified once it has been configured and issued by the enterprise. Any changes or deviation from expected configuration are remotely detected by the application server through the TPM integrity measurements and attestation protocols. Should a change be detected, the issuer can take appropriate action, such as not engaging in the critical transaction, or notifying the client that their TED has been compromised and will be revoked, etc.

Second, data and services are now available (for example, when enabled to utilize cloud computing infrastructures) to a wider cross-section of users, operating under unknown and unpredictable computing environments that lie beyond the control of a single enterprise. In many cases, the users themselves operate beyond a single organizational boundary.

These uncertainties are addressed by TED being able to be plugged into a USB port of any host computer, without the need for specialised hardware interfaces or readers, to create a known (to the issuing enterprise), trusted computing platform and associated environment and applications that are isolated (from the host's hardware up through to its operating system and applications) from the host computer.

The design and implementation of the TED prototype (both the hardware and software) are presented in detail in another paper ([11]). We summarise its salient features here.

An overview of the TED hardware and software

For completeness, the design requirements for the TED prototype (and its associated software components/system) were as follows:

DR-1 Should be small and cheap enough to be portable and easily re-issued to a client by the owner enterprise or cloud service provider.

DR-2 Must be able to physically plug into any host PC with a USB 2.0 compliant port.

DR-3 Must use the USB port *solely* for power and for establishing a secure network connection (tunnel) to well-known servers after it has successfully booted.

DR-4 Must be able execute owner enterprise or cloud service provider developed applications on an embedded operating system.

DR-5 Must include and use a TPM v1.2 compliant cryptographic microcontroller.

DR-6 Must be able to implement and participate in attestation and identity management protocols as per TCG specifications.

DR-7 Must *not* require that the host needs to be rebooted for correct operation.

DR-8 Must *not* rely on the host PC being interrupted from normal operation.

DR-9 Must be able to be inserted or removed from the host PC *at any time* without causing either the host or the TED to enter an error state.

The selection of the USB 2.0 connection was based on pragmatic reasons - USB 2.0 reduced the hardware costs, complexity and software development time substantially over other design options.

In principle, a TED may be regarded as a stand-alone networked device. According to the above design requirements, the TED really only requires the host PC for power and network connectivity (using either wired Ethernet or WiFi). It operates its own isolated memory address space, running on a separate CPU, all of which may be attested as operating within the strictly controlled environment provided by the issuing enterprise (which may be a cloud service provider). There were no requirements for having any traditional user screen or keyboards to interface to it; any such interfaces were to be provided through appropriately secured connections to the host PC.

As such, we did consider other designs, including having a keypad and single LCD screen mounted on the device that the user may interact with independent of the host PC (which again was only providing power and secure network connectivity). This design was never implemented due to time and project resourcing issues. Another design was a natural development from the "small keypad single LCD screen" version, where the TED was connected to a cellular phone platform providing power and that utilised 3G data network for secure network connectivity. However the initial design investigations revealed that the power requirements of this TED variant exceeded the capacity of a cellular phone's supply, and so this option was never pursued.

Figure 1 shows the TED prototype hardware that consisted of two boards: a motherboard containing the CPU, memory and associated control logic (out of view) and a daughterboard, carrying the TPM chip, USB interface and associated power supplies for both boards.

The TED internal software architecture is shown in Figure 2. It is based on an embedded Linux operating system, and required the development of dedicated extensions and drivers to accommodate the TPM device and USB interface. Above the operating system, the TED utilised a light-weight TCG Software Stack (TSS) Library and TSS server that allows applications to interface to the TPM functions.

A user's applications execute on the TED (again, that are under the control of the issuing cloud service provider) to access external systems. Its execution and memory spaces are isolated from the host PC, and only uses the host PC for power and to establish secured Internet connection to the cloud provider's service. The secured Internet connection is tunneled from the TED's USB port, through the host PC's network connections and finally onto the cloud provider's service.

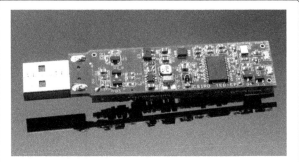

Figure 1 TED engineering prototype.

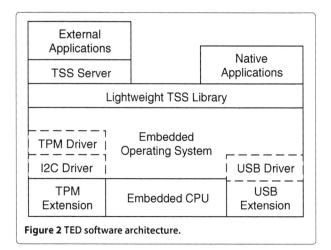

Figure 2 TED software architecture.

Integrity measurement and attestation

Without entering into details of the TCG's recommended integrity measurement and attestation (of the TED platform and its complete operational environment) [12], most (except for the Direct Anonymous Attestation protocols) follow the similar structure of the protocol given in Figure 3. Section 4.2 in the TCG Specification Architecture Overview [4] gives an excellent overview of this topic.

At step (1), a challenge message with a fresh nonce is issued to a platform (in this case, the TED) to attest its identity and integrity with the application service. Once this message is received, the TED platform at step (2) calls a TPM function to generate an Attestation Identity Key (AIK) and the TPM credentials. These credentials, along with other credentials[a] the public part of the AIK and the original challenge nonce are signed by the private TPM Endorsement Key. The resulting signed credential is then encrypted using the public part of the certifying authority's key. This is then sent at step (3) to the certifying authority as a request to validate its credentials. If successful, the certifying authority creates a signed, encrypted credential that is sent back to the platform at step (4). Step (5) is used to produce an encrypted summary of measurements of the environment held in sealed storage (the Platform Configuration Registers, or PCR) in the TPM chip. (e.g. one measurement may be a list of loaded and running processes just after boot, another measurement may be a new list of running processes several hours after boot). This encrypted measurement information is then sent back to the challenger, along with the identity credential received from the certifying authority at step (6). Upon reception of the message, the challenging application service now validates at step (7) the measured environment and compares it to its own expected measurements that it holds. During this process, the challenging application service checks the identity

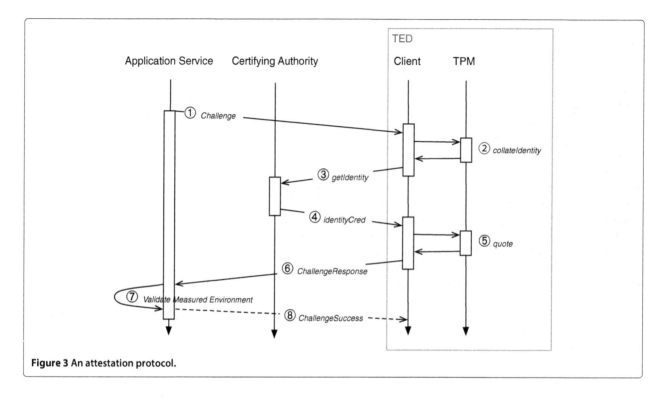

Figure 3 An attestation protocol.

credential to determine that it was signed by the certifying authority, as well as verifying the signature of the measured values and that it contains the original challenge nonce. Depending on the application requirements, step (8) may optionally be used to signal to the application client the success of the measurement and attestation process.

Architecture for cloud-based integrity measurement services using TED

As mentioned previously, we argue that another dimension of trust in identities on the Internet that must be accounted for is that of the state or condition of the platform from which a given identity is seeking services. To this end we propose a *cloud-based Integrity Measurement Service* architecture (Figure 4) coupled with TED that adds the dimension of state measurement to the process of authentication of clients by the IdP when they seek access to SPs. In the following we describe the entities, assumptions and functions within the architecture, followed by a description o the steps taken by the User/Client located within the Enterprise.

Entities, assumptions and functions

Figure 4 shows the entities operating in the ecosystem:

- *TED platform, with client and User*: The User is assumed to be an employee within the Enterprise, using the client software operating on the TED platform. The TED device is able to perform the

measurement of the client-side environment, including all application software.
- *Enterprise Directory Service* (EDS): In the architecture we assume that some form of directory services exist under the domain of control of the Enterprise. For authentication performed by the IdP, the EDS is assumed to be the authoritative source of identities for all employees in the enterprise. Although Figure 4 shows the directory service as being a separate entity located within a cloud external to the Enterprise, in practice an implementation can place the directory service (i) within the Enterprise (as has been the case in the past), (ii) within a private cloud inside or outside the physical boundary of the Enterprise (as is often proposed today), or (iii) within a hosted service in an external cloud. Regardless of the configuration of the directory service, in this architecture we assume that the Enterprise has full control of the directory, with some degree of sharing of certain employee attributes and permissions with the IdP.
- *Identity Provider* (IdP): The IdP is as understood broadly in the identity literature, and as defined more specifically by the SAML core [13] and SAML profiles [5] specifications.
  When the user performs an SSO to a Service provider (SP) and is redirected by the SP to the IdP for authentication, the IdP will perform an additional step of seeking the measurement of the Client's platform. After a successful authentication by the IdP,

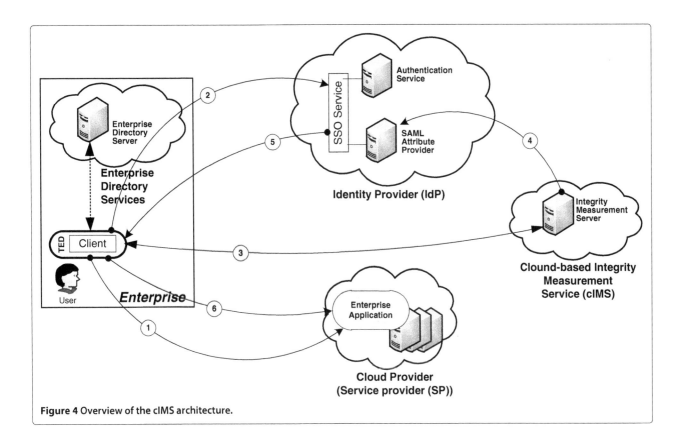

Figure 4 Overview of the cIMS architecture.

the IdP redirects the Client to the cIMS service (see below) in order to perform an integrity measurement using the TCG Trusted Connect Model (TNC) [14]. As a result of a successful authentication and measurement of the client and TED, the IdP will issue the relevant signed assertions containing among others the identity of the client, the LOA level achieved (according the defined assurance policies set at the IdP), and the protocol type used to authenticate the User and Client.

We note that the IdP may take on a similar role of the TCG's *Privacy Certifying Authority* (Privacy CA), of creating, managing and interacting with the TPM chip onboard the TED. Although another party could take on the role of a Privacy CA in principle, implementing and deploying within a SAML architecture would present difficulties due to policies, accountability requirements and responsibilities that come with operating such an authority as a separate entity.

- *Cloud-based Integrity Measurement Service* (cIMS): The cIMS is the service that performs the integrity measurement and evaluation of the Client platform. In general, we assume that the IdP has a trust relationship and a contractual business agreement with the cIMS based on a mature trust framework.

There are a number of possible outputs from an evaluation by the cIMS. Here we assume that at the very least the cIMS returns an *integrity score* based on some measurement scale agreed upon with the IdP. Although the cIMS is shown in Figure 4 as separate from the IdP, the cIMS could in fact be a service operating within the IdP. This approach would allow the IdP to offer a wider set of services while operating under a single trust framework.

- *Cloud Provider* (CP): The CP is the cloud provider, which corresponds to the *Service Provider* in the SAML2.0 terminology [5]. The CP is the relying party who depends entirely on the IdP for correct authentication and integrity evaluation of the TED platform. The CP uses the signed SAML assertions (containing the LOA values) from the IdP in order to grant/deny access to the User to resources or services at the CP (either provided by the CP itself or gated by the CP).

It is important to note that Figure 4 *does not* explicitly show the additional entities and protocols involved required to fully support the TPM functionality such as the various key and credential creation and management functions. Where required, these are presented in the text of the paper.

Overview of protocol flows

Figure 4 provides a high level view of the interactions between the client running on the TED platform with the IdP. In the following discussion, we use the terminology and scenario of the SAML2.0 Single Sign-ON (SSO) as defined in [5]. This well known SSO scenario is purposely selected in order to highlight the introduction of TED and the cIMS service.

For clarity, the Privacy Certifying Authority has been left off the diagram. As explained in a previous section, the Privacy CA service could be run by the IdP, or if required, by a separate trusted third party.

We use the term "Client" to denote the application software running on the TED platform that performs the SSO to the IdP. The Client software is the piece of software that integrates the authentication client and is entity that interacts with the SP and IdP on behalf of the user. It is also the software that triggers the integrity measurements performed by TED, and as such must always be included in any platform measurements and in integrity self-checks.

The following summarizes the interaction between the Client on TED and the entities in the ecosystem:

(1) *The Client (on TED) requests access to Cloud Provider*: Following the classic SAML 2.0 SSO scenario, the Client requests access to resources and services at the Cloud Provider (which is called the Service Provider in the SAML2.0 glossary). The CP redirects the Client to the IdP for authentication of the Client.

Within the re-directon message the CP includes a signed *integrity schema* document (or a pointer to it) [12]. The integrity schema represents the components within the client's platform that is of interest to the CP. Thus, for example, the CP may be interested in the status-information regarding the client's firmwares (e.g. BIOS, drivers, etc), in the OS patch level and in the Anti-Virus (AV) condition of the client machine.

Note that if the CP and the IdP has a back-channel established by virtue of their business relationship, the CP can communicate its set of preferred integrity schemas to the IdP via the back-channel.

(2) *Client Authenticates to IdP*: Here the Client has been redirected by the Cloud Provider (ie. SP) to the Identity Provider (IdP) for user authentication. The method for user authentication is out-of-scope in this paper, and has been well treated elsewhere (for example, see SAML2.0 SSO profile).

After successful authentication by the IdP, the Client is further re-directed to the cloud-based Integrity Measurement Service (cIMS) selected by the IdP. The cIMS is assumed to be a trusted third party

operating under the same trust framework as the IdP and Cloud provider.

In requesting that an integrity measurement be performed, the IdP needs to indicate which components in the client's environment must be measured. One possible approach is for the IdP to include (in its re-direction of the Client) an *integrity schema* [12] which indicates to the cIMS which platform components are of interest to the IdP. In this way the Client can initiate the TED platform to perform measurements following the integrity schema. Later, in compiling the integrity report, TED will format the report also following the integrity schema, and return it The integrity schema should be a core part of the client-profile that the IdP maintains for that Client.

(3) *Client is integrity-evaluated by the cIMS*: Here the Client has been re-directed by the IdP to the cIMS for the purpose of measurement of the Client and evaluation by the cIMS.

Upon receiving the indication from the cIMS that an integrity report is required, the Client performs the measurement of the components as indicated by the cIMS. Assuming that an integrity schema was returned (or pointed to) by the IdP, the TED performs the measurements following the schema. The integrity schema provides a uniform and standard manner in which to indicate which software components to measure. Examples include the measurement of the Client itself, other applications, the kernel, the firmwares, anti-virus measurements, and others. Note that a complete measurement of the entire platform could also be requested [12].

(4) *The cIMS forwards a Trust Score to IdP*: Upon completing the evaluation of the integrity report obtained from TED in the previous step, the cIMS generates a *trust score* for the Client. The trust score reflects the judgement of the cIMS (regarding the Client) as compared against some *Integrity Measurement Policies* stored at the cIMS. The cIMS logs all the measurement and evaluation events, and archives all received integrity reports and resulting trust scores in order to maintain audit and accountability information.

Note that in the multi-host situation, the IdP may have an account with the cIMS within which it defines the set of integrity measurement policies for all clients that the IdP re-directs to the cIMS. As such, the cIMS becomes a provider to multiple IdPs.

(5) *The IdP issues assertions with LOA*: Upon receiving the trust score from the cIMS, the IdP compares the trust score against the access control policies (e.g. belonging to the Enterprise) stored at the IdP.

(Alternatively, the IdP could access the relevant Enterprise access control policies from the EDS). The IdP then issues a signed assertion or claim containing the LOA value. The LOA is the result of the IdP successfully authenticating the User and the evaluation of the trust score (about the Client/TED) as received from the cIMS.

Here it is worthwhile noting that the IdP could in fact issue multiple LOAs, each refering to one aspect of the authentication event. Thus, for example, an additional LOA value could also be issued by the IdP conveying the second factor of authentication used by the user (e.g. User wielded an OTP token or biometric device).

(6) *The Client sends request to the Cloud Provider*: Upon the signed assertion (containing the LOA value) from the IdP, the Client forwards the assertion to the Cloud provider in its re-attempt to access the resources at the Cloud Provider.

Identity and trustworthy collaborations

Trustworthiness and being able of assure identity claims with high degree of confidence also arises in broader collaborative situations, where organizations have to partner with each other over a specific period of time each to achieve a set of mutually desirable outcomes. Typically, each participant will have their own respective policies in place about control and sharing of information, as well as policies that cover exceptions. When brought together, the establishment of identity, who has access to information and the control of access and the information itself forces each participant to consider how to evaluate the trustworthiness of the collaboration and the respective partners.

We believe that trustworthy collaborations are enabled if the partners have the following in place:

1. *Agreed upon contracts.* The collaborating partners must first formalise an agreement (a contract) that allows them to understand how information within the collaboration will be used between partners. This includes who has access, how information may be shared, how long does the shared information persist, what happens to shared collaborative information should a partner leave the collaboration prematurely or if a new partner joins the collaboration later, and so on. For cloud service providers, this typically constitutes an explicit SLA.

2. *Demonstrable adherance to the contract* Once a contract between participants is agreed upon, each partner and their organisations must be able to prove that they are able to behave according to the collaborative agreement, and in particular, for those transactions that are critical within the collaboration.

In this paper, we identify one particular technique that applies to cloud service providers: the assurance of the integrity of the systems that are used are within bounds of the collaboration agreement, as described in "Background: TED and integrity measurements".

3. *Resolving exceptions and disputes* Establishing that the partners demonstrated compliance against a contract and behaviour (given in points (1) and (2), above) also requires the use of a variety of differing pieces of irrefutable evidence gathered about the behaviour of each of the collaborators. This evidence needs to be irrefutable so that it can be used to settle any disputes about whether or not partners have behaved according to the collaboration agreement. From another point of view, each of the partners is held accountable for their actions. With this in mind, we developed an Accountability Service, proposed in [15], that is directly applicable to cloud service providers. This service may be used to collect and manage the evidence of critical transactions within a collaborative environment, where each participant belongs to a separate organisational domain (with its own policies).

In terms of the identity claims that are made within a collaboration, adopting the approach taken in this paper would be of benefit to each individual participant. Further, as the cloud service provider is key in establishing and maintaining the collaborative "infrastructure", the addition of services such as accountability and provenance increases the level of trust in the system and between the participants by providing (if required) additional evidence of "good" behaviour as well as irrefutable evidence of "bad" behaviour.

Conclusion and further work

The goal of this paper is to proposed the use of a cloud-based integrity management service coupled with a trustworthy client component in the form of the portable trust extension device (TED), as a means to to increase the quality of the security evaluation of a client. In addition to performing authentication of the client (e.g. as part of Single Sign-On), the IdP asks that the integrity of the client platform be computed and then be evaluated by a trustworthy and independent Cloud-based Integrity Measurement Service (cIMS).

The portable TED device performs an integrity measurement of the client platform, and sends an integrity report to the cIMS the cIMS validates the measurements performed by the TED device, reports a *trust score* to the Identity Provider (IdP). The IdP takes into account the reported trust score when the IdP computes and issues a Level of Assurance (LOA) value to the client platform.

This approach provides a path forward for Service Providers to obtain better picture of the state of client end-points, and thereby providing them better assurance of the quality of the client's computing environment.

It is our intention to demonstrate a prototype system in the near future to elaborate upon, and evaluate, the ideas presented in this paper. Of particular interest to the authors is using concepts behind this paper in extending standard authentication systems such as Kerberos to offer a higher level of assurance of identity claims made to cloud service providers.

Endnote

[a]These that are unique to each TPM hardware chip and "burnt in" during its manufacture.

Competing interests

The authors declare that they have no competing interests.

Authors' contribution

TH and JZ proposed the new system architecture and protocol extensions. TH drafted the sections on Abstract; Introduction; Architecture for Cloud-based Integrity Measurement Services using TED. JZ drafted the sections Background: TED and Integrity Measurements; Identity and Trustworthy Collaborations. TH and JZ jointly drafted the Conclusions and further work section. All authors read and approved the final manuscript.

Acknowledgement

We thank Stephen Buckley at the MIT Kerberos Consortium and John Taylor and Dimitrios Georgakopoulos from CSIRO for supporting this work.

Author details

[1]CSIRO ICT Centre, PO Box 76, Epping, NSW 1710, Australia. [2]MIT Kerberos and Internet Trust Consortium, Massachusetts Institute of Technology, Cambridge, MA 02139, USA.

References

1. Federal Identity Credentialing and Access Management (2009) Trust Framework Provider Adoption Process (TFPAP). [Online]. Available: http://www.idmanagement.gov/documents/TrustFrameworkProvider AdoptionProcess.pdf
2. Open Identity Exchange (OIX) (2011) The Respect Trust Framework. Public Review Draft [Online]. Available: http://openidentityexchange.org/frameworks
3. Burr WE, Dodson DF, Perlner RA, et al. (2008) DRAFT i Draft Special Publication 800-63-1 Electronic Authentication Guideline. [Online]. Available: http://csrc.nist.gov/publications/drafts/800-63-rev1/SP800-63-Rev1_Dec2008.pdf
4. Trusted Computing Group (2007) TCG Specification Architecture Overview Specification Revision 1.4. [Online]. Available: http://www.trustedcomputinggroup.org/resources/tcg_architecture_overview_version_14
5. Security Services Technical Committee (2005) Profiles for the OASIS Security Assertion Markup Language (SAML) V2.0. OASIS Standard, [Online]. Available: http://docs.oasis-open.org/security/saml/v2.0/saml-profiles-2.0-os.pdf
6. Ironkey (2013) Company home web page. [Online]. Available: http://www.ironkey.com/
7. Gemalto - security to be free (2013) Company home web page. [Online]. Available: http://www.gemalto.com/
8. Gratzer V, Naccache D (2007) Trust on a nationwide scale. IEEE Secur Privacy 5(5): 69–71
9. Trusted Computing Group (2013) Trusted Computing Group Home. [Online]. Available: http://www.trustedcomputinggroup.org
10. TPM Main Specification (2011). [Online]. Available: http://www.trustedcomputinggroup.org/resources/tpm_main_specification
11. Nepal S, Zic J, Liu D, Jang J (2010) Trusted computing platform in your pocket. In: Embedded and Ubiquitous Computing, IEEE/IFIP International Conference on, pp 812–817
12. TCG Infrastructure Working Group (2006) TCG Infrastructure Architecture Part II - Integrity Management, TCG Standard. [Online]. Available: http://www.trustedcomputinggroup.org/resources/
13. Security Services Technical Committee (2005) Assertions and Protocols for the OASIS Security Assertion Markup Language (SAML) V2.0, OASIS Standard. [Online]. Available: http://docs.oasis-open.org/security/saml/v2.0/saml-core-2.0-os.pdf
14. TCG Trusted Network Connect Working Group (2012) TNC Architecture for Interoperability, Version 1.5, TCG Standard. [Online]. Available: http://www.trustedcomputinggroup.org/resources/
15. Yao J, Chen S, Wang C, Levy D, Zic J (2010) Accountability as a service for the cloud. In: Services Computing, IEEE International Conference on, pp 81–88

14

A multi-level security model for partitioning workflows over federated clouds

Paul Watson

Abstract

Cloud computing has the potential to provide low-cost, scalable computing, but cloud security is a major area of concern. Many organizations are therefore considering using a combination of a secure internal cloud, along with (what they perceive to be) less secure public clouds. However, this raises the issue of how to partition applications across a set of clouds, while meeting security requirements. Currently, this is usually done on an ad-hoc basis, which is potentially error-prone, or for simplicity the whole application is deployed on a single cloud, so removing the possible performance and availability benefits of exploiting multiple clouds within a single application. This paper describes an alternative to ad-hoc approaches – a method that determines all ways in which applications structured as workflows can be partitioned over the set of available clouds such that security requirements are met. The approach is based on a Multi-Level Security model that extends Bell-LaPadula to encompass cloud computing. This includes introducing workflow transformations that are needed where data is communicated between clouds. In specific cases these transformations can result in security breaches, but the paper describes how these can be detected. Once a set of valid options has been generated, a cost model is used to rank them. The method has been implemented in a tool, which is described in the paper.

Introduction

Cloud computing is of growing interest due to its potential for delivering cheap, scalable storage and processing. However, cloud security is a major area of concern that is restricting its use for certain applications: "Data Confidentiality and Auditability" is cited as one of the top ten obstacles to the adoption of cloud computing in the influential Berkeley report [1]. While security concerns are preventing some organizations from adopting cloud computing at all, others are considering using a combination of a secure internal "private" cloud, along with (what they perceive to be) less secure "public" clouds. Sensitive applications can then be deployed on a private cloud, while those without security concerns can be deployed externally on a public cloud. However, there are problems with this approach. Currently, the allocation of applications to clouds is usually done on an ad-hoc, per-application basis, which is not ideal as it lacks rigour and auditability. Further, decisions are often made at the level of granularity of the whole application, which is allocated entirely to either a public or private cloud based on a judgment of its overall sensitivity. This eliminates the potential benefits for partitioning an application across a set of clouds, while still meeting its overall security requirements. For example, consider a medical research application in which data from a set of patients' heart rate monitors is analyzed. A workflow used to analyze the data from each patient is shown in Figure 1. The input data is a file with a header identifying the patient, followed by a set of heart rate measurements recorded over a period of time. A service (*Anonymize*) strips off the header, leaving only the measurements (this application is concerned with the overall results from a cohort of patients, not with individuals). A second service (*Analyze*) then analyzes the measurements, producing a summary.

Analyzing the heart rate data is computationally expensive, and would benefit from the cheap, scalable resources that are available on public clouds. However, most organizations would be unlikely to consider storing medical records on a public cloud for confidentiality and, in some cases, legal reasons. Therefore, one solution is to deploy the whole workflow on a secure private cloud. However, this may overload the finite resources of the private cloud,

Correspondence: Paul.Watson@ncl.ac.uk
School of Computing Science, Newcastle University, Newcastle-upon-Tyne, NE1 7RU, UK

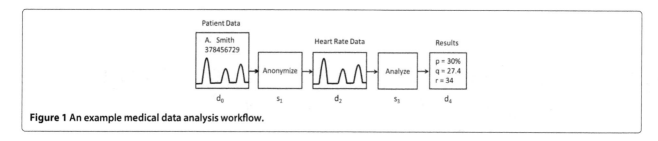

Figure 1 An example medical data analysis workflow.

resulting in poor performance, and potentially a negative impact on other applications.

An alternative solution is to partition the application between the private cloud and an external public cloud in order to exploit the strengths of both. This could be attempted in an ad-hoc fashion by a security expert but, as this paper describes, there are challenges in working out the set of partitioning options that still preserve the required security of data and services. This paper therefore describes an alternative to ad-hoc solutions – a method that takes an application consisting of a set of services and data connected in a workflow, and determines the valid set of deployments over a set of clouds, ensuring that security requirements are met. Although the paper is focused on workflows in which services communicate through passing data, the method can be applied to other types of distributed system that are composed of a set of communicating components. The method is based on Multi-Level Security models [2], specifically Bell-LaPadula [3]. The result of the method is the complete set of options that meet the organization's security requirements for the application. The method introduces transformations that need to be performed on the workflows where data is communicated between clouds; the paper identifies the security issues that can be raised as a result, and the extra security checks that need to be performed to address this. When the method results in more than one valid partitioning option, there is the issue of how to choose the best. The paper shows how a cost model can be introduced to rank the valid options; a model based on price is defined, and applied to the running medical workflow example. The full method, including the cost model, has been implemented in a tool that has been built to automate and explore its application.

The paper is structured as follows. The **Method** section gives a brief introduction to Multi-Level Security models and Bell-LaPadula. It then describes how the Bell-LaPadula rules can be applied to ensure that a workflow meets the security requirements of its constituent services and data. The method is then extended to cloud computing by assigning security levels to clouds, and building on Bell-LaPadula to define a method for determining if security requirements are met in a particular deployment of the constituent parts of a workflow onto a set of clouds.

The **Calculating valid deployment options** section then defines a method for enumerating all valid options for deploying a workflow over a set of clouds so as to meet security requirements. It highlights the issues raised when data must flow between clouds, and shows the workflow transformations and security checks that must be included in the method if security is to be guaranteed. The result is a set of valid options; the **Selecting a deployment option with a cost model** section then introduces a model that can be used to select the best option. The method is then applied to a second, more complex example (in the **A more complex example** section). A tool has been designed and built to implement the method. As described in the **Tooling** Section, it is structured as a set of rules, transforms and a cost model, allowing it to be enhanced to meet other non-functional requirements, including dependability. Following a review of related work, the paper draws conclusions and outlines further work.

Method

This section describes how the Bell-LaPadula security model can be applied to workflows, and can then be extended to the deployment of workflows on clouds. Through this section, a workflow is modeled as a directed graph in which services and data are represented as nodes. Services consume zero or more data items and generate one or more data items; the edges in the graph represent the data dependencies.

Representing security requirements

The Bell-LaPadula multi-level access control model [3] is adopted, with services modeled as the subjects (S), and data as the objects (O) [4]. The security model therefore consists of the following:

- a set of actions (A) that subjects (S) can carry out on objects (O). In the case of services operating on data in a workflow, the actions are limited to read and write. Therefore, the set of actions (A) is: $A = \{r, w\}$
- a poset of security levels: L
- a permissions matrix: $M : S \times O \rightarrow A$ (the contents of the matrix are determined by the workflow design; i.e. if service s_1 reads datum d_0 then there will be an entry in the matrix: $s_1 \times d_0 \rightarrow r$; similarly, if service

s_1 writes datum d_2 then there will be an entry in the matrix: $s_1 \times d_2 \rightarrow w$)

- an access matrix: $B : S \times O \rightarrow A$ (this is determined by the execution of the workflow: if there are no choice points then it will equal the permissions matrix, however, if there are choice points then it will equal a subset of the permissions matrix corresponding to the path taken through the workflow when it is executed.
- a clearance map: $C : S \rightarrow L$ (this represents the maximum security level at which each service can operate)
- a location map: $l : S + O \rightarrow L$ (this represents the security level of each service and datum in the workflow)

In a typical Multi-Level Security scenario, the system moves through a set of states, and the model can have different values for permissions, access, clearance and location in each state. However, here the execution of a workflow is modeled as taking place within a single state. Normally a service would be expected to have a clearance that is constant across all uses of that service in workflows, however the location can be chosen specifically for each workflow, or even (though less likely) for each invocation of a workflow. However, the model itself is general, and makes no assumptions on this.

The Bell-LaPadula model states that a system is secure with respect to the above model if the following conditions are satisfied $\forall$subjects$u \in S$ and $\forall$objects$i \in O$

$$\text{authorization:} B_{ui} \subseteq M_{ui} \qquad (1)$$

$$\text{clearance:} l(u) \le c(u) \qquad (2)$$

$$\text{no-read-up:} r \in B_{ui} \Rightarrow c(u) \ge l(i) \qquad (3)$$

$$\text{no-write-down:} w \in B_{ui} \Rightarrow l(u) \le l(i) \qquad (4)$$

For workflows, the implications of these conditions are:

(1) all actions carried out by services must conform to the permissions granted to those services
(2) a service can only operate at a security level (location) that is less than or equal to its clearance
(3) a service cannot read data that is at a higher security level than its own clearance
(4) a service cannot write data to a lower security level than its own location.

For example, consider a service s_1 which consumes datum d_0 and produces datum d_2:

$$\boxed{d_0} \rightarrow \boxed{s_1} \rightarrow \boxed{d_2}$$

(in these diagrams, the $\rightarrow$ is used to show data dependency, and each block – service or datum – is uniquely

identified by the subscript). The following rules must be met:

by (3)

$$c(s_1) \ge l(d_0) \qquad (5)$$

and by (4)

$$l(d_2) \ge l(s_1) \qquad (6)$$

The relationship between security levels is captured in Figure 2. Arrows represent $\ge$ relationships.

Whilst assigning a security level to a datum in a workflow is directly analogous to assigning a level to an object (e.g. a document) in the standard Bell-LaPadula model, assigning a security level to a service may be less intuitive. The justification is that an organization may have differing levels of confidence in the set of services they wish to use. For example, they may be very confident that a service written in-house, or provided by a trusted supplier, will not reveal the data it consumes and produces to a third party either deliberately or through poor design; in contrast, there is a risk that a service downloaded from the Internet, of unknown provenance, may do just that. Therefore, the organization can assign a high security level to the former service, and a low level to the latter.

For a specific workflow, when an organization's security experts are assigning locations to services, they may in some cases chose to set the location below that of the clearance level in order to allow a service to create data that is at a lower level than its clearance level; i.e. so that the no write down rule (4) is not violated. This may, for example, take place when the expert knows that the output data will not be sensitive, given the specific data that the service will consume as input in this specific workflow. A concrete example would be a service that summarizes textual data. This has been written to a high standard, and the security expert is confident that it will not leak data to a third party. Therefore, its clearance is high. However, in one particular workflow it is known that this service will only be used to summarise public data downloaded from the World Wide Web, which is also where its output will be published. Therefore, the security expert would set the

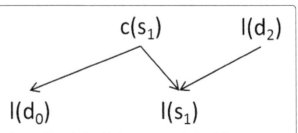

Figure 2 The relationship between security levels for a service that consumes and produces data.

service's location to an appropriately low level so that the write down rule was not violated.

Cloud security

This section describes how the Bell-LaPadula model, as applied to workflows, can be extended to encompass cloud computing.

Let us say that an organization wishes to run a particular workflow. As more than one cloud is available, a decision must be made as to where the data and services should be placed. In current practice, it is typical that a security expert or system administrator would just take a considered view on the overall security level of the workflow, and that of the clouds on which it could be deployed. For example, let us say that there are two clouds, one a highly trusted private cloud contained within the intranet of the organization, and the other a less trusted public cloud. It may seem obvious in this case that a workflow that operates on sensitive medical data should run only on the internal cloud. Similarly, a workflow that summarises public data could be deployed on the public cloud. However, there are two problems with this approach. Firstly, it is informal, being based on an expert's judgment; a systematic approach is preferable as it will give more consistent, defendable results. Secondly, the approach deploys the whole of a workflow on a single cloud. This rules out other options that may:

- reduce cost: for example by running less sensitive, but computationally intensive, sub-parts of the workflow on a public cloud if that avoids the need to purchase expensive new servers so that the internal cloud can handle the extra load
- increase reliability: for example by having the option to run on a public cloud if the private cloud has an outage
- increase performance: for example by taking advantage of the greater processing capacity of the public cloud for the computationally intensive services in a workflow

Therefore, the rest of this section extends the security model introduced earlier in order to allow systematic decisions to be taken on where the services and data within a workflow may be deployed to ensure security requirements are met.

To do this, the location map is extended to include clouds which we denote by P (to avoid confusion with the C conventionally used to denote the clearance map):

- location map: $l : S + O + P \rightarrow L$

Also, H is added to represent the mapping from each service and datum to a cloud:

$$H : S + O \rightarrow P]$$

We then add a rule that any block (service or datum) must be deployed on a cloud that is at a location that is greater than or equal to that of the block, e.g. for a block x on cloud y:

$$l(p_y) \geq l(b_x) \tag{7}$$

Returning to the example service introduced in the previous section:

$$\boxed{d_0} \rightarrow \boxed{s_1} \rightarrow \boxed{d_2}$$

if, in H, d_0 is on cloud p_a, s_1 on p_b and d_2 on cloud p_c then the following must be true:

$$l(p_a) \geq l(d_0) \tag{8}$$

$$l(p_b) \geq l(s_1) \tag{9}$$

$$l(p_c) \geq l(d_2) \tag{10}$$

This allows us to extend (6) to:

$$l(p_c) \geq l(d_2) \geq l(s_1) \tag{11}$$

The complete relationship between security levels for blocks and clouds is captured in Figure 3.

Calculating valid deployment options

Using the above model and rules, it is now possible to automatically enumerate all the valid deployment options for a workflow. These are generated in two stages. Firstly, given the following:

- the set of clouds P
- the set of services S
- the set of data O
- the map of security locations l

we can define the valid mappings of services and data onto clouds, using rule (7):

$$V : S + O \rightarrow P$$

$$V = \{b \rightarrow p | b \in S + O, p \in P, l(b) \leq l(p)\}$$

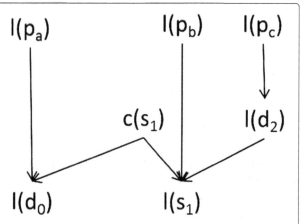

Figure 3 The relationship between cloud and workflow block security levels.

To illustrate this, we use the medical workflow of Figure 1, with two clouds. This has two services connected in a pipeline, each with one datum as input and one as output:

$$\boxed{d_0} \rightarrow \boxed{s_1} \rightarrow \boxed{d_2} \rightarrow \boxed{s_3} \rightarrow \boxed{d_4}$$

Table 1 shows an example location and clearance table (while the scheme is general, this example uses only two security levels: 0 and 1). Here, c_1 is a private cloud, which is at a higher security level than the public cloud c_0. The patient data (d_0) is at the highest security level, while the other data is at the lower level as it is not confidential. Service s_1 is cleared to access confidential data at level 1, but its location has been set to 0 in this workflow so that it can produce non-confidential output at level 0 without violating the Bell-LaPadula "no-write-down" rule (4).

Based on this mapping of blocks and clouds to locations, Table 2 then shows the possible valid placement of each block onto the two clouds.

Having determined all valid mappings of services and data to clouds, the set of all valid workflow deployments is given by:

$$W : (S + O \rightarrow P) \rightarrow \{(S + O \rightarrow P)\} =$$

$$\{w \in ||V||, \forall b \in S+O.\exists p \in P.b \rightarrow p \in w, |w| = |S+O|\}$$

Where $||V||$ is the power set of V and $|w|$ is the cardinality of w. Algorithmically, in the implementation of the method, W is computed by forming the cross-product of the block-to-cloud mappings contained in V.

All possible valid workflow deployments – as defined by W – for the running medical workflow example are shown in Figure 4. The cloud on which a datum or service is deployed is indicated as a superscript; e.g. d_j^a is datum j deployed on cloud a.

Transferring data between clouds

There is still an important issue to be addressed: the approach makes assumptions that are unrealistic for a practical distributed workflow system. It assumes that:

Table 1 Locations and clearances for the medical analysis example

	Location (l)	Clearance (c)
d_0	1	
s_1	0	1
d_2	0	
s_3	0	0
d_4	0	
c_0	0	
c_1	1	

Table 2 Valid mappings of blocks to clouds

Block	Cloud c_0	Cloud c_1
d_0		•
s_1	•	•
d_2	•	•
s_3	•	•
d_4	•	•

1. a service can generate as its output a datum directly on another cloud, without that item being first stored on the same cloud as the service
2. a service can consume as its input a datum directly from another cloud, without that item ever being stored on the same cloud as the service

This problem is solved in two stages. Firstly, a new type of service is introduced – sxfer – which will transfer data from one cloud to another (this is analogous to the exchange operator used in distributed query processing [5]). It would be implemented with sub-components running on the source and destination clouds. The sxfer service takes a datum on one cloud and creates a copy on another. All the workflows generated by W are then transformed to insert the transfer nodes whenever there is an inter-cloud edge in the workflow graph. There are four graph transformations:

$$\boxed{d_j^a} \rightarrow \boxed{s_i^a} \Rightarrow \boxed{d_j^a} \rightarrow \boxed{s_i^a} \qquad (12)$$

$$\boxed{d_j^a} \rightarrow \boxed{s_i^b} \Rightarrow \boxed{d_j^a} \rightarrow \boxed{sxfer} \rightarrow \boxed{d_j^b} \rightarrow \boxed{s_i^b} \qquad (13)$$

$$\boxed{s_i^a} \rightarrow \boxed{d_j^a} \Rightarrow \boxed{s_i^a} \rightarrow \boxed{d_j^a} \qquad (14)$$

$$\boxed{s_i^a} \rightarrow \boxed{d_j^b} \Rightarrow \boxed{s_i^a} \rightarrow \boxed{d_j^a} \rightarrow \boxed{sxfer} \rightarrow \boxed{d_j^b} \qquad (15)$$

Transforms (12) and (14) reflect the fact that if both nodes are deployed on the same cloud then no change is needed. In contrast, (13) and (15) introduce new $\boxed{sxfer}$ nodes to transfer data between clouds.

Unfortunately, the creation of new copies of data through transforms (13) and (15) introduces potential security problems. When transform (13) is applied, there is the need to check that cloud b has a sufficiently high security level to store the copy of d_j that would be created on it (the copy inherits the security level of the original). The following rule must therefore be checked to ensure this is true:

$$l(p_b) \geq l(d_j) \qquad (16)$$

Similarly, for transform 15:

$$l(p_a) \geq l(d_j) \qquad (17)$$

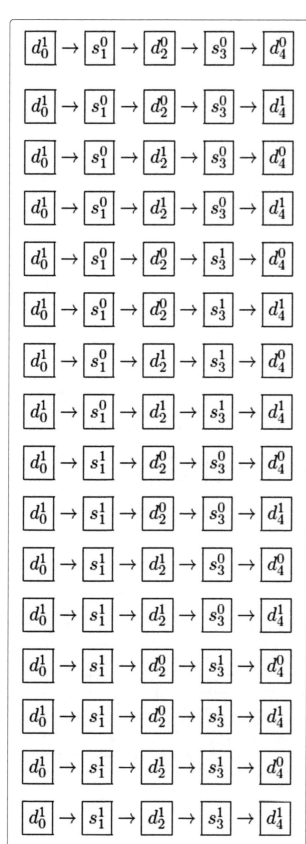

Figure 4 All valid workflows produced by mapping blocks to clouds.

If either is violated then the workflow does not meet the security requirements, and so should be removed from the set W of valid mappings of services and data to clouds. Proof that this violation can only occur in two specific cases now follows.

Firstly, consider (16). By rule (2) we have:

$$c(s_i^b) \geq l(s_i^b) \qquad (18)$$

First consider the case where:

$$c(s_i^b) = l(s_i^b) \qquad (19)$$

i.e. the clearance of the object is equal to its location.
Rules (3) and (4) give

$$c(s_i^b) \geq l(d_j) \qquad (20)$$

and

$$l(p_b) \geq l(s_i^b) \qquad (21)$$

then, by (19)

$$l(p_b) \geq l(s_i^b) \geq l(d_j) \Rightarrow l(p_b) \geq l(d_j) \qquad (22)$$

and rule (16) is satisfied. Therefore, in this case there are no violations.

However, if:

$$c(s_i^b) > l(s_i^b) \qquad (23)$$

i.e. the clearance of the service is strictly greater than its location then combining (23) with (3) and (4) in a similar way to the above, we get:

$$l(s_i^b) < c(s_i^b) \geq l(d_j) \qquad (24)$$

and

$$l(p^b) \leq l(s_i^b) < c(s_i^b) \qquad (25)$$

so it is possible that

$$l(p^b) < l(d_j) \qquad (26)$$

in which case rule (16) is violated and so that particular workflow deployment does not meet the security requirements.

Turning now to the data produced by services, rule (17) can be violated by transform (15) in the case where the service s_0 writes up data (4) to a level such that:

$$l(p_a) < l(d_j)$$

The effect of the transformations is to modify the security lattice of Figure 2 to that of Figure 5. The arc from $l(p_b)$ to $l(d_0)$ is introduced by transform (13) which adds a copy of d_0 into the workflow, while the arc from $l(p_b)$ to $l(d_2)$ is introduced by transform (15) which adds a copy of d_2.

Applying the transformations to each workflow in Figure 4, followed by rules (16) and (17) removes half of

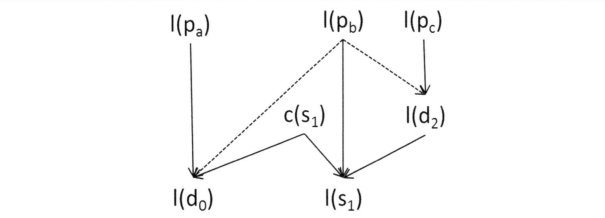

Figure 5 The relationship between security levels after transformation for inter-cloud data transfer.

the possible deployment options. Removing two duplicates created by the transformations leaves the six valid options shown in Figure 6. Another view of the remaining options is shown in Figure 7. As services can have multiple inputs and outputs, the arcs in the diagrams are labelled with the input / output number. These diagrams were generated automatically by the tool we have built to implement the methods described in this paper. The aim is to provide a security expert with an easy to understand view of the possible options.

Whilst a simple, linear workflow has been used here to illustrate the method, it is applicable to all workflows that can be represented by a directed graph, whatever their structure. The discussion so far does however still leave open the issue of how to choose between these valid options? The next section therefore describes how a cost model (also implemented in the tool) can be used to select the best option based on the charges made by the cloud providers.

Selecting a deployment option with a cost model

Once all valid options for allocating services and data to clouds have been determined, one must be selected, and used to enact the workflow. This decision could be made by a deployment expert, but this section describes how it can be achieved automatically through the use of a cost model. Different criteria may be important for different applications (e.g. dependability, performance), but this section illustrates the approach by describing a model that minimizes price.

Cloud pricing is measured using the metrics by which cloud providers allocate charges. For a cloud (p) this is represented as:

- volume of data transferred into a cloud: e^p_{dxi}
- volume of data transferred out of a cloud: e^p_{dxo}
- volume of data stored, per unit of time for which it is stored: e^p_{ds}

$$d^1_0 \rightarrow s^1_1 \rightarrow d^1_2 \rightarrow sxfer \rightarrow d^0_2 \rightarrow s^0_3 \rightarrow d^0_4$$

$$d^1_0 \rightarrow s^1_1 \rightarrow d^1_2 \rightarrow sxfer \rightarrow d^0_2 \rightarrow s^0_3 \rightarrow d^0_4 \rightarrow sxfer \rightarrow d^1_4$$

$$d^1_0 \rightarrow s^1_1 \rightarrow d^1_2 \rightarrow sxfer \rightarrow d^0_2 \rightarrow sxfer \rightarrow d^1_2 \rightarrow s^1_3 \rightarrow d^1_4 \rightarrow sxfer \rightarrow d^0_4$$

$$d^1_0 \rightarrow s^1_1 \rightarrow d^1_2 \rightarrow sxfer \rightarrow d^0_2 \rightarrow sxfer \rightarrow d^1_2 \rightarrow s^1_3 \rightarrow d^1_4$$

$$d^1_0 \rightarrow s^1_1 \rightarrow d^1_2 \rightarrow s^1_3 \rightarrow d^1_4 \rightarrow sxfer \rightarrow d^0_4$$

$$d^1_0 \rightarrow s^1_1 \rightarrow d^1_2 \rightarrow s^1_3 \rightarrow d^1_4$$

Figure 6 The Workflows that remain valid after Transfer Blocks are Added.

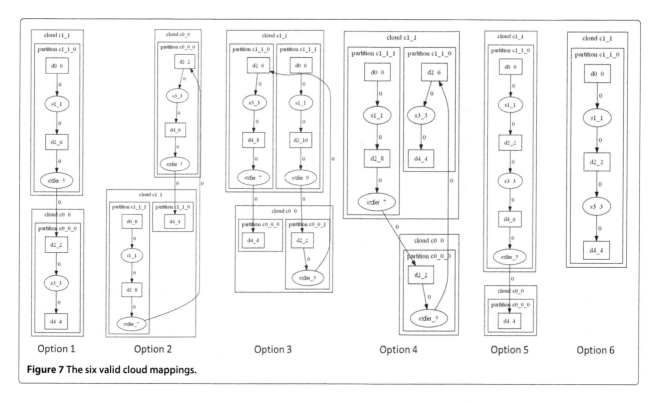

Option 1   Option 2   Option 3   Option 4   Option 5   Option 6

Figure 7 The six valid cloud mappings.

- time units of cpu consumed in the execution of a service: e_{cpu}^{p}

Cost metrics are characterised for a datum (d) as:

- data size: size(d)
- data longevity – the length of time the datum is stored: longevity(d)

Finally, the cost metric for a service (s) is characterised as:

- time units of cpu consumed in the execution of a service: cpu(s)

The cost model for a workflow execution can then be defined as:

$$cost = \sum_{d=0}^{d=k-1} e_{ds}^{p}.size(d).longevity(d)+$$

$$\sum_{s=0}^{s=m-1} e_{cpu}^{p}.cpu(s)+$$

$$\sum_{x=0}^{x=q-1} (e_{dxo}^{ps} + e_{dxi}^{pd}).size(d)$$

where k is the number of data items in the workflow, and m is the number of services, while q is the number of

inter-cloud data transfers. In the third term that calculates data transfer costs, ps represents the source cloud and pd the destination cloud for the transfer.

Using the cost model requires estimates of data sizes and cpu costs. This is realistic for many workflows, and producing these estimates is made easier if performance and capacity are logged for each run, so allowing statistical analysis to generate predictions. This is, for example, done by the e-Science Central cloud platform [6] which logs data on all data sizes, and service execution times.

Two examples now highlight the use of the model. Consider the valid mapping options shown in Figure 7 for the running medical workflow example. In the simplest case, if the performance and cost of both clouds are equal (as in Table 3), then the cost difference between options is dependent only on the number of inter-cloud communications. Table 4 gives example values for the blocks in the workflow. The size of d_0 will be known as it is the input to the workflow, while that for d_2 and d_4 are estimates, perhaps based on the results of previous runs. To set the longevity values, it is assumed that the input (d_0)

Table 3 Cloud costs: Example 1

Cloud	Storage (GB / Month)	Transfer in (/GB)	Transfer out (/GB)	CPU (/s)
c_0	10	10	10	10
c_1	10	10	10	10

Table 4 Block info

Block	Size (GB)	Longevity (months)	CPU (s)
d_0	10	12	
s_1			100
d_2	5	0	
s_3			50
d_4	1	12	

and output data (d_4) is stored for a year, while intermediate data (d_2) (along with any intermediate copies of data created by transforms) is immediately discarded once it has been consumed by a service: in this case s_2.

Table 5 shows the results when the cost model is applied. Each row represents the cost of an option in Figure 6. The final column of the table gives the order of the options (from lowest to highest cost). This confirms that the cheapest is option 6, in which all the blocks are deployed on the same cloud, and so there are no inter-cloud transfer costs.

While it may seem that an option in which all services and data are deployed on a single cloud will always be the cheapest, if CPU costs vary between clouds, then inter-cloud transfers may be worthwhile. Table 6 shows clouds with a different set of cost parameters. Here, a private cloud (c_1) has higher security, but higher CPU and data costs, compared to a public cloud (c_0). The effect of plugging these values into the cost model is shown in Table 7. The result is that the best option is now the one that allocates as much work as possible to the public cloud, which has lower CPU costs.

A more complex example

The medical example used to date consists to a purely linear workflow: each service reads and writes only one data item. However, the method supports arbitrary workflows, and this is now demonstrated through the example of a more complex workflow,which is based on that introduced in [4]. It is shown in Figure 8.

Table 6 Cloud costs: Example 2

Cloud	Storage (GB / Month)	Transfer in (/GB)	Transfer out (/GB)	CPU (/s)
c_0	5	5	5	5
c_1	10	5	5	10

With security settings shown in Table 8, the workflow meets the Bell-LaPadula criteria, and produces the three workflow partitionings shown in Figure 9.

With block costs from Table 9 and cloud costs from Table 6 (as in the previous example), the costs of the three partitioning options are shown in Table 10. This example illustrates the importance of the use of the cost model in allowing an expert or automatic deployment system to filter out valid but inefficient workflow partitionings such as option 2.

Tooling

The method described in this paper has been implemented in a tool which takes the workflow and security requirements as input, and generates as output the set of valid partitions with costs. The tool is implemented in the functional language Haskell [7], with workflows represented as directed graphs. This section explains how the tool implements the multi-level security method that is the focus of this paper, and then goes on to explain how it can be used to process other classes of non-functional requirements.

The tool is structured so that three types of functions are used to process the initial workflow:

1. **Transformation** functions take a workflow as input and generate a set of workflows derived from it. In the multi-level security method they are used for two purposes: to generate the candidate workflow partitionings from the initial workflow (Figure 4); and to insert the inter-cloud transfers according to (13) and (15).
2. **Rules** are implemented as filter functions that take a workflow as input and return a boolean indicating whether the workflow meets the rule. Workflows that do not meet a rule are removed from the set of

Table 5 Workflow deployment options costs: Example 1

Option	Storage	Transfer	CPU	Total	Order
1	1320	100	1500	2920	3
2	1320	120	1500	2940	4
3	1320	220	1500	3040	6
4	1320	200	1500	3020	5
5	1320	20	1500	2840	2
6	1320	0	1500	2820	1

Table 7 Workflow deployment options costs: Example 2

Option	Storage	Transfer	CPU	Total	Order
1	1260	75	1250	2585	1
2	1320	90	1250	2660	2
3	1260	165	1500	2925	5
4	1320	150	1500	2970	6
5	1260	15	1500	2775	3
6	1320	0	1500	2820	4

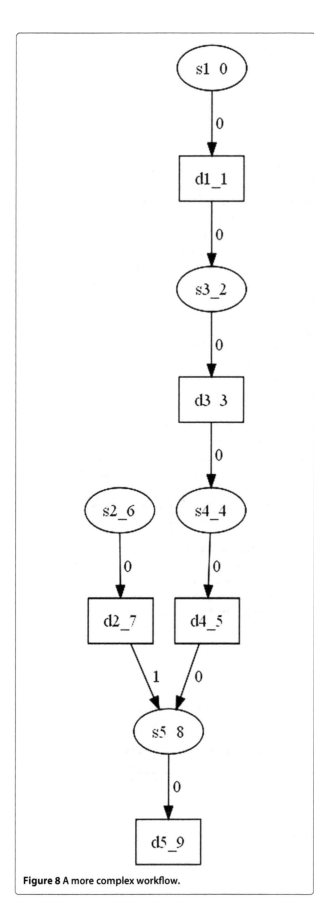

Figure 8 A more complex workflow.

Table 8 Block locations and clearances

	Location (*l*)	Clearance (*c*)
$s1_0$	0	1
$s2_6$	0	0
$s3_2$	1	1
$s4_4$	0	1
$s5_8$	1	1
$d1_1$	1	
$d2_7$	0	
$d3_3$	1	
$d4_5$	1	
$d5_9$	1	

valid workflows. In the methods described in this paper, they are used to check that the initial workflow conforms to Bell-LaPadula (Figure 2), and that the candidate workflow partitionings conform to Figure 3.

3. **Cost Model** functions take in a candidate workflow and assign a cost. They are used to implement the model described in Section "Selecting a deployment option with a cost model".

Overall, the tool takes the initial workflow (e.g. that of Figure 1) and security requirements, applies the set of transformations and rules, and then uses the cost model function to rank the valid workflows.

The tool also automatically generates the diagrams that are shown in Figure 7 using the GraphViz software library [8]; these visualisations have proved to be a useful way to review the available options. It can also generate an html report for a security review, containing all the information generated by the method, including the diagrams, security tables and ranked cost tables. Finally, it can automatically generate LaTeXtables. Therefore all the tables and diagrams used in this paper have been automatically generated by the tool. Automatically generating diagrams and tables eliminates the risk of transcription errors [9] when conveying results through reports and papers. These reports can be used by system administrators to configure the partitions manually onto the clouds, but we are also currently developing a tool to do this automatically, as described in the next section.

Generalising the approach

While this paper focuses on meeting security requirements, the structure of the tool,with its three types of functions described above, allows it to be utilised as a general system for generating partitions of workflows over clouds that meet non-functional requirements. As well as security, those requirements can include dependability

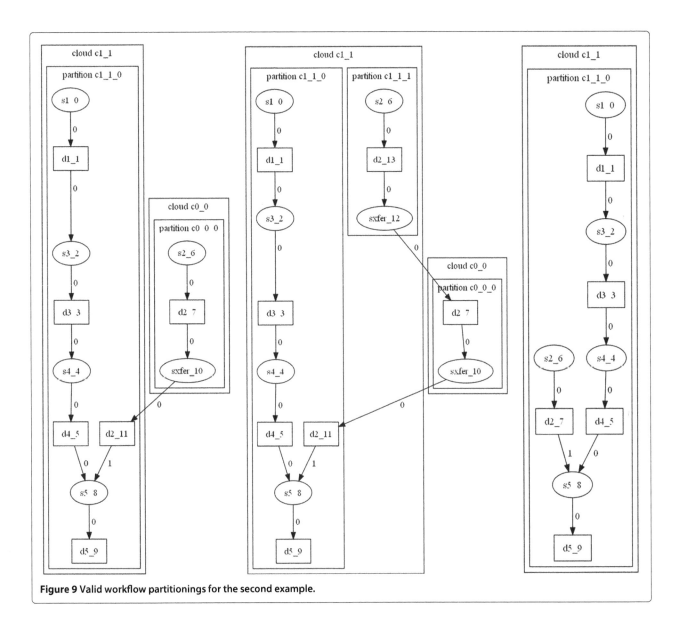

Figure 9 Valid workflow partitionings for the second example.

and performance. For example, the tool is currently being extended to encompass dependability requirements. One example requirement came out of discussions with the designer of an application in which the key workflow was very similar to that of Figure 1, but with the additional constraint that the input and output data for the workflow as a whole (e.g. d_0 and d_4 in Figure 1) must **not** be stored on the same cloud. We were able to meet this requirement simply by adding one extra rule into the tool. This is a function *apart* that takes three arguments:

- the set of blocks that need to be kept apart on different clouds
- the mapping of blocks onto clouds
- the workflow to be checked against the rule

The result of the function is true if every block contained in the first argument is deployed on a different cloud. One subtlety is that the function must take into account the fact that transformations may create one or more copies of the blocks that have been specified by the user as needing to be kept apart. For example, transforms (13) and (15) can create such copies. It is important that those copies are also included in the set of blocks that need to be kept apart. This is is achieved by exploiting the fact that the tool assigns blocks a name and identifier pair, e.g. '(*xfer*,14)'. While the identifier of each block is unique, the name can be shared by multiple blocks. When a block is copied by a transformation, it is given the same name but a new, unique identifier (similarly, separate deployments of the same service share the same name,

Table 9 Block Costs

	Size	Longevity	CPU
$d1$	10	12	
$d2$	5	12	
$d3$	1	0	
$d4$	20	0	
$d5$	20	12	
$s1$			100
$s2$			50
$s3$			10
$s4$			40
$s5$			60

but have a different unique identifier), e.g. a transform copying data item $(d,14)$ could generate $(d,27)$ where 27 is a unique identifier, not shared with another block. The *apart* function therefore works by comparing whether two blocks with the same name are stored on the same cloud, irrespective of their identifiers. For the running medical workflow example, adding the rule that d_0 and d_4 in Figure 1 must be deployed on different clouds results in only allowing the single partitioning option shown in Figure 10.

Figure 11 shows the architecture of the generalised tool. The Deployment Manager takes in the workflow and the user's non-functional requirements. It uses the rules and transformations to generate a set of valid partitionings over the available clouds, and then applies a cost model to rank them. The 'best' workflow is then executed across the set of clouds.

To achieve this, each cloud must run software that can store data and execute workflows. In this work the e-Science Central cloud platform [6] is used. This has the advantage of providing a portable platform that can be deployed on a range of clouds including public clouds (Amazon and Windows Azure) but also private clouds. Figure 12 shows the e-Science Central Architecture.

This is a cloud Platform-as-a-Service that provides users with the ability to store, share and analyse data in the cloud. Data can be uploaded and tagged with structured or unstructured metadata. Tools are provided to allow services, written in a variety of languages, to be packaged and loaded into the platform. Users can then create workflows from those services and execute them in the

Table 10 Workflow partitioning option costs

Option	Storage	Transfer	CPU	Total	Rank
1	4500	50	2350	6900	2
2	5100	100	2600	7800	3
3	4200	0	2600	6800	1

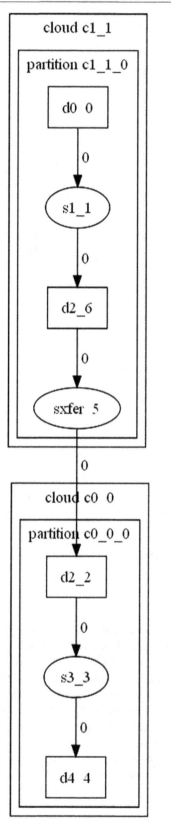

Figure 10 The only valid workflow partitioning if d_0 and d_4 must not be deployed on the same cloud.

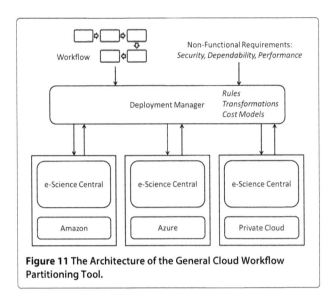

Figure 11 The Architecture of the General Cloud Workflow Partitioning Tool.

cloud; a graphical, in-browser editor is provided to allow users to create new workflows. e-Science Central provides scalable cloud computing as it can distribute the execution of a set of workflows across a set of nodes. This is mainly used to scale throughput (to increase the number of workflow executions per second), but it can also be used to reduce response time where there are opportunities to execute sub-workflows in parallel. The system has achieved scalability at over 90% efficiency, when running on up to 190 cloud nodes, each with two cores.

All accesses to e-Science Central system are policed by a Security service. This ensures that access to all data, services and workflows can be controlled by users. The basis for this is a social networking system that allows users to connect to each other, as well as to create and join groups. Users can chose to keep data, services and workflows private, or can share them with other users, or with groups to which they are connected.

All actions carried out in e-Science Central are recorded in an audit/provenance log. Users can view and query the subset of this log that the security system permits them to see. This allows users to determine exactly how each data item was created (e.g. the graph of service/workflow executions) and how it has been used.

e-Science Central has a Software-as-a-Service interface that allows users to perform all actions through a web browser. In addition, there is an API so that programs can drive the system. This includes all the actions needed to deploy and execute partitioned workflows over federated clouds: storing data, creating and executing workflows. The portability of e-Science Central means that the 'Deployment Manager' in Figure 11 can create and trigger the execution of the workflow partitions in exactly the same way, irrespective of the underlying cloud on which the partition is deployed and executed.

Figure 11 shows two way communication between the 'Deployment Manager' and 'e-Science Central'. The above description of the tool describes the flow of information

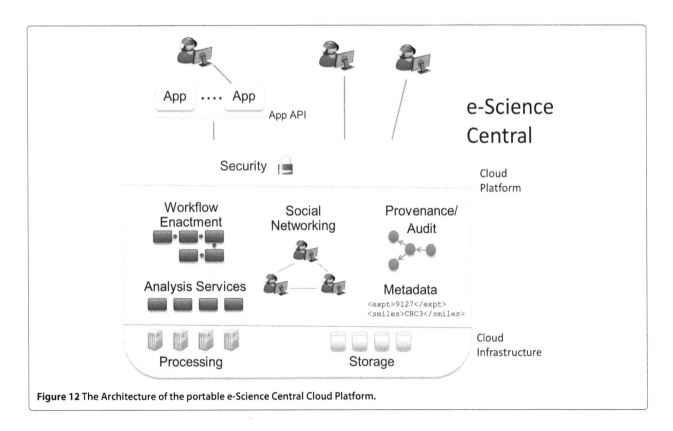

Figure 12 The Architecture of the portable e-Science Central Cloud Platform.

from the 'Deployment Manager' to the 'e-Science Central' instances in the form of workflow partitions to be executed. Information flowing in the reverse direction can include cost updates. If cloud providers start to vary their pricing models frequently, and provide APIs to access it, this information could also be fed back into the Deployment Manager so that the cost models can be kept up-to-date. e-Science Central also has a sophisticated provenance capture and analysis system [10]; this includes collecting information on data sizes and service execution times that can be used to improve the accuracy of the estimated block costs that feed into the cost models.

The Deployment Manager could also monitor the availability of the clouds, for example by sending regular "ping" requests to the e-Science Central deployments, or by including time-outs in the calls to execute a workflow partition on a cloud. This would then allow it to select dynamically between possible workflow partitionings based on which clouds are currently available. Of course, there is a danger that all valid options depend on the availability of one particular cloud (as in the running medical workflow example). Rather than discover this at run-time, it is possible to determine this statically using the tool. This can be done by running the tool multiple times, each time omitting one cloud. This will determine whether the execution of a workflow is critically dependent on a single cloud (in this case the tool will generate no valid options). Having done this, an organization for whom the workflow is business-critical could ensure that the cloud in question has sufficiently high levels of availability, or identify (or create) a second cloud with a sufficiently high security clearance that could also be used by the workflow if the other failed.

Related work

The motivation for this paper came from the author's experience of cloud applications with security constraints (e.g. healthcare applications in the 'Social Inclusion through the Digital Economy' (SiDE) project [11]). However, the general concern that security was a barrier to use of the cloud for many organizations and applications has been widely discussed [1]. The general issues associated with security and clouds are discussed in [12]. A high-level approach to deciding where an application could be deployed is discussed in [13]. Another approach to eliciting and exploiting information on the security and other properties of clouds is described in [14]. These methodologies could be valuable in assigning security levels to clouds, services and data: something which is orthogonal to the scheme described in this paper.

In [4], Bell-LaPadula is also applied to workflow security. Petri Nets are used to model the workflow, rather than the approach taken in this paper. However, the key difference is that its scope does **not** extend to considering the deployment of blocks within a workflow across a set of computational resources, as this paper does. It also differs in including *clearance* but not *location* in its embodiment of Bell-LaPadula.

There has been a large body of work on using cost models to predict execution times in order to select between options for deploying workflows over grids and clouds [15,16]. However, perhaps due to the relatively recent introduction of pay-as-you-go cloud computing, there is much less work on using price-based cost models. In [17], both execution time and price-based models are used to compare a set of options for allocating a workflow over local resources and a public cloud. The work in [18] uses non-linear programming to generate options for using clouds to execute a workflow. Security is not a consideration in any of these papers.

Once the partitioning of a workflow over a set of clouds has been decided, a distributed workflow enactment engine is needed to actually run the workflow. The issues around this are discussed in [19] and a solution is proposed.

Conclusions

This paper has described a new method for automatically determining valid options for partitioning a workflow of services and data across a set of clouds based on security requirements. A cost model is then used to choose between the available options. The main contribution is to show how multi-level security, which has previously been applied to workflows, can be extended to encompass the allocation of workflow services and data to clouds. This has demonstrated that the need for inter-cloud data transfers raises interesting potential security violations that need to be addressed; in the running medical workflow example, this ruled out over half of the possible partitioning options. Although the paper focuses on workflows, the method can be applied to other distributed systems whose components are to be partitioned over a set of clouds.

The tool developed to implement the method has proved invaluable in two ways. Firstly, it removes the chance of human error in applying the various stages of the method to the input workflow. To reinforce this advantage, it can automatically generate both html and LATEXtables, diagrams and reports (the LATEXtables were used in this paper). Secondly, developing the tool forced us to think about how best to structure the implementation of the method, which resulted in a very general system that operates on rules, transforms and cost models. Whilst the focus of this paper is on the multi-level security rules and transforms, as described in sub-section "Generalising the approach", we have been exploring the extension of the approach to other non-functional requirements such as dependability. Whilst this work is ongoing, even in its current form the method can illuminate dependability issues; for example, analysing the set of valid options can highlight the dependency of the workflow on a specific cloud (as in the running medical workflow example). This will allow an organization which is dependent on the workflow to ensure that this cloud has sufficiently high levels of availability, or encourage it to identify a second cloud with a sufficiently high security clearance that could also be used by the workflow.

Overall, the hope is that the approach described in this paper can move the process of partitioning workflows over federated clouds from one in which a human administrator makes an informed but ad-hoc choice, to one in which a tool, such as the one built to implement this method, can determine the valid options based on a rigorous underlying set of rules, and then suggest which is the best, based on a cost model. The approach therefore has the advantage that it can reduce both security violations and execution costs.

Competing interests
The author declare that he have no competing Interests.

Acknowledgements
The author would like to thank Leo Freitas, John Mace, Paolo Missier, Chunyan Mu, Sophie Watson, Feng Hao, Zhenyu Wen, Simon Woodman and Hugo Hiden for their comments and suggestions. This work was funded by the Research Councils UK 'Social Inclusion through the Digital Economy' project EP/G066019/1.

References
1. Armbrust M, Fox A, Griffith R, Joseph AD, Katz RH, Konwinski A, Lee G, Patterson DA, Rabkin A, Stoica I, Zaharia M (2009) Above the clouds: a berkeley View of Cloud Computing, Technical Report UCB/EECS-2009-28, EECS Department, University of California, Berkeley. http://www.eecs.berkeley.edu/Pubs/TechRpts/2009/EECS-2009-28.html
2. Landwehr CE (1981) Formal models for computer security. ACM Comput Surveys 13: 247–278
3. Bell DE, LaPadula LJ (1973) Secure Computer Systems: Mathematical Foundations. Tech. rep., MITRE Corporation
4. Knorr K (2001) Multilevel Security and Information Flow in Petri Net Workflows. In: Proceedings of the 11th Conference on Advanced Information Systems Engineering
5. Graefe G (1990) Encapsulation of parallelism in the Volcano query processing system. In: Proceedings of the 1990 ACM SIGMOD international conference on, Management of data, SIGMOD '90. ACM New York, pp 102–111. http://doi.acm.org/10.1145/93597.98720
6. Watson P, Hiden H, Woodman S (2010) e-Science Central for CARMEN: science as a service. Concurr Comput: Pract Exper 22: 2369–2380. http://dx.doi.org/10.1002/cpe.v22:17
7. Jones SP (2003) Haskell 98 language and libraries: the Revised Report. Cambridge University Press. ISBN 0521826144
8. Ellson J, Gansner E, Koutsofios L, North SC, Woodhull G (2002) Graphviz – open source graph drawing tools. Graph Drawing 2265: 483–484. http://www.springerlink.com/index/bvdkvy7uj1plml8n.pdf
9. Kelly MC (1989) The Works of Charles Babbage. William Pickering, London
10. Woodman S, Hiden H, Watson P, Missier P (2011) Achieving reproducibility by combining provenance with service and workflow versioning. In: 6th Workshop on Workflows in Support of Large-Scale Science
11. Social Inclusion through the Digital Economy. www.side.ac.uk
12. Mace J, van Moorsel A, Watson P (2011) The case for dynamic security solutions in public cloud workflow deployments, dsnw. IEEE/IFIP 41st International Conference on Dependable Systems and Networks Workshops. pp 111–116. http://csdl2.computer.org/csdl/proceedings/dsnw/2011/0374/00/05958795-abs.html
13. Capgemeni (2010) Putting Cloud security in perspective. Tech. rep., Capgemeni
14. Pearson S, Sander T (2010) A mechanism for policy-driven selection of service providers in SOA and cloud environments. In: New Technologies of Distributed Systems (NOTERE), 2010 10th Annual International Conference on. pp 333–338
15. Yu J, Buyya R, Tham CK (2005) Cost-based scheduling of scientific workflow applications on utility grids. In: First International Conference on e-Science and Grid Computing (e-Science'05). pp 140–147
16. Singh G, Kesselman C, Deelman E (2007) A provisioning model and its comparison with best-effort for performance-cost optimization in grids. In: Proceedings of the 16th international symposium on High performance distributed computing - HPDC '07. ACM Press, New York, pp 117–126
17. Deelman E, Singh G, Livny M, Berriman B, Good J (2008) The cost of doing science on the cloud: the Montage example. In: Proceedings of the 2008 ACM/IEEE conference on Supercomputing, SC '08. IEEE Press, Piscataway, pp 50:1–50:12. http://dl.acm.org/citation.cfm?id=1413370.1413421
18. Pandey S, Gupta K, Barker A, Buyya R (2009) Minimizing Cost when Using Globally Distributed Cloud Services: A Case Study in Analysis of Intrusion Detection Workflow Application. Tech. rep., Cloud Computing and Distributed Systems Laboratory, The University of Melbourne, Australia, Melbourne, Australia
19. Woodman S (2008) A programming system for process coordination in virtual organisations. PhD thesis, School of Computing Science, Newcastle University

15

Trust as a facilitator in cloud computing: a survey

Sheikh Mahbub Habib*, Sascha Hauke, Sebastian Ries and Max Mühlhäuser

Abstract

Cloud computing offers massively scalable, elastic resources (e.g., data, computing power, and services) over the internet from remote data centres to the consumers. The growing market penetration, with an evermore diverse provider and service landscape, turns Cloud computing marketplaces a highly competitive one. In this highly competitive and distributed service environment, the assurances are insufficient for the consumers to identify the dependable and trustworthy Cloud providers.

This paper provides a landscape and discusses incentives and hindrances to adopt Cloud computing from Cloud consumers' perspective. Due to these hindrances, potential consumers are not sure whether they can trust the Cloud providers in offering dependable services. Trust-aided unified evaluation framework by leveraging trust and reputation systems can be used to assess trustworthiness (or dependability) of Cloud providers. Hence, cloud-related specific parameters (QoS+) are required for the trust and reputation systems in Cloud environments. We identify the essential properties and corresponding research challenges to integrate the QoS+ parameters into trust and reputation systems. Finally, we survey and analyse the existing trust and reputation systems in various application domains, characterizing their individual strengths and weaknesses. Our work contributes to understanding 1) why trust establishment is important in the Cloud computing landscape, 2) how trust can act as a facilitator in this context and 3) what are the exact requirements for trust and reputation models (or systems) to support the consumers in establishing trust on Cloud providers.

Keywords: Cloud computing, Cloud taxonomy, Trust evaluation, Reputation system, Trust management, Trust models

Introduction

Cloud computing offers dynamic, scalable, shared, and elastic resources (e.g., computing power, storage, software, etc.) over the internet from remote data centres to the users (e.g., business organizations, government authorities, individuals, etc.). The opportunities afforded by cloud computing are too attractive for the consumers (which we also refer to as "customers") to ignore in today's highly competitive service environments (which we also refer to as "marketplaces"). The way to realizing these opportunities, however, is not free of obstacles.

The highly distributed and non-transparent nature of cloud computing represents a considerable obstacle to the acceptance and market success of cloud services. Potential users of these services often feel that they lose control over

their data and they are not sure whether cloud providers can be trusted. Particularly, they are concerned and confused about the capabilities of Cloud providers [1]. Additionally, a recent survey [2], conducted among more than 3000 Cloud consumers from 6 countries, shows that 84% of the consumers are concerned about their data storage location and 88% of the consumers worry about who has access to their data. The business market is growing rapidly with new players entering the Cloud computing marketplaces and it is expected that Cloud providers are going to compete for customers by providing services with similar primary functionality. However, there can be huge differences regarding the provided quality level of those services. Thus, there will be a need to reliably identify the dependable service providers in such a competitive marketplace [3]. The ability to do so will establish confidence of the consumers in adopting

*Correspondence: sheikh.habib@cased.de
Technische Universität Darmstadt/CASED, Telecooperation Group, Darmstadt, Germany

cloud-based services and support consumers in selecting the appropriate service providers.

Similar issues of establishing trust and confidence are already known from the Internet of Services (as well as from P2P and eCommerce). Trust and reputation (TR) systems [4] are successfully used in numerous application scenarios to support users in identifying the dependable (or trustworthy) providers, e.g., on eBay, Amazon, and app markets for mobile applications. Related concepts are needed to support customers in selecting appropriate trustworthy Cloud providers. Industry experts and academic researchers have already coined the need for regulation, monitoring and trust establishment in the Cloud computing environments, as outlined exemplarily in the following. The need for a third party assurance body to accredit Cloud providers is mentioned in [5]. In [6], the author has discussed ways for evaluating the service quality of Cloud providers based on parameters like response time, availability and elasticity. A recent article [1] has highlighted the challenges and given an outline of solutions using emerging technologies for establishing trust in Cloud computing. Another article [7] has discussed several security and privacy challenges in Cloud computing environments and suggested considering a trust-based framework for supporting adaptive policy integration. Additionally, a number of research articles aimed at revealing security weaknesses [8,9], providing security guidance [10], and giving recommendations [11] regarding Cloud computing. Most of the articles mentioned above outline different challenges and possible solutions or recommendations regarding security, privacy, and trust issues in Cloud computing. However, there are only a few research articles that focus on the evaluation of Cloud providers or on finding appropriate solutions to establish confidence and trust between the consumers and the Cloud providers. We focus on this particular issue in this paper.

This article is the first survey focusing on the hindrances for adopting Cloud computing and how the trust concepts can support the consumers in overcoming these hindrances. Our work contributes to the understanding of why trust establishment is important in the Cloud computing landscape, how trust can act as a facilitator in this context to overcome the hindrances and what are the exact requirements for the trust and reputation models (or systems) in Cloud environments to support the consumers in establishing trust on Cloud providers. Particularly:

1. We propose a Cloud taxonomy to provide a clear idea about the involved players, their roles and offerings as well as the diversity of Cloud marketplaces in general.
2. We classify the current trends of trust establishment in Cloud computing. By analysing them in the context

of a healthcare provider (a potential Cloud consumer) we identified the limitations of these trends.
3. We classify the QoS+ [12] parameters (in the sense of consumers' requirements) in terms of their information sources (based on the Cloud taxonomy) and approaches (based on the current trends) to derive the information.
4. We identified the required properties of TR models in Cloud environments for integrating the QoS+ parameters and outline the corresponding challenges.
5. We characterize the existing TR models and systems based on the essential properties. We also discuss each model's and system's strengths and weaknesses based on the property characterization.

The rest of the paper is organized as follows: Section "Cloud computing landscape" gives a brief introduction to Cloud computing. Section "Adoption of cloud computing" briefly depicts the incentives and hindrances to adopt Cloud computing and discusses how trust concepts is used to mitigate those hindrances. Section "Trust in cloud computing" describes the importance of trust concepts for service provider selection with an example and analyse the current trends for trust establishment. Section "TR models for cloud marketplaces: requirements and challenges" provides a list of relevant parameters (i.e., QoS+) and required properties along with their corresponding challenges for trust models in Cloud environments. Section "Survey and analysis of TR Systems/Models" surveys and analyses the existing trust models and systems. Finally, we present our concluding remarks in Section "Conclusions".

Cloud computing landscape

This section describes the landscape of Cloud computing from our perspective. In particular, it illustrates the building blocks and a taxonomy of Cloud computing.

Cloud computing building blocks

The basic building blocks of Cloud computing are illustrated in the following three sub-sections named:

- Service delivery models,
- Service deployment models, and
- Cloud entities

Before describing the building blocks, we give a brief overview of Cloud computing.

Definition

Defining *Cloud computing* stringently has not been an easy task in IT industry. However, IBM, Forrester Research, NIST (National Institute of Standards and Technology) and ENISA (European Network and Information Security Agency) came up with concrete definitions

[11,13,14]. While these definitions show a significant degree of overlap, each leaves out one or another attribute that the others demand and which we consider essential in order to define *Cloud computing* clearly. Thus, we propose to define *Cloud computing* by adopting those existing definitions as follows:

Definition 1 (Cloud Computing). Cloud computing is a computing paradigm that involves data and/or computation outsourcing over the network (Intranet or Internet) based on virtualization and distributed computing techniques, especially fulfilling the following five special attributes:

1. *Multitenancy or sharing of resources:* Multiple users share resources at the network, host and application level.
2. *Elasticity:* Users can rapidly increase or decrease their resources (e.g., computing, storage, bandwidth, and etc.) whenever they need.
3. *Broad network of access:* Resources can be accessed from heterogeneous thin or thick client platforms (e.g., smartphones, notebooks, PDAs, and etc.)
4. *Pay-as-you-go feature:* Users pay only what they use in terms of computing cycles or usage duration.
5. *On-demand self-provisioning of resources:* Users can provision the resources on self-service basis whenever they want.

Service delivery models
Cloud computing enables and facilitates the provisioning of numerous kinds and diverse flavours of services. It is however possible to group these services as per the mode of their delivery. According to the NIST [14], Cloud services are delivered within three types of delivery models which are SaaS, PaaS, and IaaS. Aside from these three categories, three further service delivery models have been introduced in a distinguished talk by industry expert Stephen Hanna of Juniper Networks [15]. Adopting all these categories, Cloud service delivery models are categorized in six types which are Software as a Service (SaaS), Data as a Service (DaaS), Network as a Service (NaaS), Platform as a Service (PaaS), Identity and Policy Management as a Service (IPMaaS), and Infrastructure as a Service (IaaS). For further details regarding specific delivery models we refer the readers to [14,15].

Deployment models
Cloud deployment models are basically categorized into four different types [14] based on specific requirements of the consumers. These are: Public Cloud, Private Cloud, Community Cloud, and Hybrid Cloud. For further details, we refer the readers to [14].

Cloud entities
Cloud providers and consumers are the two primary entities in the business market. However, aside from these, brokers and resellers are two other emerging entities in Cloud computing market [12]. Recently, NIST has mentioned Cloud Auditors and Cloud Carriers as further two entities (or actors) in their updated reference architecture of Cloud computing [16]. The different types of Cloud entities are briefly discussed in the following.

Cloud Providers (CPs) Cloud providers host and manage the underlying infrastructure and offer Cloud services (e.g., SaaS, PaaS, and IaaS) to consumers, service brokers or resellers. Note that Cloud Brokers (CBs), Cloud Resellers (CRs), and Cloud Consumers (CCs) may act as CPs in certain contexts, which are discussed in the following sections.

Cloud Brokers (CBs) Generally, two types of brokers in a Cloud market can be distinguished. Firstly, there are brokers that concentrate on negotiating relationships between consumers and providers without owning or managing the Cloud infrastructure. They provide, for example, consultancy services to the potential CCs for moving their IT resources into a suitable Cloud. Secondly, there are brokers that add extra services on top of a CPs' infrastructure / platform / software to enhance and secure the Cloud environment for the consumers. For example, a broker might offer identity and access management service on top of CP's basic service offerings to consumers. As an example, such a broker may develop APIs in order to make Cloud services interoperable and portable. In both cases, the broker act as a CP that offer value added or bundled services to the CCs. DaaS, IPMaaS and NaaS are three types of service delivery models that offer services on top of other services (e.g., SaaS, PaaS, and IaaS). Thus, the CPs, that offer add-on services (e.g., DaaS, IPMaaS, and NaaS), plays the role as a broker in Cloud computing market.

Cloud Resellers (CRs) Resellers provide services on behalf of a Cloud provider. They can become an important factor in the Cloud market when CPs expand their businesses into new markets, for instance across continents. CPs may choose local IT consultancy firms or resellers of their existing products to act as resellers for their Cloud-based products in a particular region. Thus, on the one hand, resellers may realize business opportunities of massive Cloud investments rolling into their market, for instance in order to harness strategic partnerships, establish themselves in a new business field or supplement their existing infrastructures. On the other hand, CPs can use the brand recognition, marketing and reselling expertise of the resellers to strengthen their position in the Cloud market. In the case of reselling the Cloud services and offering customer support on behalf of a provider, a reseller may act as a CP to Cloud consumers.

Cloud Consumers (CCs) CCs can be broadly categorized into two types: i) end consumers and ii) Cloud-based service providers (CbSPs). Business organizations, government authorities, educational institutions, and individuals belong to the category of end consumers who may use Cloud services to meet their business, national, educational and personal needs (without offering any new services to others). On the other hand, CbSPs offer new services to the consumers that are entirely hosted in Cloud. The role of CbSPs is different than that of the CBs, as CBs just offer the add-ons on the top of existing services, where as CbSPs develop their own business model based on the services they offer (cf. Figure 1).

Cloud Auditors (CAs) Auditors conduct independent assessment of other entities (including Cloud Carriers) in terms of Cloud services, information systems operations, performance and security of the Cloud implementations. For example, a Cloud auditor can make assessment of security controls in the information system to determine the level of controls implemented correctly or not. Based on the assessment they issue a particular audit certificate which is extremely important for the consumer who outsource in-house application to the Cloud.

Cloud Carriers (CCas) These intermediate entities ensure seamless service provisioning by providing connectivity among Cloud entities. For example, CCas provide network, telecommunication and other devices for accessing Cloud services. Network and telecommunication operators are also part of this category as they ensure service distribution through their network.

In the next section, Cloud taxonomy is provided to give a clear picture of the Cloud computing marketplaces.

Taxonomy of the cloud computing market

Existing Cloud taxonomy [17] by OpenCrowd community covers three basic service delivery models (e.g., SaaS, PaaS, IaaS) and Cloud softwares to provide an extensive list of CPs. We further extend the taxonomy by including the Cloud entities and other service delivery models (e.g., NaaS, IPMaaS, and DaaS) to provide a more concrete picture of Cloud computing marketplaces.

According to OpenCrowd's Cloud taxonomy, CPs are classified into four categories based on the type of services they offer. In this taxonomy, providers of three non-canonical service models – DaaS, NaaS and IPMaaS – are missing. Moreover, except CPs, the other Cloud entities mentioned in section "Cloud entities" are not part of the

taxonomy. Our objective is to provide a taxonomy where all the entities can be incorporated based on the types of services they are related with. We omit the category "Cloud softwares" as the providers belong to that category easily fit into our taxonomy with extended service delivery models.

The Cloud taxonomy (cf. Figure 1) illustrates the entities of today's Cloud marketplaces. The entities are categorized based on the roles they are playing in Cloud marketplaces. Each of the entities is further categorized based on the types of services they are offering or consuming. A brief discussion regarding the taxonomy is given as follows.

In the first row, CPs are listed according to the service delivery models (see section "Service delivery models"). In each of the service delivery models, there are various types of services that are offered by the CPs. For example, it can be seen that Zoho offers a particular type of *SaaS* products, *desktop productivity*, but is not one of the companies providing, for instance, *social networks* as a service.

In the second row, CBs are listed according to the types of services they are brokering. For example, Right Scale provides a Cloud management platform which gives consumers the flexibility of managing their infrastructures (e.g., virtual OS images) hosted by different Cloud infrastructure providers.

In the third row, CRs are listed under the respective CPs for whose offerings they act as resellers. Only a few of the CPs publicize a list of their resellers.

In the fourth row, CCs are depicted according to the business model they follow. For example, Animoto, a video rendering service provider hosted in the Amazon Cloud (thus, acting as a service provider to its customers, but consuming Cloud-based computing services from Amazon), is offering rendering services to its end consumers for creating video slides from the given images. End consumers, however, consume Cloud services but do not provide Cloud services to other customers as part of their primary business model. For example, educational institutions (e.g., Chalmers University of Technology or the University of Amsterdam), business organizations (e.g., Eli Lilly [15]) and government authorities (e.g., Los Angeles city government [18]) use Cloud resources for their IT needs but not selling the services outside their boundary or to the consumers outside the organizations.

In the fifth row, a range of cloud audit standards (or services) are listed according to the audit related resources from the Cloud Security Alliance [19]. Note that the list is not limited to these standards or services.

The Cloud taxonomy presented here gives a clear idea about the diversified market structure of Cloud computing. This obviously appear as one of the incentives for the consumers to adopt Cloud computing business model through many alternatives. However, there are

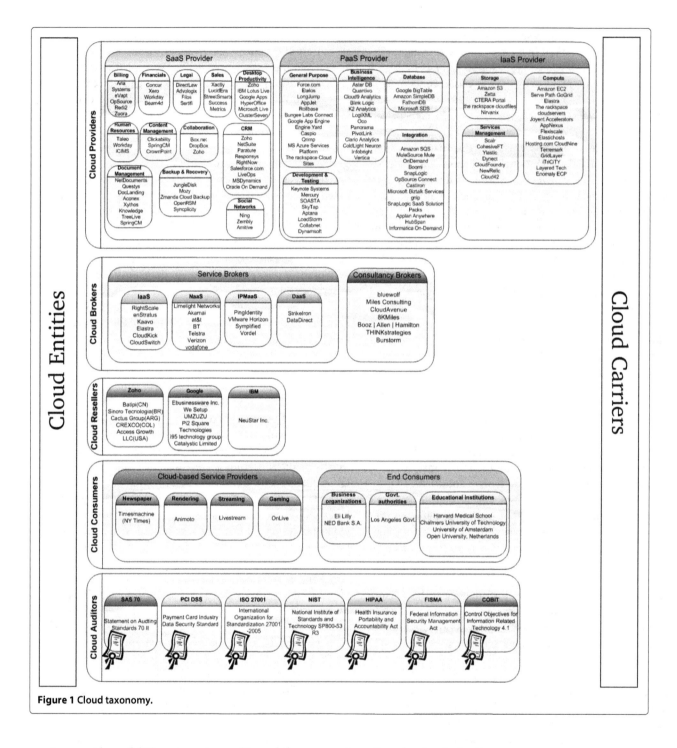

Figure 1 Cloud taxonomy.

service providers of different service quality and the non-transparent nature of Cloud computing introduce considerable obstacles which make the consumers sceptic to adopt Cloud computing as a part of their business model.

Adoption of cloud computing
Cloud computing offers incentives for each of the Cloud entities. However, these incentives are not free of obstacles (hindrances for cloud adoption).

Incentives for cloud adoption
Primary incentives for Cloud entities depend on the role of these entities in the service provisioning process. In such a process, an entity is either a consumer or provider of a particular service. The immediate benefit for entities fulfilling the provider role, i.e., CPs, CBs, CRs, and CCas primarily lies in enabling their business and offering new business opportunities. Organizational CPs stand to gain from providing Cloud services, generating profit

by making their expertise in IT and unused computing capabilities available to consumers.

From a Cloud Consumer (CC) point of view, the adoption of Cloud computing by individuals is already widespread. Organizational Cloud Consumers, ranging from start-ups to SMEs (Small and Medium-sized Enterprises) to large companies and NGOs (Non-Government Organizations), are outsourcing IT resources in the Cloud in order to leverage a number of key benefits, ultimately related to both cost and capabilities. We see the following key benefits: cost reduction, dynamic resource sharing, pay-per-use, fast roll out of new services, dynamic resource availability which are detailed in [12].

Hindrances for cloud adoption

As outlined above, CCs, particularly on the institutional level, can leverage considerable benefits by switching to applications run in the Cloud. This has prompted Gartner Inc. to identify Cloud computing as one of the top strategic technologies for the year 2010 [20], thereby further highlighting the importance for companies and other institutional consumers.

However, actual adoption of Cloud computing by businesses is still lagging. A number of concerns contribute to this, generally showing that confidence in the new technology still has to grow. Some of these concerns have been identified in recent articles. Researchers from the RAD lab of UC Berkeley, for instance, have identified 10 specific concerns (i.e., availability, data lock-in, data confidentiality & auditability, data transfer bottlenecks, etc.) [21] regarding the adoption of cloud-based services. Recently, another group of researchers identified a number of threats and risks (i.e., security & privacy threats, weak Service Level Agreements (SLAs), lack of reliability, etc.) to adopt cloud-based services and discussed how these affect the consumers' trust on cloud providers [12]. As a further example, another survey [22] about Cloud computing, from the perspective of SMEs, shows that security and the liability for incidents involving the infrastructure are major concerns for potential Cloud consumers among SMEs at present.

With enterprises hesitant to move into Cloud computing, CPs are unable to realize the full potential of the Cloud market. By identifying and addressing customer concerns, CPs have thus the opportunity to increase their profits. The same reasoning also applies to potential CBs and CRs. They do, however, act in a dual role, both consuming Cloud Services and providing them. They have, as service providers, a vested interest to attract customers to their offerings. However, they are not controlling the entire service provisioning process because they have to rely on the CPs that supply the services they expand or resell. The Cloud enables their business models, while at the same time, concerns regarding Cloud adoption hamper their success.

The issues faced by both providers and prospective consumers of Cloud services boil down to an unwillingness on the part of the consuming party to depend on the providing party. Thus, the overall acceptance, and thus the success of enterprise service provisioning in Cloud computing, hinges on whether or not consumers are willing to relinquish control over potentially business relevant information, data or internal processes. Often, losing this control exposes the depending party to a considerable risk if internal, sensitive data is divulged or (time-critical) services are not being rendered adequately by the provider. In order to overcome this significant challenge, consumers have to be put in a position where they can reliably assess the dependability of a service provider [3]. At the same time, service providers have to be able to truthfully represent their dependability. If both these objectives can be achieved, consumers have a basis for making well-founded decisions about whether or not to depend on a particular service providers.

Trust as a facilitator

Predicting the future behaviour of a partner in a situation involving uncertain outcomes is usually achieved, in social contexts, through the concept of trust. Various factors contribute to the establishment of a trust relationship between two partners, ranging from general assumptions about the legal or social environment, to the immediate public reputation of each of the partners, to concrete, actual prior experiences made during previous interactions [23]. Particularly the last factor, direct prior experience, represents a strong indicator of the dependability of a potential partner.

In the Cloud environment, however, entities potentially initiate transactions with each other without having had prior contacts. Due to the resulting lack of direct experience shared among a particular pairing of consumer and provider, consumers often hold insufficient information for reliably predicting the quality of a service and the trustworthiness of its provider. Lack of experience with a service provider, for instance regarding data privacy and security policies, thus represents a specific hurdle to the adoption of Cloud computing.

This situation is exacerbated by CPs seemingly giving overcommitted assurances while at the same time limiting liability for failure to achieve the assured levels of service in their SLAs. In other words, providers today tend to make promises that they are unwilling to back up. Several CPs, for instance, promise high availability, such as 100% or 99.99% availability of a service – the latter translates to 52 minutes downtime a year. In the light of recently reported Cloud service outages [24]), this seems unreasonably optimistic (if not to say, wholly unrealistic).

Thus, Cloud Providers currently do not represent their dependability truthfully. The lack of *meaningful* information results in *mis*trust. Dedicated trust management, in the sense of [25], leveraging trust and reputation concepts, is required to permit consumers to fully embrace Cloud Computing.

Trust and the related concept of reputation are two essential mechanisms in the facilitation of decision making in many economic and social fields, from ancient fish markets to modern eCommerce. In order to be applicable, however, the somewhat broad term 'trust' has to be specified a bit further. A common definition of trust [4,26,27] in computational applications describes it is a subjective expectation of one entity about another within a specific context at a given time. Thus, trust can serve as an estimation of future behavior.

Reputation is defined as what is believed about an entity's standing by the community [4]. This belief can be derived from previous experience, using past behavior to predict future actions. This experience can be either direct or indirect. Direct experience connotes what has been learned by an evaluating entity about another from previous interactions between these two entities. Meanwhile, indirect experience is built from either (*a*) observations of interactions between the entity under evaluation and a third or (*b*) recommendations given to the evaluating entity by another member of its community. Usually, determining trust, i.e., computing a subjective expectation of another entity's future actions, is based upon the reputation that entity has – thus, reputation directly affects trust. However, trust, as a subjective, dyadic relation between entities, also affects reputation. Trust represents the opinion of one entity towards a specific other, while the collective opinions of (all) entities constitute reputation. Thus, trust affects the reputation of an entity and vice versa [28].

Reputation clearly is an important aspect of trust establishment, a fact evident in the numerous reputation-based computational trust models in existence [4]. It is, however, not the only important one. Aside from reputation, the intentions, capabilities and competencies of the partners in a potential interaction also contribute to the assessment of trust. A consumer, for instance, is more likely to trust a service provider to deliver a satisfactory performance, if the service provider can credibly represent its ability to meet the consumer's requirements. It can do so by relying on its public standing and general history of delivering a service well, i.e. its reputation. However, it can also provide documents, certificates or audits to show that its capabilities are sufficient for the consumer.

Trust in cloud computing

Trust issues become particularly important when data processing is decentralized across geographically dispersed data centres and resources are distributed beyond a definable and controllable perimeter, which is especially true in the Cloud computing scenario. In the next section, we illustrate an example to show the importance of trust establishment in Cloud computing, in particular establishing trust on Cloud providers.

Motivating example

The example we illustrate here is of a healthcare provider who wants to outsource their in-house application that deal with medical records to a Cloud-based service. The main goal is to minimize the IT expenditure as well as allow seamless access to these medical records using the Cloud-based service to doctors, patients, and insurance companies. The medical records consist of private information and by outsourcing them in a Cloud-based service one has to make sure that the most dependable Cloud provider host the service. The healthcare provider require assurances regarding compliance (e.g., HIPAA (Health Insurance Portability and Accountability Act)), data protection through security and privacy controls, geographical location (data should not leave the political border) and high availability of the services. The healthcare provider considers the CPs trustworthy if they are dependable in fulfilling the assurances.

Since the Cloud computing market for offering medical record services is competitive, the healthcare provider is facing the challenge of selecting a potential provider that is best-suited and most appropriate for them, from numerous alternatives. Assume that all of these providers have the same functionality and provide the assurances according to the healthcare provider's requirements. In order to select the trustworthy Cloud provider, the consumer (i.e., the healthcare provider) has to compare the offered services or solutions independently which is, in fact, a cumbersome task. This task includes analysing the SLAs and finding out the clauses according to their requirements, checking whether the provider abide by the specific audit standards or studying the CAIQ (Consensus Assessments Initiative Questionnaire) [29] from STAR (Security, Trust & Assurance Registry) [30] by CSA (Cloud Security Alliance) to learn about the present security controls of the Cloud provider.

Current trends for trust establishment

There are ad-hoc approaches to support the consumers in selecting trustworthy (or dependable) CPs. We classify and briefly analyse these approaches as follows.

- **SLAs:** In practice, one way to establish trust on CPs is the fulfilment of SLAs. SLA validation [31] and monitoring [32] schemes are used to quantify what exactly a CP is offering and which assurances are actually met. In Cloud computing environments, customers are responsible for monitoring SLA violations and informing the providers for compensation. The compensation clauses in SLAs are written by the CPs in such a way so that the customers merely get the advantage of applying for compensation (e.g., service credits) due to SLA violation. This problem arise for not having standardized SLAs for the stakeholders in Cloud computing marketplace. Although, the problem is addressed by industry driven initiative [33] for establishing standardized SLAs, this initiative is far from implementation in practice.

- **Audits:** CPs use different audit standards (e.g., SAS 70 II, FISMA, ISO 27001) to assure users about their offered services and platforms. For example, Google lists SAS 70 II and FISMA certification to ensure users about the security and privacy measures taken for Google Apps. The audit SAS 70 II covers only the operational performance (e.g., policies and procedures inside datacenters) and relies on a highly specific set of goals and standards. They are not sufficient to alleviate the users' security concerns [34] and most of the CPs are not willing to share the audit reports, which also leads to a lack of transparency.

- **Measuring & Ratings:** Recently, a Cloud marketplace [35] has been launched to support consumers in identifying dependable CPs. They are rated based on a questionnaire that needs to be filled in by current CCs. In the future, Cloud Commons aims to combine consumer feedback with technical measurements for assessing and comparing the trustworthiness of CPs. Furthermore, there is a new commercial Cloud marketplace named SpotCloud [36] that provides a platform where CCs can choose among potential providers in terms of cost, quality, and location. Here, the CPs' ratings are given in an Amazon-like "star" interface with no documentation on how the ratings are computed.

- **Self-assessment Questionnaires:** The CSA proposed a detailed questionnaire for ensuring security control transparency of CPs – called the CAIQ (Consensus Assessment Initiative Questionnaire). This questionnaire provides means for assessing the capabilities and competencies of CPs in terms of different attributes (e.g., compliance, information security, governance). However, the CSA metrics working group does not provide any proposals for a metric to evaluate CAIQ yet. This is necessary for comparing the potential CPs based on the answered assessment questionnaire stored in the STAR. Furthermore, the information stored in the STAR repository can be checked against the CCM (Cloud Control Matrix) [19]. This will provide the assurance whether services offered by the CPs comply with the industry-accepted security standards, audits, regulations, control frameworks (cf. Figure 1) or not.

Limitations of current trends

The trends currently followed by the CPs are mostly ad-hoc. These trends are either considering technical and functional features or the user feedback for establishing trust on CPs. Thus, these trends are lacking a unified approach (i.e., trust evaluation framework) where all these trends can be considered complementary to support the consumers in evaluating the providers and selecting the most trustworthy (or dependable) one. Moreover, the current approaches (e.g., analysing the SLAs or studying the audit reports) are time consuming and cumbersome. Therefore, the CCs (e.g., the healthcare provider) may skip the idea of outsourcing the in-house application to the Cloud. Figure 2 visualizes the current trends for trust establishment from the perspective of the healthcare provider.

In the next section, the technical solutions are envisioned to overcome the limitations of current trends and support the consumers in selecting trustworthy providers.

Overcoming the limitations of current trends

To overcome the limitations of the current trends the technical solutions should go beyond simply selecting a service provider based upon purely technical features, such as classical QoS (quality of service) parameters. Rather, trust has to be established, both regarding individual service providers and the Cloud computing paradigm in general. This trust extends to CPs supplying reliable services, maintaining confidentiality, integrity and availability, conforming to contracts and SLAs, etc. On a more abstract plane, consumers have to trust that Cloud computing is a secure and economically sound paradigm in order to facilitate Cloud computing as a business model. On a technical, but also on a commercial side, trust has to be made measurable, in order to represent it in decision making contexts (e.g., for provider selection). If Cloud services are not transparent with regard to their features (e.g., security, service performance, geographical location, etc.), underlying service compositions and the technical infrastructure, trust and quality cannot be factored to decision making processes (e.g., provider selection). Lack of transparency of a service creates an asymmetry between consumer and provider. The consequences of such an asymmetry have been described by Ackerloff in his article *A Market for Lemons* [37]. While the original example describe the effects with regard to the sale of used cars, the results are nonetheless transferable to modern eCommerce. In [37], expensive but high quality products are driven out of the market in favour of low-cost alternatives, because customers are unable to assess the reliability of the sellers. In another article [5], the author points out a

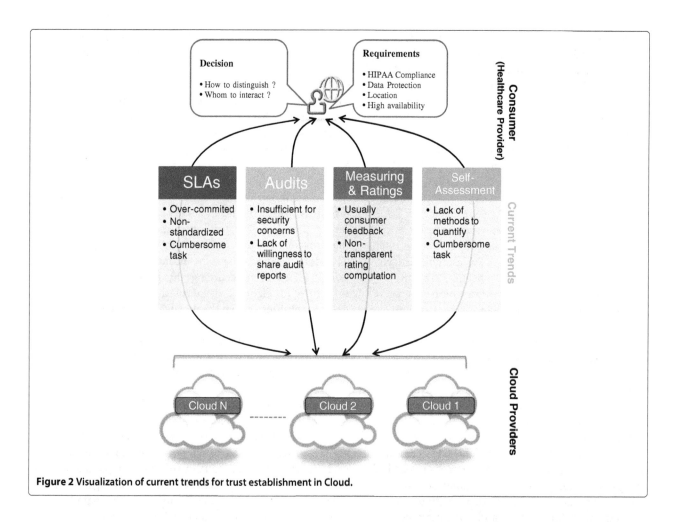

Figure 2 Visualization of current trends for trust establishment in Cloud.

typical scenario where a Cloud provider can offer a "wonderfully" secure service while another may not. In analogy to the market of lemons example, if the latter charges half the price, the majority of organizations will opt for this cheaper competitor as there is no practicable way to explore the difference. To assist customers in exploring the differences and selecting the most trustworthy Cloud provider, a trust-aided unified evaluation framework is needed. Trust and Reputation (TR) models used in various application environments represent a promising and essential basis for such a framework .

Figure 3 visualizes the trust-aided technical solution for supporting the consumers (e.g., healthcare provider) in interacting with the most trustworthy Cloud provider.

TR models for cloud marketplaces: requirements and challenges

TR models have been proven useful for decision making in numerous service environments (e.g., e-commerce, p2p networks, product reviews) [4,38]. The concepts have also been adapted in grid computing [39,40], inter-cloud computing environments [41], and selecting web services [42]. These trust models mainly consider interaction

experiences and behavioural (e.g., p2p networks) or technical (e.g., grid computing, web services) observations for selecting trustworthy entities. Both of these aspects and related parameters are equally important to consider when selecting trustworthy service providers in Cloud marketplaces.

Cloud based services are hosted in massively distributed and complex systems (highly abstract and non-transparent). Because of this distributed complex service oriented architecture, consumers have to consider the parameters which are related to both aspects (i.e., inter-action experiences and technical) for current TR models in numerous service environments. Moreover, TR models for Cloud computing environments need to take specific cloud-related parameters into account for trustworthy service provider selection. These parameters go beyond the usual QoS parameters [43], which are considered when selecting web service providers.

QoS+ Parameters for TR models

Recently, researchers proposed QoS+ (beyond the usual QoS) parameters for TR models in Cloud environments [12]. These parameters are identified based on the state-

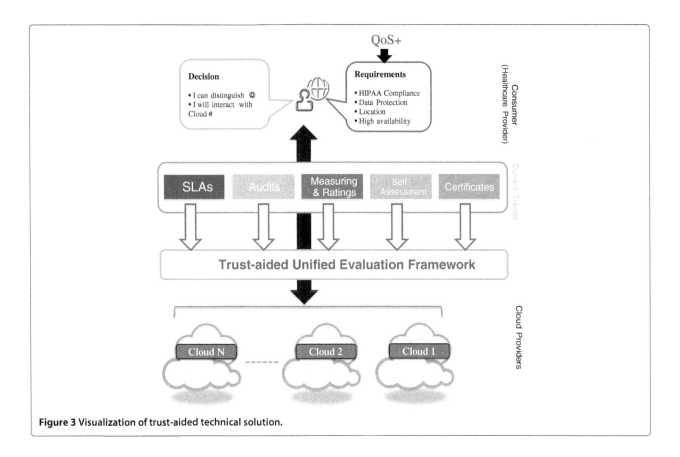

Figure 3 Visualization of trust-aided technical solution.

of-the-art survey of threats and risks discussed in [12]. Moreover, a recent article [3] published a list of functional and non-functional trust affectors based on a extensive survey conducted among the Cloud entities. This survey clearly shows the consumers' interest and need of reckoning the trust affectors for establishing trust on Cloud providers. The QoS+ parameters map quite closely to the trust affectors identified in the survey article. The mapping shows the usefulness and absolute need of such parameters for selecting trustworthy service providers in Cloud environments. Therefore, considering the cloud-specific parameters (i.e., QoS+) for trust models in Cloud environments in turn support the consumers to know the capabilities and competencies of the CPs before interacting with them.

TR models require direct and indirect information (i.e., experiences, observations, opinions) regarding the QoS+ parameters for trust computation and evaluation phase. The information about the parameters are often available from multiple entities and parties (e.g., CPs, CCs, CAs, CBs, CCas). They provide the information through different measures or approaches. Hence, the approaches followed in current trends (cf. Section "Current trends for trust establishment") are considered complimentary for trust establishment. In Table 1 , the QoS+parameters are listed along with their corresponding sources of

information, the existing approaches used for deriving the information. The parameters are discussed briefly in the following:

1. **SLAs:** The entities that are providing services are required to follow standardized SLA, e.g., proposed by Cloud Computing Use Cases community [33]. The SLA specification of CPs then can be assessed based on the compliance to the standardized format. This compliance is further factored into trust assessment of CPs. The information regarding the SLAs is considered to be direct, as these agreements are usually between the corresponding entities (e.g., CCs and CPs, CPs and CBs, CPs and CCas).

2. **Compliance:** CPs use audit standards as an assurance for the existence of technical (e.g., security) and organizational controls related to their offered services. The CAs assess these controls and issue certificates for the CPs based on the assessment reports. Otherwise, the information about those controls are provided by CPs in the STAR repository and can be checked against the CCM initiated by CSA. The results about the audit compliance can be obtained directly from the CPs or indirectly from the CSA.

Table 1 QoS+ Parameters: information sources and approaches

QoS+ Parameters	Who provide the information?	How to derive the information?
SLA	CPs, CBs, CCs, CCas	Standardized SLAs
Compliance	CAs, CSA	Audit Standards, CCM
Portability Interoperability Geographical Location	CPs	SLAs
Customer Support	CCs, CPs, CBs, CCas	SLAs, User Feedback
Performance	CBs, Independent Third-party, CCs, CPs	Measurement, User Feedback
Federated IdM	CPs	SLAs
Security	CSA, CPs, CAs	CSA CAIQ, Certificate-based Attestation mechanism, Audits
User Feedback	CCs	Measurement and Ratings (User Feedback)
Service Deployment Models Service Delivery Models	CCs, CBs, CRs	Context Dependency and Similarity techniques

3. **Portability, Interoperability, and Geographical Location:** The information regarding these parameters are directly obtainable from the CPs. The existence of terms and clauses related to these parameters documented in the SLAs are the valid form of information in this case.

4. **Customer Support:** CPs usually provide assurances about terms and clauses related to "customer support" in their SLAs. TCBs and CCas are also required to include similar terms in their SLAs for their respective consumers (e.g., CPs or CBs or CCs). The SLA-based terms and clauses can be complemented by considering experiences from the existing consumers and factor into overall trust computation of CPs or CCas.

5. **Performance:** In Cloud computing environments, the information about the performance related parameter (e.g., availability, latency, bandwidth, elasticity) is obtained using service monitoring technologies. CPs and CBs usually provide the application for monitoring such parameters which are usually used after the service provisioning contract. CCs also can hire the independent third-party brokers (if required) to monitor those parameters before provisioning the services. In this case, the monitored or observed data regarding the performance parameters can be compared among the potential providers or with the agreed data stated in the SLAs to validate them [44]. The validation result (i.e., success or failure) or the comparison of performances then may influence the evaluation of trustworthiness of CPs.

6. **Federated IdM:** The information regarding this particular parameter is provided by the CPs through their SLAs. This parameter is required for the federated enterprises using common cloud-based services.

7. **Security:** CCs want to know about the existence of certain security controls when outsourcing their IT resources to the cloud. The CSA initiated CAIQ [29], a self-assessment questionnaire designed for the CPs to document their security controls, to increase transparency between the providers and consumers by publishing it in a public repository. Moreover, CPs host services in trusted virtualized platforms using the trusted computing (TC) technology. In a distributed service environments (e.g, Cloud computing), consumers can learn about the security or non-security related behaviour of the software components running on those platforms using remote-attestation mechanism, e.g., [45].

8. **User Feedback:** Feedback, recommendation, reviews from the consumers are valuable for service selection in e-marketplaces. This concept is also adapted in Cloud marketplaces (e.g., CloudCommons, SpotCloud) where CCs share their experiences about the cloud services they provisioned. The information about their experiences may appear as quantitative (e.g., satisfaction score) and/or qualitative (e.g., reviews) forms. Consumers' experiences can be used to evaluate the CPs as a whole or with respect to each QoS+ parameter.

9. **Service Deployment and Delivery Models:** Trust models are usually context-specific and it is important to consider in the TR models for service selection in Cloud environments. The service delivery models (cf. Section "Service delivery models") and service deployment models (cf. Section "Deployment models") should be factored as a contextual parameter in trust models. Hence, the

context dependency and similarity techniques [46,47] are considered complementary for the trust models in Cloud environments.

Properties and challenges of TR models

TR models require specific properties to incorporate QoS+ parameters for trust establishment in Cloud environments. The integration of these parameters into a TR model specifically tailored to the use in Cloud environments introduces further challenges. The following sections comprise essential properties and related challenges for consideration:

1. **Multi-faceted Trust Computation:** The computation of trust should consider the parameters listed in Section "QoS+ Parameters for TR models", which refer to the competencies and capabilities of a service provider in certain aspects, for instance, providing security measures, accreditation, bandwidth or customer support. Integrating these different aspects brings up multi-faceted challenges regarding computation of trust, which are as follows.

   - Multi-criteria: The assessment of the trustworthiness of an entity should consider all relevant parameters, which usually means to take into account multiple parameters describing different qualities of a service (composition) or its provider. Especially the aggregation of objective parameters (e.g., expert ratings or real-time measurements) and subjective parameters (e.g., recommendations by other consumers) is a major challenge.
   - Multi-root: When integrating multiple parameters into a TR model, one has to consider that the quantitative or qualitative information, being factored into the trust establishment process, can be derived from different roots. Furthermore, one has to consider that those roots might have very different characteristics; for instance, information derived from a trusted platform module (TPM) or certificates provided by a property attestation authority (sometimes referred to as hard trust) need to be handled differently from trust information derived from user feedback (sometimes referred to as soft trust). Therefore, the combination of information from different roots poses another major challenge.
   - Multi-context: As a single service provider may offer different services that require different competencies, a computational model should be able to reflect the context in which a service provider has established trust. In Cloud

computing, the different context can refer to different service delivery models. For example, a service provider might be trustworthy in delivering SaaS but not PaaS or IaaS. Moreover, if a trust model is able to consider that an entity has different trust values in different contexts, the model should be able to reason about the overall trustworthiness of an entity, or about the trustworthiness of a newly deployed service (e.g., based on the knowledge which components that are already used in other contexts are re-used for the new service).

2. **Customization and Aggregation:** Another issue that is relevant when selecting or designing of trust or reputation mechanism relates to how much customization should be supported and where should the trust values be aggregated.

   - Trust Customization (Global reputation vs Local/Subjective trust values): When trust is derived from different parameters, it is possible to consider *subjective* interests and requirements that *dependent* on the entity evaluating the trustworthiness of a service provider. This leads to a *local* (subjective) trust value. However, a *global* trust value is independent from who evaluates trustworthiness of a service provider. On the one hand, the *local (i.e., subjective)* trust values provide means for considering the preference of each user in detail. Customization allows users to define the parameters relevant for trust establishment from their point of view, to weight the parameters according to his preferences and to consider which sources of information the user believes to be more trustworthy. For example, one customer might give preference (a higher weight) to security measures, whereas for another customer a high-quality customer support is more important. On the other hand, service providers might be more interested in the calculation of a *global trust (or reputation)* value, as this might be more directly influenced and observed by the companies.
   - Trust Aggregation (Centralized vs Decentralized): Usually, there are two different fundamental approaches to store and aggregate trust-related information; The first one is to host the information in a *centralized* repository, the other is to use a

decentralized approach. Both have distinct advantages and disadvantages: In *centralized* trust models – requiring a trusted third party – users cannot manipulate the data except by providing ratings to the central system. The aggregation methodology can be kept secret and the individual ratings of an entity are (usually and ideally) not published or distributed. However, the trusted authority hosting the centralized repository may manipulate the results and represent a single point for attacks. *Decentralized* trust models do not require a trusted third party, however, one has to trust in the mechanisms which are used for distributing the ratings and to consider the costs for distributing the ratings among the entities. The latter can be solved by applying algorithms that aggregate the individual ratings by only communicating with an entity's local neighbourhood [48]. A disadvantage of *decentralized* models is that preserving privacy is much harder as more information is distributed between the participating entities.

3. **Trust Evaluation:** For complex, distributed environments (e.g., Cloud computing) we introduce a categorization of mechanisms that are relevant for trust evaluation that – to the best of our knowledge – have not been discussed in this context before:

- Black box approach: Following this approach, the trustworthiness of an entity or a service is evaluated taking into account only the observed output, for example by only considering user feedback. Models in this class treat the service as a black box, and do not require (or consider) any knowledge about the internal processes and components of the service.
- Inside-out approach: Following this approach, the trustworthiness of an entity or a service is derived based on the knowledge about the architecture of the service and the trustworthiness of its components (or subsystems). For recent approaches following this idea, see [49,50].
- Outside-in approach: A model that is following this approach requires knowledge about the internal architecture of a service and its components as input as well as information stating the observed behaviour of the overall service. The goal of this kind of model is to derive the trustworthiness of internal components of a service composition based on its external behaviour (cf. [51]). This is far from

trivial, but can be successful when some components are re-used in multiple services and if certain errors in the behaviour of the service composition can be backtracked to the originating component.

4. **Transferring Trust between Contexts:** As stated above, customer trust in a service provider depends on the specific application context or the scope of interaction. Transfer of trust across those contexts is a significant challenge for trust and reputation systems. Consider, for example, a service provider offering an email service and a video rendering service – both belonging to the SaaS category. Both application contexts require different competencies, for example spam protection and storage for the email context, whereas for video rendering context, latency, bandwidth and parameters dealing with performance matters (e.g., response time, CDN (Content Delivery Node) facilities, etc.) are important. Here, transferring trust established in one context (email) to the other one (video rendering) is not a trivial task, and could, for instance, be supported by combining the outside-in and the inside-out evaluation.

5. **Attack Resistance:** As soon as the influence of trust and reputation models on the decision of customers will grow, the interests in manipulating those values in Cloud environment will grow accordingly, as already seen in other service environments earlier [52]. A number of different attacks (e.g., playbooks, proliferation attacks, reputation lag attacks, false praise or accusation (collusion), whitewashing (re-entry), sybil attacks, etc.) against trust and reputation systems have been discussed [52,53]. These types of attacks will also be of concern when designing trust and reputation system for Cloud computing environments. Thus, attack resiliency is a central design goal for developers of these kind of systems.

6. **Transparent Trust Representation:** The derived trust values or reputation scores must be transparent to and comprehensible enough for the consumers, so that they can easily and confidently make trust-based decision. To make the trust values transparent and comprehensible, users need to be supplied with an intuitive representation of trust together with enough information regarding the relevant parameters.

In the next section, we survey and summarize state-of-the-art trust and reputation systems and models from different fields of application. Particularly, attention is given to the characteristics of the models whether they satisfy the above mentioned properties whole or in part.

Survey and analysis of TR systems/models

There are a number of commercial TR models, as well as numerous proposals in different research communities, targeting various application areas (e.g. eCommerce, product review sites, Peer to Peer (P2P) networks, Online Social Networks (OSNs), Wireless Sensor Networks (WSNs), ubiquitous and grid computing). In the following, we choose seventeen promising models from different application fields for our analysis with respect to the properties mentioned in section "Properties and challenges of TR models": eBay [54], Epinions [55], Beta reputation [56], CertainTrust [27,28], FIRE [57], EigenTrust [58], socialREGRET [59,60], TidalTrust [61], RFSN [62], GridEigenTrust [63], Abawajy's model [41], TESM [45], Unitec [64], BNTM [65], Buchegger's model [66], Billhardt's model [67], Hang's model [51].

Trust customization and *trust aggregation* properties are the two most generic properties for *TR* models in commercial applications or research community proposals. Most of the commercial *TR* models (e.g., *eBay, Epinions*) support a single *reputation (i.e., Global trust)* score for each customers; this score is calculated and stored in a centralized system. Most of the TR models proposed by the research community support *local (subjective)* trust values considering the customer preference in detail while measuring the trustworthiness of a service provider except *Eigentrust, GridEigentTrust, Abawajy's model*, and *Unitec.* However, all the TR models from the research community, we surveyed, support distributed computation and storage for trust-related information.

Most of the TR models, either in commercial applications or proposed by the research community, consider trust information from just a single *root (soft trust)*. However, only two trust models (*FIRE* and *TESM*) from the research community consider two roots (from soft and hard trust) in trust computation. Regarding *trust evaluation*, most TR models (commercial and research proposals) use the *black box approach*. A few models from the research community, notably *GridEigenTrust* and *TESM*, evaluate trust using the *inside-out approach*. One particular among the surveyed models, (*Hang's model*), uses the *outside-in approach* for trust evaluation.

Taking *multiple criterias* into account, when calculating trust in TR models, is not common in the trust community. Commercial applications (e.g., *eBay* and *Epinions*) support multi-criterial computation of trust. However, eBay's seller ratings, displayed in four distinct categories (i.e., item described, communication, shipping time, shipping and handling charges), don't affect the general rating system (i.e., categorical ratings are not taken into account to compute the overall rating). Only three models – (*socialREGRET, TESM,* and *BNTM*) – proposed by the research community, support multiple criteria in trust computation.

Commercial models like *Epinions* aggregate trust ratings from *multiple contexts* to provide an overall reputation score for an entity. However, commercial models like *eBay* and most of the TR models proposed by the research community, do not support the feature. A few TR models from the research community (e.g., *GridEigenTrust* and *BNTM*) consider trust values from *multiple contexts* to compute an overall trust score. However, neither *GridEigenTrust* nor *BNTM* can *transfer trust* across contexts. Conversely, *Billhardt's model* does not support the *multi-context* feature but is capable of transferring trust across contexts. Thus, significant improvement is needed regarding TR models for Cloud environments that are to support both features.

Most of the trust models are subject to different kinds of attacks, while a few of them are resistant to particular attacks like false praise or accusation (FPA), sybil and whitewashing attacks. Thus, we limit our scope to those three attacks to keep the comparisons concise in Table 2. *CertainTrust* model is resistant to sybil and FPA attacks, while *EigenTrust* is resistant to sybil and *Buchegger's model* and *socialREGRET* are resistant to FPA attacks only. None of the models are resistant to whitewashing attacks.

Commercial models like *eBay* and *Epinions* provide a graphical interface (e.g., star rating) together with detailed information (e.g., detailed seller ratings, detailed opinions) to the customers. On the one hand, the graphical interface in commercial models does not provide comprehensive trust information but with the help of detailed information the models mitigate that problem. On the other hand, most of the trust models from the research community do not provide a graphical interface for trust representation except the *CertainTrust* model and the *Beta reputation system*.

Table 2 summarizes the comparison among *TR* models from commercial applications and research community's proposals with respect to the above mentioned trust properties.

Discussion

From the analysis of different *TR* models in the previous section, it can be evidenced that most of the models we surveyed in this paper need significant improvement to be used in the Cloud computing environments. Specifically, multi-faceted trust computation and *transfer of trust* properties are important in order to accommodate different service delivery contexts and multiple parameters that are needed to establish trust on Cloud providers. Trust evaluation approaches, especially the *outside-in* approach, are essential to evaluate the trustworthiness of Cloud providers of complex composite services or distributed systems. Thus, trust evaluation approaches should consider the trustworthiness of underlying subsystems and components of complex

Table 2 Characterization of existing trust and reputation (TR) models and systems

Properties TR models	Trust computation			Trust customization Global trust (G) vs Local trust (L)	Trust aggregation Centralized (C) vs Decentralized (D)	Trust evaluation (Bb vs Io vs Oi)[2]	Transfer trust across contexts	Attack resistance (FPA/S/W)[3]	Transparent trust information[4] (UI/C)
	Multi-criteria	Multi-root (S/H)[1]	Multi-context						
eBay	N	S/-	N	G	C	Bb	No	-/-/-	UI/C
Epinions	Y	S/-	Y	G	C	Bb	No	-/-/-	UI/C
Beta Reputation	N	S/-	N	G	C	Bb	No	-/-/-	UI/-
CertainTrust	N	S/-	N	L	D	Bb	No	FPA/S/-	UI/C
FIRE	N	S/H	N	L	D	Bb	No	-/-/-	-/-
EigenTrust	N	S/-	N	G	D	Bb	No	-/S/-	-/-
socialREGRET	Y	S/-	N	L	D	Bb	No	FPA/-/-	-/-
TidalTrust	N	S/-	N	L	D	Bb	No	-/-/-	-/-
RFSN	N	S/-	N	L	D	Bb	No	-/-/-	-/-
GridEigenTrust	N	S/-	Y	G	D	Io	No	-/-/-	-/-
Abawajy's model	N	S/-	N	G	C	Bb	No	-/-/-	-/-
TESM	Y	S/H	N	L	D	Io	No	-/-/-	-/-
Unitec	N	S/-	N	G	D	Bb	No	-/-/-	-/-
BNTM	Y	S/-	Y	L	D	Bb	No	-/-/-	-/-
Buchegger's model	N	S/-	N	L	D	Bb	No	FPA/-/-	-/-
Billhardt's model	N	S/-	N	L	D	Bb	Yes	-/-/-	-/-
Hang's model	N	S/-	N	L	D	Oi	No	-/-/-	-/-

[1] (S=Soft trust; H=Hard trust).
[2] (Bb=Black box; Io=Inside-out; Oi=Outside-in).
[3] (FPA=False Praise Accusation; S=Sybil attack; W=Whitewashing attack).
[4] (UI=User Interface; C=Comprehensiveness).

systems. Attack resistance is also an essential property for trust models in general. Trust model in Cloud environments should also possess this property to ensure reliable trust score for consumers. Finally, consumers need an intuitive trust representation (graphical interface with comprehensive trust information) which is also very important in terms of transparency and usability. All these specific properties are essential for integrating in a unified trust evaluation framework (cf. Figure 3) (i.e., trust management system [25]) by means of TR models.

Conclusions

This article is the first survey focusing on the technical solution to the obstacles for adopting Cloud computing by means of TR models and systems. We provide a extended Cloud taxonomy to better understand the diversified market structure and how it is related to the adoption of Cloud computing. We have discussed the necessity of trust establishment and its influence on the adoption of Cloud computing from the perspective of Cloud entities. We have classified the current trends of trust establishment and identified their limitations by means of a use case where a healthcare provider face the challenge of selecting the most trustworthy Cloud provider. We have demonstrated the value of unified trust evaluation framework (i.e., a trust management system) by means of TR models and their required properties for establishing trust in Cloud environments. These properties and corresponding challenges are valuable for future research in designing trust-aided evaluation framework for Cloud environments.

TR models and systems provide mean for trustworthy interactions in online communities. Understanding the existing models/systems and their comparison in terms of required properties is an important first step towards developing robust systems in the future. This article has aimed to provide rigid properties to compare the existing models/systems and bring understanding of these systems to a broader Cloud computing community, including trust-aided system developers and practitioners.

Abbreviations
TR: Trust and Reputation; SaaS: Software as a Service; PaaS: Platform as a Service; IaaS: Infrastructure as a Service; DaaS: Data as a Service; NaaS: Network as a Service; IPMaaS: Identity and Policy Management as a Service; VPN: Virtual Private Lan; CPs: Cloud Providers; CBs: Cloud Brokers; CRs: Cloud Resellers; CCs: Cloud Consumers; OS: Operating System; IT: Information Technology; SLAs: Service Level Agreements; SMEs: Small and Medium-sized Enterprises; HIPAA: Health Insurance Portability and Accountability Act; CAIQ: Consensus Assessments Initiative Questionnaire; STAR: Security, Trust & Assurance Registry; CSA: Cloud Security Alliance; SAS 70: Statement on Auditing Standards (SAS) No. 70; FISMA: Federal Information Security Management Act; ISO 27001: International Organization for Standardization 27001; CCM: Cloud Control Matrix; PCI: Payment Card Industry; NIST: National Institute of Standards and Technology; QoS: Quality of Service; TPM: Trusted Platform Module; CDN: Content Delivery Node; P2P: Peer to Peer; OSN: Online Social Networks; WSN: Wireless Sensor Networks.

Competing interests
The authors declare that they have no competing interests.

Authors' contributions
SMH carried out the studies of cloud computing, trust and reputation models from various application fields, drafted the manuscript, and coordinated the task among authors. SH has critically reviewed the paper and drafted the manuscript, especially the "Adoption of cloud computing" section. SR has critically reviewed the paper and drafted the article, especially the trust related sections. MM has contributed to the concept of "trust in cloud computing" and reviewed the manuscript. All authors read and approved the final manuscript.

Authors' information
Sheikh Mahbub Habib is a doctoral researcher at the Center for Advanced Security Research Darmstadt (CASED) and research assistant at the Telecooperation Lab (TK) of Technische Universitt Darmstadt Germany. He is working on computational trust models and how those models can be adapted in trust management for complex distributed service environments (e.g., cloud computing). Earlier, he earned M.Sc. in Networks and Distributed Systems, specializing in security and distributed systems from Chalmers University of Technology Sweden. His current research interests includes trust and reputation models, logical reasoning of trust, trust management techniques, trust enhanced security techniques and their application in complex distributed systems.
Sascha Hauke is a doctoral researcher and research assistant at the Center for Advanced Security Research Darmstadt (CASED) and the Telecooperation Lab (TK) of Technische Universitt Darmstadt, Germany. He is working on developing techniques for extending reputation-based trust models into advanced trust management solutions. He received the degree of Diplom-Informatiker (Dipl.-Inform.) from the Westflische Wilhelms-Universitt Mnster (WWU), specializing in machine learning, soft computing and linguistics. His current research interests include reputation-based trust management, the application of machine learning techniques for prediction and their application in service oriented environments.
Sebastian Ries was born in 1979. At the time of writing this article, he was the coordinator of the research area Secure Services at the Center for Advanced Security Research Darmstadt (since 2009). Furthermore he was the head of the research group Smart Security & Trust at the Telecooperation Lab (TK), Technische Universität Darmstadt, Germany, since 2008, and a principle investigator at CASED since 2010. He obtained his Doctor and Diploma degrees in Computer Science from Technische Universität Darmstadt obtained in 2009 and 2005, respectively. He was awarded with research scholarships by the German National Science Foundation (DFG) and CASED, while preparing his dissertation. His research interests include trust and reputation models, trust establishment in complex systems, as well as challenges in the fields of identity management, privacy, and usable security.
Max Mühlhäuser is a full professor at the Technische Universitt Darmstadt, Germany, where he heads the Telecooperation Lab (TK) and coordinates a division of the Center for Advanced Security Research Darmstadt (CASED). After his doctorate and a leading position in industrial research, he held permanent or visiting professorships in Kaiserslautern (D), Karlsruhe (D), Linz (A), Montral, Sophia Antipolis (F), and San Diego. With his team, he covers a broad range of Ubiquitous Computing research topics in three complementary fields: 1) ubiquitous interaction issues such as interaction concepts for future devices, proactive, context aware, and multi device interaction; 2) issues of large scale networks (OSN, P2P, WSN) and smart spaces such as middleware, context and location awareness, discovery and composition, and knowledge work; 3) ubiquitous privacy and trust, and resilience for critical infrastructures.

Acknowledgements
This work is supported by Center for Advanced Security Research Darmstadt (CASED). Additionally, the authors would like to thank the anonymous reviewers for their comments and suggestions to enhance the quality of this manuscript.

References

1. Khan KM, Malluhi Q (2010) Establishing trust in cloud computing. IT Professional 12: 20–27
2. Fujitsu Research Institute (2010) Personal data in the cloud: A global survey of consumer attitudes. Technical Report, Fujitsu Research Institute
3. Uusitalo I, Karppinen K, Juhola A, Savola R (2010) Trust and cloud services - an interview study. In: Cloud Computing Technology and Science (CloudCom), 2010 IEEE Second International Conference on, p. 712–720
4. Jøsang A, Ismail R, Boyd C (2007) A survey of trust and reputation systems for online service provision. Decision Support Syst 43(2): 618–644
5. Everett C (2009) Cloud computing - a question of trust. Computer Fraud & Security 2009(6): 5–7
6. Mouline I (2009) Why assumptions about cloud performance can be dangerous to your business. Cloud Comp J 2(3): 24–28
7. Takabi H, Joshi J, Ahn G (2010) Security and privacy challenges in cloud computing environments. Security Privacy. IEEE 8(6): 24–31
8. Ristenpart et al. (2009) Hey, you, get off of my cloud! exploring information leakage in third-party compute clouds. In: Proceedings of the 16th ACM CCS 2009. ACM Press, Newyork, p. 199–212
9. Chow R, Golle P, Jakobsson M, Shi E, Staddon J, Masuoka R, Molina J (2009) Controlling data in the cloud: outsourcing computation without outsourcing control. In:Proceedings of the 2009 ACM workshop on Cloud computing security. ACM Press, p. 85–90
10. CSA (2009) Security guidance for critical areas of focus in cloud computing v2.1. Technical report, Cloud Security Alliance
11. ENISA (2009) Cloud computing- benefits risks and recommendations for information security. Technical report, ENISA
12. Habib SM, Ries S, Muhlhauser M (2010) Cloud computing landscape and research challenges regarding trust and reputation. Ubiquitous Autonomic and Trusted Computing, Symposia and Workshops on, 410–415
13. Bias R (2009) Challenges embracing cloud storage. SNIA Cloud Storage Summit- Winter Symposium 2009
14. Mell P, Grance T (2009) The nist definition of cloud computing. Nat Inst Standards Technol 53(6): 50
15. Hanna S (2009) Cloud computing: Finding the silver lining. http://www.ists.dartmouth.edu/events/abstract-hanna.html. Accessed 11 Aug 2012
16. National Institute of Standards and Technology (2011) Nist cloud computing reference architecture: Version 1. NIST Meeting Report
17. OpenCrowd Cloud taxonomy (2012) OpenCrowd Web Portal. http://cloudtaxonomy.opencrowd.com/taxonomy/ Accessed 30 July 2012
18. Schmitz R (2009) Los angeles moves to gmail and 'cloud' computing. http://www.npr.org/templates/story/story.php?storyId=114300948. Accessed 11 Aug 2012
19. CSA (2011) Cloud Controls Matrix. https://cloudsecurityalliance.org/research/initiatives/cloud-controls-matrix/ Accessed 15 July 2012
20. Gartner Inc. (2010) Gartner highlights key predictions for it organizations and users in 2010 and beyond. http://www.gartner.com/it/page.jsp?id=1278413. Accessed 11 Aug 2012
21. Armbrust et al. (2009) Above the clouds: A berkeley view of cloud computing. Technical report, EECS Department, University of California, Berkeley
22. ENISA (2009) An sme perspective on cloud computing-survey. Technical report, ENISA
23. McKnight DH, Chervany NL (1996) The meanings of trust. Technical report, Management Information Systems Research Center, University of Minnesota, USA
24. Mark Williams (2010) Reported cloud outages for Amazon, Google, Microsoft and Salesforce.com in 2008 and 2009. http://blog.muoncloud.com/2010/01/31/reported-cloud-outages-for-amazon-google-microsoft-and-salesforce-com-in-2008-and-2009/. Accessed 11 Aug 2012
25. Jøsang A, Keser C, Dimitrakos T (2005) Can we manage trust?. In: Herrmann P, Issarny V, Shiu S (eds) Trust Management, Third International Conference, iTrust 2005, 93–107. Proceedings, Springer, Paris, France, May 23-26, 2005
26. Gambetta D (2000) Can We Trust Trust? In: Trust: Making and Breaking Cooperative Relations, Department of Sociology, University of Oxford. pp. 213–237
27. Ries S (2009) Extending bayesian trust models regarding context-dependence and user friendly representation. In: Proceedings of the 2009 ACM Symposium on Applied Computing. ACM, New York. pp 1294–1301
28. Ries S (2009) Trust in Ubiquitous Computing. PhD thesis, Technische Universität Darmstadt
29. CSA (2011) Consensus Assessments Initiative. https://cloudsecurityalliance.org/research/initiatives/consensus-assessments-initiative/ Accessed 15 July 2012
30. CSA (2011) Security, Trust & Assurance Registry. https://cloudsecurityalliance.org/research/initiatives/star-registry/ Accessed 25 July 2012
31. Haq IU, Brandic I, Schikuta E (2010) Sla validation in layered cloud infrastructures. In: GECON. Lecture Notes in Computer Science. Springer-Verlag, Berlin, Heidelberg. 153–164
32. 3Tera Applogic (2009) 3tera's Cloud Computing SLA goes live. http://blog.3tera.com/computing/175/. Accessed 11 Aug 2012
33. Cloud Computing Use Cases Discussion Group (2010) Cloud computing use cases white paper Version 4.0. Cloud Computing Use Cases Discussion Group
34. SearchCIO (2009) Amazon gets SAS 70 Type II audit stamp, but analysts not satisfied. http://searchcloudcomputing.techtarget.com/news/1374629/Amazon-gets-SAS-70-Type-II-audit-stamp-but-analysts-not-satisfied Accessed 11 Aug 2012
35. Cloud Commons (2011) Cloud Commons Learn About SMI. http://beta-www.cloudcommons.com/web/cc/about-smi Accessed 15 July 2012
36. SpotCloud (2011) Cloud Capacity Marketplace. http://www.spotcloud.com/ Accessed 15 July 2012
37. Akerlof G (1970) A market for lemons. Q J Economics 84(3): 488–500
38. Ruohomaa S, Kutvonen L, Koutrouli E (2007) Reputation management survey In: The Second International Conference on Availability, Reliability and Security (ARES). pp 103–111
39. Haq IU, Alnemr R, Paschke A, Schikuta E, Boley H, Meinel C (2010) Distributed trust management for validating sla choreographies. In: Grids and Service-Oriented Architectures for Service Level Agreements. Springer, US, pp 45–55
40. Teacy WTL, Patel J, Jennings NR, Luck M (2006) Travos: Trust and reputation in the context of inaccurate information sources. Autonomous Agents and Multi-Agent Syst 12(2): 183–198
41. Abawajy J (2009) Determining service trustworthiness in intercloud computing environments. Int Symp Parallel Architectures, Algorithms, and Networks 0: 784–788
42. Wang SX, Zhang L, Wang S, Qiu X (2010) A cloud-based trust model for evaluating quality of web services. J Comput Sci Technol 25: 1130–1142
43. Wang Y, Vassileva J (2007) A review on trust and reputation for web service selection. IEEE Computer Society, Washington. pp 25
44. Bin L, Lee G, Loughlin JO (2010) Towards application-specific service level agreements: Experiments in clouds and grids. In: Antonopoulos N Gillam L (eds) Cloud Computing. Volume 0 of Computer Communications and Networks. Springer, London, pp 361–372
45. Nagarajan A, Varadharajan V (2011) Dynamic trust enhanced security model for trusted platform based services. Future Gener Comput Syst 27: 564–573
46. Tavakolifard M, Knapskog S, Herrmann P (2008) Trust transferability among similar contexts. In: Proceedings of the 4th ACM symposium on QoS and security for wireless and mobile networks. ACM Press, Newyork, pp 91–97
47. Jeh G, Widom J (2002) Simrank: a measure of structural-context similarity. KDD '02. ACM, New York, pp 538–543
48. Gergö T (2007) Specification and state of the art report for the club concept. http://p2p-fusion.mokk.bme.hu/w/images/archive/9/92/20070614214657!Trust_systems.pdf Accessed 11 Aug 2012
49. Schryen G, Volkamer M, Ries S, Habib SM (2011) A formal approach towards measuring trust in distributed systems. In: Proceedings of the 2011 ACM Symposium on Applied Computing. SAC '11. ACM Press, Newyork, pp 1739–1745
50. Ries S, Habib SM, Mühlhäuser M, Varadharajan V (2011) Certainlogic: A logic for modeling trust and uncertainty (short paper). In: Trust and Trustworthy Computing. Volume 6740 of Lecture Notes in Computer Science. Springer, Berlin / Heidelberg, pp 254–261
51. Hang CW, Singh MP (2011) Trustworthy service selection and composition. ACM Transactions on Autonomous and Adaptive Systems Volume 6(Issue 1). Article 5, 17 pages

52. Kerr R, Cohen R (2009) Smart cheaters do prosper: defeating trust and reputation systems. In: AAMAS '09: Proceedings of The 8th International Conference on Autonomous Agents and Multiagent Systems, pp. 993–1000

53. Jøsang A, Golbeck J (2009) Challenges for robust of trust and reputation systems. In: Proceedings of the 5th Int. Workshop on Security and Trust Management (STM2009)

54. eBay Inc (2011) eBay homepage. http://www.ebay.com Accessed 20 July 2012

55. Epinions (2011) Epinions homepage. http://www.epinions.com Accessed July 20 2012

56. Jøsang A, Ismail R (2002) The beta reputation system. In: Proceedings of the 15th Bled Conference on Electronic Commerce

57. Huynh TD, Jennings NR, Shadbolt NR (2006) An integrated trust and reputation model for open multi-agent systems. Autonomous Agents and Multi-Agent Syst 13(2): 119–154

58. Kamvar SD, Schlosser MT, Garcia-Molina H The eigentrust algorithm for reputation management in p2p networks. ACM Press, Newyork, pp 640–651

59. Sabater J, Sierra C (2002) Reputation and social network analysis in multi-agent systems. In: Proceedings of the first international joint conference on Autonomous agents and multiagent systems: part 1. ACM Press, pp. 475–482

60. Sabater J (2003) Trust and reputation for agent societies. Universitat Autnoma de Barcelona, Spain

61. Golbeck J (2005) Computing and Applying Trust in Web-Based Social Networks. University of Maryland, USA

62. Ganeriwal S, Balzano LK, Srivastava MB (2008) Reputation-based framework for high integrity sensor networks. ACM Trans Sen Netw 4(3): 1–37

63. von Laszewski G, Alunkal BE, Veljkovic I (2005) Towards reputable grids. calable Comput: Pract and Experience 6(3): 95–106

64. Kinateder M, Baschny E, Rothermel K Towards a Generic Trust Model Comparison of Various Trust Update Algorithms. In: Proceedings of the Third International Conference on Trust Management: iTrust'05; Rocquencourt, France, May 23-26, 2005. Springer-Verlag, Berlin, Heidelberg, pp 119–134

65. Wang Y, Vassileva J (2003) Bayesian network-based trust model. IEEE Computer Society, Washington, pp 372–378

66. Buchegger S, Le Boudec J Y (2004) A Robust Reputation System for Peer-to-Peer and Mobile Ad-hoc Networks. In: P2PEcon 2004

67. Billhardt H, Hermoso R, Ossowski S, Centeno R (2007) Trust-based service provider selection in open environments. In: SAC '07: Proceedings of the 2007. ACM Symposium on Applied Computing. ACM Press, Newyork,. pp. 1375–1380

Permissions

All chapters in this book were first published in JCC, by Springer; hereby published with permission under the Creative Commons Attribution License or equivalent. Every chapter published in this book has been scrutinized by our experts. Their significance has been extensively debated. The topics covered herein carry significant findings which will fuel the growth of the discipline. They may even be implemented as practical applications or may be referred to as a beginning point for another development.

The contributors of this book come from diverse backgrounds, making this book a truly international effort. This book will bring forth new frontiers with its revolutionizing research information and detailed analysis of the nascent developments around the world.

We would like to thank all the contributing authors for lending their expertise to make the book truly unique. They have played a crucial role in the development of this book. Without their invaluable contributions this book wouldn't have been possible. They have made vital efforts to compile up to date information on the varied aspects of this subject to make this book a valuable addition to the collection of many professionals and students.

This book was conceptualized with the vision of imparting up-to-date information and advanced data in this field. To ensure the same, a matchless editorial board was set up. Every individual on the board went through rigorous rounds of assessment to prove their worth. After which they invested a large part of their time researching and compiling the most relevant data for our readers.

The editorial board has been involved in producing this book since its inception. They have spent rigorous hours researching and exploring the diverse topics which have resulted in the successful publishing of this book. They have passed on their knowledge of decades through this book. To expedite this challenging task, the publisher supported the team at every step. A small team of assistant editors was also appointed to further simplify the editing procedure and attain best results for the readers.

Apart from the editorial board, the designing team has also invested a significant amount of their time in understanding the subject and creating the most relevant covers. They scrutinized every image to scout for the most suitable representation of the subject and create an appropriate cover for the book.

The publishing team has been an ardent support to the editorial, designing and production team. Their endless efforts to recruit the best for this project, has resulted in the accomplishment of this book. They are a veteran in the field of academics and their pool of knowledge is as vast as their experience in printing. Their expertise and guidance has proved useful at every step. Their uncompromising quality standards have made this book an exceptional effort. Their encouragement from time to time has been an inspiration for everyone.

The publisher and the editorial board hope that this book will prove to be a valuable piece of knowledge for researchers, students, practitioners and scholars across the globe.

List of Contributors

David W Chadwick
School of Computing, University of Kent, Canterbury
CT2 7NF, UK

Matteo Casenove
School of Computing, University of Kent, Canterbury
CT2 7NF, UK

Kristy Siu
School of Computing, University of Kent, Canterbury
CT2 7NF, UK

Jingwei Huang
Information Trust Institute, University of Illinois at
Urbana-Champaign 1308 West Main Street, Urbana,
Illinois 61801, USA

David M Nicol
Information Trust Institute, University of Illinois at
Urbana-Champaign 1308 West Main Street, Urbana,
Illinois 61801, USA

Robert Denz
Thayer School of Engineering at Dartmouth College,
Hanover, NH, America

Stephen Taylor
Thayer School of Engineering at Dartmouth College,
Hanover, NH, America

Lee Gilla
Department of Computing, University of Surrey,
Guildford, Surrey GU2 7XH, UK

Bin Li
Department of Computing, University of Surrey,
Guildford, Surrey GU2 7XH, UK

John O'Loughlin
Department of Computing, University of Surrey,
Guildford, Surrey GU2 7XH, UK

Anuz Pratap Singh Tomar
Department of Computing, University of Surrey,
Guildford, Surrey GU2 7XH, UK

Craig A Lee
Computer Systems Research Department, The Aerospace
Corporation, P.O. Box 92957, El Segundo, CA 90009, USA

Alan F Sill
High Performance Computing Center, Texas Tech
University, Lubbock, TX 79409, USA

Tansel Dokeroglu
Middle East Technical University Computer Engineering
Department, Cankaya, Ankara, Turkey

Serkan Ozal
Middle East Technical University Computer Engineering
Department, Cankaya, Ankara, Turkey

Murat Ali Bayir
Microsoft Research Redmond, One Microsoft Way,
Redmond, Washington 98052, USA

Muhammet Serkan Cinar
Hacettepe University Computer Engineering Department,
Cankaya, Ankara, Turkey

Ahmet Cosar
Middle East Technical University Computer Engineering
Department, Cankaya, Ankara, Turkey

Xing Chen
College of Mathematics and Computer Science, Fuzhou
University, Fuzhou 350116, China
Fujian Provincial Key Laboratory of Networking
Computing and Intelligent Information Processing
(Fuzhou University), Fuzhou 350116, China

Ying Zhang
Key Laboratory of High Confidence Software Technologies
(Ministry of Education), Beijing 100871, China.
School of Electronics Engineering and Computer Science,
Peking University, Beijing 100871, China

Gang Huang
Key Laboratory of High Confidence Software Technologies
(Ministry of Education), Beijing 100871, China.
School of Electronics Engineering and Computer Science,
Peking University, Beijing 100871, China

Xianghan Zheng
College of Mathematics and Computer Science, Fuzhou
University, Fuzhou 350116, China
Fujian Provincial Key Laboratory of Networking
Computing and Intelligent Information Processing
(Fuzhou University), Fuzhou 350116, China

Wenzhong Guo
College of Mathematics and Computer Science, Fuzhou
University, Fuzhou 350116, China
Fujian Provincial Key Laboratory of Networking
Computing and Intelligent Information Processing
(Fuzhou University), Fuzhou 350116, China

Chunming Rong
Department of Computer Science and Electronic Engineering, University of Stavanger, Stavanger 4036, Norway

Anant V Nimkar
School of Information Technology, IIT Kharagpur, Kharagpur, India

Soumya K Ghosh
School of Information Technology, IIT Kharagpur, Kharagpur, India

Mohamad Gebai
Department of Computer and Software Engineering, Polytechnique Montreal, 2900 Boulevard Edouard-Montpetit, Montreal, QC H3T 1J4, Canada

Francis Giraldeau
Department of Computer and Software Engineering, Polytechnique Montreal, 2900 Boulevard Edouard-Montpetit, Montreal, QC H3T 1J4, Canada

Michel R Dagenais
Department of Computer and Software Engineering, Polytechnique Montreal, 2900 Boulevard Edouard-Montpetit, Montreal, QC H3T 1J4, Canada

Zaheer Khan
Centre for Complex Cooperative Systems, Faculty of Environment And Technology, University of the West of England, Coldharbour Lane, BS16 1QY Bristol, UK

Saad Liaquat Kiani
Department of Computer Science and Creative Technologies, Faculty of Environment And Technology, University of the West of England, Coldharbour Lane, BS16 1QY Bristol, UK.

Kamran Soomro
Centre for Complex Cooperative Systems, Faculty of Environment And Technology, University of the West of England, Coldharbour Lane, BS16 1QY Bristol, UK

Owen Rogers
Department of Computer Science, University of Bristol, Merchant Venturers Building, Bristol, UK

Dave Cliff
Department of Computer Science, University of Bristol, Merchant Venturers Building, Bristol, UK

Ting Wang
Hong Kong University of Science and Technology, Hong Kong SAR, China

Bo Qin
Hong Kong University of Science and Technology, Hong Kong SAR, China

Zhiyang Su
Hong Kong University of Science and Technology, Hong Kong SAR, China

Yu Xia
Hong Kong University of Science and Technology, Hong Kong SAR, China

Mounir Hamdi
Hong Kong University of Science and Technology, Hong Kong SAR, China
Hamad Bin Khalifa University, Doha, Qatar

Sebti Foufou
Qatar University, Doha, Qatar

Ridha Hamila
Qatar University, Doha, Qatar

John Zic
CSIRO ICT Centre, PO Box 76, Epping, NSW 1710, Australia

Thomas Hardjono
MIT Kerberos and Internet Trust Consortium, Massachusetts Institute of Technology, Cambridge, MA 02139, USA